BEAKER POTTERY OF GREAT BRITAIN AND IRELAND

The Rillaton gold cup, Cornwall—a cup of the Wessex II Subculture—found with a skeleton, a pot, faience (?) beads, and an ogival bronze dagger; compare with the clay Food Vessel imitation, fig. 1081. Cup height, 8·5 cms

BEAKER POTTERY
OF GREAT BRITAIN
AND IRELAND

D. L. CLARKE
Fellow of Peterhouse, Cambridge

VOLUME 2

CAMBRIDGE
AT THE UNIVERSITY PRESS
1970

Published by the Syndics of the Cambridge University Press
Bentley House, 200 Euston Road, London N.W.1
American Branch: 32 East 57th Street, New York, N.Y.10022

Library of Congress Catalogue Card Number: 69-11269

Standard Book Numbers:

521 07443 6 vol. 1
521 07444 4 vol. 2
521 07249 2 set of two vols.

Printed in Great Britain
at the University Printing House, Cambridge
(Brooke Crutchley, University Printer)

CORPUS ILLUSTRATIONS

Introductory notes

The *c.* 1200 illustrations are from original full-size drawings by the author, with the exceptions noted below. These exceptions are objects now lost, destroyed, not available, or in fields not immediately related to the topic of the work; this class of material has therefore been illustrated from existing drawings, including: figs. 42, 91, 140–2, 158, 166, 178, 180, 185, 186, 195, 200, 210, 271, 274, 316, 341, 381, 384, 387–8, 416, 461, 469, 687–8, 744, 746, 943–6, 1019, 1058.

All drawings of beakers and artefacts are reproduced at a one-third reduction, unless the caption states to the contrary.

The standard form of caption is laid out as follows:

> figure number. beaker group corpus number,
> site name, county.

The site name is necessarily an abbreviated form of the full designation to be found in the corpus under the appropriate corpus number.

A large plus sign linking figures with the same site name indicates important associations, usually from one grave.

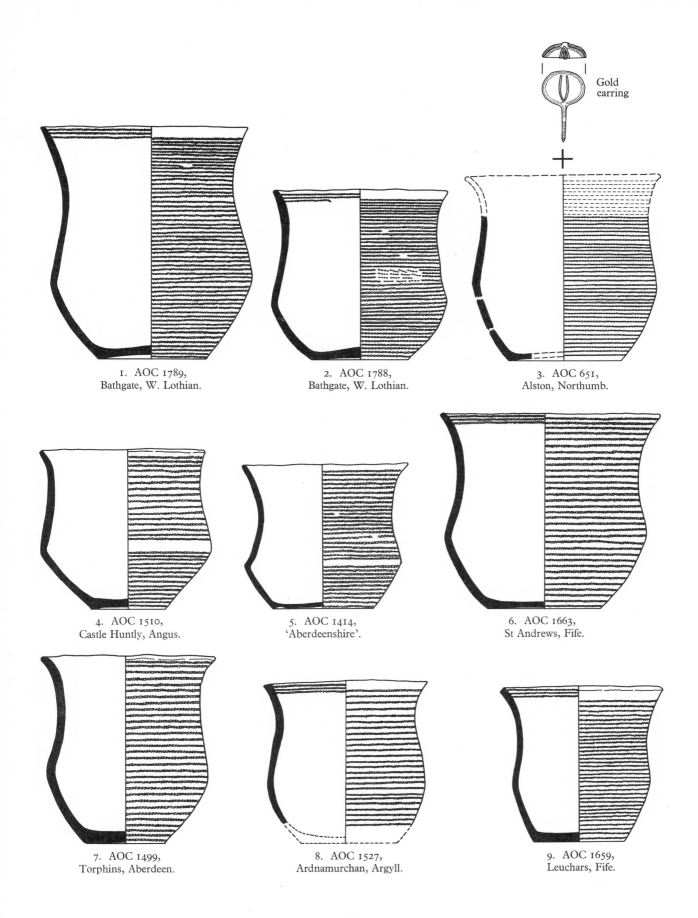

Gold
earring

1. AOC 1789,
Bathgate, W. Lothian.

2. AOC 1788,
Bathgate, W. Lothian.

3. AOC 651,
Alston, Northumb.

4. AOC 1510,
Castle Huntly, Angus.

5. AOC 1414,
'Aberdeenshire'.

6. AOC 1663,
St Andrews, Fife.

7. AOC 1499,
Torphins, Aberdeen.

8. AOC 1527,
Ardnamurchan, Argyll.

9. AOC 1659,
Leuchars, Fife.

10. AOC 1376,
Rudstone 67, Yorks.

11. AOC 1085,
Bulford, Wilts.

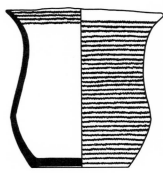

12. AOC 980,
Mortlake, Surrey.

13. AOC 43,
Hitcham, Bucks.

14. AOC 730,
Cassington, Oxon.

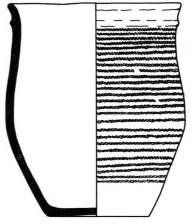

15. AOC 1445,
Inverurie, Aberdeen.

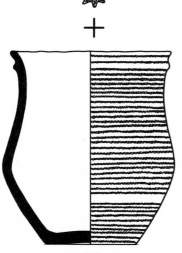

16. AOC 1582,
Forglen, Banff.

17. AOC 1738,
Auchterarder, Perth.

18. AOC 1259,
Cave, Yorks.

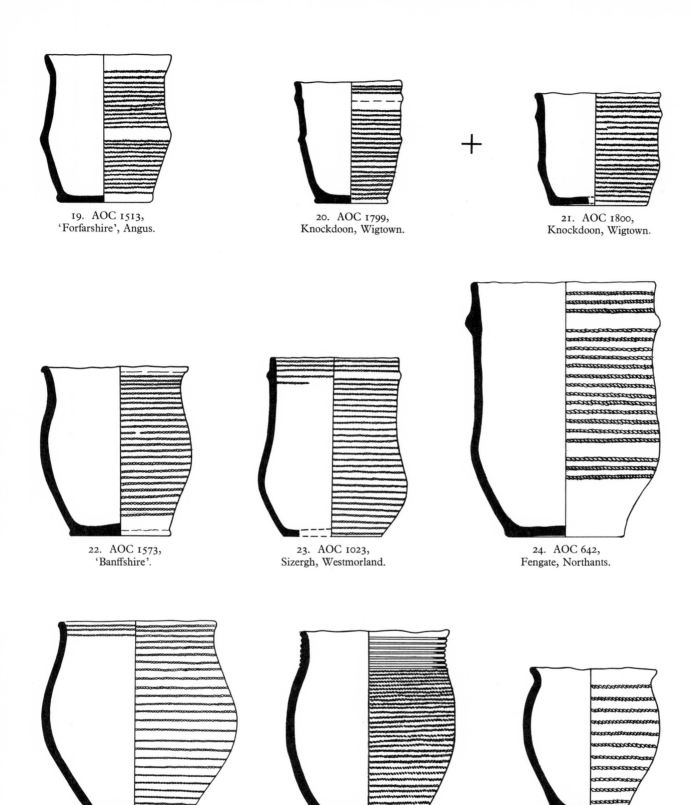

19. AOC 1513,
'Forfarshire', Angus.

20. AOC 1799,
Knockdoon, Wigtown.

21. AOC 1800,
Knockdoon, Wigtown.

22. AOC 1573,
'Banffshire'.

23. AOC 1023,
Sizergh, Westmorland.

24. AOC 642,
Fengate, Northants.

25. AOC Netherlands,
Nieuw Roden, Roden.

26. AOC 1574,
Scatterty (?), Banff.

27. AOC 976,
Mortlake, Surrey.

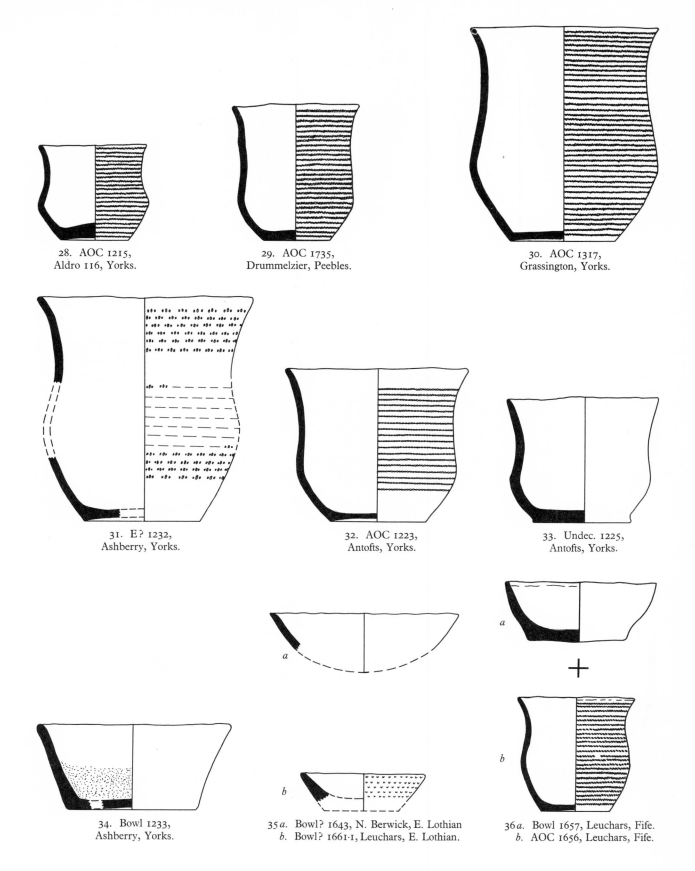

28. AOC 1215,
Aldro 116, Yorks.

29. AOC 1735,
Drummelzier, Peebles.

30. AOC 1317,
Grassington, Yorks.

31. E? 1232,
Ashberry, Yorks.

32. AOC 1223,
Antofts, Yorks.

33. Undec. 1225,
Antofts, Yorks.

34. Bowl 1233,
Ashberry, Yorks.

35 a. Bowl? 1643, N. Berwick, E. Lothian
b. Bowl? 1661·1, Leuchars, E. Lothian.

36 a. Bowl 1657, Leuchars, Fife.
b. AOC 1656, Leuchars, Fife.

37. Food Vessel
Amesbury, Wilts.

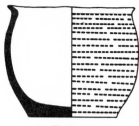

38. E. Ang. 407,
Ightham, Kent.

39. AOC 1408,
Willerby 235, Yorks.

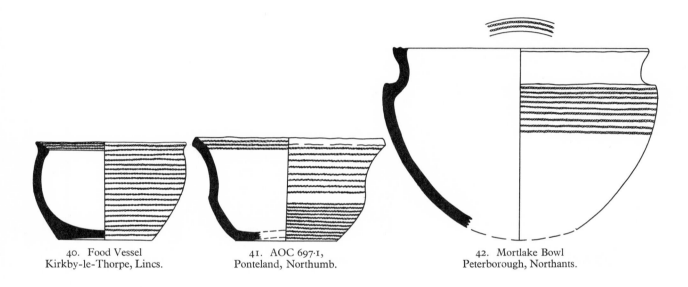

40. Food Vessel
Kirkby-le-Thorpe, Lincs.

41. AOC 697·1,
Ponteland, Northumb.

42. Mortlake Bowl
Peterborough, Northants.

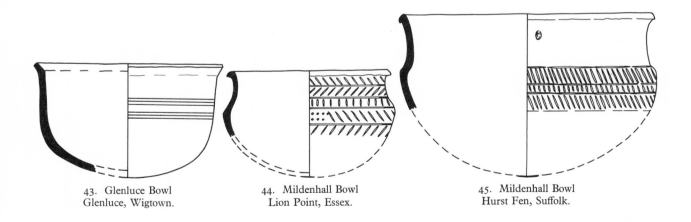

43. Glenluce Bowl
Glenluce, Wigtown.

44. Mildenhall Bowl
Lion Point, Essex.

45. Mildenhall Bowl
Hurst Fen, Suffolk.

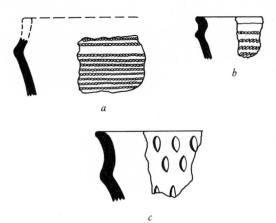

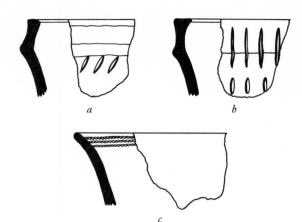

46 *a*. AOC 457, Manton Warren, Lincs.
  b. AOC 1780, Falkirk, Stirling.
  c. FN 1538, Coll Is., Argyll.

47 *a*. FN Germany, Rüsselsheim.
  b. FN Germany, near Darmstadt.
  c. Undec. Germany, Urmitz.

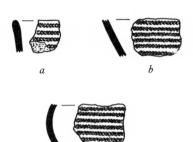

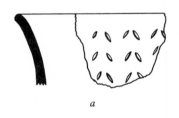

48 *a*. AOC 192, Hilton, Dorset.
  b. AOC 1617, Archerfield, E. Lothian.
  c. AOC 1813, Glenluce, Wigtown.

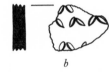

49 *a*. FN 1627, Hedderwick, E. Lothian.
  b. FN 1619, Archerfield, E. Lothian.

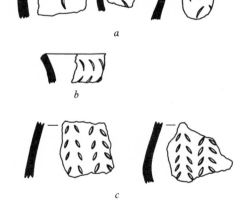

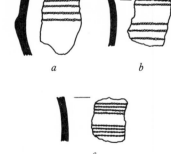

52 *a–c*. AOC rim profiles.

50 *a*. FN 700, Ross Links, Northumb.
  b. FN 1642, Tusculum, E. Lothian.
  c. FN 1814, Glenluce, Wigtown.

51. *a* AOC 1808, Glenluce, Wigtown.
  b. AOC 1808, Glenluce, Wigtown.
  c. AOC 1536, Coll Is, Argyll.

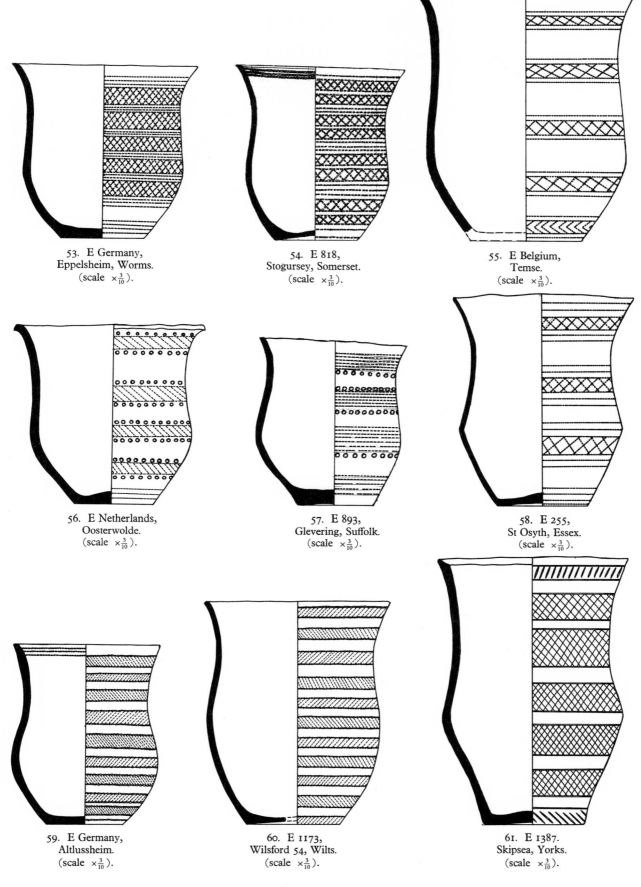

53. E Germany,
Eppelsheim, Worms.
(scale ×³⁄₁₀).

54. E 818,
Stogursey, Somerset.
(scale ×³⁄₁₀).

55. E Belgium,
Temse.
(scale ×³⁄₁₀).

56. E Netherlands,
Oosterwolde.
(scale ×³⁄₁₀).

57. E 893,
Glevering, Suffolk.
(scale ×³⁄₁₀).

58. E 255,
St Osyth, Essex.
(scale ×³⁄₁₀).

59. E Germany,
Altlussheim.
(scale ×³⁄₁₀).

60. E 1173,
Wilsford 54, Wilts.
(scale ×³⁄₁₀).

61. E 1387.
Skipsea, Yorks.
(scale ×³⁄₁₀).

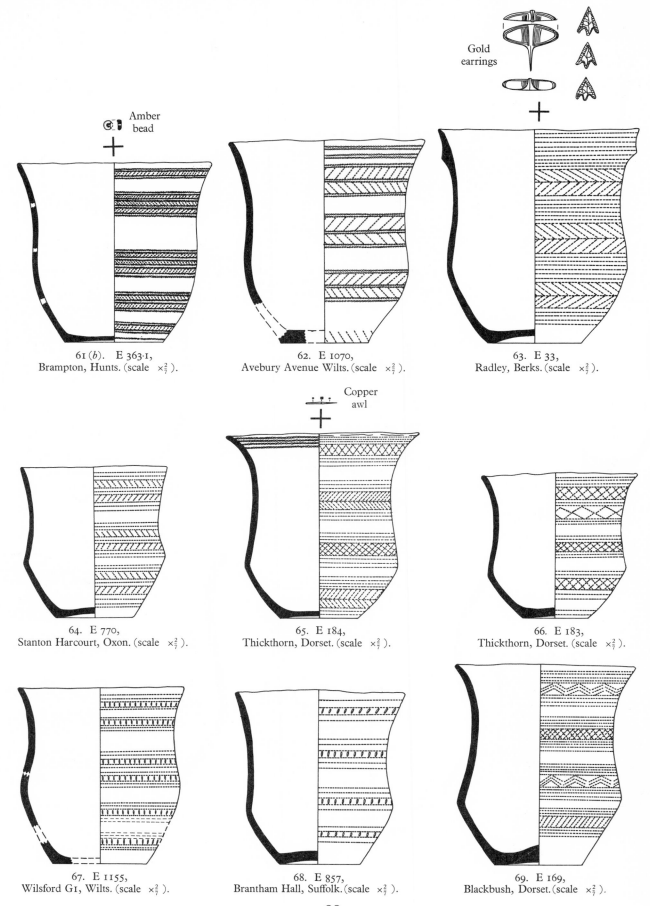

Amber
bead

61 (b). E 363·1,
Brampton, Hunts. (scale ×²⁄₇).

62. E 1070,
Avebury Avenue Wilts. (scale ×²⁄₇).

Gold
earrings

63. E 33,
Radley, Berks. (scale ×²⁄₇).

64. E 770,
Stanton Harcourt, Oxon. (scale ×²⁄₇).

Copper
awl

65. E 184,
Thickthorn, Dorset. (scale ×²⁄₇).

66. E 183,
Thickthorn, Dorset. (scale ×²⁄₇).

67. E 1155,
Wilsford G1, Wilts. (scale ×²⁄₇).

68. E 857,
Brantham Hall, Suffolk. (scale ×²⁄₇).

69. E 169,
Blackbush, Dorset. (scale ×²⁄₇).

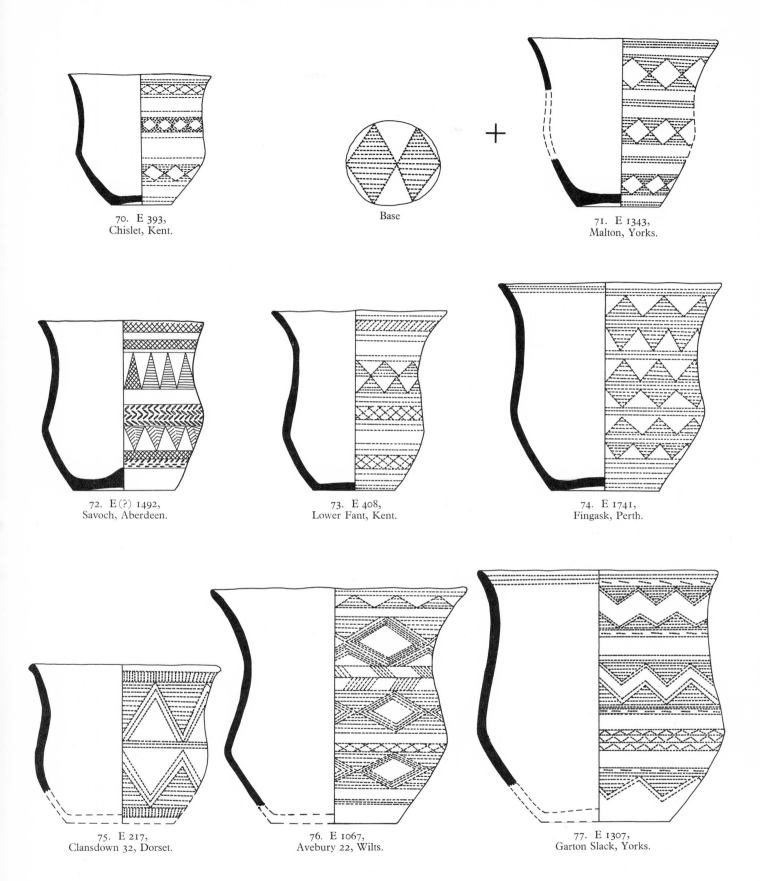

70. E 393,
Chislet, Kent.

Base

71. E 1343,
Malton, Yorks.

72. E (?) 1492,
Savoch, Aberdeen.

73. E 408,
Lower Fant, Kent.

74. E 1741,
Fingask, Perth.

75. E 217,
Clansdown 32, Dorset.

76. E 1067,
Avebury 22, Wilts.

77. E 1307,
Garton Slack, Yorks.

289

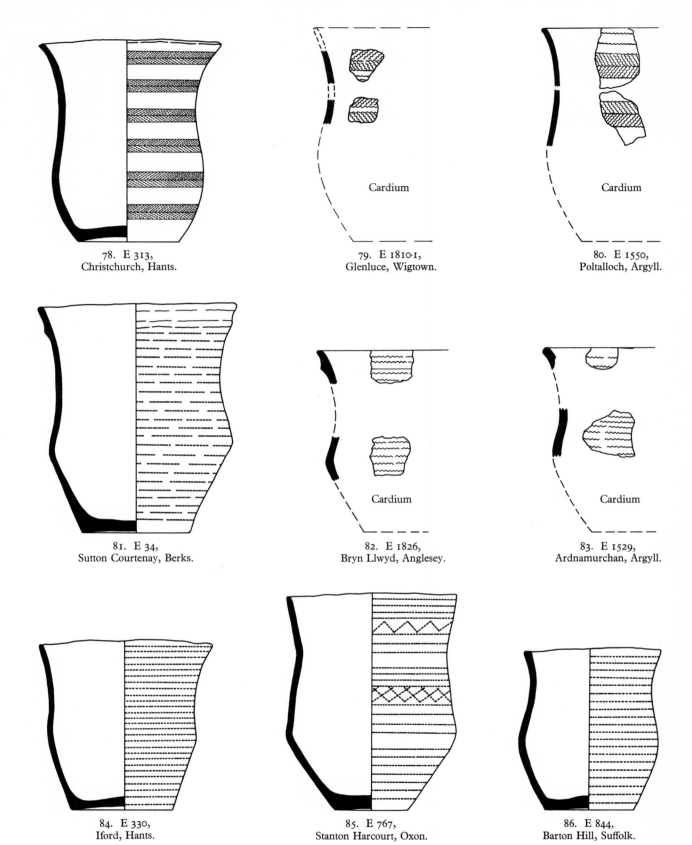

78. E 313,
Christchurch, Hants.

79. E 1810·1,
Glenluce, Wigtown.

Cardium

80. E 1550,
Poltalloch, Argyll.

Cardium

81. E 34,
Sutton Courtenay, Berks.

82. E 1826,
Bryn Llwyd, Anglesey.

Cardium

83. E 1529,
Ardnamurchan, Argyll.

Cardium

84. E 330,
Iford, Hants.

85. E 767,
Stanton Harcourt, Oxon.

86. E 844,
Barton Hill, Suffolk.

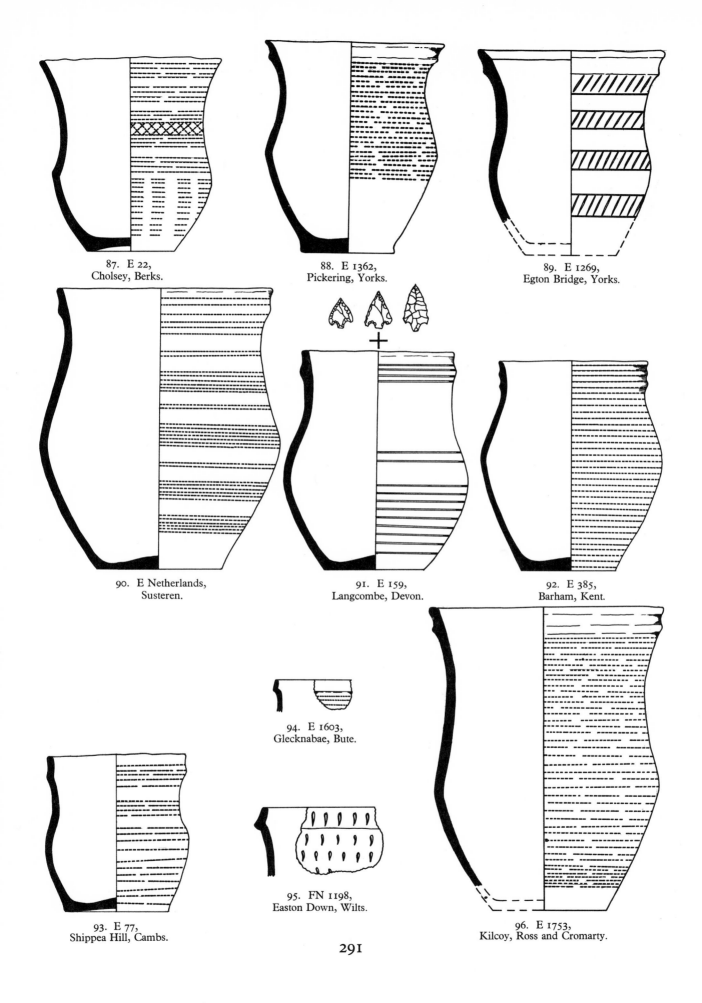

87. E 22,
Cholsey, Berks.

88. E 1362,
Pickering, Yorks.

89. E 1269,
Egton Bridge, Yorks.

90. E Netherlands,
Susteren.

91. E 159,
Langcombe, Devon.

92. E 385,
Barham, Kent.

94. E 1603,
Glecknabae, Bute.

93. E 77,
Shippea Hill, Cambs.

95. FN 1198,
Easton Down, Wilts.

96. E 1753,
Kilcoy, Ross and Cromarty.

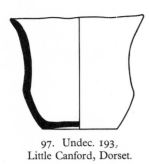

97. Undec. 193,
Little Canford, Dorset.

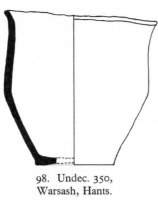

98. Undec. 350,
Warsash, Hants.

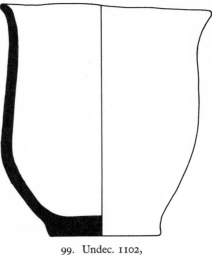

99. Undec. 1102,
Durrington Walls, Wilts.

100. Undec. 422,
Glaston, Rutland.

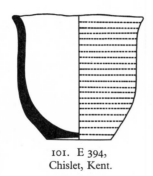

101. E 394,
Chislet, Kent.

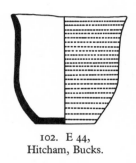

102. E 44,
Hitcham, Bucks.

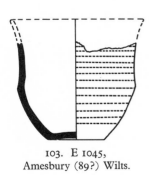

103. E 1045,
Amesbury (89?) Wilts.

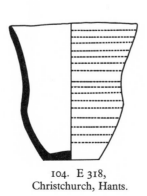

104. E 318,
Christchurch, Hants.

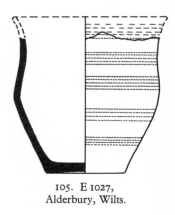

105. E 1027,
Alderbury, Wilts.

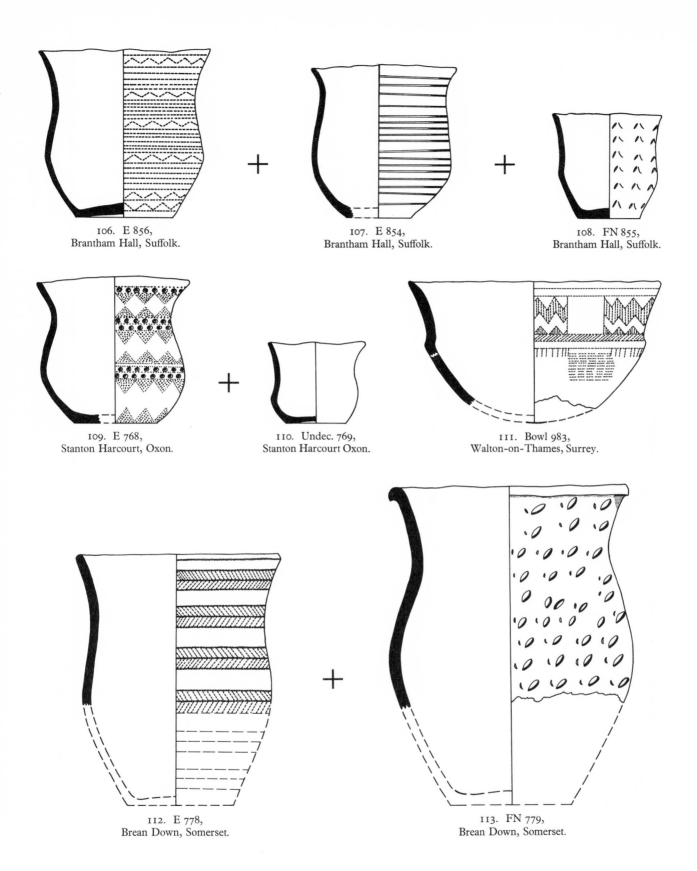

106. E 856,
Brantham Hall, Suffolk.

107. E 854,
Brantham Hall, Suffolk.

108. FN 855,
Brantham Hall, Suffolk.

109. E 768,
Stanton Harcourt, Oxon.

110. Undec. 769,
Stanton Harcourt Oxon.

111. Bowl 983,
Walton-on-Thames, Surrey.

112. E 778,
Brean Down, Somerset.

113. FN 779,
Brean Down, Somerset.

293

114. FN 620,
Tottenhill, Norfolk.

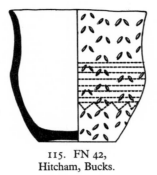

115. FN 42,
Hitcham, Bucks.

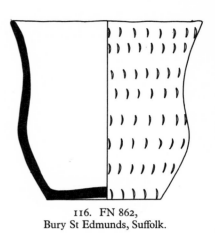

116. FN 862,
Bury St Edmunds, Suffolk.

117. FN 866,
Butley, Suffolk.

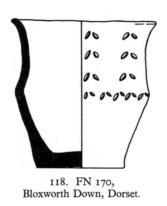

118. FN 170,
Bloxworth Down, Dorset.

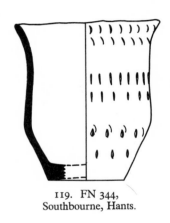

119. FN 344,
Southbourne, Hants.

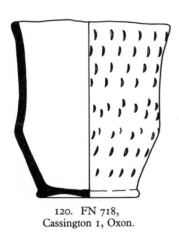

120. FN 718,
Cassington 1, Oxon.

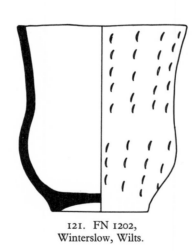

121. FN 1202,
Winterslow, Wilts.

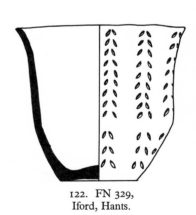

122. FN 329,
Iford, Hants.

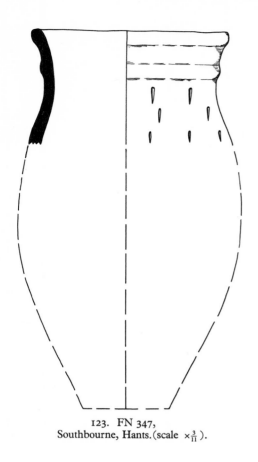

123. FN 347,
Southbourne, Hants. (scale $\times \frac{3}{11}$).

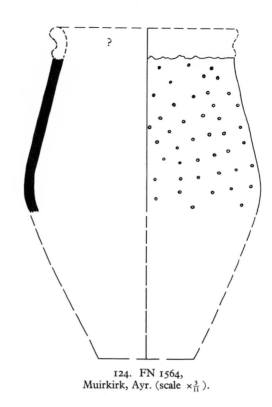

124. FN 1564,
Muirkirk, Ayr. (scale $\times \frac{3}{11}$).

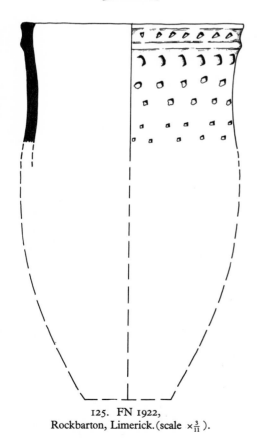

125. FN 1922,
Rockbarton, Limerick. (scale $\times \frac{3}{11}$).

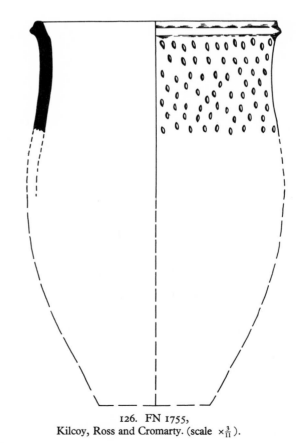

126. FN 1755,
Kilcoy, Ross and Cromarty. (scale $\times \frac{3}{11}$).

295

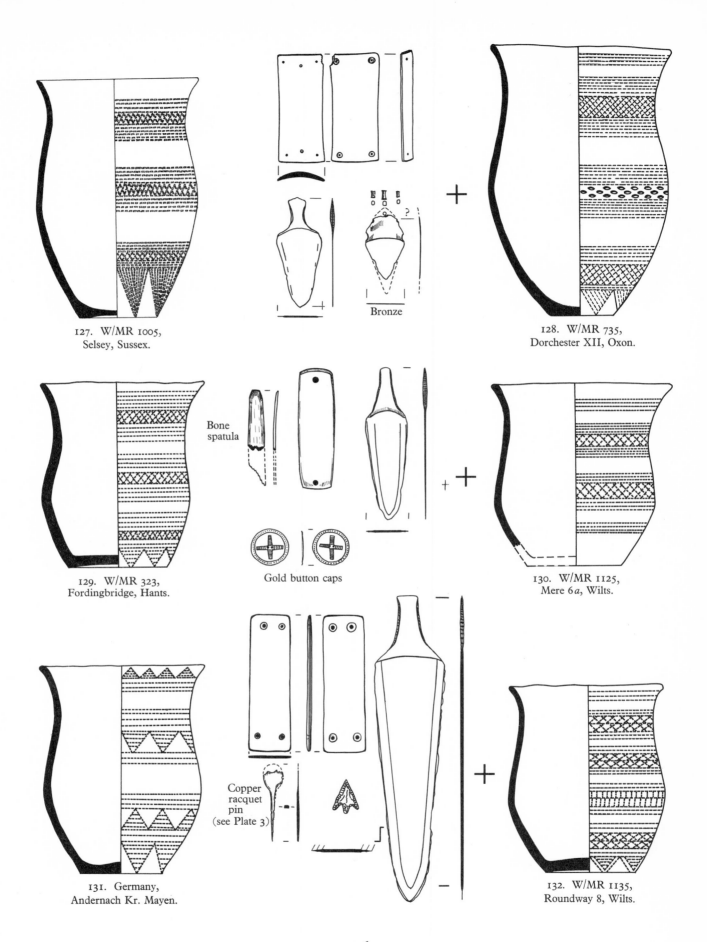

127. W/MR 1005,
Selsey, Sussex.

Bronze

128. W/MR 735,
Dorchester XII, Oxon.

Bone
spatula

Gold button caps

129. W/MR 323,
Fordingbridge, Hants.

130. W/MR 1125,
Mere 6a, Wilts.

Copper
racquet
pin
(see Plate 3)

131. Germany,
Andernach Kr. Mayen.

132. W/MR 1135,
Roundway 8, Wilts.

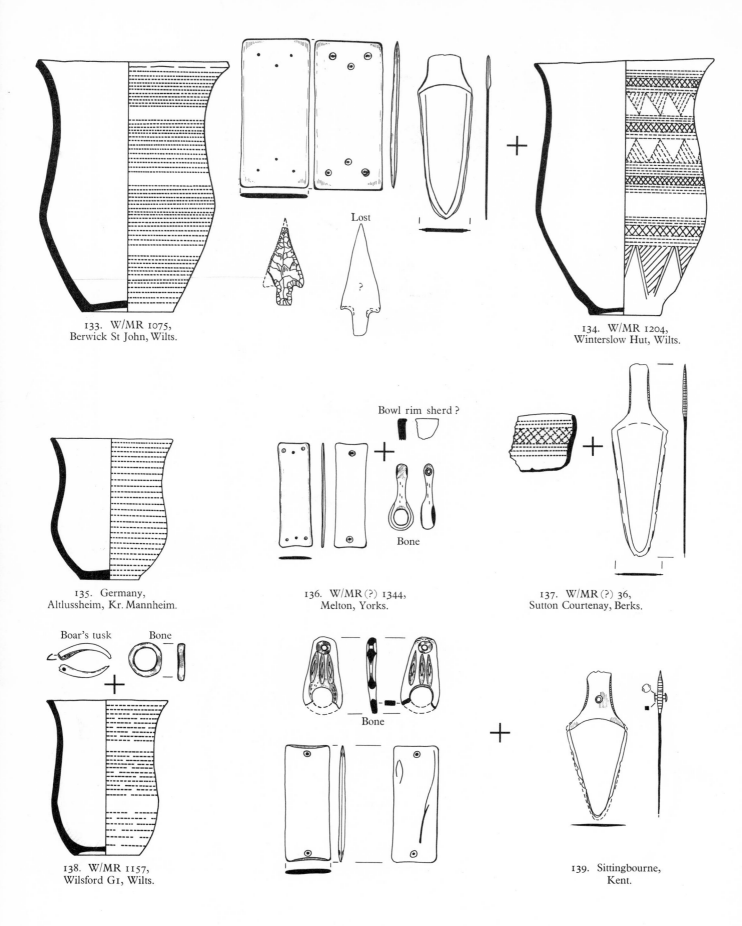

133. W/MR 1075,
Berwick St John, Wilts.

Lost

134. W/MR 1204,
Winterslow Hut, Wilts.

135. Germany,
Altlussheim, Kr. Mannheim.

Bowl rim sherd ?

Bone

136. W/MR (?) 1344,
Melton, Yorks.

137. W/MR (?) 36,
Sutton Courtenay, Berks.

Boar's tusk   Bone

Bone

138. W/MR 1157,
Wilsford G1, Wilts.

139. Sittingbourne,
Kent.

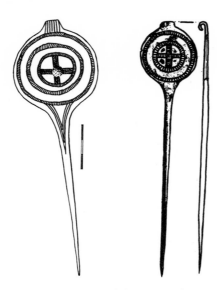

a

b

c

140. Aunjetitz bronze pins
(scale ×$\frac{5}{16}$).

141. Gold button caps from
  a. Douglas, Co. Cork. (scale ×$\frac{2}{3}$).
  b. Ballyshannon, Co. Kildare. (scale ×$\frac{3}{5}$).
  c. Kilmuckridge, Co. Wexford. (scale ×$\frac{4}{9}$).

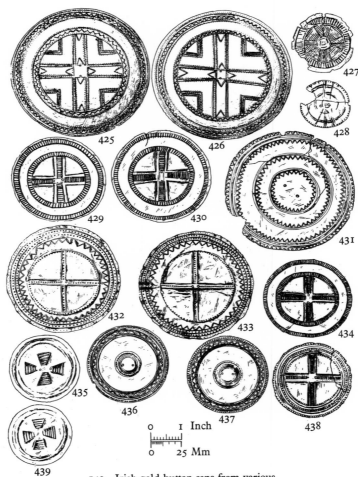

425

426

427

428

429

430

431

432

433

434

435

436

437

438

439

0 1 Inch

0 25 Mm

142. Irish gold button caps from various
Irish sites in Cos Cork (427, 431, 436,
437); Mayo (429, 430); Monaghan (425,
426); Roscommon (435, 439) and
Wexford (432, 433).

298

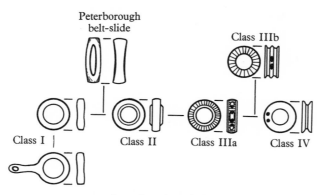

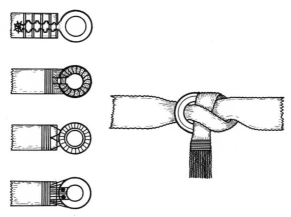

143. A typology for British belt rings.

144. A hypothetical reconstruction of beaker belt rings in use, illustrating the skeuomorphic decoration suggested by the binding.

Below, a fragmentary stone menhir illustrating a girdled kilt of beaker type, from Sion, Petit-Chasseur, Switzerland, associated with a beaker cist burial (*Bollettino del Centro Camuno di Studi Preistorici*, III (1967)).

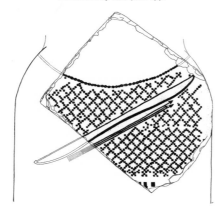

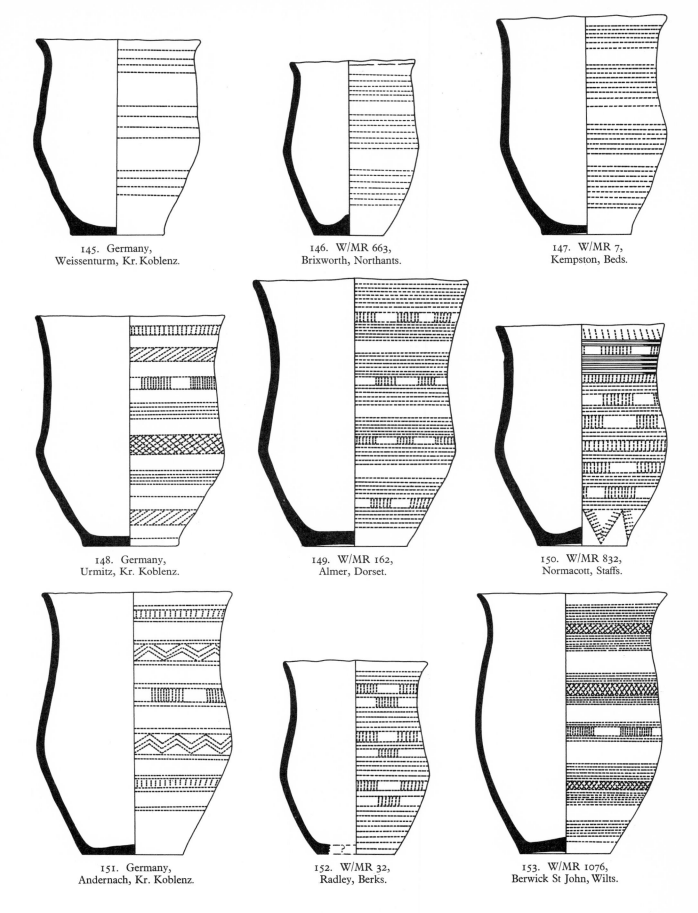

145. Germany,
Weissenturm, Kr. Koblenz.

146. W/MR 663,
Brixworth, Northants.

147. W/MR 7,
Kempston, Beds.

148. Germany,
Urmitz, Kr. Koblenz.

149. W/MR 162,
Almer, Dorset.

150. W/MR 832,
Normacott, Staffs.

151. Germany,
Andernach, Kr. Koblenz.

152. W/MR 32,
Radley, Berks.

153. W/MR 1076,
Berwick St John, Wilts.

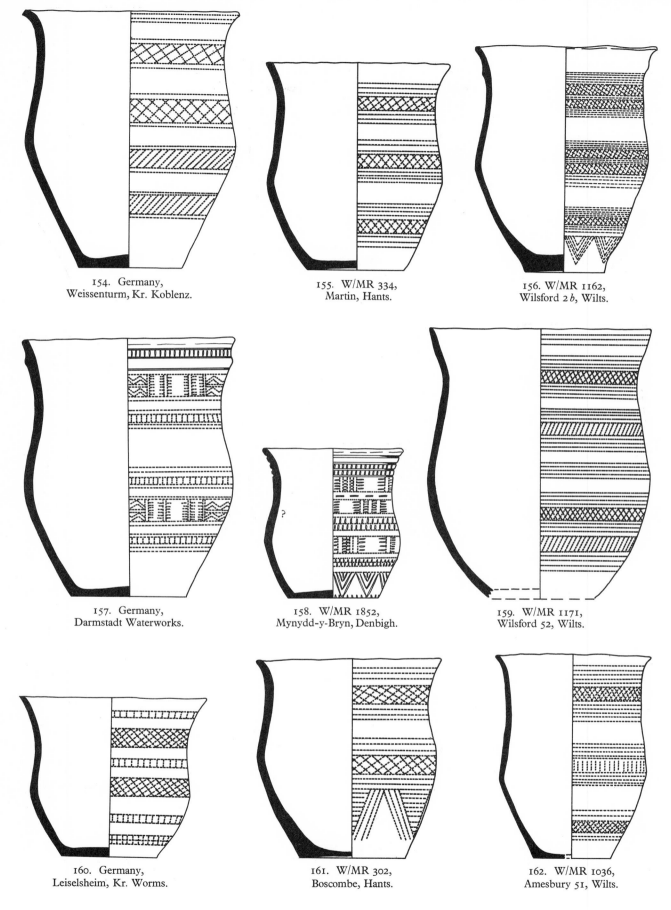

154. Germany,
Weissenturm, Kr. Koblenz.

155. W/MR 334,
Martin, Hants.

156. W/MR 1162,
Wilsford 2 *b*, Wilts.

157. Germany,
Darmstadt Waterworks.

158. W/MR 1852,
Mynydd-y-Bryn, Denbigh.

159. W/MR 1171,
Wilsford 52, Wilts.

160. Germany,
Leiselsheim, Kr. Worms.

161. W/MR 302,
Boscombe, Hants.

162. W/MR 1036,
Amesbury 51, Wilts.

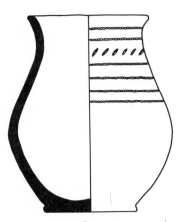

163. Germany,
Frankfurt-Praunheim.

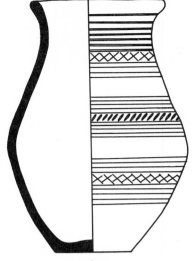

164. W/MR 755,
Little Rollright, Oxon.

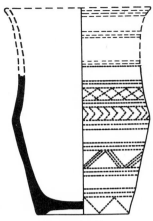

165. W/MR 716,
Cassington, Oxon.

Wooden bead cores

Sheet
copper

Shale beads

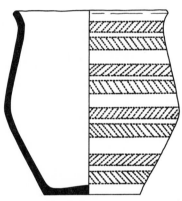

166. Germany,
Logabirum Kr. Leer.

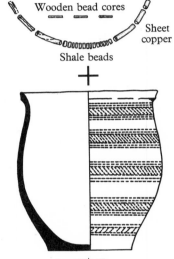

167. W/MR 991,
Devil's Dyke, Sussex.

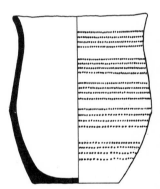

168. W/MR 19,
Brightwell, Berks.

169. Germany,
Worms-Herrnsheim.

170. W/MR 1084,
Bulford, Wilts.

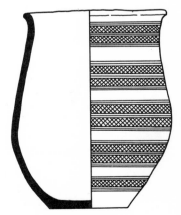

171. W/MR 1151,
Upton Lovell 2c, Wilts.

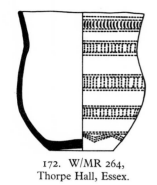

172. W/MR 264,
Thorpe Hall, Essex.

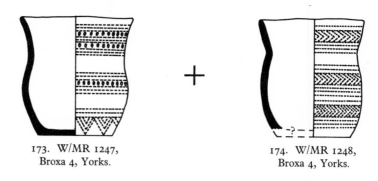

173. W/MR 1247,
Broxa 4, Yorks.

+

174. W/MR 1248,
Broxa 4, Yorks.

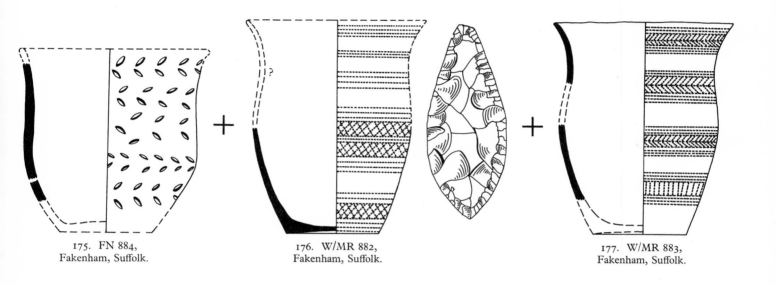

175. FN 884,
Fakenham, Suffolk.

+

176. W/MR 882,
Fakenham, Suffolk.

+

177. W/MR 883,
Fakenham, Suffolk.

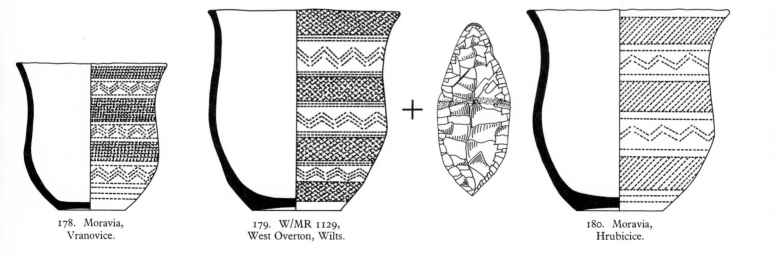

178. Moravia,
Vranovice.

179. W/MR 1129,
West Overton, Wilts.

+

180. Moravia,
Hrubicice.

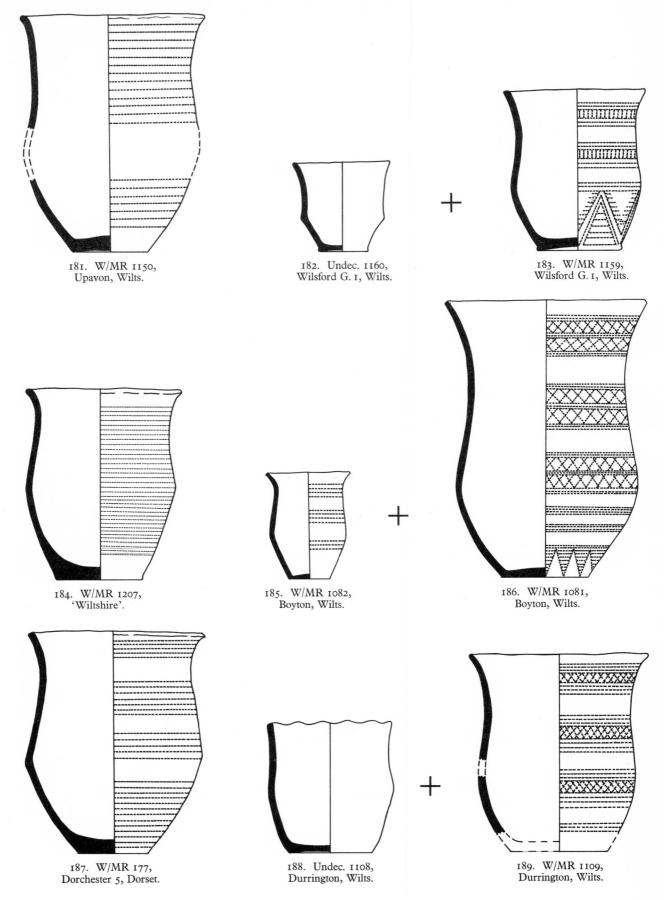

181. W/MR 1150,
Upavon, Wilts.

182. Undec. 1160,
Wilsford G. 1, Wilts.

183. W/MR 1159,
Wilsford G. 1, Wilts.

184. W/MR 1207,
'Wiltshire'.

185. W/MR 1082,
Boyton, Wilts.

186. W/MR 1081,
Boyton, Wilts.

187. W/MR 177,
Dorchester 5, Dorset.

188. Undec. 1108,
Durrington, Wilts.

189. W/MR 1109,
Durrington, Wilts.

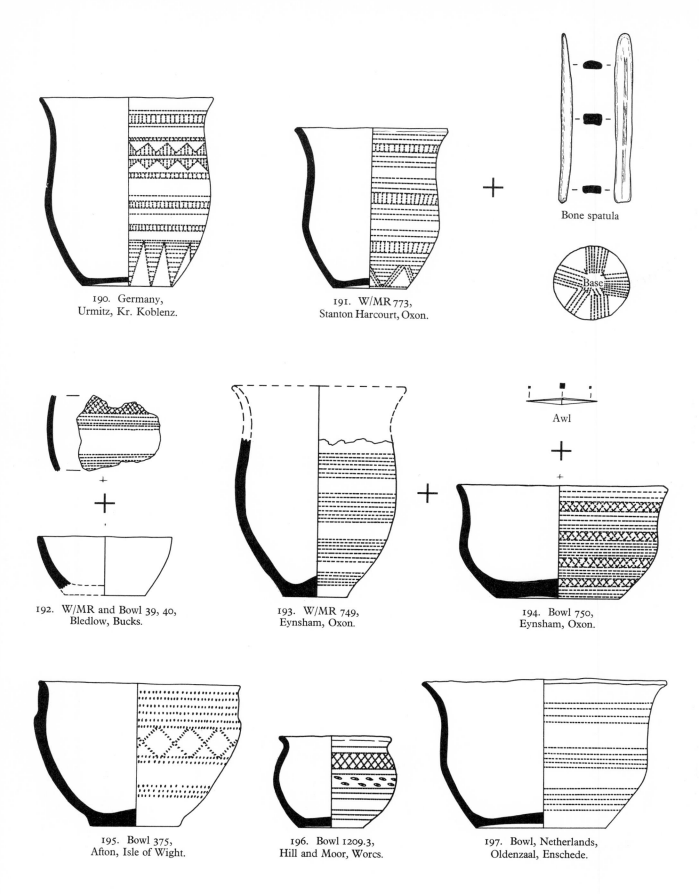

Bone spatula

Base

190. Germany,
Urmitz, Kr. Koblenz.

191. W/MR 773,
Stanton Harcourt, Oxon.

Awl

192. W/MR and Bowl 39, 40,
Bledlow, Bucks.

193. W/MR 749,
Eynsham, Oxon.

194. Bowl 750,
Eynsham, Oxon.

195. Bowl 375,
Afton, Isle of Wight.

196. Bowl 1209.3,
Hill and Moor, Worcs.

197. Bowl, Netherlands,
Oldenzaal, Enschede.

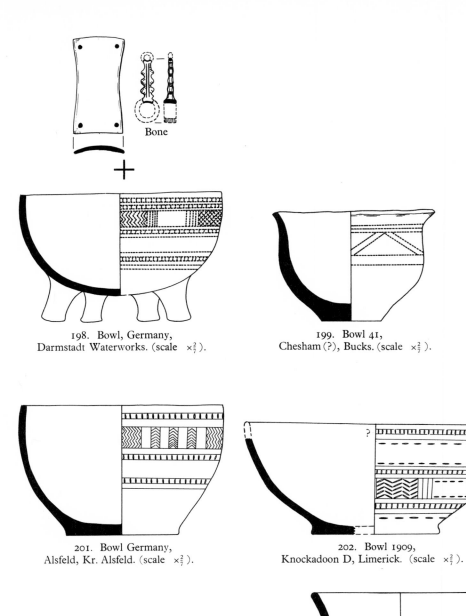

Bone

198. Bowl, Germany,
Darmstadt Waterworks. (scale ×$\frac{2}{7}$).

199. Bowl 41,
Chesham (?), Bucks. (scale ×$\frac{2}{7}$).

200. Bowl 1868,
Tinkinswood, Glamorgan. (scale ×$\frac{2}{7}$).

Polypod?

201. Bowl Germany,
Alsfeld, Kr. Alsfeld. (scale ×$\frac{2}{7}$).

202. Bowl 1909,
Knockadoon D, Limerick. (scale ×$\frac{2}{7}$).

203. Bowl Germany,
Miesenheim Kr. Mayen. (scale ×$\frac{2}{7}$).

See colour plate Vol. I

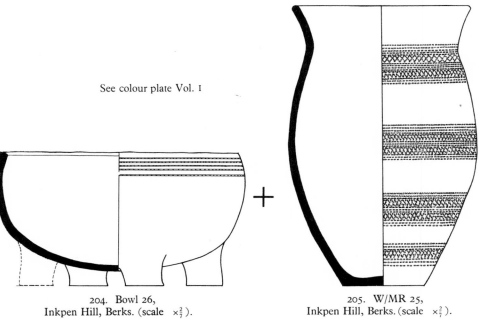

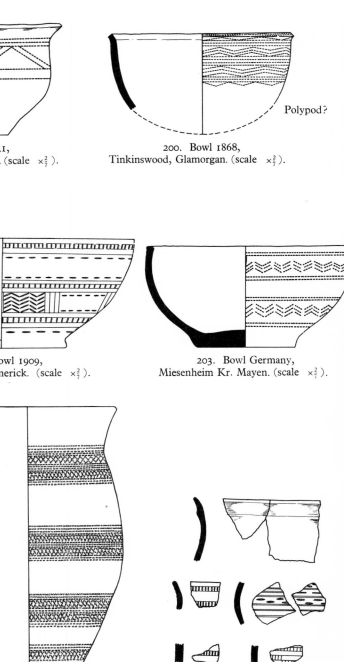

204. Bowl 26,
Inkpen Hill, Berks. (scale ×$\frac{2}{7}$).

205. W/MR 25,
Inkpen Hill, Berks. (scale ×$\frac{2}{7}$).

206. W/MR (?) 1910-12,
Knockadoon, Limerick. (scale ×$\frac{2}{7}$).

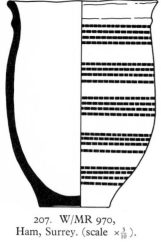

207. W/MR 970,
Ham, Surrey. (scale ×$\frac{3}{10}$).

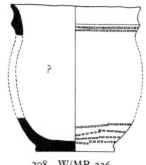

208. W/MR 336,
Otterbourne, Hants. (scale ×$\frac{3}{10}$).

209. W/MR 337,
Otterbourne, Hants. (scale ×$\frac{3}{10}$).

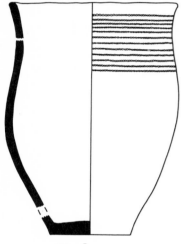

210. Germany,
Brauel-Offensen, Kr. Zeven. (scale ×$\frac{3}{10}$).

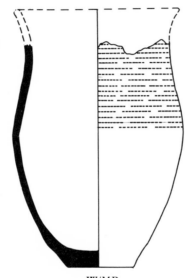

211. W/MR 420,
Glaston, Rutland. (scale ×$\frac{3}{10}$).

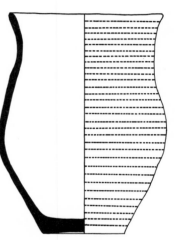

212. W/MR 547,
Heacham, Norfolk. (scale ×$\frac{3}{10}$).

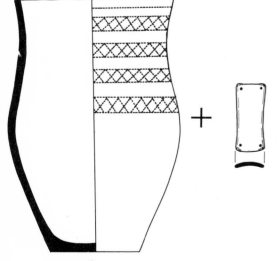

213. Germany,
Urmitz, Kr. Koblenz. (scale ×$\frac{3}{10}$).

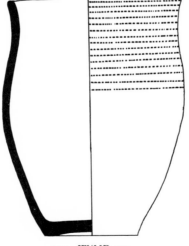

214. W/MR 503,
Bardolph Fen, Norfolk. (scale ×$\frac{3}{10}$).

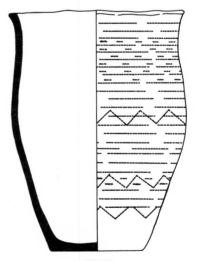

215. W/MR 201,
Tarrant Launceston, Dorset. (scale ×$\frac{3}{10}$).

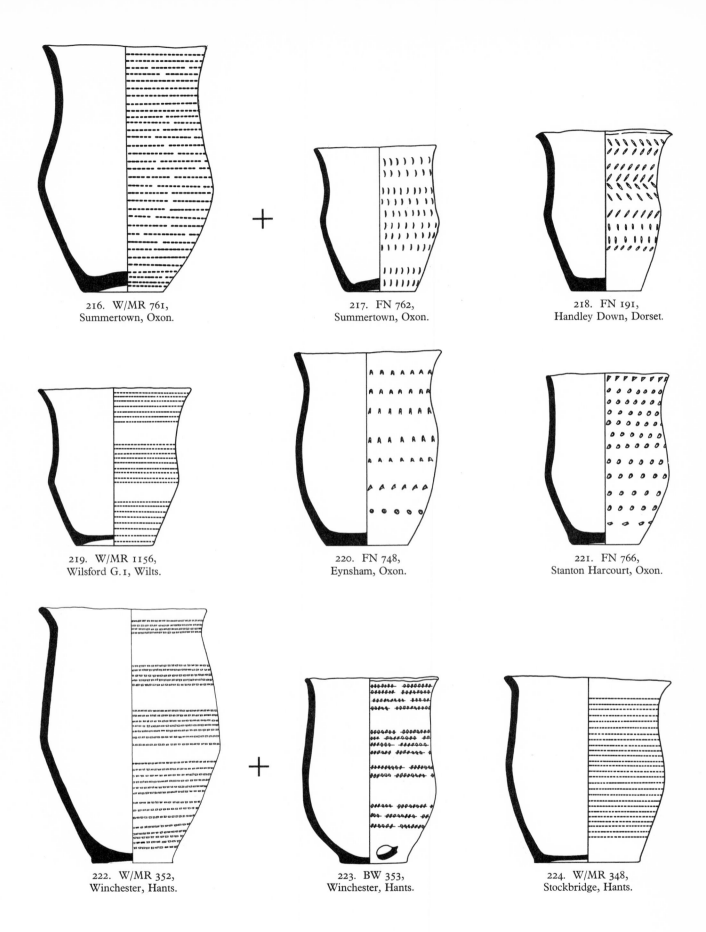

216. W/MR 761,
Summertown, Oxon.

217. FN 762,
Summertown, Oxon.

218. FN 191,
Handley Down, Dorset.

219. W/MR 1156,
Wilsford G.1, Wilts.

220. FN 748,
Eynsham, Oxon.

221. FN 766,
Stanton Harcourt, Oxon.

222. W/MR 352,
Winchester, Hants.

223. BW 353,
Winchester, Hants.

224. W/MR 348,
Stockbridge, Hants.

225. Undec. 180,
Frampton 1, Dorset.
(scale ×$\frac{3}{11}$).

226. Undec. 995,
Hassocks, Sussex.
(scale ×$\frac{3}{11}$).

227. Undec. 1003,
Rodmell, Sussex.
(scale ×$\frac{3}{11}$).

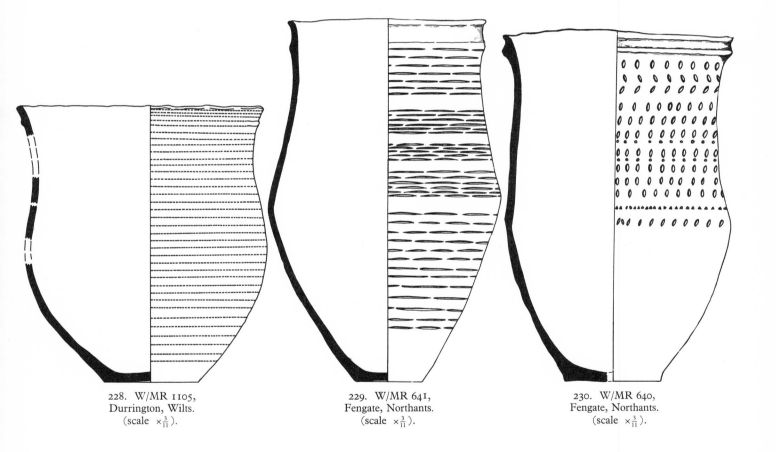

228. W/MR 1105,
Durrington, Wilts.
(scale ×$\frac{3}{11}$).

229. W/MR 641,
Fengate, Northants.
(scale ×$\frac{3}{11}$).

230. W/MR 640,
Fengate, Northants.
(scale ×$\frac{3}{11}$).

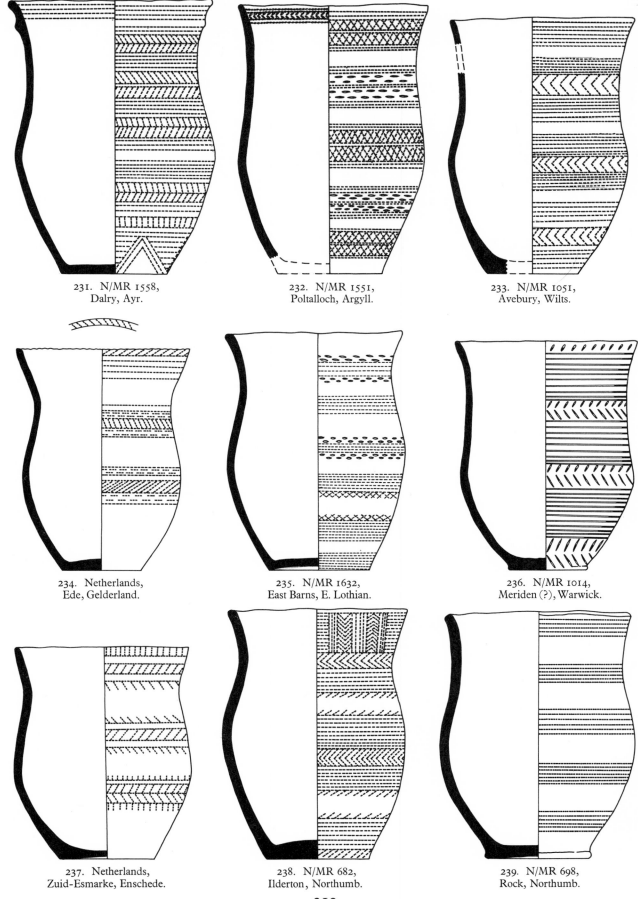

231. N/MR 1558,
Dalry, Ayr.

232. N/MR 1551,
Poltalloch, Argyll.

233. N/MR 1051,
Avebury, Wilts.

234. Netherlands,
Ede, Gelderland.

235. N/MR 1632,
East Barns, E. Lothian.

236. N/MR 1014,
Meriden (?), Warwick.

237. Netherlands,
Zuid-Esmarke, Enschede.

238. N/MR 682,
Ilderton, Northumb.

239. N/MR 698,
Rock, Northumb.

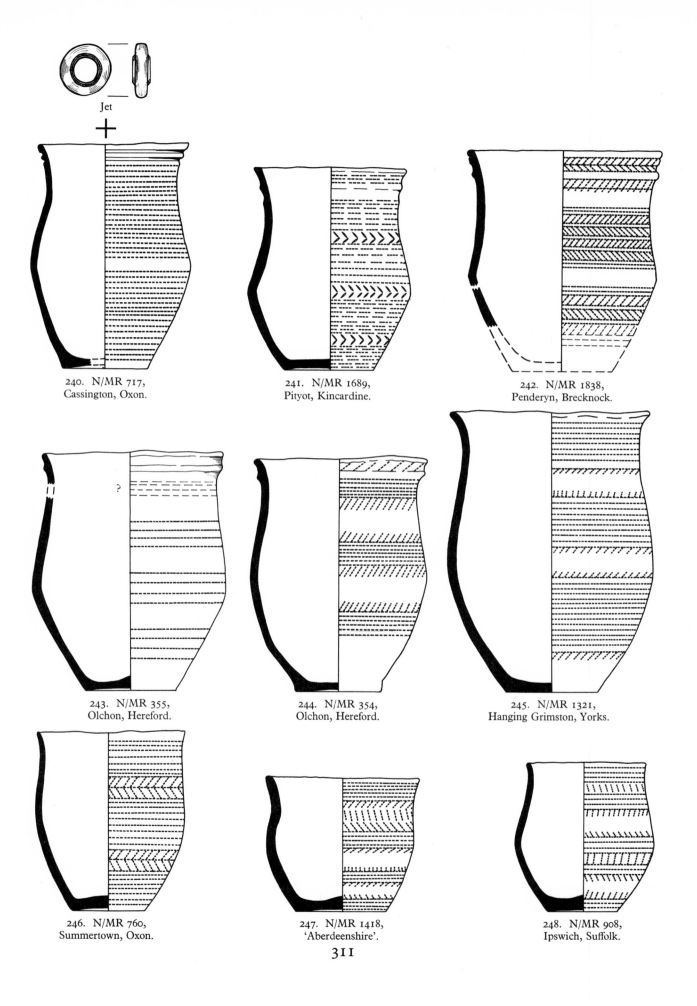

Jet

240. N/MR 717,
Cassington, Oxon.

241. N/MR 1689,
Pityot, Kincardine.

242. N/MR 1838,
Penderyn, Brecknock.

243. N/MR 355,
Olchon, Hereford.

244. N/MR 354,
Olchon, Hereford.

245. N/MR 1321,
Hanging Grimston, Yorks.

246. N/MR 760,
Summertown, Oxon.

247. N/MR 1418,
'Aberdeenshire'.

248. N/MR 908,
Ipswich, Suffolk.

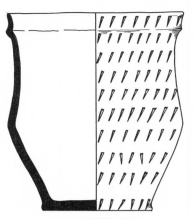

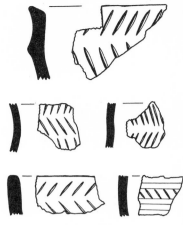

249. Netherlands,
Bargeroosterveld, Emmen.

250. N/MR 1882,
Talbenny, Pembroke.

251. N/MR? 1910-12,
Knockadoon, Limerick.

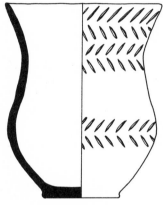

252. Germany,
Beuern, Kr. Giessen.

253. N/MR 694,
Norham, Northumb.

254. N/MR 389,
Canterbury, Kent.

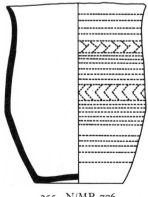

255. N/MR 776,
Yarnton, Oxon.

256. Undec. 1686,
Dunnottar, Kincardine.

257. N/MR 1781,
Buckieburn, Stirling.

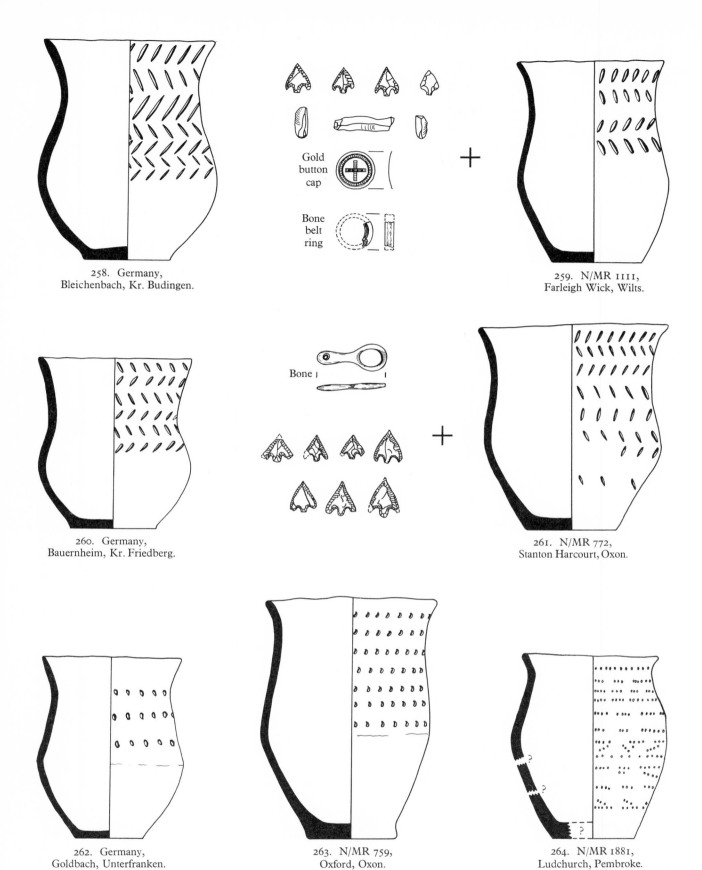

258. Germany,
Bleichenbach, Kr. Budingen.

Gold
button
cap

Bone
belt
ring

259. N/MR 1111,
Farleigh Wick, Wilts.

260. Germany,
Bauernheim, Kr. Friedberg.

Bone

261. N/MR 772,
Stanton Harcourt, Oxon.

262. Germany,
Goldbach, Unterfranken.

263. N/MR 759,
Oxford, Oxon.

264. N/MR 1881,
Ludchurch, Pembroke.

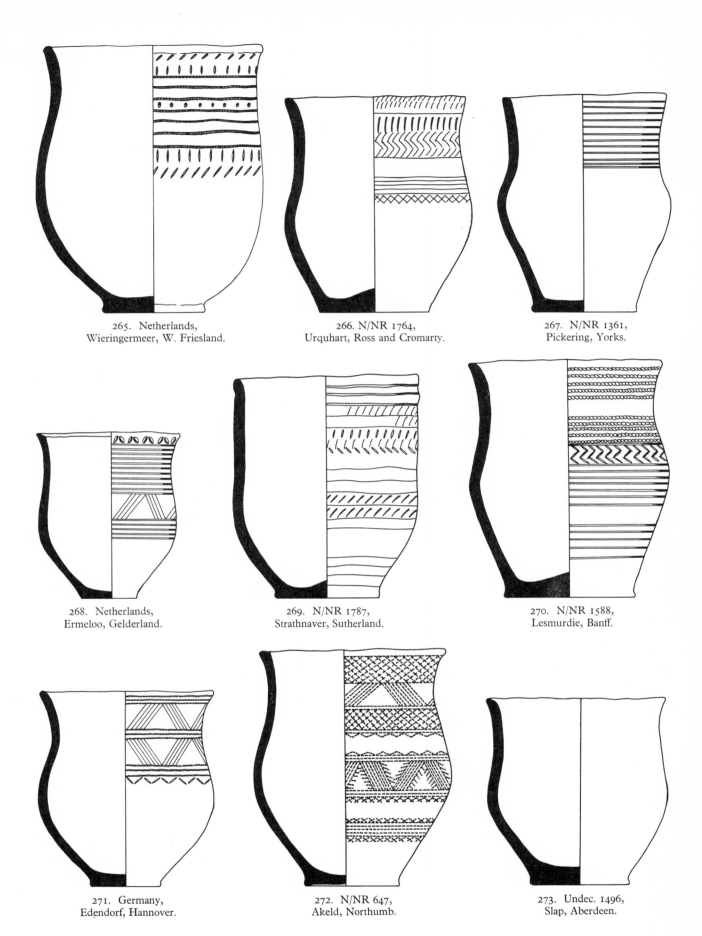

265. Netherlands,
Wieringermeer, W. Friesland.

266. N/NR 1764,
Urquhart, Ross and Cromarty.

267. N/NR 1361,
Pickering, Yorks.

268. Netherlands,
Ermeloo, Gelderland.

269. N/NR 1787,
Strathnaver, Sutherland.

270. N/NR 1588,
Lesmurdie, Banff.

271. Germany,
Edendorf, Hannover.

272. N/NR 647,
Akeld, Northumb.

273. Undec. 1496,
Slap, Aberdeen.

274. Germany, Schalkholz,
Kr. Norderdithmarschen.

275. N/NR 1783,
Dornoch, Sutherland.

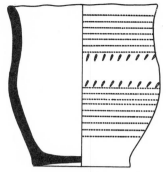

276. N/NR 1746,
Dalmore, Ross and Cromarty.

Stone

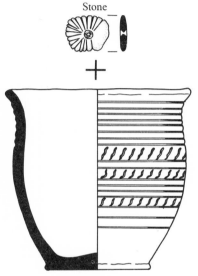

277. N/NR 1491,
Ruthven, Aberdeen.

Bone awl

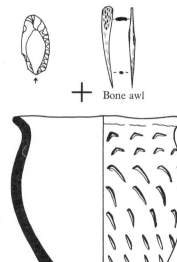

278. FN 221,
Hasting Hill, Durham.

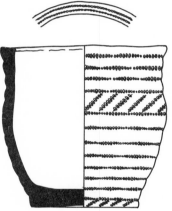

279. Food Vessel
Tentsmuir, Fife.

280. N/NR 1715,
Gordonstown, Moray.

281. N/NR 1430,
Blackhills, Aberdeen.

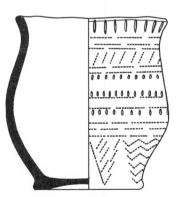

282. N/NR 669,
Doddington, Northumb.

283. Germany,
Mainz-Kastel.

284. N/NR 1213,
Aldro 54, Yorks.

285. N/NR 108,
Ainstable, Cumberland.

286. Germany,
Frankfurt-Zeilsheim.

287. N/NR 1739,
Bridge of Allan, Perth.

288. N/NR 1300,
Garton Slack 81, Yorks.

289. N/NR 1281,
Folkton 245, Yorks.

290. N/NR 1299,
Garton Slack 80, Yorks.

291. N/NR 453.1,
Kirkby-on-Bain, Lincs.

Jet

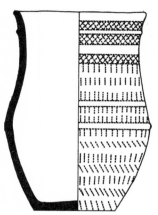

292. Netherlands,
Oudemolen, Vries.
(scale ×$\frac{3}{10}$).

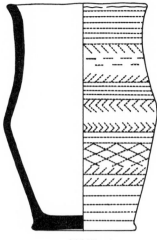

293. N/NR 1246,
Broxa 4, Yorks.
(scale ×$\frac{3}{10}$).

294. N/NR 1624,
Drem, E. Lothian.
(scale ×$\frac{3}{10}$).

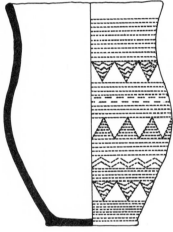

295. N/NR 114,
Newton Penrith, Cumberland.
(scale ×$\frac{3}{10}$).

296. N/NR 373,
Stanground, Hunts.
(scale ×$\frac{3}{10}$).

297. N/NR 693,
Norham, Northumb.
(scale ×$\frac{3}{10}$).

298. N/NR 1369,
Rudstone 62, Yorks.
(scale ×$\frac{3}{10}$).

299. N/NR 647.1,
Chatton, Northumb.
(scale ×$\frac{3}{10}$).

300. N/NR 647.2,
Chatton, Northumb.
(scale ×$\frac{3}{10}$).

317

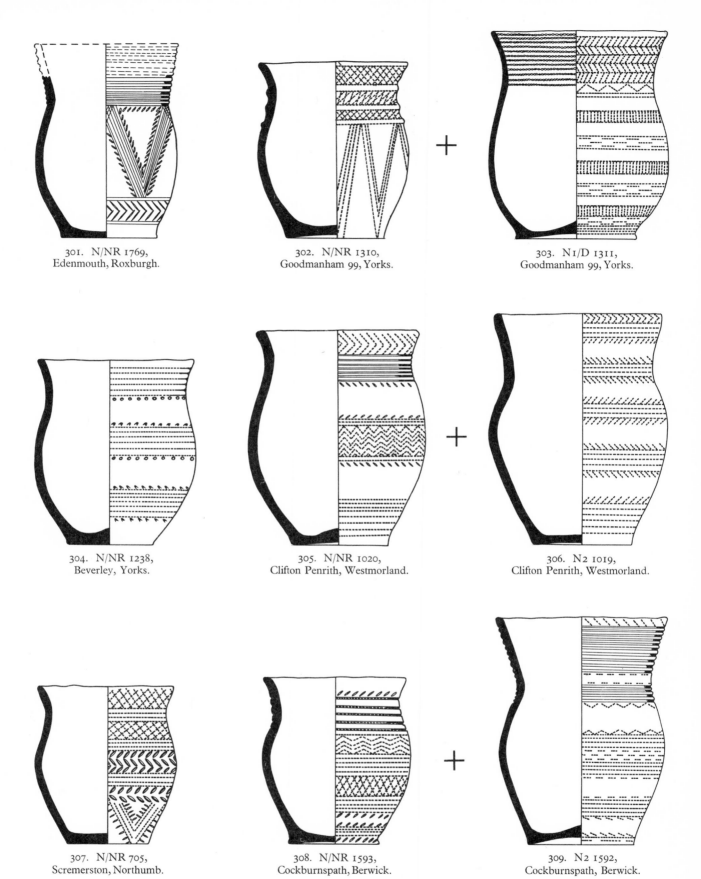

301. N/NR 1769,
Edenmouth, Roxburgh.

302. N/NR 1310,
Goodmanham 99, Yorks.

303. N1/D 1311,
Goodmanham 99, Yorks.

304. N/NR 1238,
Beverley, Yorks.

305. N/NR 1020,
Clifton Penrith, Westmorland.

306. N2 1019,
Clifton Penrith, Westmorland.

307. N/NR 705,
Scremerston, Northumb.

308. N/NR 1593,
Cockburnspath, Berwick.

309. N2 1592,
Cockburnspath, Berwick.

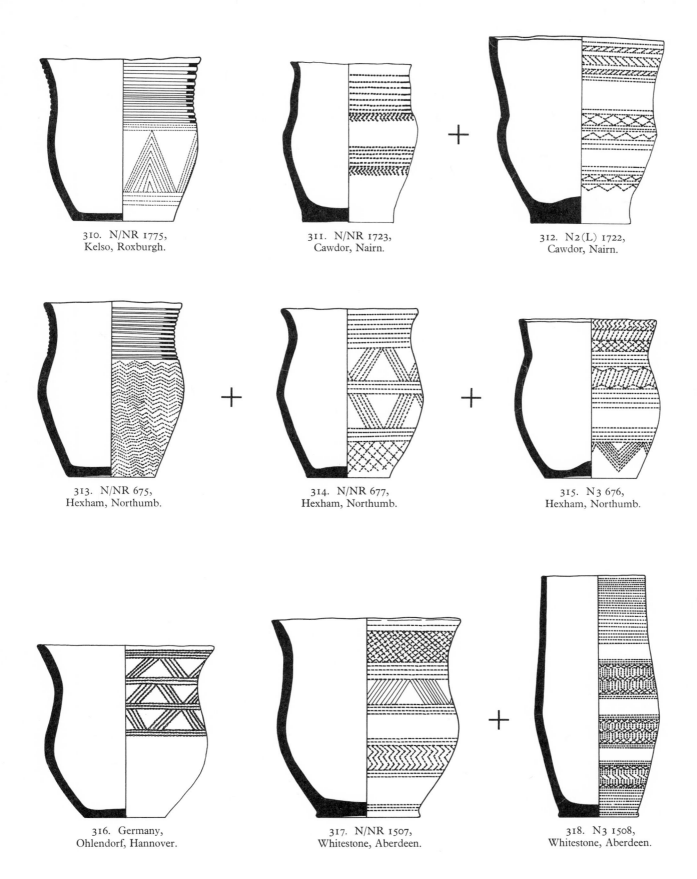

310. N/NR 1775,
Kelso, Roxburgh.

311. N/NR 1723,
Cawdor, Nairn.

312. N2(L) 1722,
Cawdor, Nairn.

313. N/NR 675,
Hexham, Northumb.

314. N/NR 677,
Hexham, Northumb.

315. N3 676,
Hexham, Northumb.

316. Germany,
Ohlendorf, Hannover.

317. N/NR 1507,
Whitestone, Aberdeen.

318. N3 1508,
Whitestone, Aberdeen.

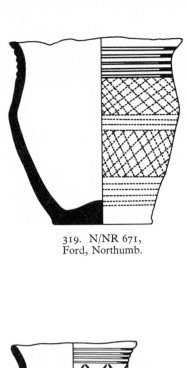

319. N/NR 671,
Ford, Northumb.

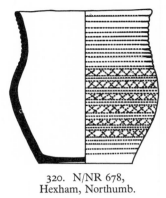

320. N/NR 678,
Hexham, Northumb.

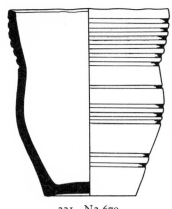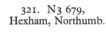

321. N3 679,
Hexham, Northumb.

322. N/NR 1685,
Dunnottar, Kincardine.

323. N3 (L) 1684,
Dunnottar, Kincardine.

324. N3 (L) 1683,
Dunnottar, Kincardine.

325. Netherlands,
Uddelermeer, Gelderland.

326. N/NR 741,
Eynsham, Oxon.

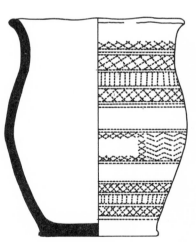

327. N/NR 1761,
Rosemarkie, Ross and Cromarty.

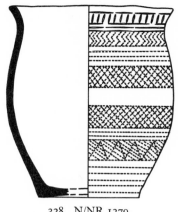

328. N/NR 1279,
Flixton, Yorks.

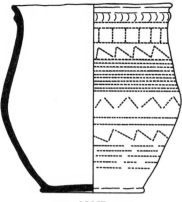

329. N/NR 1391,
Staxton, Yorks.

330. N/NR 650,
Alwinton, Northumb.

331. N/NR 1377,
Rudstone 67, Yorks.

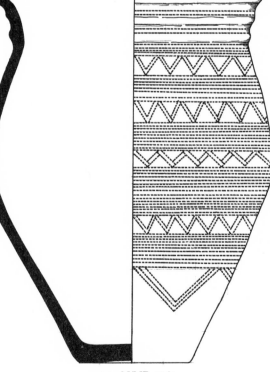

334. N/NR 1365,
Rossington, Yorks.

332. Germany,
Rethwischdorf,
Kr. Aschendorf-Hümmling.

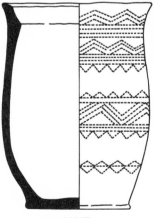

333. N/NR 1790,
Cairnpapple, W. Lothian.

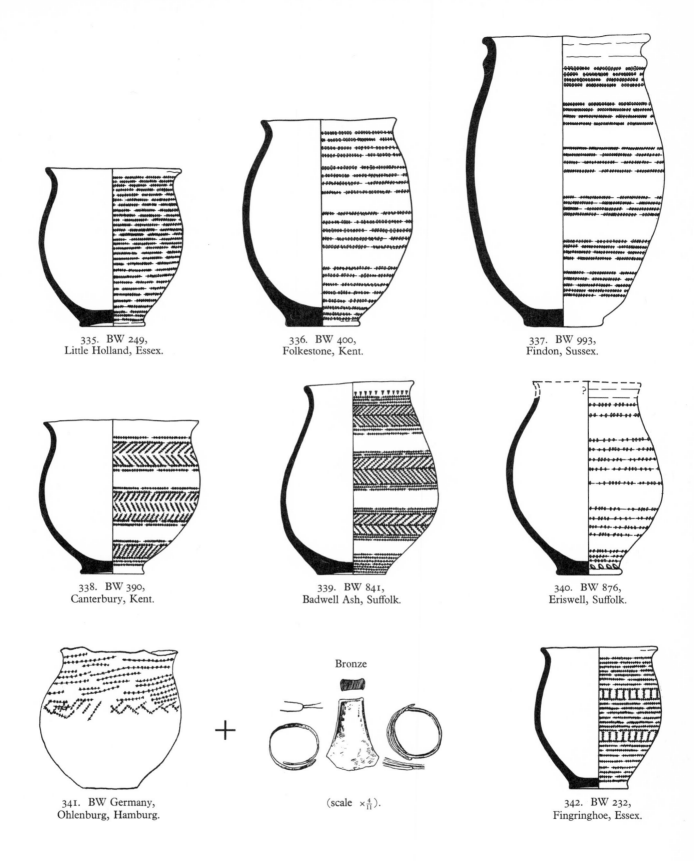

335. BW 249,
Little Holland, Essex.

336. BW 400,
Folkestone, Kent.

337. BW 993,
Findon, Sussex.

338. BW 390,
Canterbury, Kent.

339. BW 841,
Badwell Ash, Suffolk.

340. BW 876,
Eriswell, Suffolk.

341. BW Germany,
Ohlenburg, Hamburg.

Bronze

+

(scale ×$\frac{4}{11}$).

342. BW 232,
Fingringhoe, Essex.

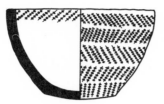
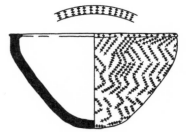

343. BW 902,
Ipswich, Suffolk.

344. BW Bowl 981,
Mortlake, Surrey.

345. BW Bowl 982,
Putney, Surrey.

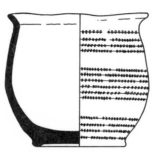

346. BW 889,
Felixstowe, Suffolk.

347. BW 1063,
Avebury Sanctuary, Wilts.

348. BW 519,
Cley-next-Sea, Norfolk.

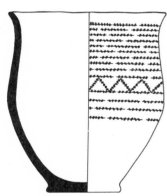

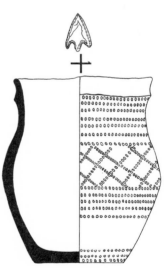

349. BW Netherlands,
Weerselo, Oldenzaal.

350. BW 413,
Tovil, Kent.

351. BW 992,
Falmer, Sussex.

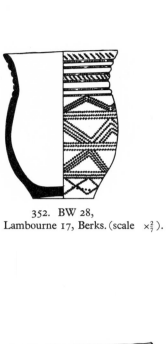

352. BW 28,
Lambourne 17, Berks. (scale ×$\frac{2}{7}$).

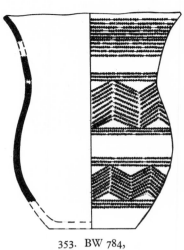

353. BW 784,
Burrington, Somerset. (scale ×$\frac{2}{7}$).

354. BW 817,
Stoford Barwick, Somerset. (scale ×$\frac{2}{7}$).

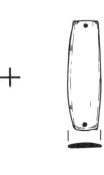

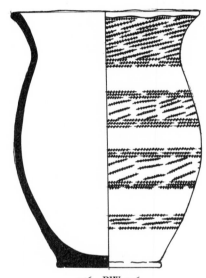

355. BW 1869,
Ty-Llwyd, Glamorgan. (scale ×$\frac{2}{7}$).

356. BW 156,
Chagford, Devon. (scale ×$\frac{2}{7}$).

357. BW? Bowl 243,
Linford Essex. (scale ×$\frac{2}{7}$).

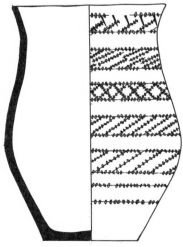

+

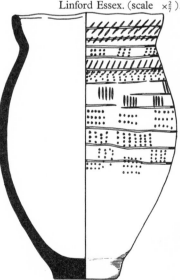

358. BW Germany,
Mülheim, Löschacker. (scale ×$\frac{2}{7}$).

359. BW? 1857,
Llancaiach-Isaf, Glamorgan. (scale ×$\frac{2}{7}$).

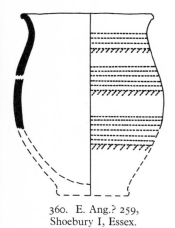

360. E. Ang.? 259,
Shoebury I, Essex.

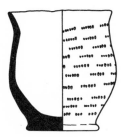

361. E. Ang.? 259,
Shoebury I, Essex.

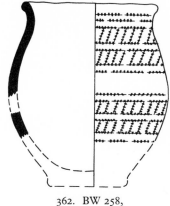

362. BW 258,
Shoebury I, Essex.

363. BW 260,
Shoebury I, Essex.

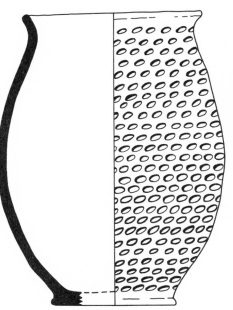

364. E. Ang.? 950,
Stutton, Suffolk.

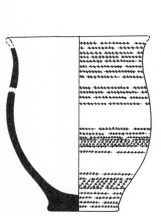

365. BW 258,
Shoebury I, Essex.

366. FN 256,
Shoebury I, Essex.

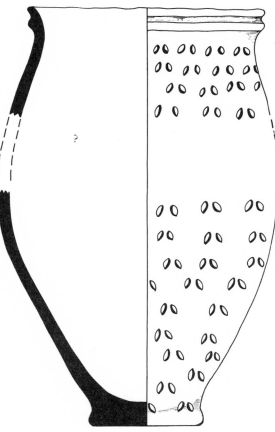

367. FN 257,
Shoebury I, Essex.

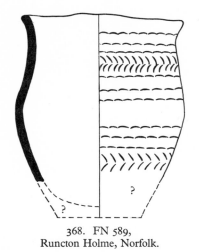

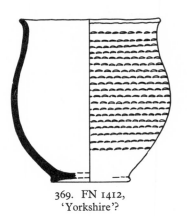

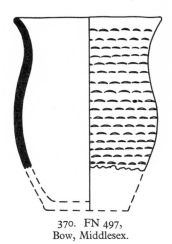

368. FN 589,
Runcton Holme, Norfolk.

369. FN 1412,
'Yorkshire'?

370. FN 497,
Bow, Middlesex.

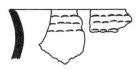

372. FN 888,
Felixstowe, Suffolk.

371. Germany,
Selm, Kr. Lüdinghausen.

373. FN 248,
Lion Point, Essex.

374. Fengate Ware
Astrop, Northants.

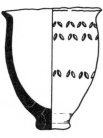

375. Germany,
Urmitz, Kr. Koblenz.

376. FN 499,
Hammersmith, London.

377. Fengate Ware
Fengate, Northants.

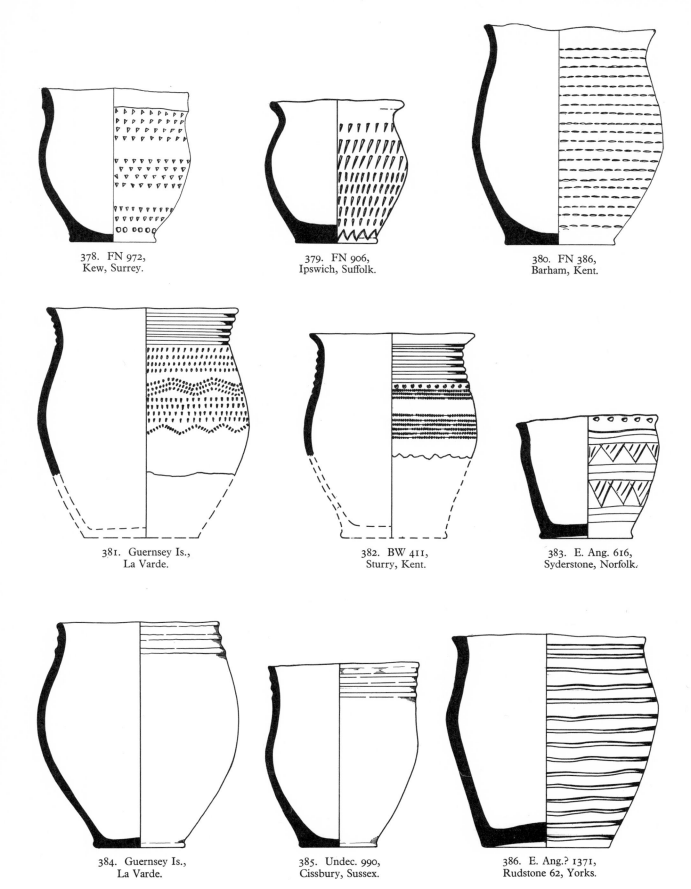

378. FN 972,
Kew, Surrey.

379. FN 906,
Ipswich, Suffolk.

380. FN 386,
Barham, Kent.

381. Guernsey Is.,
La Varde.

382. BW 411,
Sturry, Kent.

383. E. Ang. 616,
Syderstone, Norfolk.

384. Guernsey Is.,
La Varde.

385. Undec. 990,
Cissbury, Sussex.

386. E. Ang.? 1371,
Rudstone 62, Yorks.

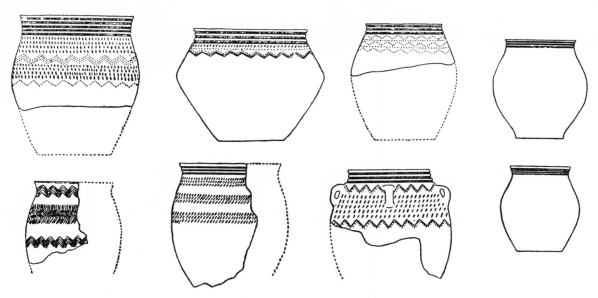

387. Vessels from La Varde megalith   (scale $\times \frac{1}{5}$).

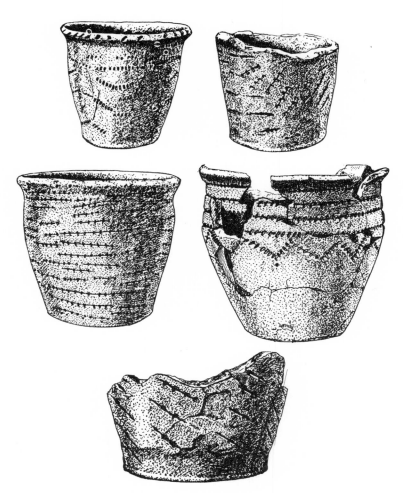

388. Vessels from various Swedish Long Cists   (scale $\times \frac{4}{11}$).

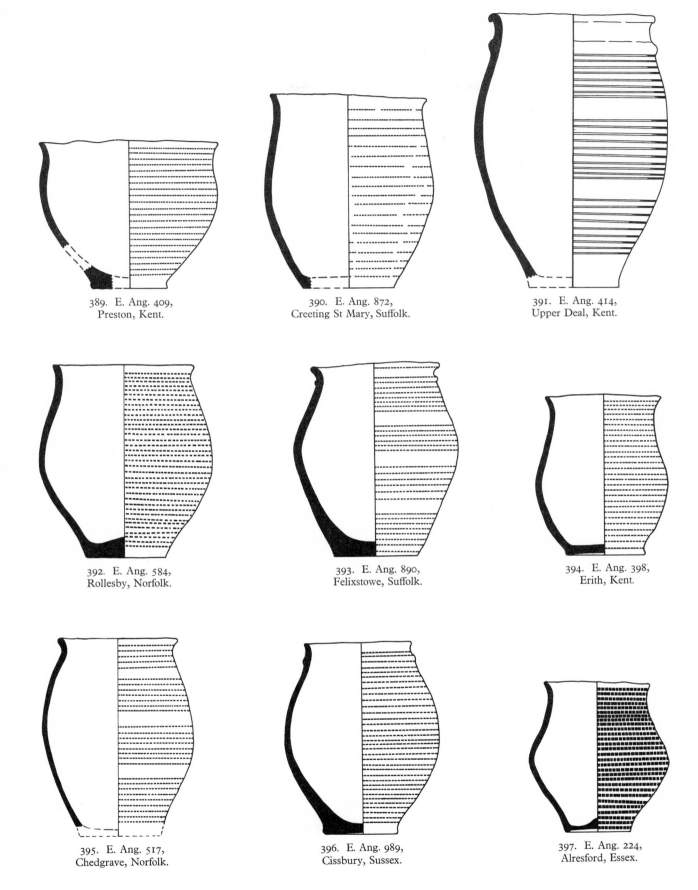

389. E. Ang. 409,
Preston, Kent.

390. E. Ang. 872,
Creeting St Mary, Suffolk.

391. E. Ang. 414,
Upper Deal, Kent.

392. E. Ang. 584,
Rollesby, Norfolk.

393. E. Ang. 890,
Felixstowe, Suffolk.

394. E. Ang. 398,
Erith, Kent.

395. E. Ang. 517,
Chedgrave, Norfolk.

396. E. Ang. 989,
Cissbury, Sussex.

397. E. Ang. 224,
Alresford, Essex.

329

398. Germany,
Worms-Herrnsheim.

399. E. Ang. 1007,
Shoreham-by-Sea, Sussex.

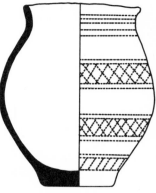

400. E. Ang. 921,
Kirton, Suffolk.

401. E. Ang. 961,
Woolpit, Suffolk.

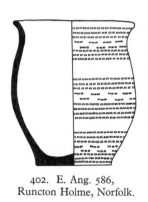

402. E. Ang. 586,
Runcton Holme, Norfolk.

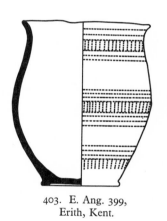

403. E. Ang. 399,
Erith, Kent.

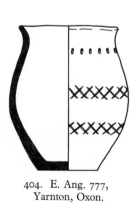

404. E. Ang. 777,
Yarnton, Oxon.

405. E. Ang. 613,
Stowbridge, Norfolk.

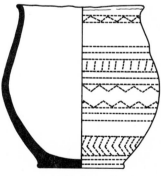

406. E. Ang. 388,
Bromley, Kent.

407. Netherlands,
Emmen, Drenthe.

408. E. Ang. 891,
Felixstowe, Suffolk.

409. E. Ang. 225,
Ardleigh, Essex.

410. Netherlands,
Eext, Anloo.

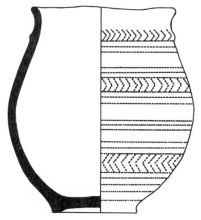

411. E. Ang. 496,
Brentford, Middlesex.

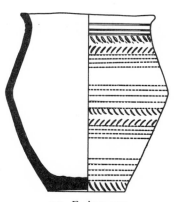

412. E. Ang. 905,
Ipswich, Suffolk.

413. E. Ang. 892,
Felixstowe, Suffolk.

414. E. Ang. 250,
Little Holland, Essex.

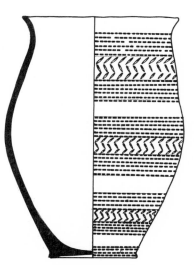

415. E. Ang. 920,
Kettleburgh, Suffolk.

416. Germany,
Klein-Hehlen, Kr. Celle.

417. E. Ang. 848,
Bawdsey, Suffolk.

418. E. Ang. 909,
Ipswich, Suffolk.

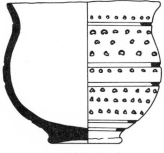

419. Netherlands,
Varsseveld, Zwarte Moor.

420. E. Ang. 850,
Boyton, Suffolk.

421. E. Ang. 903,
Ipswich, Suffolk.

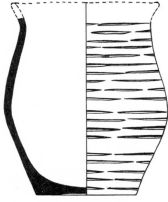

422. E. Ang. 588,
Runcton Holme, Norfolk.

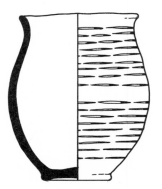

423. E. Ang. 406,
Gt. Mongeham, Kent.

424. E. Ang. 603,
Stalham, Norfolk.

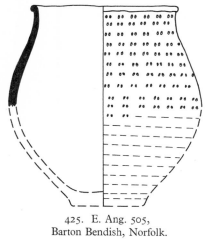

425. E. Ang. 505,
Barton Bendish, Norfolk.

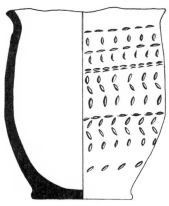

426. E. Ang. 54,
'Cambridgeshire'.

427. FN 996,
Kingston Buci, Sussex.

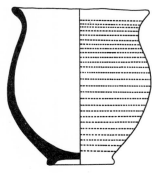

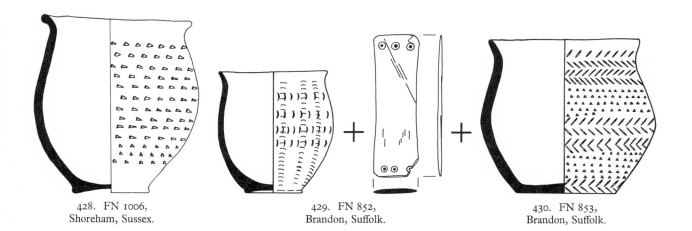

428. FN 1006,
Shoreham, Sussex.

429. FN 852,
Brandon, Suffolk.

430. FN 853,
Brandon, Suffolk.

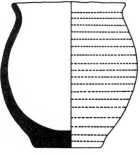

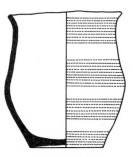

431. E. Ang. 886,
Felixstowe, Suffolk.

432. E. Ang. 847,
Bawdsey, Suffolk.

433. E. Ang. 765,
Stanton Harcourt, Oxon.

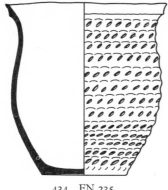

434. FN 235,
Great Clacton, Essex.

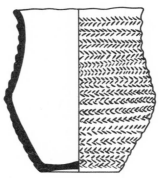

435. FP 396,
Dover, Kent.

436. FP 922,
Lakenheath, Suffolk.

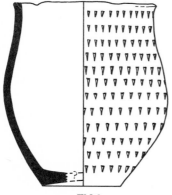

437. FN 871,
Creeting St Mary, Suffolk.

438. FN 368,
Houghton, Hunts.

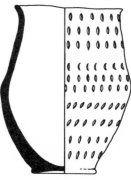

439. FN 569,
Methwold, Norfolk.

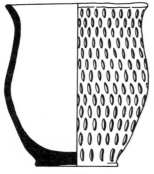

440. FN 241,
Halstead, Essex.

441. FN 951,
Sudbury, Suffolk.

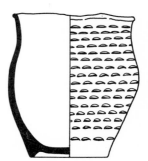

442. FN 919,
Kersey, Suffolk.

334

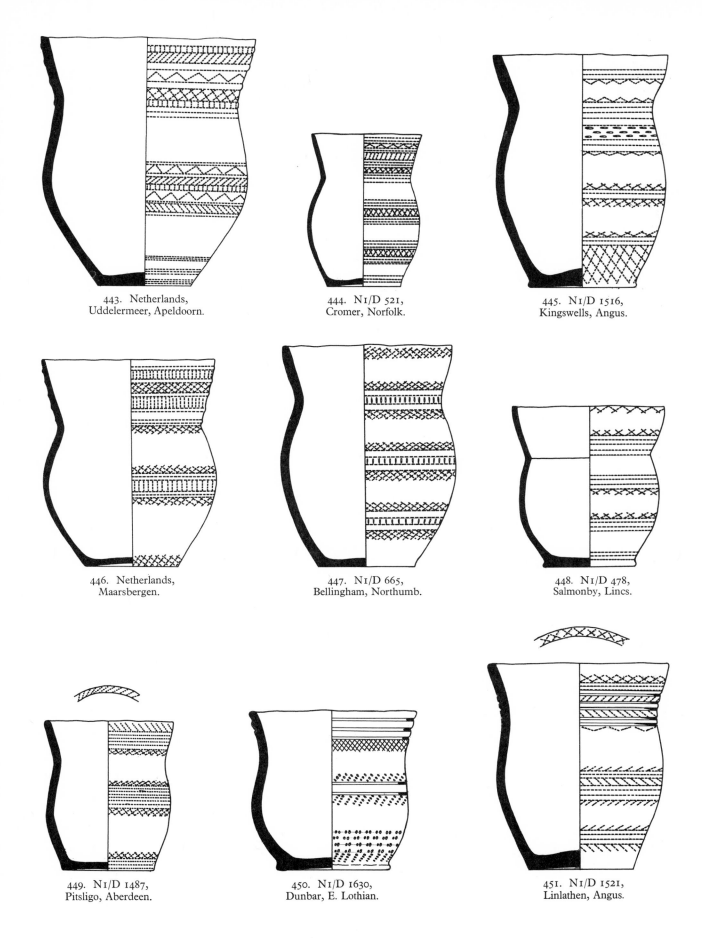

443. Netherlands,
Uddelermeer, Apeldoorn.

444. NI/D 521,
Cromer, Norfolk.

445. NI/D 1516,
Kingswells, Angus.

446. Netherlands,
Maarsbergen.

447. NI/D 665,
Bellingham, Northumb.

448. NI/D 478,
Salmonby, Lincs.

449. NI/D 1487,
Pitsligo, Aberdeen.

450. NI/D 1630,
Dunbar, E. Lothian.

451. NI/D 1521,
Linlathen, Angus.

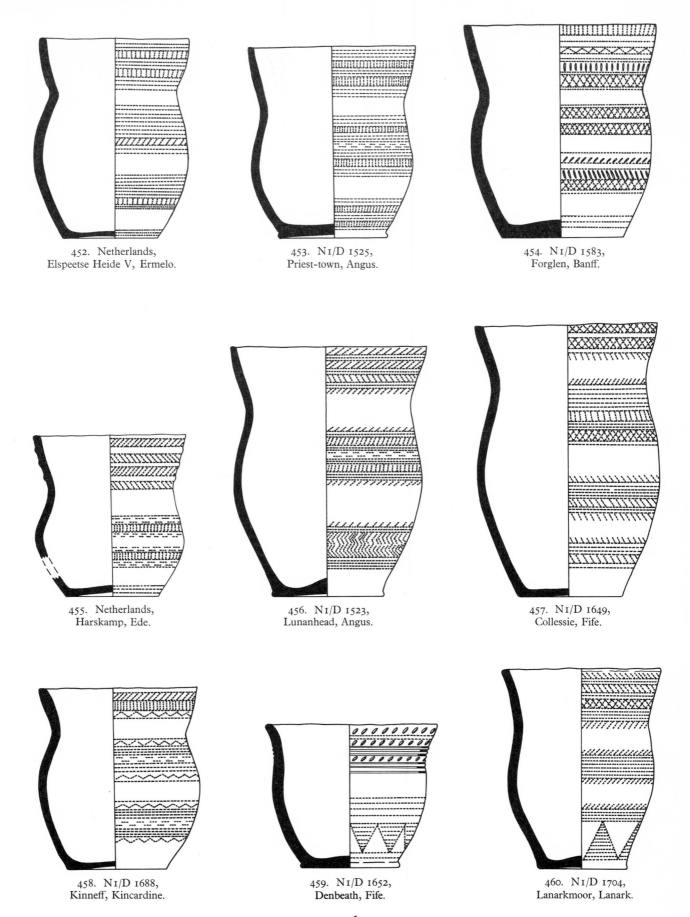

452. Netherlands,
Elspeetse Heide V, Ermelo.

453. NI/D 1525,
Priest-town, Angus.

454. NI/D 1583,
Forglen, Banff.

455. Netherlands,
Harskamp, Ede.

456. NI/D 1523,
Lunanhead, Angus.

457. NI/D 1649,
Collessie, Fife.

458. NI/D 1688,
Kinneff, Kincardine.

459. NI/D 1652,
Denbeath, Fife.

460. NI/D 1704,
Lanarkmoor, Lanark.

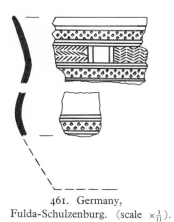

461. Germany,
Fulda-Schulzenburg. (scale ×$\frac{3}{11}$).

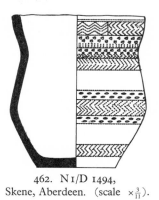

462. N1/D 1494,
Skene, Aberdeen. (scale ×$\frac{3}{11}$).

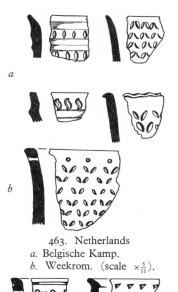

463. Netherlands
a. Belgische Kamp.
b. Weekrom. (scale ×$\frac{3}{11}$).

464. Netherlands,
Mook, Nijmegen. (scale ×$\frac{3}{11}$).

465. Netherlands,
Nijmegen. (scale ×$\frac{3}{11}$).

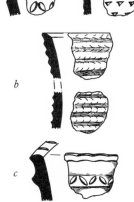

466. Netherlands
a. Duesburger, S. Veluwe.
b. Ederheide, S. Veluwe.
c. Apeldoorn. (scale ×$\frac{3}{11}$).

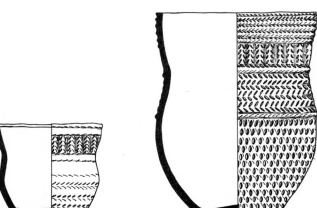

467. Netherlands,
Hazekampje, Nijmegen. (scale ×$\frac{3}{11}$).

468. FP 1413.1,
'Scotland'? (scale ×$\frac{3}{11}$).

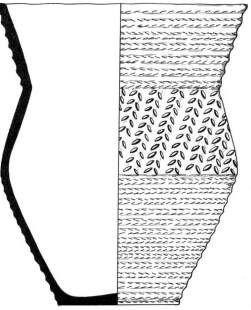

469. Germany,
Winnekendonk, Kr. Geldern. (scale ×$\frac{3}{11}$).

337

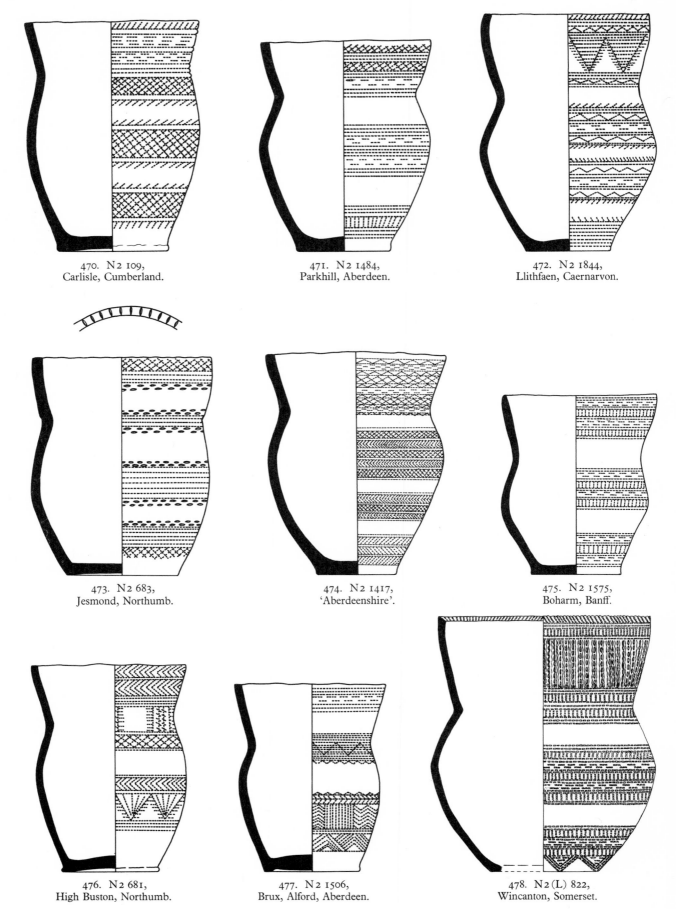

470. N2 109,
Carlisle, Cumberland.

471. N2 1484,
Parkhill, Aberdeen.

472. N2 1844,
Llithfaen, Caernarvon.

473. N2 683,
Jesmond, Northumb.

474. N2 1417,
'Aberdeenshire'.

475. N2 1575,
Boharm, Banff.

476. N2 681,
High Buston, Northumb.

477. N2 1506,
Brux, Alford, Aberdeen.

478. N2 (L) 822,
Wincanton, Somerset.

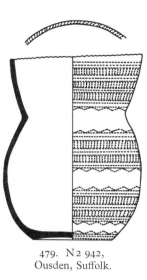

479. N2 942,
Ousden, Suffolk.

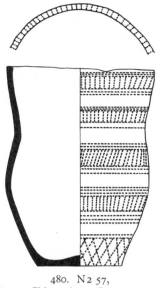

480. N2 57,
Chippenham, Cambs.

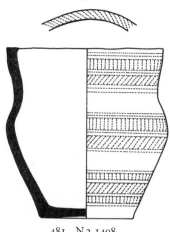

481. N2 1498,
Stoneywood, Aberdeen.

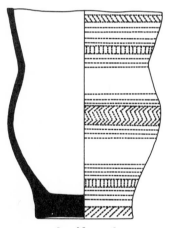

482. N2 1578,
Buckie, Banff.

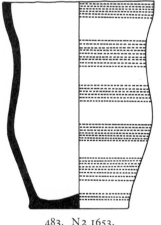

483. N2 1653,
Dunshelt, Fife.

484. N2 1552,
Poltalloch, Argyll.

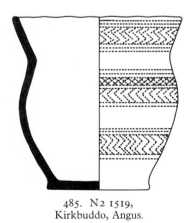

485. N2 1519,
Kirkbuddo, Angus.

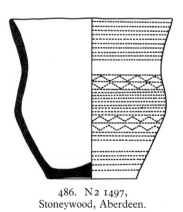

486. N2 1497,
Stoneywood, Aberdeen.

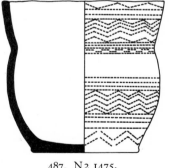

487. N2 1475,
Kildrummy, Aberdeen.

339

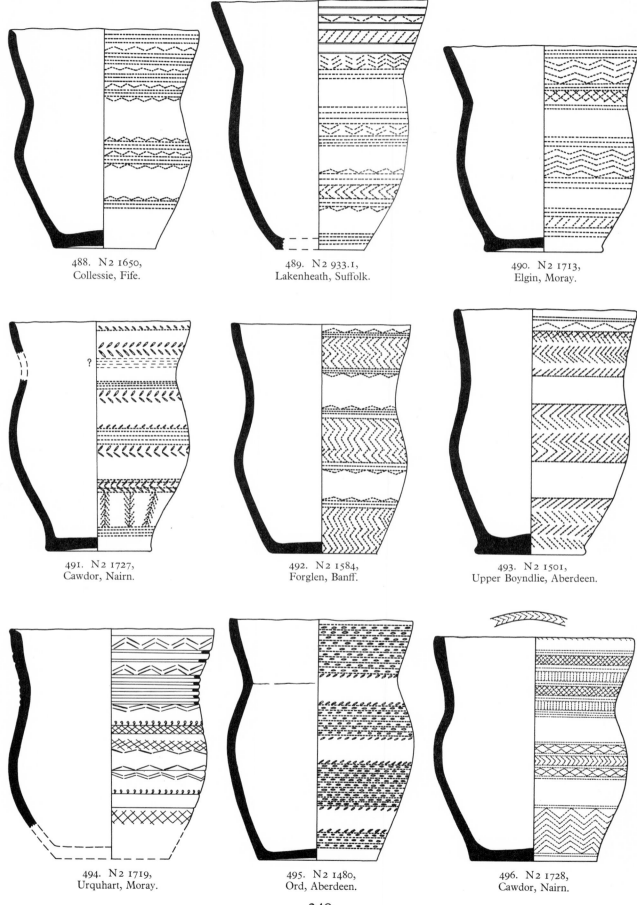

488. N2 1650,
Collessie, Fife.

489. N2 933.1,
Lakenheath, Suffolk.

490. N2 1713,
Elgin, Moray.

491. N2 1727,
Cawdor, Nairn.

492. N2 1584,
Forglen, Banff.

493. N2 1501,
Upper Boyndlie, Aberdeen.

494. N2 1719,
Urquhart, Moray.

495. N2 1480,
Ord, Aberdeen.

496. N2 1728,
Cawdor, Nairn.

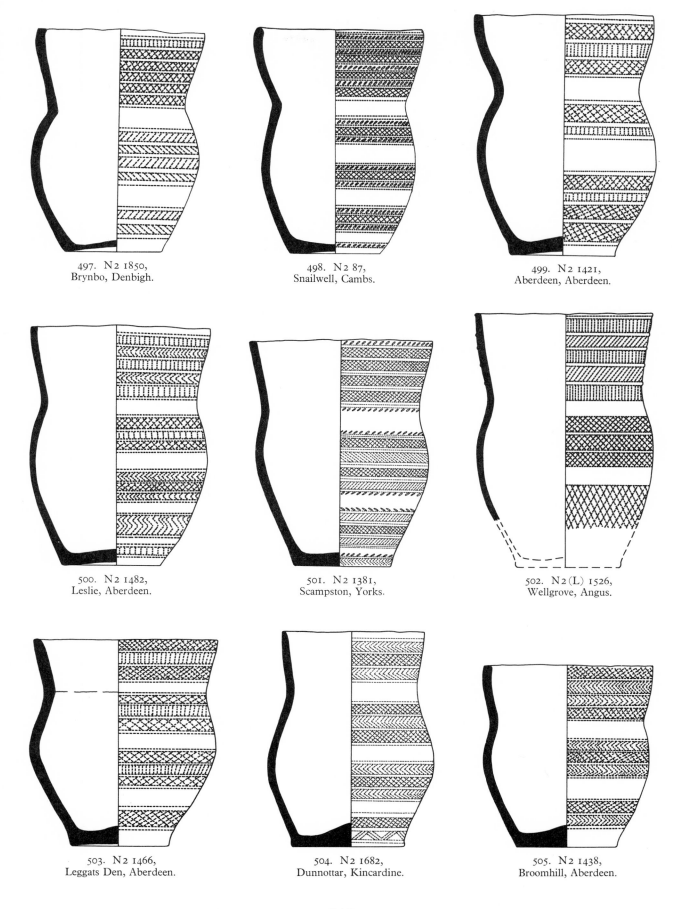

497. N2 1850,
Brynbo, Denbigh.

498. N2 87,
Snailwell, Cambs.

499. N2 1421,
Aberdeen, Aberdeen.

500. N2 1482,
Leslie, Aberdeen.

501. N2 1381,
Scampston, Yorks.

502. N2 (L) 1526,
Wellgrove, Angus.

503. N2 1466,
Leggats Den, Aberdeen.

504. N2 1682,
Dunnottar, Kincardine.

505. N2 1438,
Broomhill, Aberdeen.

341

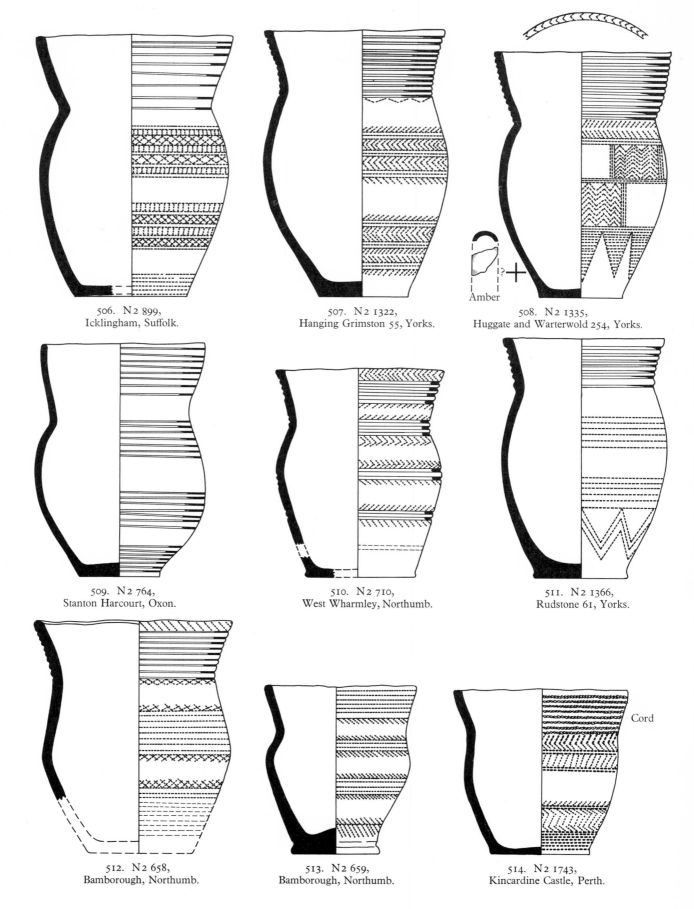

506. N2 899,
Icklingham, Suffolk.

507. N2 1322,
Hanging Grimston 55, Yorks.

508. N2 1335,
Huggate and Warterwold 254, Yorks.

Amber

509. N2 764,
Stanton Harcourt, Oxon.

510. N2 710,
West Wharmley, Northumb.

511. N2 1366,
Rudstone 61, Yorks.

512. N2 658,
Bamborough, Northumb.

513. N2 659,
Bamborough, Northumb.

514. N2 1743,
Kincardine Castle, Perth.

Cord

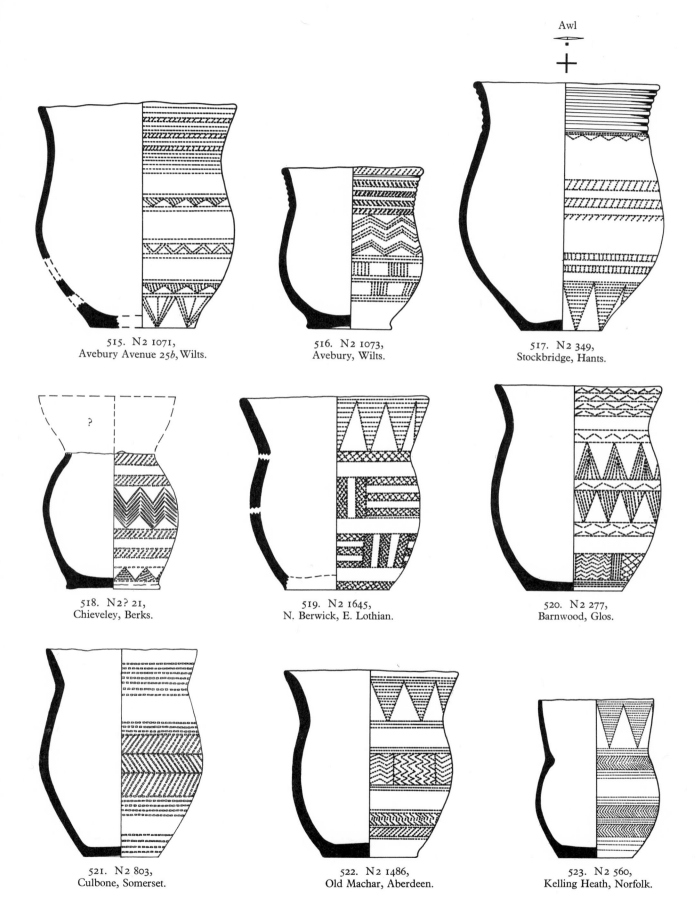

Awl

515. N2 1071,
Avebury Avenue 25*b*, Wilts.

516. N2 1073,
Avebury, Wilts.

517. N2 349,
Stockbridge, Hants.

518. N2? 21,
Chieveley, Berks.

519. N2 1645,
N. Berwick, E. Lothian.

520. N2 277,
Barnwood, Glos.

521. N2 803,
Culbone, Somerset.

522. N2 1486,
Old Machar, Aberdeen.

523. N2 560,
Kelling Heath, Norfolk.

343

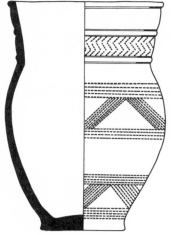

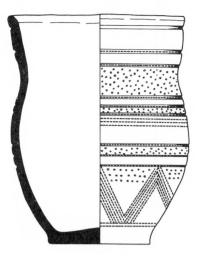

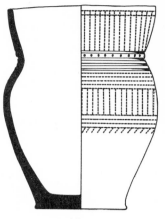

524. N2 1405,
Weaverthorpe 297, Yorks.
(scale ×$\frac{3}{10}$).

525. N2 1635,
Innerwick, E. Lothian.
(scale ×$\frac{3}{10}$).

526. N2 1375,
Rudstone 66, Yorks.
(scale ×$\frac{3}{10}$).

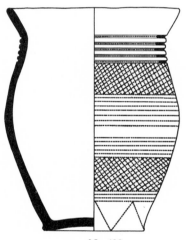

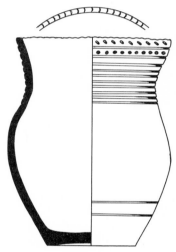

527. N2 688,
Lilburn Hill, Northumb. (scale ×$\frac{3}{10}$).

528. N2 1756,
Kilcoy, Ross and Cromarty.
(scale ×$\frac{3}{10}$).

529. N2 135,
Longstone, Derby.
(scale ×$\frac{3}{10}$).

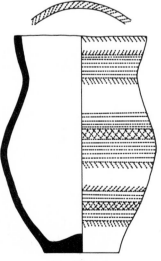

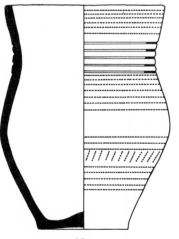

530. N2 1367,
Rudstone 62, Yorks.
(scale ×$\frac{3}{10}$).

531. N2 1334,
Huggate and Warterwold 254, Yorks.
(scale ×$\frac{3}{10}$).

532. N2 (L) 227,
Colchester (?), Essex.
(scale ×$\frac{3}{10}$).

344

533. N2 1402,
Towthorpe 211½, Yorks. (scale ×³⁄₁₀).

534. N2 1212,
Aldro 54, Yorks. (scale ×³⁄₁₀).

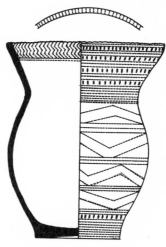

535. N2 518,
Cley, Norfolk. (scale ×³⁄₁₀).

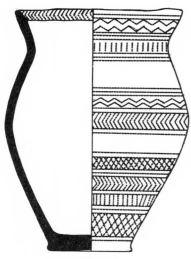

536. N2 1368,
Rudstone 62, Yorks. (scale ×³⁄₁₀).

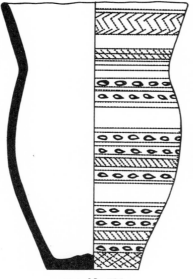

537. N2 686,
Lesbury, Northumb. (scale ×³⁄₁₀).

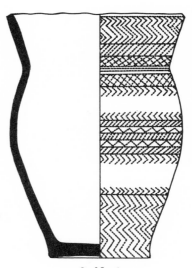

538. N2 649,
Alnwick, Northumb. (scale ×³⁄₁₀).

539. N2 1221,
Amotherby, Yorks. (scale ×³⁄₁₀).

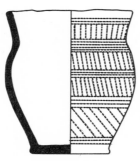

540. N2 684,
Lesbury, Northumb. (scale ×³⁄₁₀).

541. N2 1384,
Sherburn 7, Yorks. (scale ×³⁄₁₀).

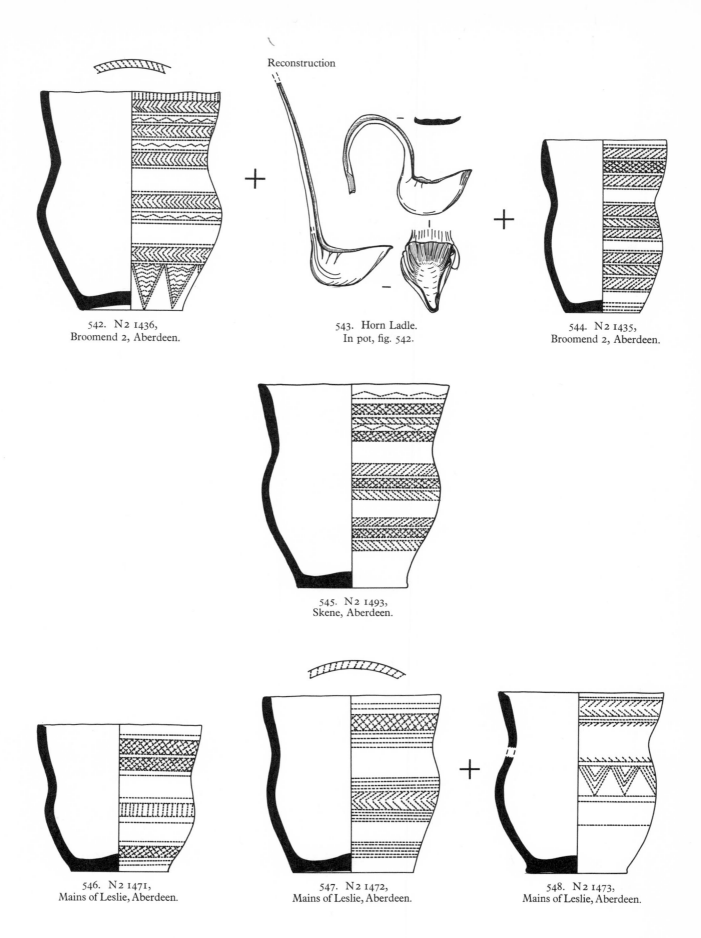

Reconstruction

542. N2 1436,
Broomend 2, Aberdeen.

543. Horn Ladle.
In pot, fig. 542.

544. N2 1435,
Broomend 2, Aberdeen.

545. N2 1493,
Skene, Aberdeen.

546. N2 1471,
Mains of Leslie, Aberdeen.

547. N2 1472,
Mains of Leslie, Aberdeen.

548. N2 1473,
Mains of Leslie, Aberdeen.

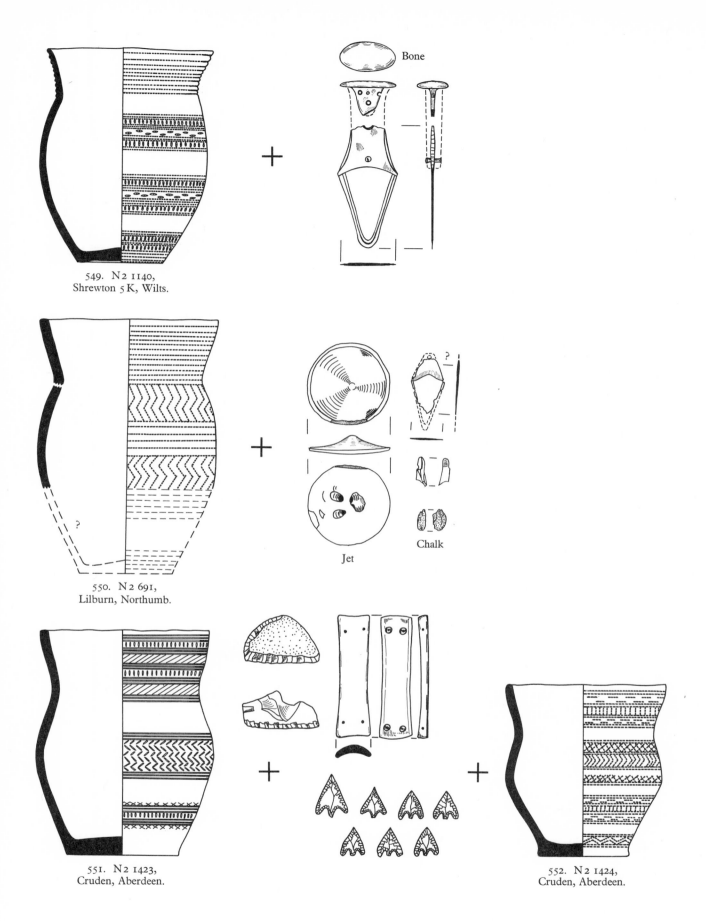

549. N2 1140,
Shrewton 5 K, Wilts.

Bone

550. N2 691,
Lilburn, Northumb.

Jet

Chalk

551. N2 1423,
Cruden, Aberdeen.

552. N2 1424,
Cruden, Aberdeen.

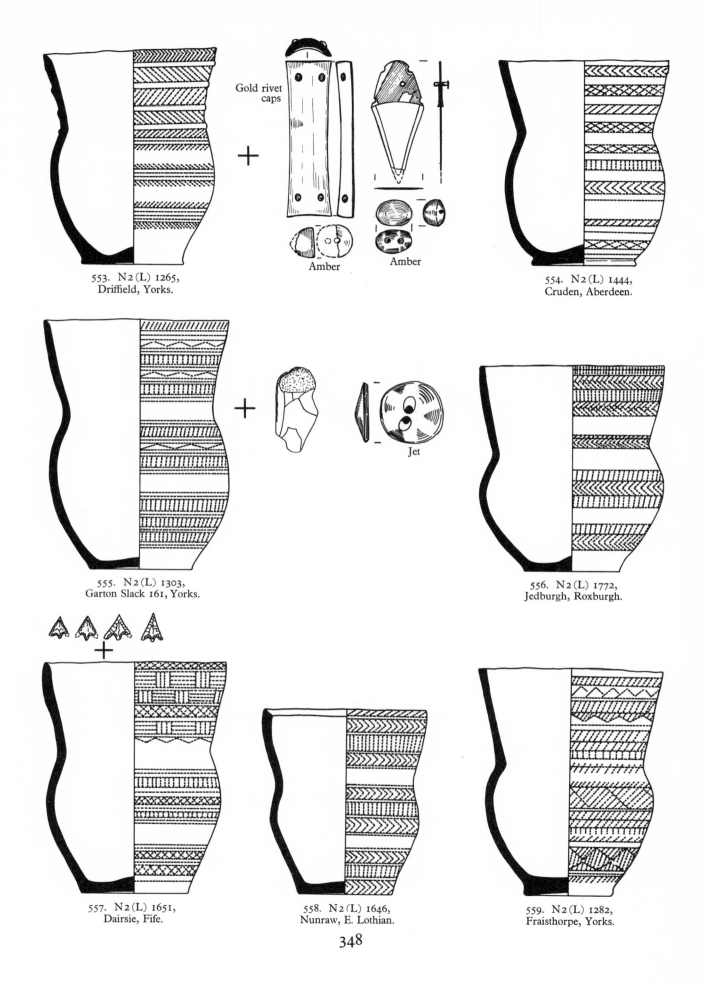

553. N2(L) 1265,
Driffield, Yorks.

Gold rivet caps

Amber   Amber

554. N2(L) 1444,
Cruden, Aberdeen.

555. N2(L) 1303,
Garton Slack 161, Yorks.

Jet

556. N2(L) 1772,
Jedburgh, Roxburgh.

557. N2(L) 1651,
Dairsie, Fife.

558. N2(L) 1646,
Nunraw, E. Lothian.

559. N2(L) 1282,
Fraisthorpe, Yorks.

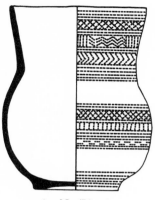

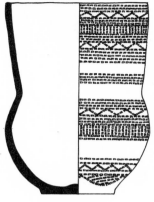

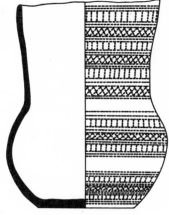

560. N2(L) 563,
Little Massingham, Norfolk.

561. N2(L) 94,
Wilburton Fen, Cambs.

562. N2(L) 988,
Burpham, Sussex.

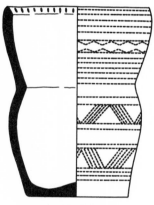

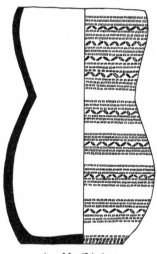

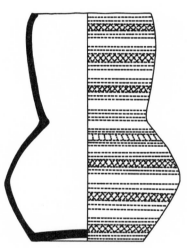

563. N2(L) 1718,
Knockando, Moray.

564. N2(L) 69,
Ely, Cambs.

565. N2(L) 242,
Langham, Essex.

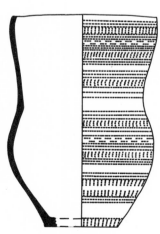

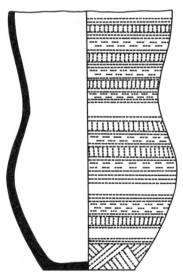

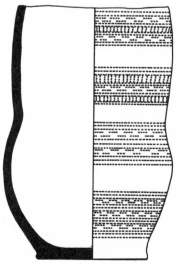

566. N2(L) 367,
Houghton, Hunts.

567. N2(L) 870,
Coddenham, Suffolk.

568. N2(L) 140,
Minning Low, Derby.

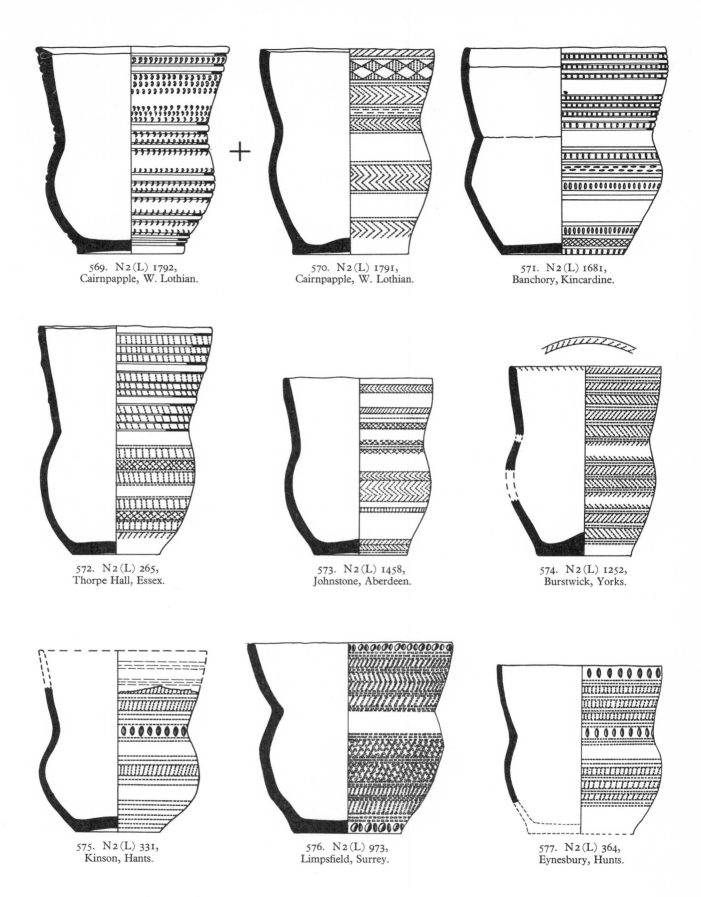

569. N2(L) 1792,
Cairnpapple, W. Lothian.

570. N2(L) 1791,
Cairnpapple, W. Lothian.

571. N2(L) 1681,
Banchory, Kincardine.

572. N2(L) 265,
Thorpe Hall, Essex.

573. N2(L) 1458,
Johnstone, Aberdeen.

574. N2(L) 1252,
Burstwick, Yorks.

575. N2(L) 331,
Kinson, Hants.

576. N2(L) 973,
Limpsfield, Surrey.

577. N2(L) 364,
Eynesbury, Hunts.

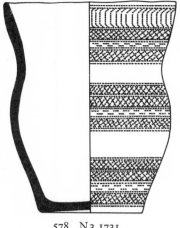

578. N3 1731,
Cuthbertown, Nairn.

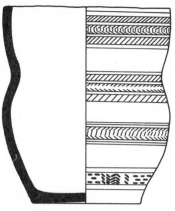

579. N3 1667,
Lochend, Inverness.

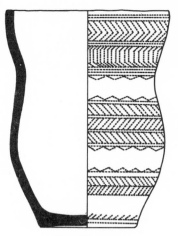

580. N3 1509,
Bandoch, Angus.

581. N3 1636,
Innerwick, E. Lothian.

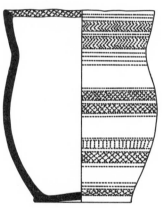

582. N3 1419,
'Aberdeenshire'.

583. N3 1633,
Humbie, E. Lothian.

584. N3 1676,
Skye, Inverness.

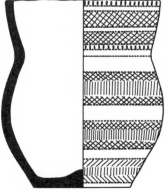

585. N3 1485,
Parkhill, Aberdeen.

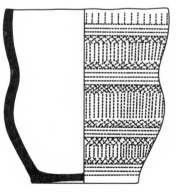

586. N3 1693,
Tillyochie, Kinross.

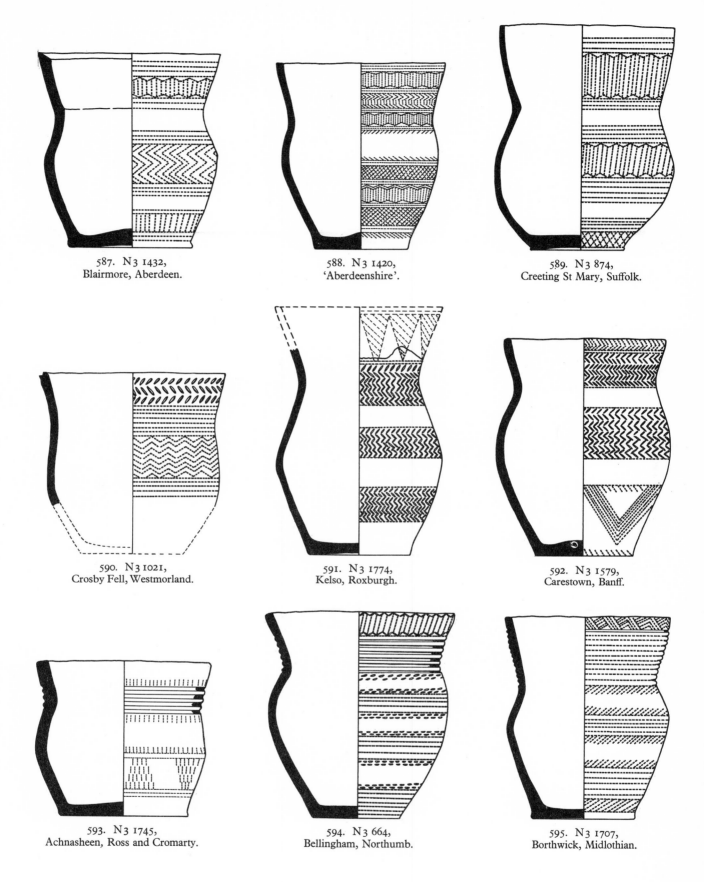

587. N3 1432,
Blairmore, Aberdeen.

588. N3 1420,
'Aberdeenshire'.

589. N3 874,
Creeting St Mary, Suffolk.

590. N3 1021,
Crosby Fell, Westmorland.

591. N3 1774,
Kelso, Roxburgh.

592. N3 1579,
Carestown, Banff.

593. N3 1745,
Achnasheen, Ross and Cromarty.

594. N3 664,
Bellingham, Northumb.

595. N3 1707,
Borthwick, Midlothian.

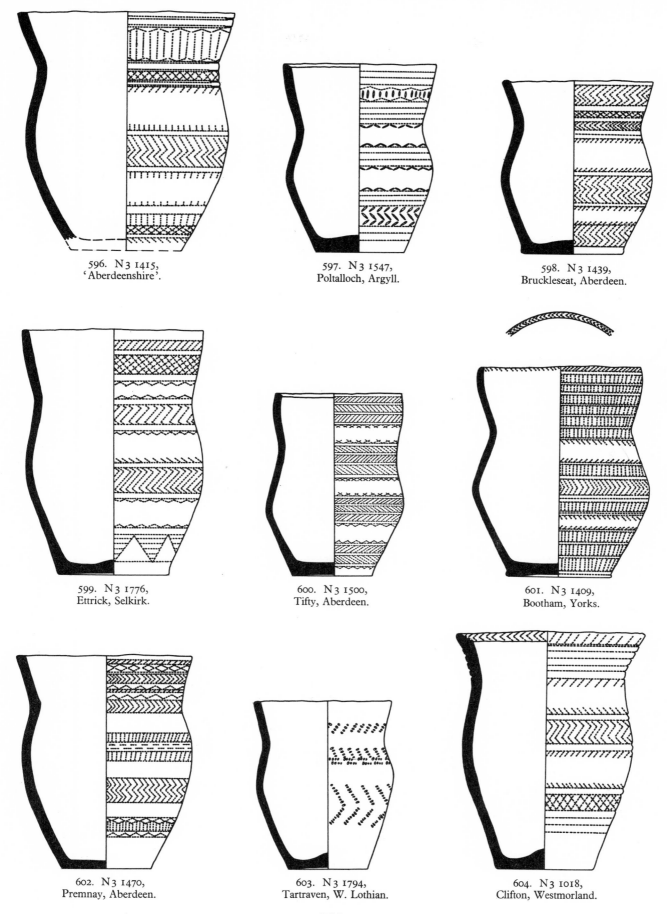

596. N3 1415,
'Aberdeenshire'.

597. N3 1547,
Poltalloch, Argyll.

598. N3 1439,
Bruckleseat, Aberdeen.

599. N3 1776,
Ettrick, Selkirk.

600. N3 1500,
Tifty, Aberdeen.

601. N3 1409,
Bootham, Yorks.

602. N3 1470,
Premnay, Aberdeen.

603. N3 1794,
Tartraven, W. Lothian.

604. N3 1018,
Clifton, Westmorland.

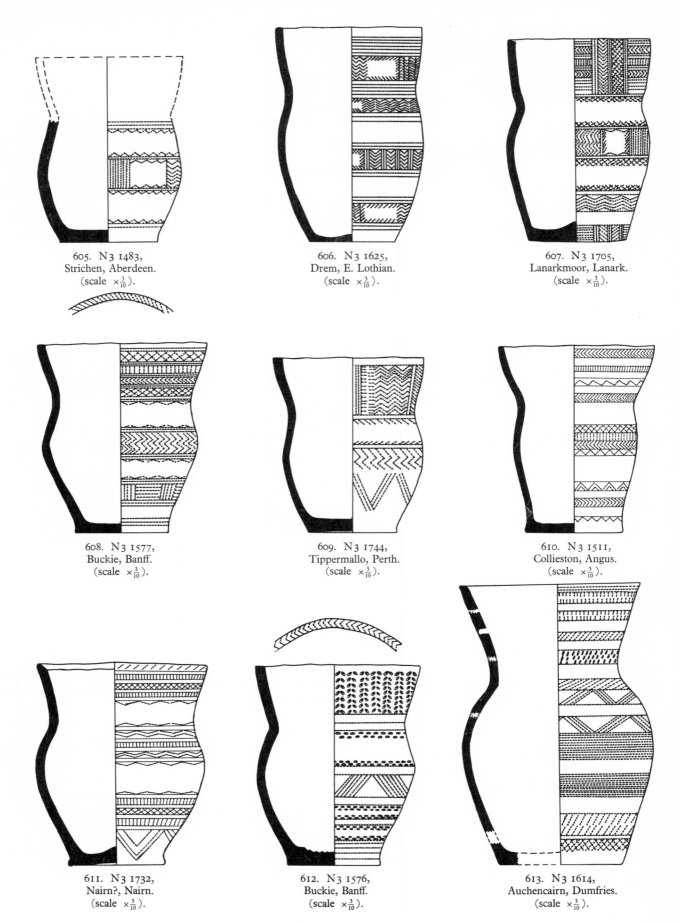

605. N3 1483,
Strichen, Aberdeen.
(scale ×$\frac{3}{10}$).

606. N3 1625,
Drem, E. Lothian.
(scale ×$\frac{3}{10}$).

607. N3 1705,
Lanarkmoor, Lanark.
(scale ×$\frac{3}{10}$).

608. N3 1577,
Buckie, Banff.
(scale ×$\frac{3}{10}$).

609. N3 1744,
Tippermallo, Perth.
(scale ×$\frac{3}{10}$).

610. N3 1511,
Collieston, Angus.
(scale ×$\frac{3}{10}$).

611. N3 1732,
Nairn?, Nairn.
(scale ×$\frac{3}{10}$).

612. N3 1576,
Buckie, Banff.
(scale ×$\frac{3}{10}$).

613. N3 1614,
Auchencairn, Dumfries.
(scale ×$\frac{3}{10}$).

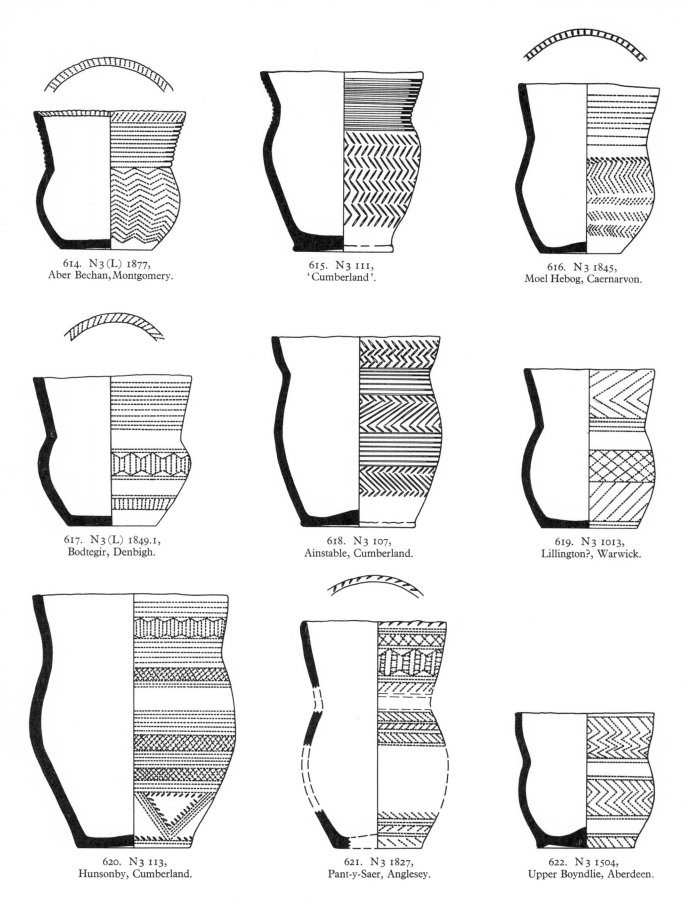

614. N3 (L) 1877,
Aber Bechan, Montgomery.

615. N3 111,
'Cumberland'.

616. N3 1845,
Moel Hebog, Caernarvon.

617. N3 (L) 1849.1,
Bodtegir, Denbigh.

618. N3 107,
Ainstable, Cumberland.

619. N3 1013,
Lillington?, Warwick.

620. N3 113,
Hunsonby, Cumberland.

621. N3 1827,
Pant-y-Saer, Anglesey.

622. N3 1504,
Upper Boyndlie, Aberdeen.

355

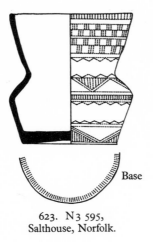

623. N3 595,
Salthouse, Norfolk.

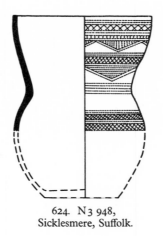

624. N3 948,
Sicklesmere, Suffolk.

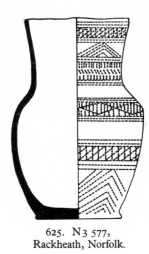

625. N3 577,
Rackheath, Norfolk.

626. Netherlands,
Wijchen.

627. N3 397,
Dover, Kent.

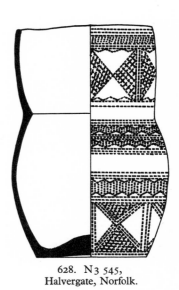

628. N3 545,
Halvergate, Norfolk.

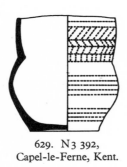

629. N3 392,
Capel-le-Ferne, Kent.

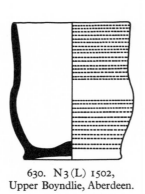

630. N3 (L) 1502,
Upper Boyndlie, Aberdeen.

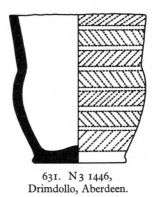

631. N3 1446,
Drimdollo, Aberdeen.

356

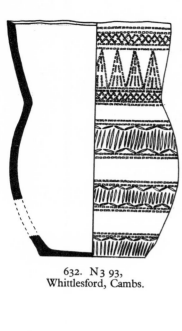

632. N3 93,
Whittlesford, Cambs.

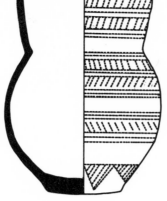

633. N3 401,
Folkestone, Kent.

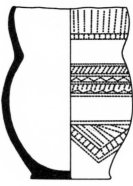

634. N3 842,
Barnham Cross, Suffolk.

635. N3 900,
Icklingham, Suffolk.

636. N3 508,
Blakeney, Norfolk.

637. N3 509,
Blakeney, Norfolk.

638. N3 1209.1,
Pershore, Worcs.

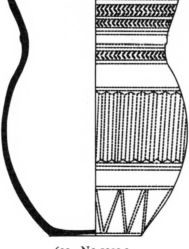

639. N3 1209.2,
Pershore, Worcs.

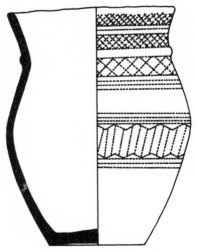

640. N3 1403,
Weaverthorpe 42, Yorks.

357

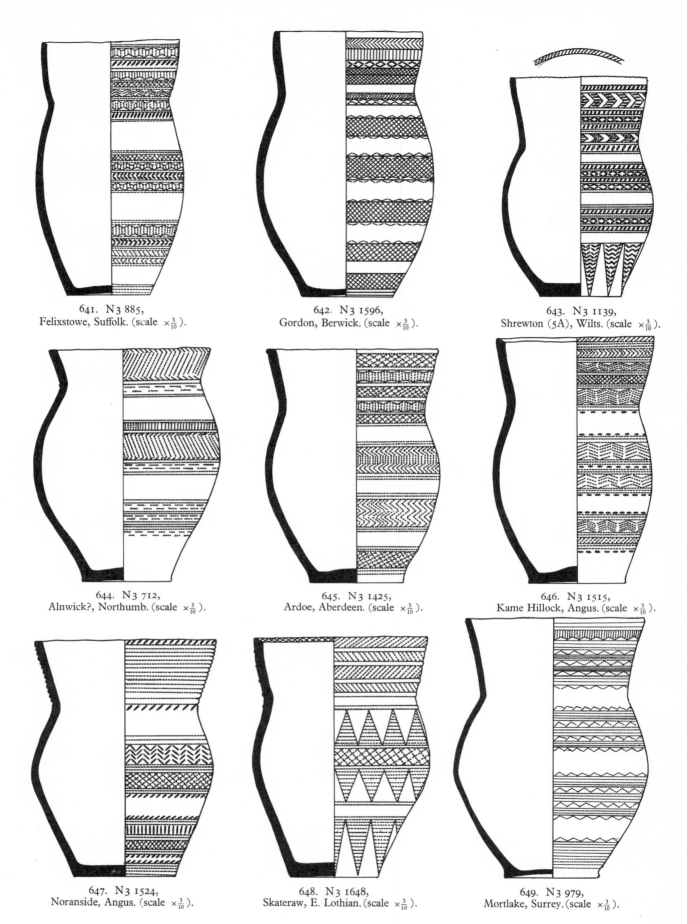

641. N3 885,
Felixstowe, Suffolk. (scale ×$\frac{3}{10}$).

642. N3 1596,
Gordon, Berwick. (scale ×$\frac{3}{10}$).

643. N3 1139,
Shrewton (5A), Wilts. (scale ×$\frac{3}{10}$).

644. N3 712,
Alnwick?, Northumb. (scale ×$\frac{3}{10}$).

645. N3 1425,
Ardoe, Aberdeen. (scale ×$\frac{3}{10}$).

646. N3 1515,
Kame Hillock, Angus. (scale ×$\frac{3}{10}$).

647. N3 1524,
Noranside, Angus. (scale ×$\frac{3}{10}$).

648. N3 1648,
Skateraw, E. Lothian. (scale ×$\frac{3}{10}$).

649. N3 979,
Mortlake, Surrey. (scale ×$\frac{3}{10}$).

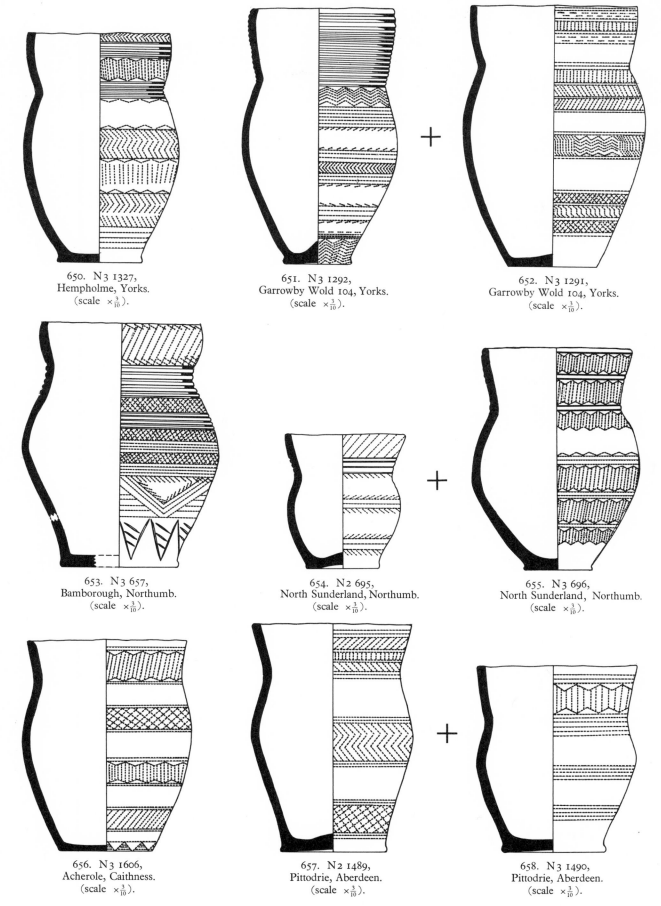

650. N3 1327,
Hempholme, Yorks.
(scale ×$\frac{3}{10}$).

651. N3 1292,
Garrowby Wold 104, Yorks.
(scale ×$\frac{3}{10}$).

652. N3 1291,
Garrowby Wold 104, Yorks.
(scale ×$\frac{3}{10}$).

653. N3 657,
Bamborough, Northumb.
(scale ×$\frac{3}{10}$).

654. N2 695,
North Sunderland, Northumb.
(scale ×$\frac{3}{10}$).

655. N3 696,
North Sunderland, Northumb.
(scale ×$\frac{3}{10}$).

656. N3 1606,
Acherole, Caithness.
(scale ×$\frac{3}{10}$).

657. N2 1489,
Pittodrie, Aberdeen.
(scale ×$\frac{3}{10}$).

658. N3 1490,
Pittodrie, Aberdeen.
(scale ×$\frac{3}{10}$).

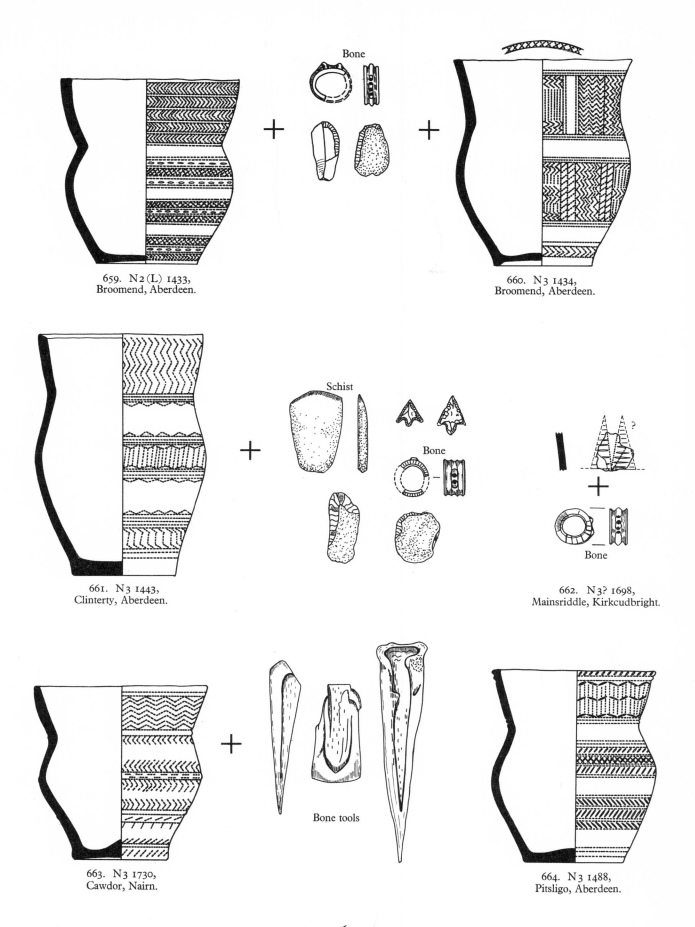

659. N2(L) 1433,
Broomend, Aberdeen.

Bone

660. N3 1434,
Broomend, Aberdeen.

661. N3 1443,
Clinterty, Aberdeen.

Schist

Bone

662. N3? 1698,
Mainsriddle, Kirkcudbright.

Bone

663. N3 1730,
Cawdor, Nairn.

Bone tools

664. N3 1488,
Pitsligo, Aberdeen.

360

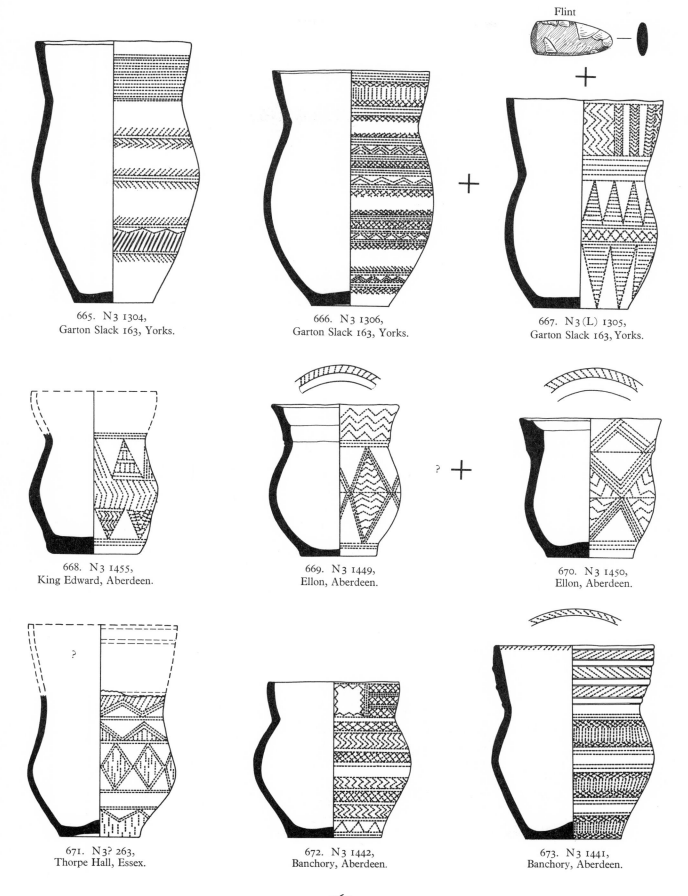

Flint

665. N3 1304,
Garton Slack 163, Yorks.

666. N3 1306,
Garton Slack 163, Yorks.

667. N3 (L) 1305,
Garton Slack 163, Yorks.

668. N3 1455,
King Edward, Aberdeen.

669. N3 1449,
Ellon, Aberdeen.

670. N3 1450,
Ellon, Aberdeen.

671. N3? 263,
Thorpe Hall, Essex.

672. N3 1442,
Banchory, Aberdeen.

673. N3 1441,
Banchory, Aberdeen.

361

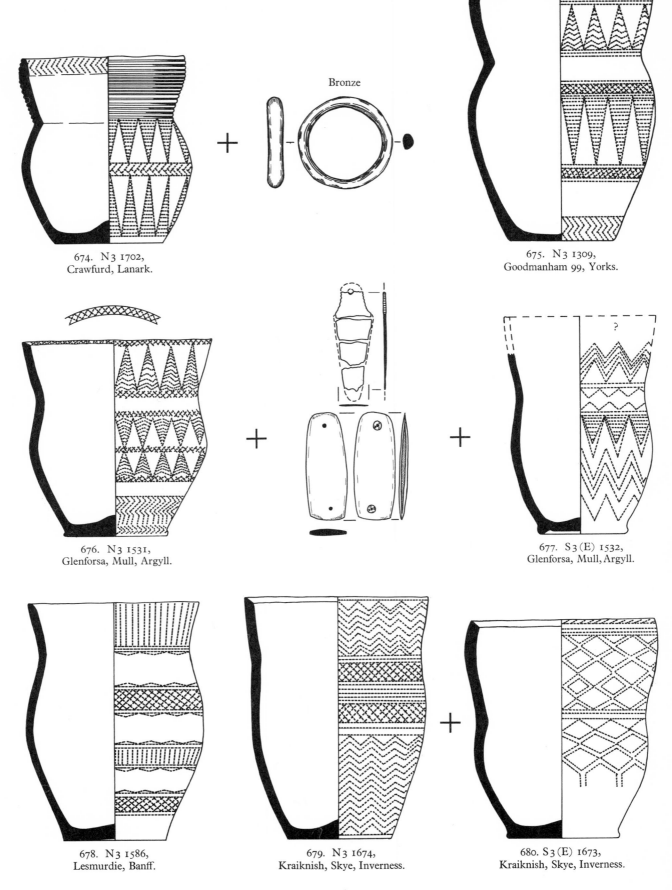

Bronze

674. N3 1702,
Crawfurd, Lanark.

675. N3 1309,
Goodmanham 99, Yorks.

676. N3 1531,
Glenforsa, Mull, Argyll.

677. S3(E) 1532,
Glenforsa, Mull, Argyll.

678. N3 1586,
Lesmurdie, Banff.

679. N3 1674,
Kraiknish, Skye, Inverness.

680. S3(E) 1673,
Kraiknish, Skye, Inverness.

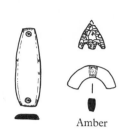

Amber

681. Netherlands,
Garderen, Barneveld.

682. N3 1457,
Inveramsay, Aberdeen.

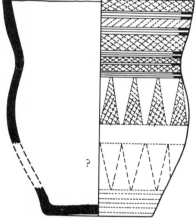

683. N3 1505,
Turriff, Aberdeen.

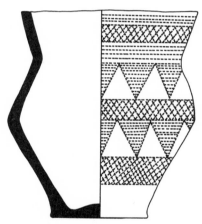

684. N3 656,
Ancroft, Northumb.

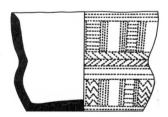

685. S2(W) 1841,
Bwlch-y-Gwrhyd, Caernarvon.

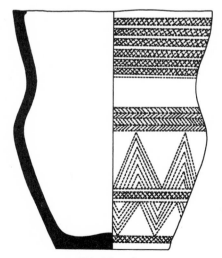

686. N3 1782,
Cambusbarron, Stirling.

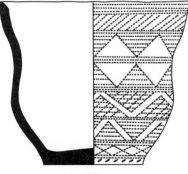

687. N3 1932,
Largantea, Londonderry.

688. S3(W) 1933,
Largantea, Londonderry.

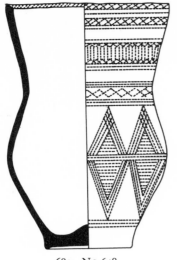

689. N3 648,
Alnwick, Northumb.
(scale ×²⁄₇).

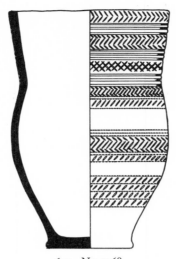

690. N3 1768,
Eckford, Roxburgh.
(scale ×²⁄₇).

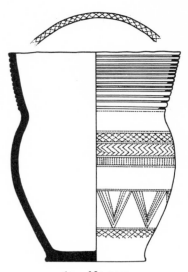

691. N3 1477,
Newlands, Aberdeen.
(scale ×²⁄₇).

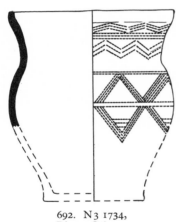

692. N3 1734,
Rinyo, Orkney.
(scale ×²⁄₇).

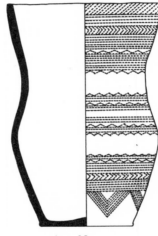

693. N3 1773,
Jedburgh, Roxburgh.
(scale ×²⁄₇).

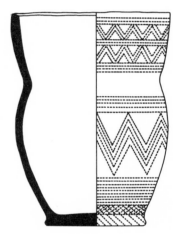

694. N3 1454,
Glasterberry, Aberdeen.
(scale ×²⁄₇).

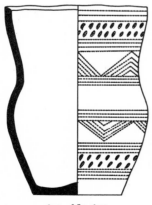

695. N3 655,
Amble, Northumb.
(scale ×²⁄₇).

696. N3 1767,
Eckford, Roxburgh.
(scale ×²⁄₇).

Base

364

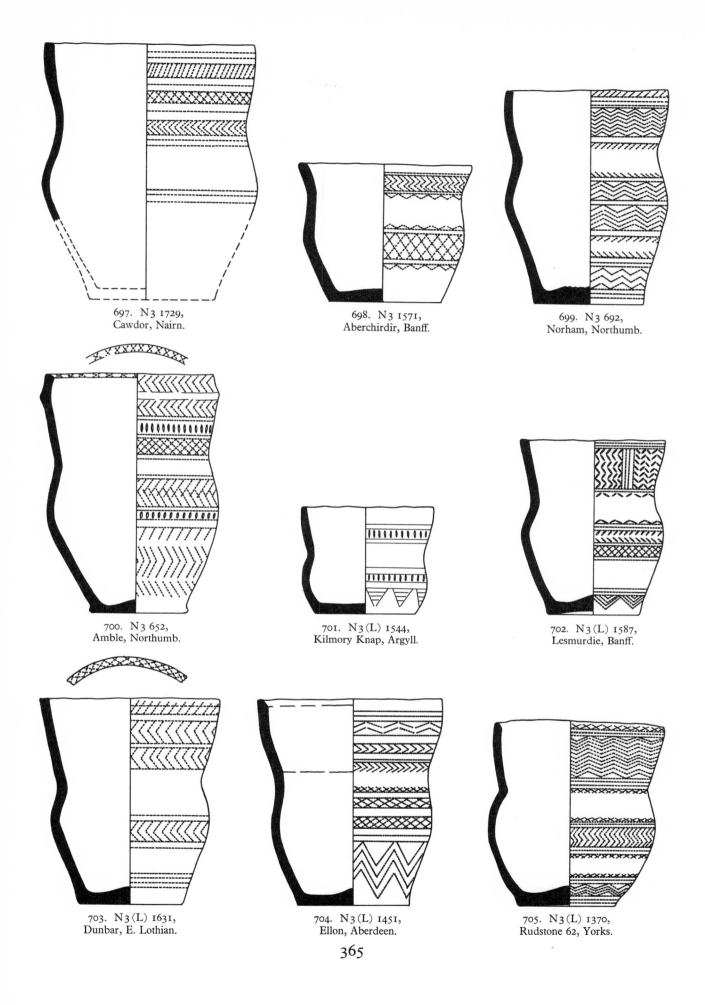

697. N3 1729,
Cawdor, Nairn.

698. N3 1571,
Aberchirdir, Banff.

699. N3 692,
Norham, Northumb.

700. N3 652,
Amble, Northumb.

701. N3(L) 1544,
Kilmory Knap, Argyll.

702. N3(L) 1587,
Lesmurdie, Banff.

703. N3(L) 1631,
Dunbar, E. Lothian.

704. N3(L) 1451,
Ellon, Aberdeen.

705. N3(L) 1370,
Rudstone 62, Yorks.

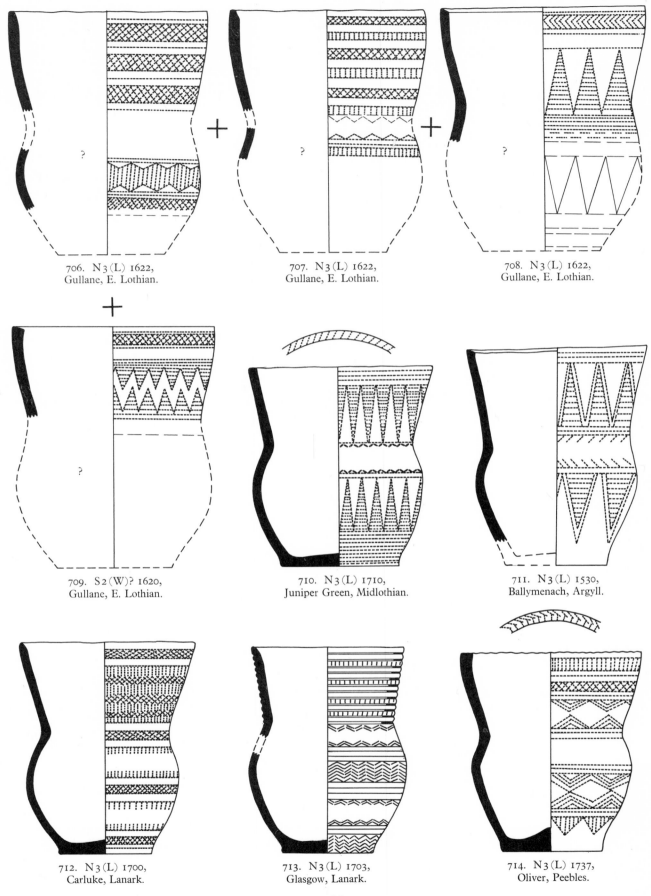

706. N3(L) 1622,
Gullane, E. Lothian.

707. N3(L) 1622,
Gullane, E. Lothian.

708. N3(L) 1622,
Gullane, E. Lothian.

709. S2(W)? 1620,
Gullane, E. Lothian.

710. N3(L) 1710,
Juniper Green, Midlothian.

711. N3(L) 1530,
Ballymenach, Argyll.

712. N3(L) 1700,
Carluke, Lanark.

713. N3(L) 1703,
Glasgow, Lanark.

714. N3(L) 1737,
Oliver, Peebles.

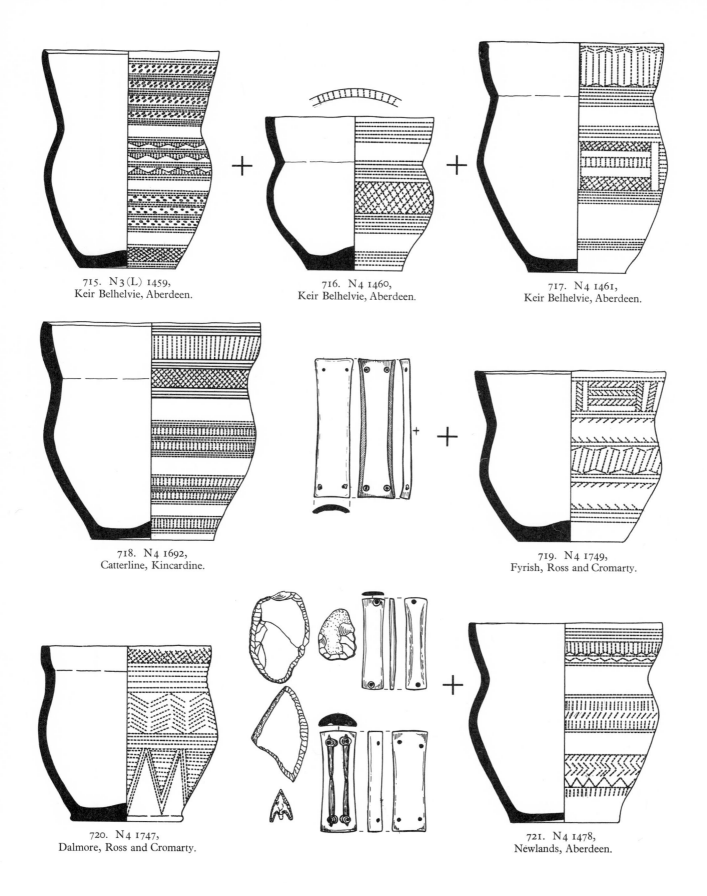

715. N3 (L) 1459,
Keir Belhelvie, Aberdeen.

716. N4 1460,
Keir Belhelvie, Aberdeen.

717. N4 1461,
Keir Belhelvie, Aberdeen.

718. N4 1692,
Catterline, Kincardine.

719. N4 1749,
Fyrish, Ross and Cromarty.

720. N4 1747,
Dalmore, Ross and Cromarty.

721. N4 1478,
Newlands, Aberdeen.

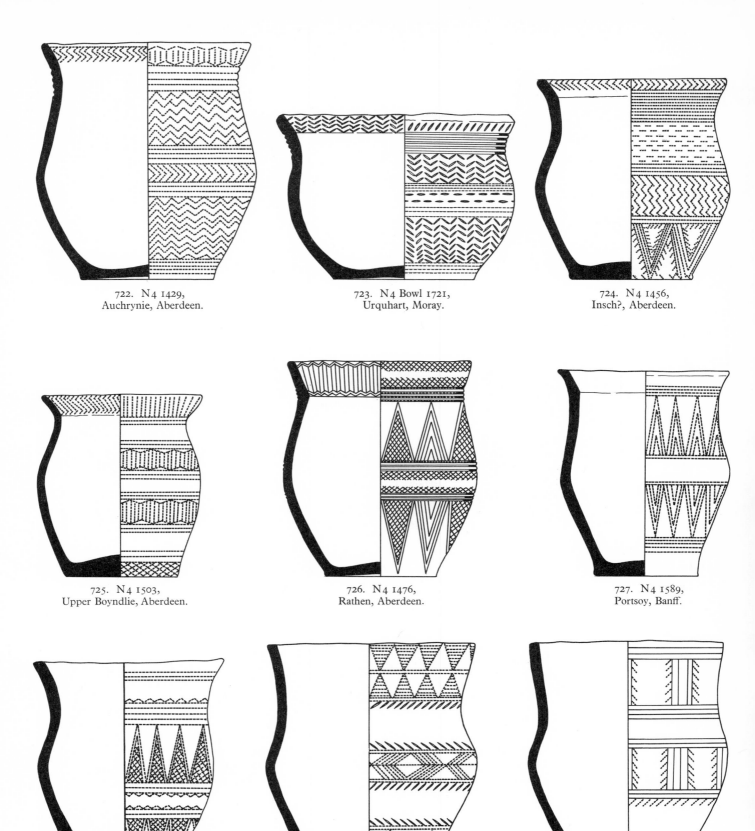

722. N4 1429,
Auchrynie, Aberdeen.

723. N4 Bowl 1721,
Urquhart, Moray.

724. N4 1456,
Insch?, Aberdeen.

725. N4 1503,
Upper Boyndlie, Aberdeen.

726. N4 1476,
Rathen, Aberdeen.

727. N4 1589,
Portsoy, Banff.

728. N4 1572,
Afforsk, Banff.

729. N4 1708,
Borthwick, Midlothian.

730. N4 1675,
Skye, Inverness.

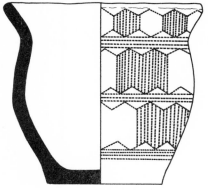

731. N4 1609,
Heathfield, Caithness.

732. N4 1580,
Cullen, Banff.

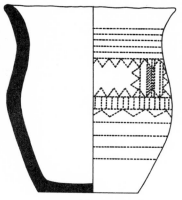

733. N4 1745.1,
Bruachaig, Ross and Cromarty.

734. Food Vessel
Fettercairn, Kincardine.

735. Food Vessel
'Ireland'.

736. Food Vessel
Darnhall, Peebles.

737. Food Vessel
Newhaven, Midlothian.

738. Food Vessel
Tyrie, Aberdeen.

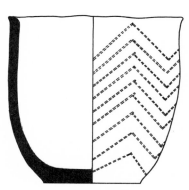

739. Food Vessel
Birsay, Orkney.

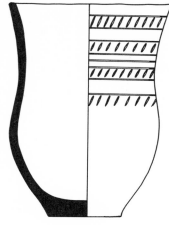

740. Netherlands,
Rhee, Drenthe.

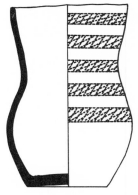

741. S 1 391,
Capel-le-Ferne, Kent.

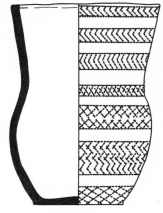

742. S 1 827,
Deepdale, Staffs.

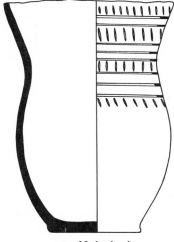

743. Netherlands,
Ginkel, Gelderland.

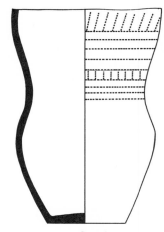

744. S 1 1350,
Newton Mulgrave?, Yorks.

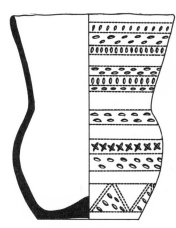

745. S 1 1127,
Netheravon, Wilts.

746. Germany,
Altenburg, Kr. Altenburg.

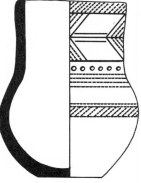

747. S 1? 501,
Leadenhall, London.

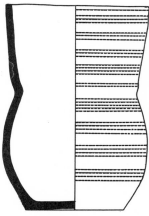

748. S 1 1126,
Netheravon, Wilts.

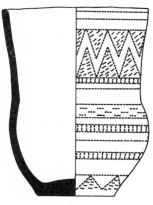

749. S1 1194,
Winterbourne Stoke (35), Wilts.

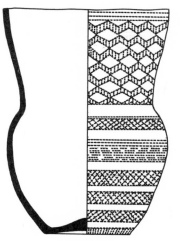

750. S1 1113,
Figheldean (31), Wilts.

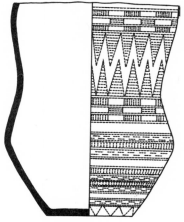

751. S1 92,
Soham, Cambs.

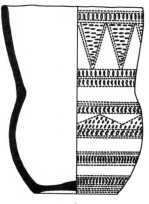

752. S1 559,
Hockwold, Norfolk.

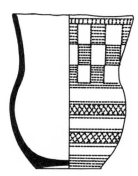

753. S1 967,
Worlington, Suffolk.

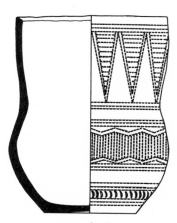

754. S1 826,
Deepdale, Staffs.

755. S1 1216,
Aldro 116, Yorks.

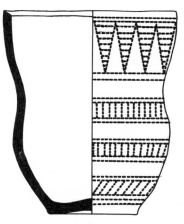

756. S1 1390,
Staxton, Yorks.

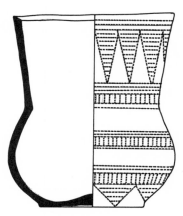

757. S1 117,
Bakewell, Derby.

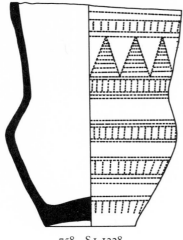

758. S1 1328,
Heslerton 55, Yorks.

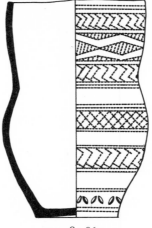

759. S1 860,
Brantham Hall, Suffolk.

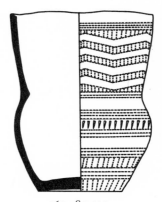

760. S1 445,
Denton, Lincs.

761. S1 1389,
Staxton, Yorks.

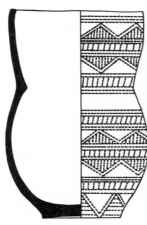

762. S1 425,
Melton Mowbray?, Leics.

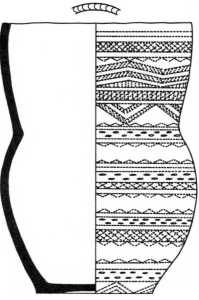

763. S1 1298,
Garton Slack 75, Yorks.

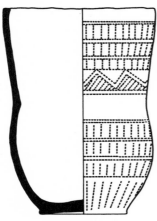

764. S1 1275,
Ferry Friston 161, Yorks.

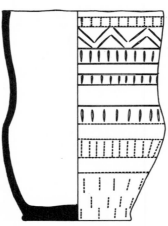

765. S1 1190,
Winterbourne Stoke (10), Wilts.

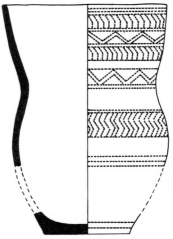

766. S1 66,
Doddington, Cambs.

372

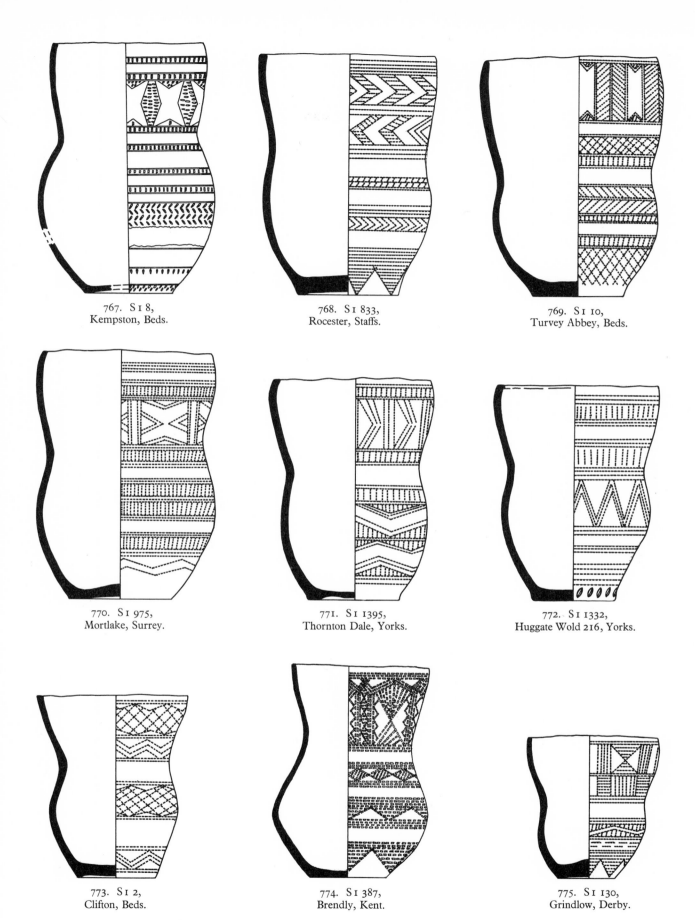

767. S 1 8,
Kempston, Beds.

768. S 1 833,
Rocester, Staffs.

769. S 1 10,
Turvey Abbey, Beds.

770. S 1 975,
Mortlake, Surrey.

771. S 1 1395,
Thornton Dale, Yorks.

772. S 1 1332,
Huggate Wold 216, Yorks.

773. S 1 2,
Clifton, Beds.

774. S 1 387,
Brendly, Kent.

775. S 1 130,
Grindlow, Derby.

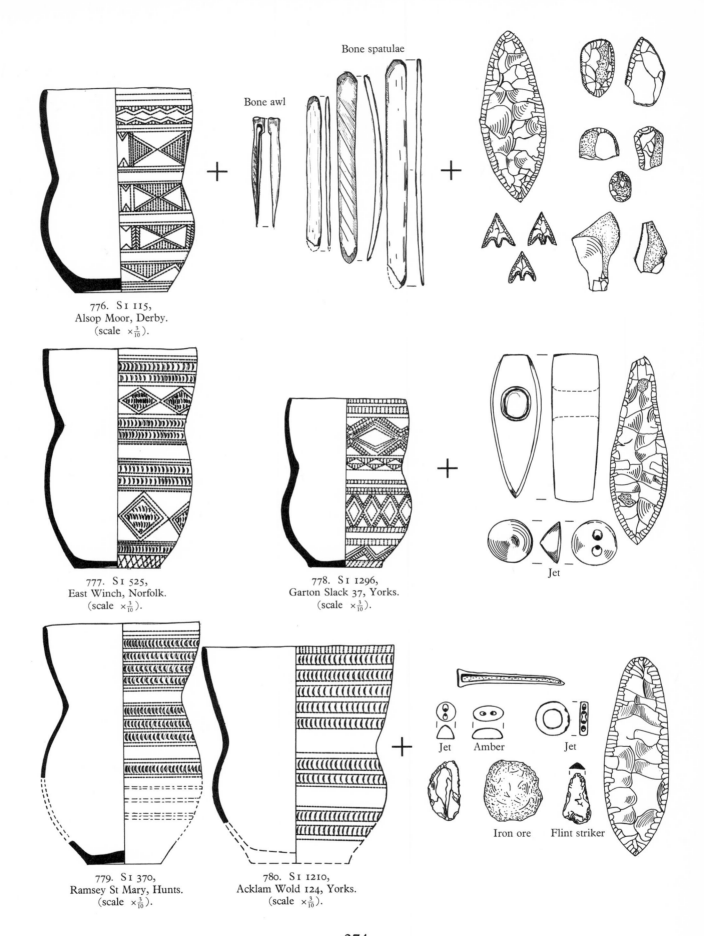

Bone spatulae

Bone awl

776. S1 115,
Alsop Moor, Derby.
(scale ×$\frac{3}{10}$).

777. S1 525,
East Winch, Norfolk.
(scale ×$\frac{3}{10}$).

778. S1 1296,
Garton Slack 37, Yorks.
(scale ×$\frac{3}{10}$).

Jet

779. S1 370,
Ramsey St Mary, Hunts.
(scale ×$\frac{3}{10}$).

780. S1 1210,
Acklam Wold 124, Yorks.
(scale ×$\frac{3}{10}$).

Jet   Amber   Jet

Iron ore   Flint striker

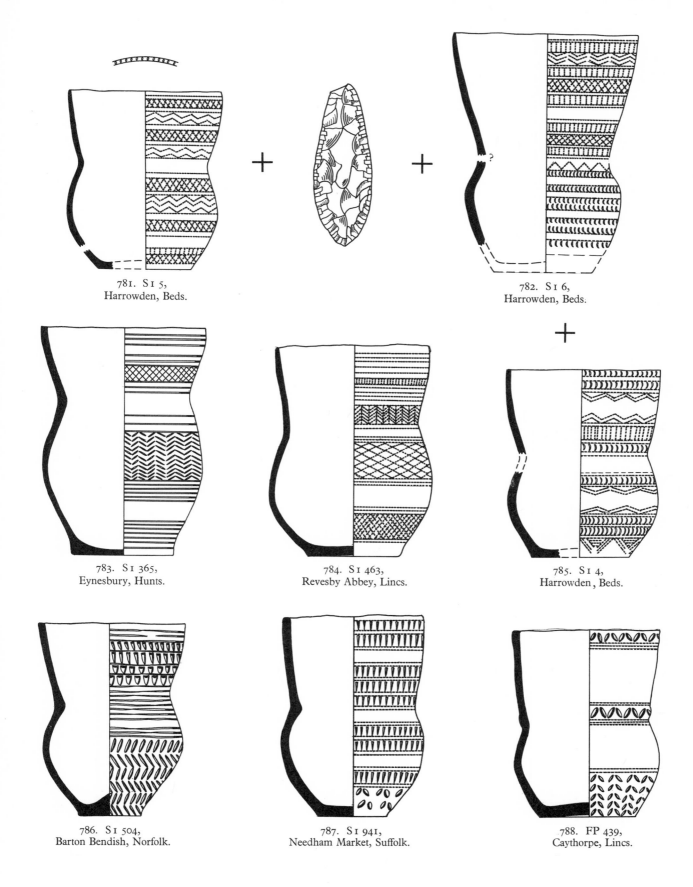

781. S 1 5,
Harrowden, Beds.

782. S 1 6,
Harrowden, Beds.

783. S 1 365,
Eynesbury, Hunts.

784. S 1 463,
Revesby Abbey, Lincs.

785. S 1 4,
Harrowden, Beds.

786. S 1 504,
Barton Bendish, Norfolk.

787. S 1 941,
Needham Market, Suffolk.

788. FP 439,
Caythorpe, Lincs.

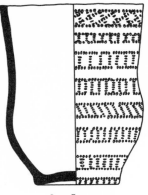

789. S 1 1352,
Painsthorpe Wold 4, Yorks.

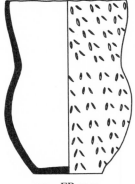

790. FP 1353,
Painsthorpe Wold 4, Yorks.

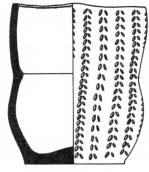

791. FP 86,
Snailwell, Cambs.

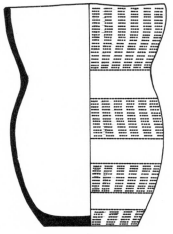

792. S 1 523,
East Tuddenham, Norfolk.

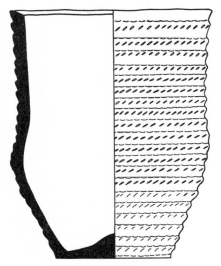

793. FP 524,
East Tuddenham, Norfolk.

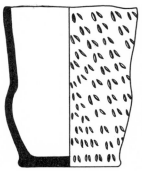

794. FP 1168,
Wilsford (51), Wilts.

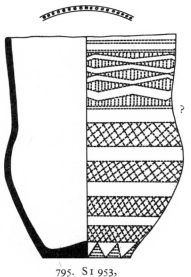

+

795. S 1 953,
Undley, Suffolk.

796. FP 954,
Undley, Suffolk.

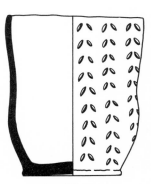

797. FP 1411,
Yorkshire?

376

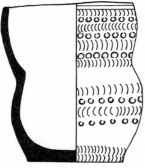

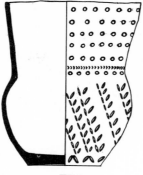

798. FP 507,
Bergh Apton, Norfolk.

799. FP 614,
Sutton, Norfolk.

800. FP 360,
Tewin, Herts.

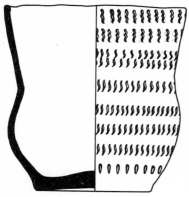

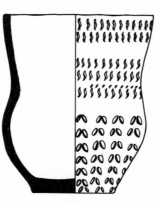

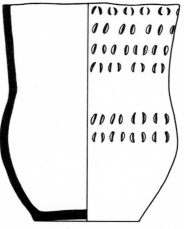

801. FP 203,
Tarrant Launceston (8), Dorset.

802. FP 1114,
Figheldean (25), Wilts.

803. FP 960,
Wherstead, Suffolk.

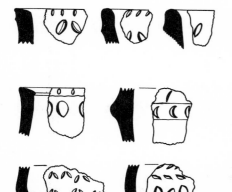

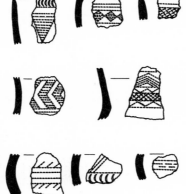

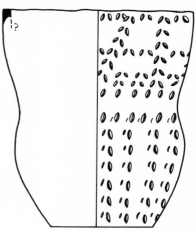

804. FP 926,
Lakenheath, Suffolk.

805. S 1? 925,
Lakenheath, Suffolk.

806. FP 1273,
Elloughton, Yorks.

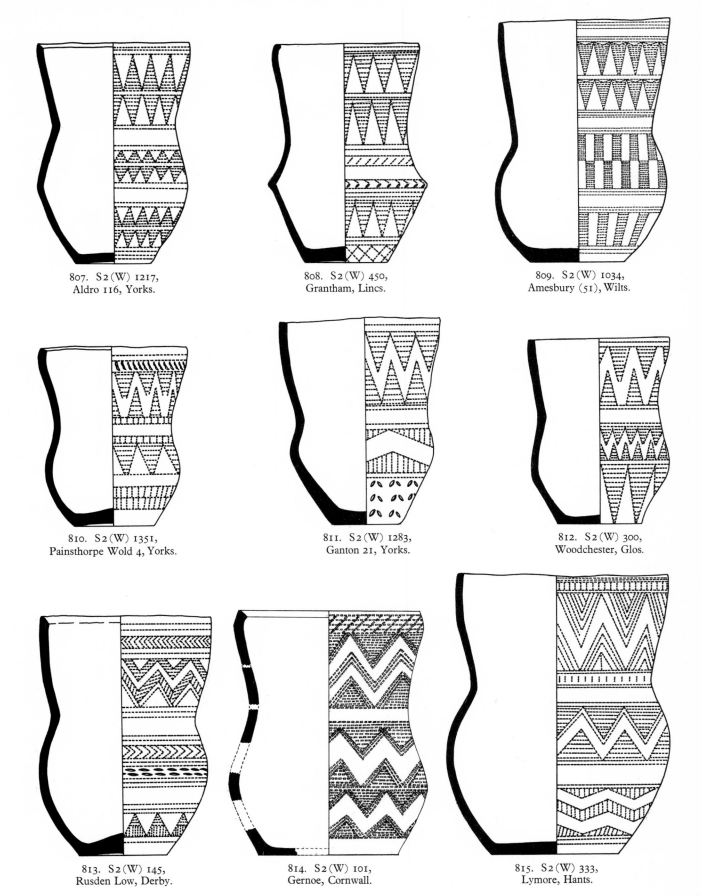

807. S2(W) 1217,
Aldro 116, Yorks.

808. S2(W) 450,
Grantham, Lincs.

809. S2(W) 1034,
Amesbury (51), Wilts.

810. S2(W) 1351,
Painsthorpe Wold 4, Yorks.

811. S2(W) 1283,
Ganton 21, Yorks.

812. S2(W) 300,
Woodchester, Glos.

813. S2(W) 145,
Rusden Low, Derby.

814. S2(W) 101,
Gernoe, Cornwall.

815. S2(W) 333,
Lymore, Hants.

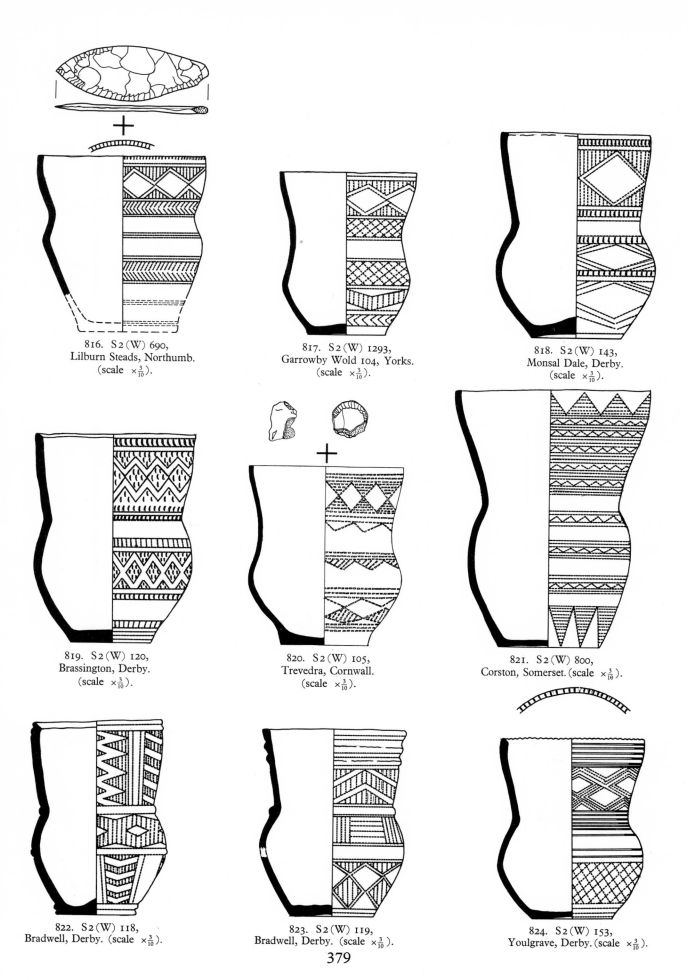

816. S2 (W) 690,
Lilburn Steads, Northumb.
(scale ×$\frac{3}{10}$).

817. S2 (W) 1293,
Garrowby Wold 104, Yorks.
(scale ×$\frac{3}{10}$).

818. S2 (W) 143,
Monsal Dale, Derby.
(scale ×$\frac{3}{10}$).

819. S2 (W) 120,
Brassington, Derby.
(scale ×$\frac{3}{10}$).

820. S2 (W) 105,
Trevedra, Cornwall.
(scale ×$\frac{3}{10}$).

821. S2 (W) 800,
Corston, Somerset. (scale ×$\frac{3}{10}$).

822. S2 (W) 118,
Bradwell, Derby. (scale ×$\frac{3}{10}$).

823. S2 (W) 119,
Bradwell, Derby. (scale ×$\frac{3}{10}$).

824. S2 (W) 153,
Youlgrave, Derby. (scale ×$\frac{3}{10}$).

379

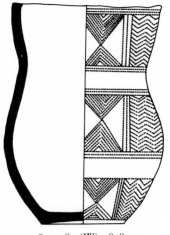

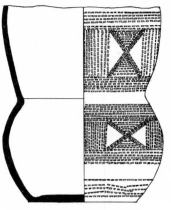

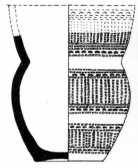

825. S2(W) 1858,
Llanharry, Glam.
(scale ×3/10).

826. S2(W) 986,
Brighton, Sussex.
(scale ×3/10).

827. S2(W) 987,
Brighton, Sussex.
(scale ×3/10).

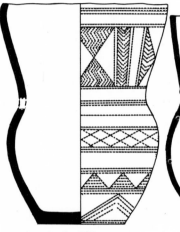

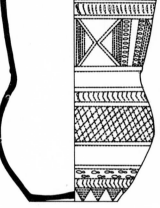

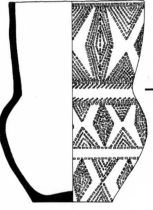

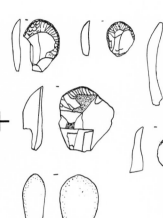

828. S2(W) 1400,
Towthorpe 21, Yorks.
(scale ×3/10).

829. S2(W) 1101,
Durrington (36), Wilts.
(scale ×3/10).

830. S2(W) 820,
Stogursey, Somerset.
(scale ×3/10).

Pebble hammer

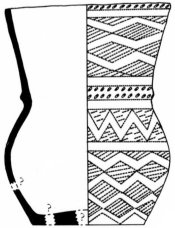

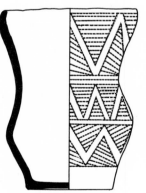

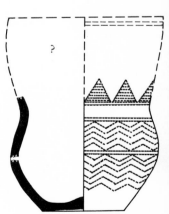

831. S2(W) 1875,
Llanelltyd, Merioneth.
(scale ×3/10).

832. S2(W) 1870,
Ty-Newydd, Glam.
(scale ×3/10).

833. S2(W)? 1856,
Hendre'r Gelli, Glam.
(scale ×3/10).

380

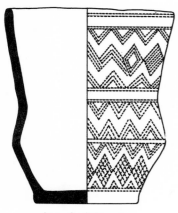

834. S2(W) 1087,
Calne Without (2c), Wilts.

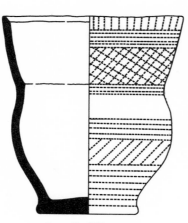

835. S2(W) 1324,
Hanging Grimston 55, Yorks.

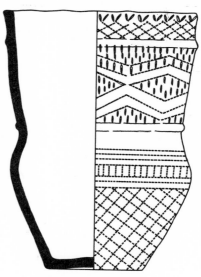

836. S2(W) 1399,
Tinshill, Yorks.

837. S2(E) 904,
Ipswich?, Suffolk.

838. S2(W) 894,
Gravel, Suffolk.

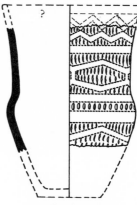

839. S2(W) 1078,
Bishops Cannings (54), Wilts.

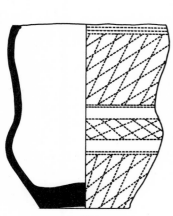

840. S2(W) 1046,
Amesbury, Wilts.

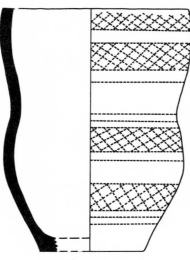

841. S2(W) 1770,
Edgerston, Roxburgh.

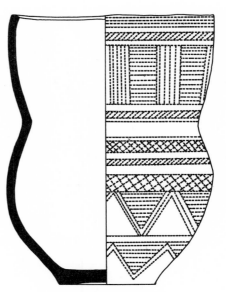

842. S2(W) 139,
Middleton, Derby.

843. S2(E) 9,
Shefford, Beds.

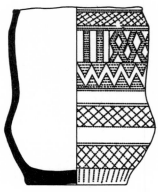

844. S2(E) 363,
Ware, Herts.

845. S2(E) 229,
Colchester, Essex.

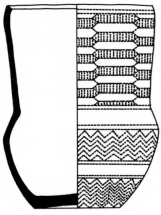

846. S2(E) 1037,
Amesdury (51), Wilts.

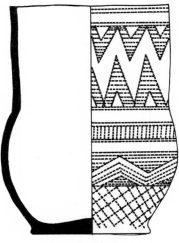

847. S2(E) 621,
Trowse-with-Newton, Norfolk.

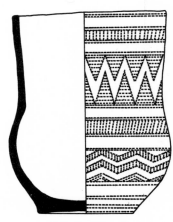

848. S2(E) 358,
Hitchin?, Herts.

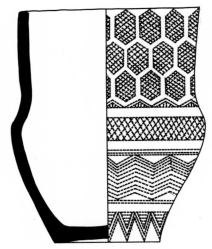

849. S2(E) 328,
Iford, Hants.

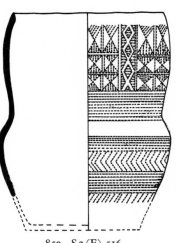

850. S2(E) 516,
Castle Acre, Norfolk.

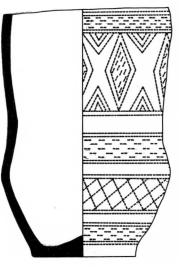

851. S2(E) 1146,
Swindon, Wilts.

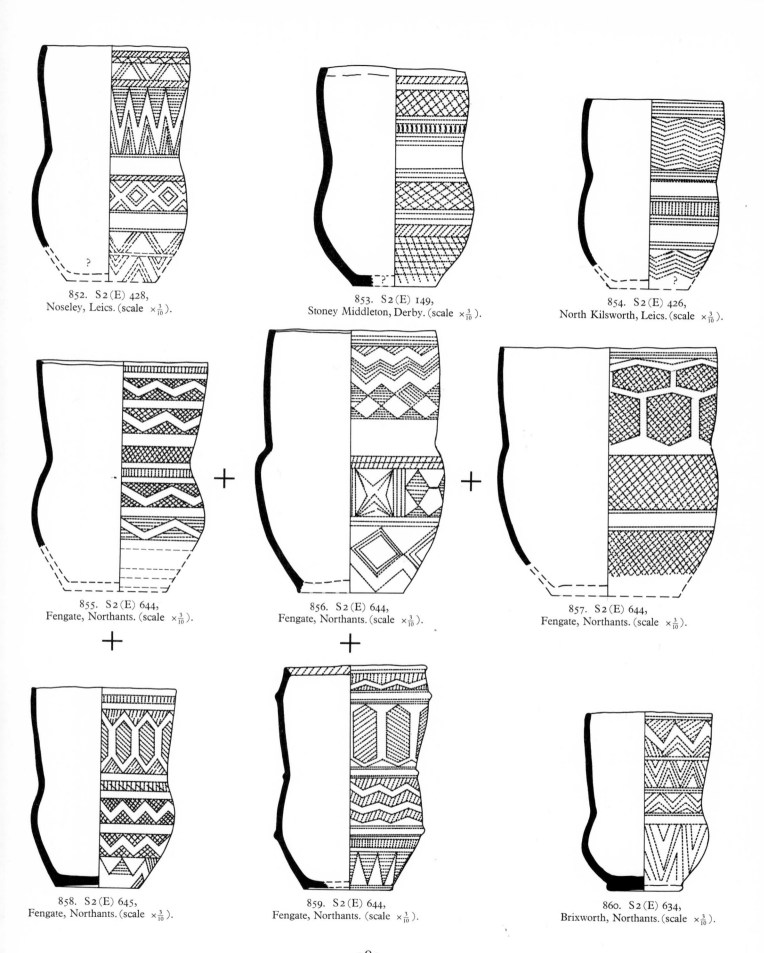

852. S2(E) 428,
Noseley, Leics. (scale ×$\frac{3}{10}$).

853. S2(E) 149,
Stoney Middleton, Derby. (scale ×$\frac{3}{10}$).

854. S2(E) 426,
North Kilsworth, Leics. (scale ×$\frac{3}{10}$).

855. S2(E) 644,
Fengate, Northants. (scale ×$\frac{3}{10}$).

856. S2(E) 644,
Fengate, Northants. (scale ×$\frac{3}{10}$).

857. S2(E) 644,
Fengate, Northants. (scale ×$\frac{3}{10}$).

858. S2(E) 645,
Fengate, Northants. (scale ×$\frac{3}{10}$).

859. S2(E) 644,
Fengate, Northants. (scale ×$\frac{3}{10}$).

860. S2(E) 634,
Brixworth, Northants. (scale ×$\frac{3}{10}$).

383

861. S2(E) 835,
Wetton, Staffs.
(scale ×$\frac{3}{11}$).

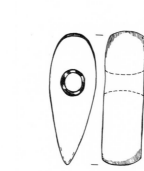

Bone
spatulae

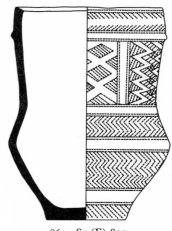

+

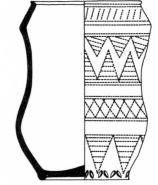

862. S2(E) 825,
Deepdale, Staffs.
(scale ×$\frac{3}{11}$).

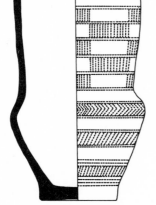

863. S2(E) 1320,
Hanging Grimston 56, Yorks.
(scale ×$\frac{3}{11}$).

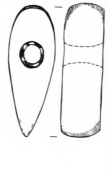

+

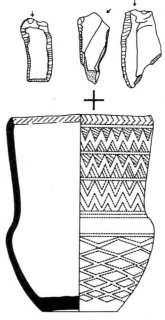

864. S2(E) 1103,
Durrington, Wilts.
(scale ×$\frac{3}{11}$).

865. S2(E) 1374,
Rudstone 66, Yorks.
(scale ×$\frac{3}{11}$).

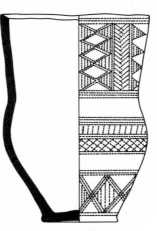

866. S2(E) 707,
Seahouses, Northumb.
(scale ×$\frac{3}{11}$).

+

867. S2(E) 1849,
Llannon, Carmarthen.
(scale ×$\frac{3}{11}$).

868. S2(E) 1331,
Huggate and Warterwold 3, Yorks.

869. S2(E) 711,
Woodhorn, Northumb.

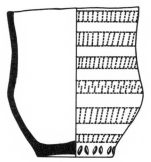

870. S2(E) 14,
Abingdon, Berks.

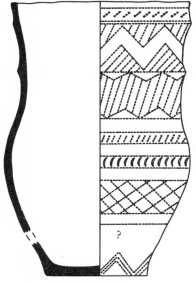

871. S2(E) 1397,
Thwing 60, Yorks.

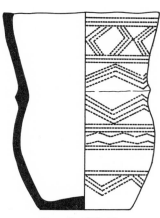

872. S2(W) 660,
Beanley, Northumb.

873. S2(E) 1323,
Hanging Grimston 55, Yorks.

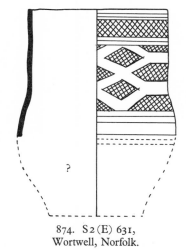

874. S2(E) 631,
Wortwell, Norfolk.

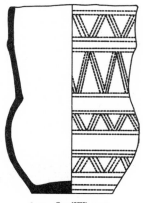

875. S2(W) 971,
Kew, Surrey.

Base

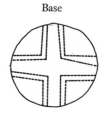

385

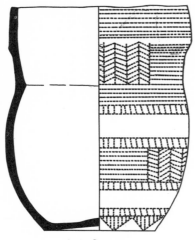

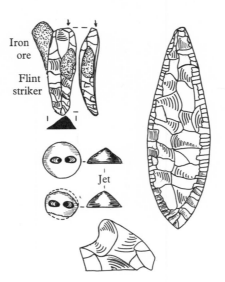

876. S2 1347,
Middleton-on-the-Wolds, Yorks.

Iron ore

Flint striker

Jet

877. S2 522,
East Harling, Norfolk.

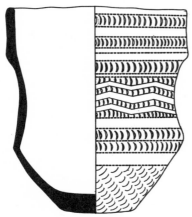

878. S2 366,
Houghton, Hunts.

a

b   *c*

879. S2 (?) 929*a*, and *b*, 931*c*,
Lakenheath, Suffolk.

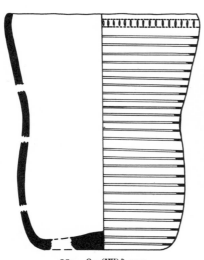

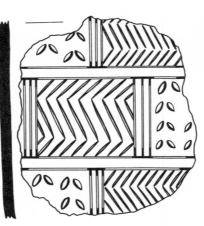

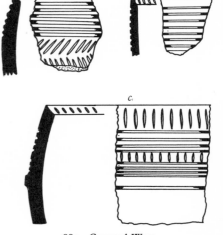

880. S2 (W)? 155,
Broad Down, Devon.

881. Grooved Ware
Woodhenge, Wilts.

a   *b*

c

882. Grooved Ware
a. Peterborough, Northants.
b. Creeting St. Mary, Suffolk.
c. Stanton Harcourt, Oxon.

386

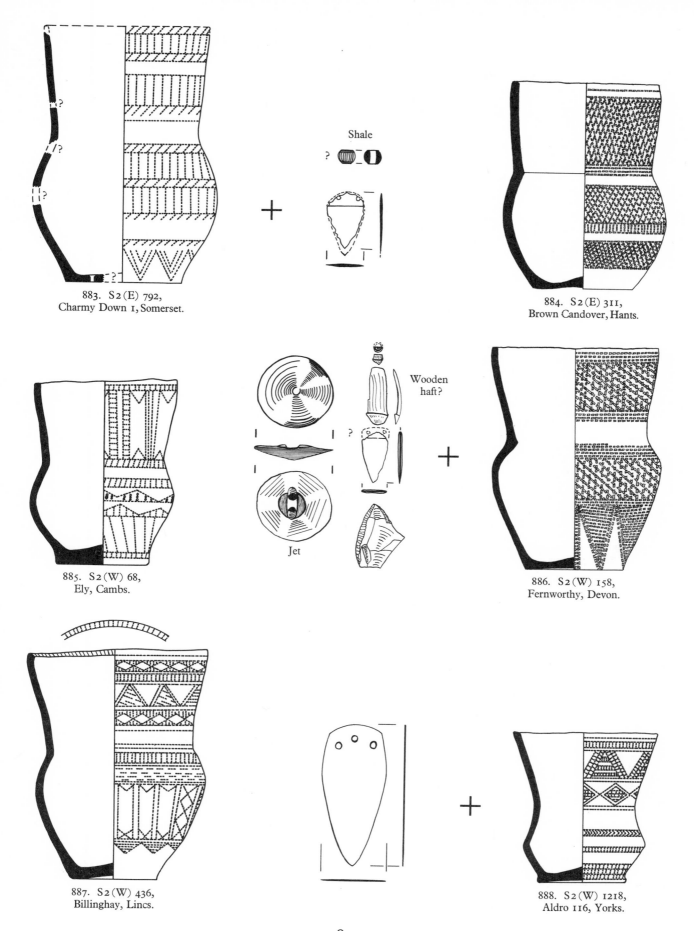

883. S2 (E) 792,
Charmy Down 1, Somerset.

Shale

884. S2 (E) 311,
Brown Candover, Hants.

885. S2 (W) 68,
Ely, Cambs.

Jet

Wooden
haft?

886. S2 (W) 158,
Fernworthy, Devon.

887. S2 (W) 436,
Billinghay, Lincs.

888. S2 (W) 1218,
Aldro 116, Yorks.

387

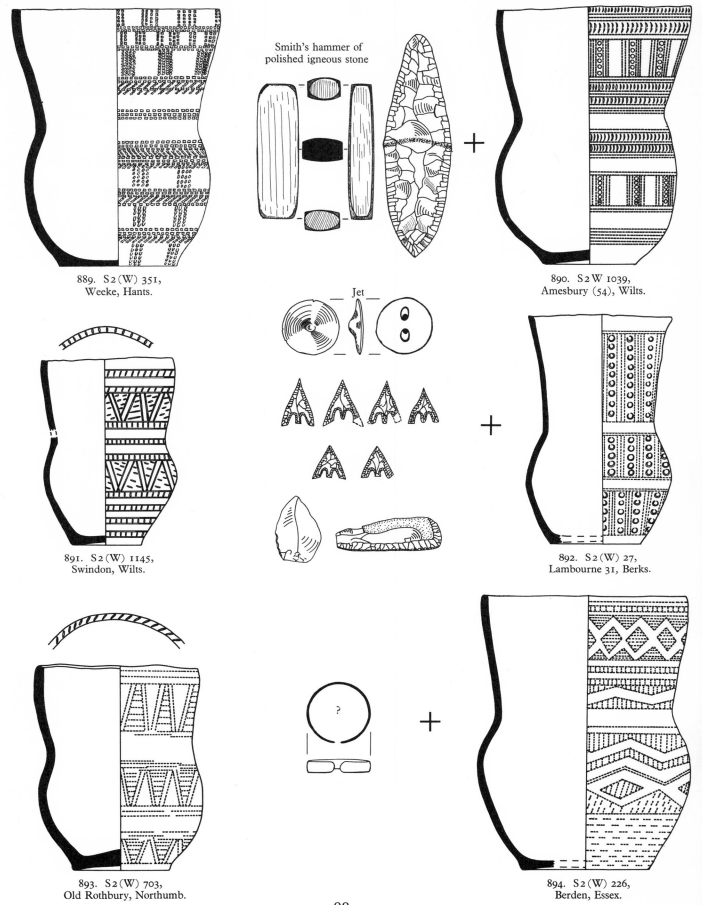

Smith's hammer of polished igneous stone

Jet

889. S2(W) 351,
Weeke, Hants.

890. S2W 1039,
Amesbury (54), Wilts.

891. S2(W) 1145,
Swindon, Wilts.

892. S2(W) 27,
Lambourne 31, Berks.

893. S2(W) 703,
Old Rothbury, Northumb.

894. S2(W) 226,
Berden, Essex.

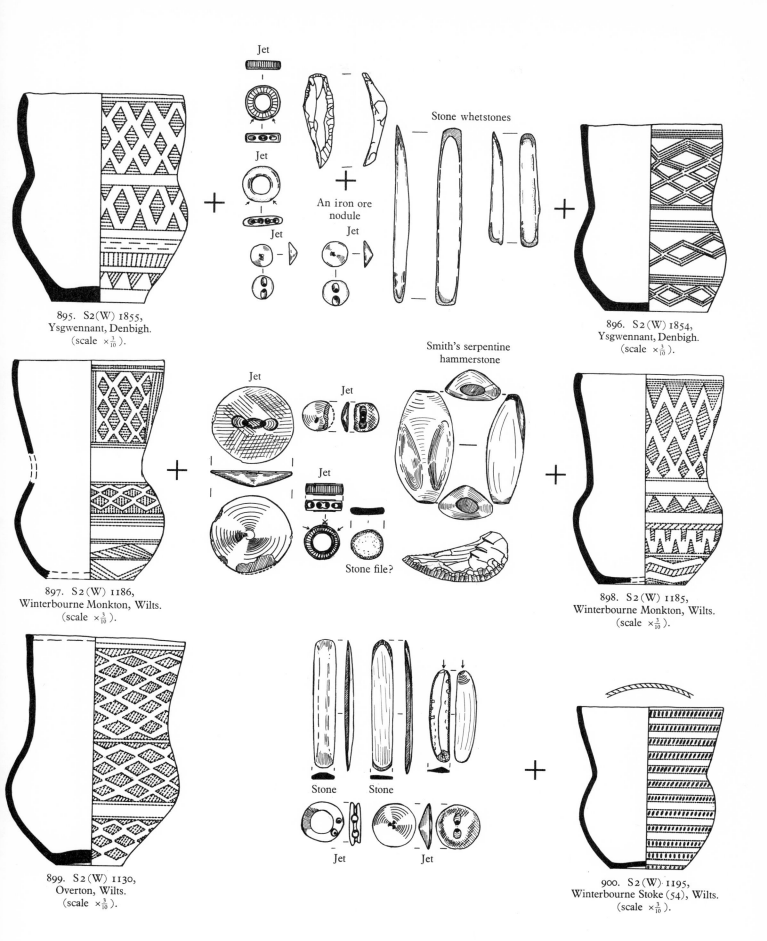

Jet

Jet

Jet　　Jet

An iron ore nodule

Stone whetstones

895. S2(W) 1855,
Ysgwennant, Denbigh.
(scale ×$\frac{3}{10}$).

896. S2(W) 1854,
Ysgwennant, Denbigh.
(scale ×$\frac{3}{10}$).

Jet

Jet

Jet

Smith's serpentine
hammerstone

Stone file?

897. S2(W) 1186,
Winterbourne Monkton, Wilts.
(scale ×$\frac{3}{10}$).

898. S2(W) 1185,
Winterbourne Monkton, Wilts.
(scale ×$\frac{3}{10}$).

Stone　　Stone

Jet　　Jet

899. S2(W) 1130,
Overton, Wilts.
(scale ×$\frac{3}{10}$).

900. S2(W) 1195,
Winterbourne Stoke (54), Wilts.
(scale ×$\frac{3}{10}$).

389

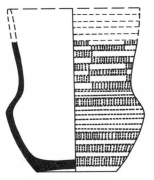

901. S2(W) 64,
Chippenham 5, Cambs.

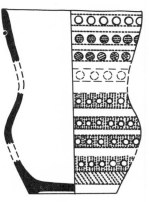

902. S2(W) 64,
Chippenham 5, Cambs.

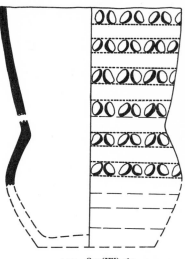

903. S2(W) 64,
Chippenham 5, Cambs.

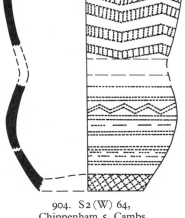

904. S2(W) 64,
Chippenham 5, Cambs.

905. SH2(?) 63,
Chippenham 5, Cambs.

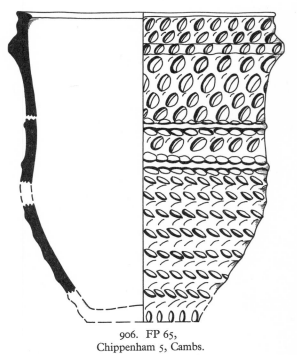

906. FP 65,
Chippenham 5, Cambs.

390

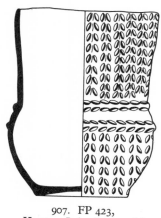

907. FP 423,
Harston, Leics. (scale ×$\frac{3}{10}$).

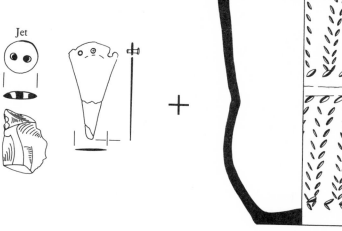

Jet

+

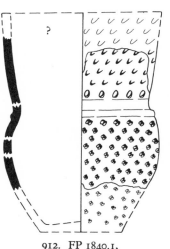

908. FP 1828,
Pentraeth, Anglesey. (scale ×$\frac{3}{10}$).

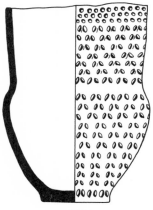

909. FP 244,
Lion Point, Essex. (scale ×$\frac{3}{10}$).

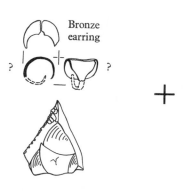

Bronze
earring

? ?

+

910. FP 122,
Buxton, Derby. (scale ×$\frac{3}{10}$).

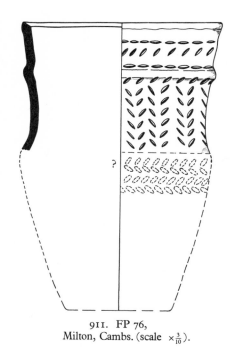

911. FP 76,
Milton, Cambs. (scale ×$\frac{3}{10}$).

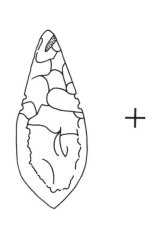

+

?

912. FP 1840.1,
Ystradfellte, Brecknock. (scale ×$\frac{3}{10}$).

391

913. 132,
Hartington, Derby.

Base

914. 1562,
Muirkirk 2, Ayr.

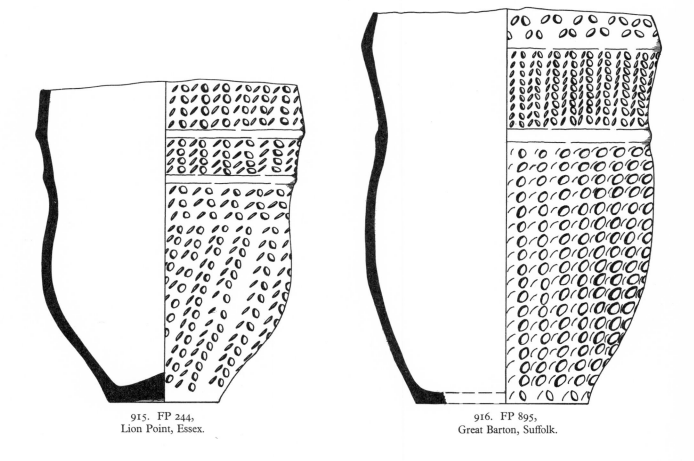

915. FP 244,
Lion Point, Essex.

916. FP 895,
Great Barton, Suffolk.

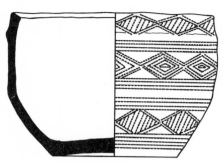

917. Bowl (S2?) 164,
Bincombe (11), Dorset.
(scale ×$\frac{3}{10}$).

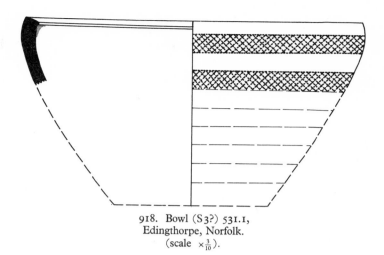

918. Bowl (S3?) 531.1,
Edingthorpe, Norfolk.
(scale ×$\frac{3}{10}$).

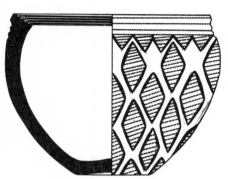

919. Food Vessel
Alnwick, Northumb.
(scale ×$\frac{3}{10}$).

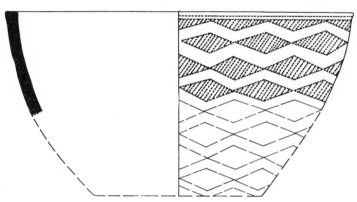

920. Bowl (S3?) 930.1,
Lakenheath, Suffolk.
(scale ×$\frac{3}{10}$).

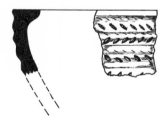

921. Bowl FP 327,
Holdenhurst, Hants.
(scale ×$\frac{3}{10}$).

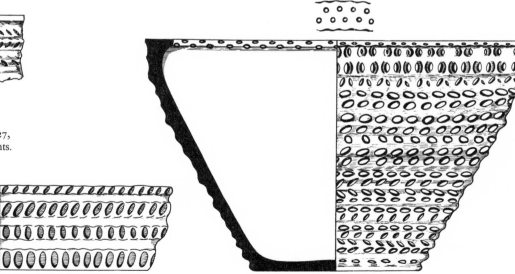

922. Fengate (?) Ware
Windmill Hill, Avebury, Wilts.
(scale ×$\frac{3}{10}$).

923. Bowl FP 310,
Bournemouth, Hants.
(scale ×$\frac{3}{10}$).

393

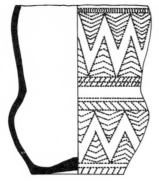

924. S3 (E) 234,
Gt. Chesterford, Essex.

925. S3 (E) 278,
Bourton, Glos.

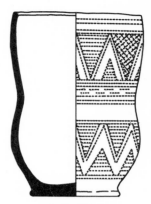

926. S3 (E) 437,
Broughton, Lincs.

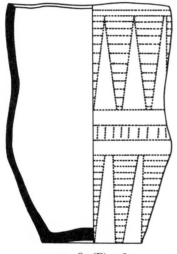

927. S3 (E) 1284,
Ganton 21, Yorks.

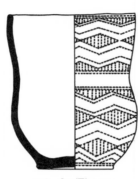

928. S3 (E) 1272,
Elloughton, Yorks.

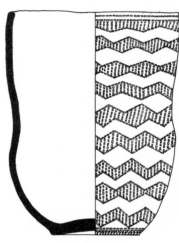

929. S3 (E) 47,
Barnwell, Cambs.

930. S3 (E) 493,
Woolsthorpe?, Lincs.

931. S3 (E) 758,
Oxford, Oxon.

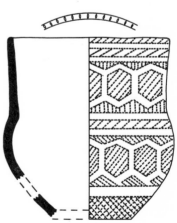

932. S3 (E) 172,
Bradford Peverell (30), Dorset.

933. S3 (E) 585,
Runcton Holme, Norfolk.

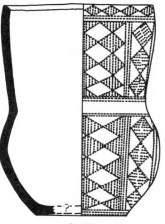

934. S3 (E) 128,
Dowel, Derby.

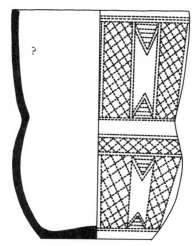

935. S3 (E) 380,
Freshwater, Isle of Wight.

936. S3 (E) 587,
Runcton Holme, Norfolk.

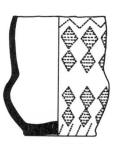

937. S3 (E) 646,
Fengate, Northants.

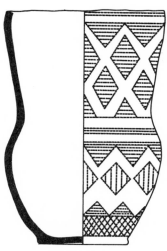

938. S3 (E) 756,
North Stoke, Oxon.

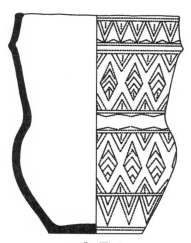

939. S3 (E) 834,
Swinscoe, Staffs.

940. S3 (E) 514,
Castle Acre, Norfolk.

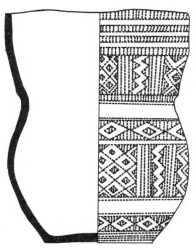

941. S3 (E) 877,
Eriswell, Suffolk.

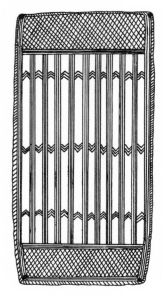

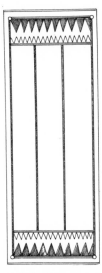

942. Wessex gold manchette,
Upton Lovell, Wilts. (scale ×$\frac{11}{21}$).

943. Aunjetitz bronze manchette,
Peigarten, Lower Austria. (scale ×$\frac{7}{25}$).

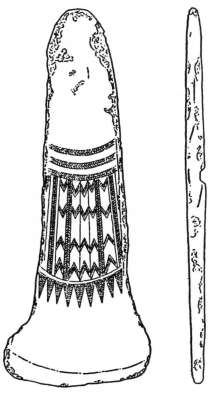

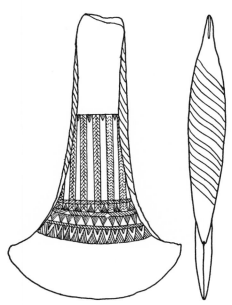

944. Decorated bronze axe,
Trenovissick, Cornwall. (scale ×$\frac{11}{21}$).

945. Decorated bronze axe,
Stuntney, Cambs. (scale ×$\frac{1}{2}$).

a

b

c

d

e

f

946. Late beaker bronze bracelets and one necklet—*d.* (scale ×$\frac{4}{9}$).

    a. Bridlington, Yorks.
    b. Knipton, Leics.
    c. Normanton, Wilts.
    d. Garton Slack, Yorks.
    e. Castern, Staffs.
    f. Mill of Laither, Banff.

397

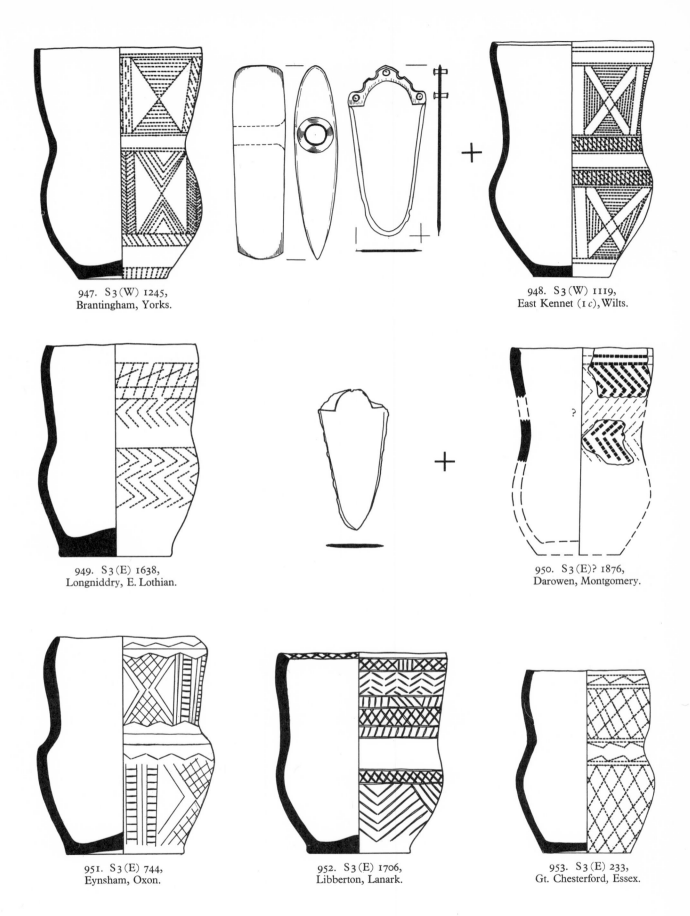

947. S3(W) 1245,
Brantingham, Yorks.

948. S3(W) 1119,
East Kennet (1c), Wilts.

949. S3(E) 1638,
Longniddry, E. Lothian.

950. S3(E)? 1876,
Darowen, Montgomery.

951. S3(E) 744,
Eynsham, Oxon.

952. S3(E) 1706,
Libberton, Lanark.

953. S3(E) 233,
Gt. Chesterford, Essex.

954. S3 (E) 1860,
Merthyr Mawr, Glam.

Bronze

955. S3 (W) 424,
Knipton, Leics.

956. S3 (E) 1861,
Merthyr Mawr, Glam.

957. S3 (W) 821,
Stogursey, Somerset.

Jet

Jet

958. S3 (W) 914,
Isleham, Suffolk.

959. S3 (W) 72,
Little Downham, Cambs.

399

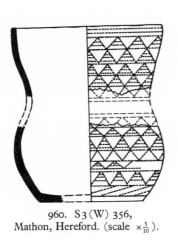

960. S3 (W) 356,
Mathon, Hereford. (scale ×$\frac{3}{10}$).

961. S3 (W) 104,
St Buryan, Cornwall. (scale ×$\frac{3}{10}$).

962. S3 (W) 1164,
Wilsford (34), Wilts. (scale ×$\frac{3}{10}$).

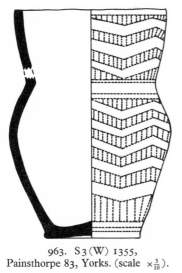
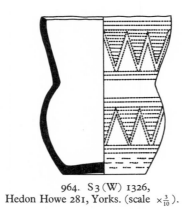
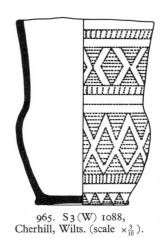

963. S3 (W) 1355,
Painsthorpe 83, Yorks. (scale ×$\frac{3}{10}$).

964. S3 (W) 1326,
Hedon Howe 281, Yorks. (scale ×$\frac{3}{10}$).

965. S3 (W) 1088,
Cherhill, Wilts. (scale ×$\frac{3}{10}$).

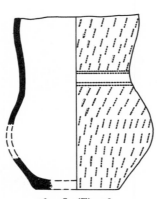

966. S3 (W) 813,
Nettlebridge, Somerset. (scale ×$\frac{3}{10}$).

967. S3 (E) 998,
Park Brow, Sussex. (scale ×$\frac{3}{10}$).

968. S3 (E) 1672,
Kilmarie, Skye, Inverness. (scale ×$\frac{3}{10}$).

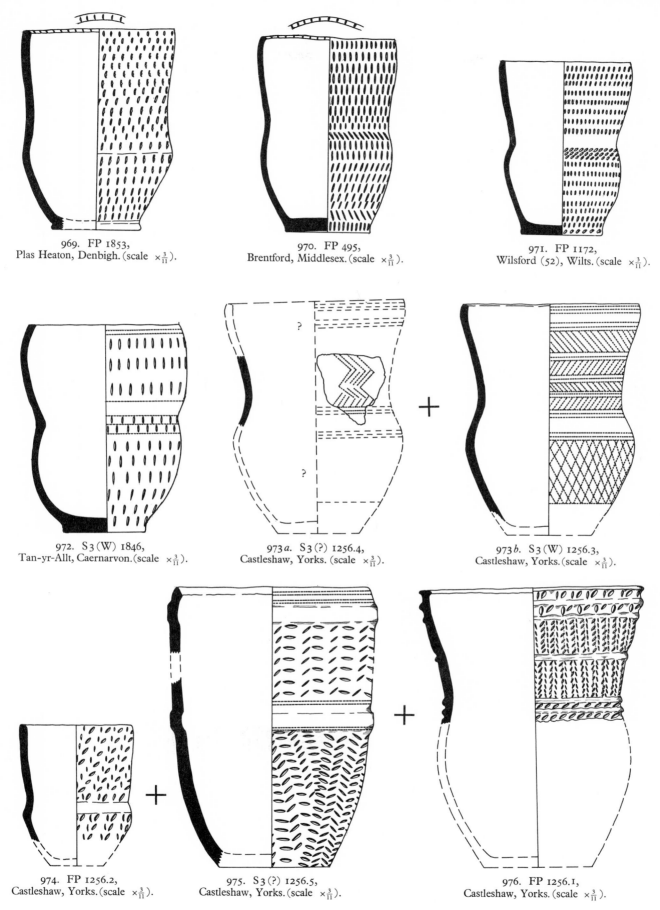

969. FP 1853,
Plas Heaton, Denbigh. (scale ×3/11).

970. FP 495,
Brentford, Middlesex. (scale ×3/11).

971. FP 1172,
Wilsford (52), Wilts. (scale ×3/11).

972. S3 (W) 1846,
Tan-yr-Allt, Caernarvon. (scale ×3/11).

973a. S3 (?) 1256.4,
Castleshaw, Yorks. (scale ×3/11).

973b. S3 (W) 1256.3,
Castleshaw, Yorks. (scale ×3/11).

974. FP 1256.2,
Castleshaw, Yorks. (scale ×3/11).

975. S3 (?) 1256.5,
Castleshaw, Yorks. (scale ×3/11).

976. FP 1256.1,
Castleshaw, Yorks. (scale ×3/11).

977. S4 719,
Cassington, Oxon.

978. S4 1083,
Brigmerston, Wilts.

979. S4 1280,
Folkton 242, Yorks.

980. S4 1545,
Kerrera Is., Argyll.

981. S4 751,
Eynsham, Oxon.

982. S4 1072,
Avebury, Wilts.

983. S4 1392,
Staxton, Yorks.

984. S4 713,
Clumber Park, Notts.

985. S4 714,
Clumber Park, Notts.

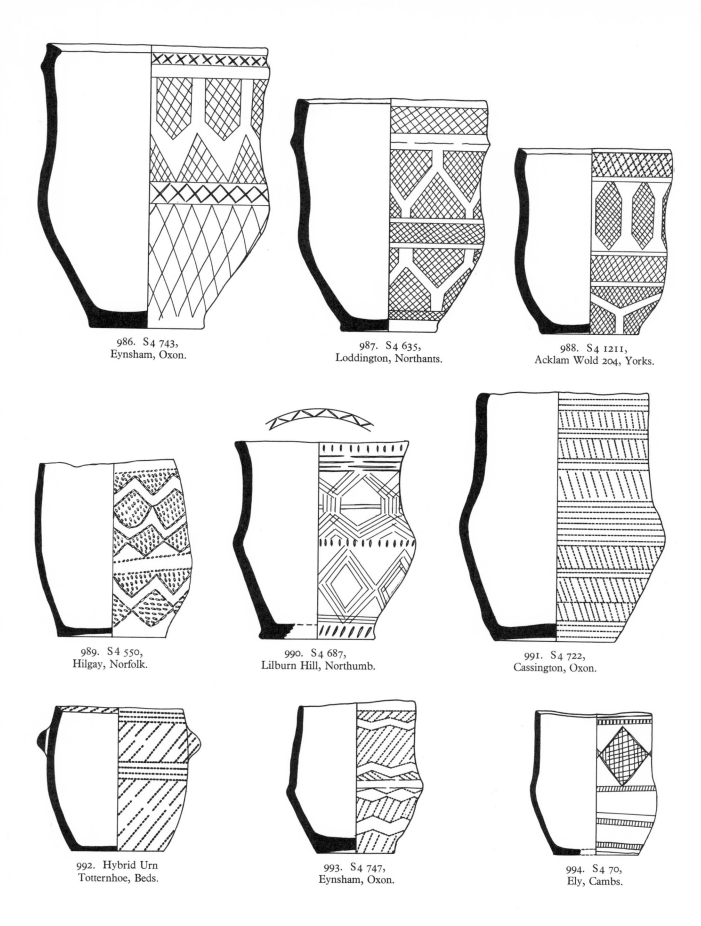

986. S4 743,
Eynsham, Oxon.

987. S4 635,
Loddington, Northants.

988. S4 1211,
Acklam Wold 204, Yorks.

989. S4 550,
Hilgay, Norfolk.

990. S4 687,
Lilburn Hill, Norfhumb.

991. S4 722,
Cassington, Oxon.

992. Hybrid Urn
Totternhoe, Beds.

993. S4 747,
Eynsham, Oxon.

994. S4 70,
Ely, Cambs.

995. S4 729,
Cassington, Oxon.

996. S4 731,
Cassington, Oxon.

997. S4 37,
Theale, Berks.

998. S4 204,
nr. Weymouth, Dorset.

999. S4 745,
Eynsham, Oxon.

1000. S4 176,
Dorchester, Dorset.

1001. S4 332,
Kinson, Hants.

1002. S4 1197,
Winterbourne Stoke?, Wilts.

1003. S4 308,
Bournemouth, Hants.

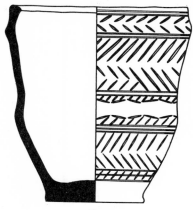

1004. S4 1413.2
'Scotland'.

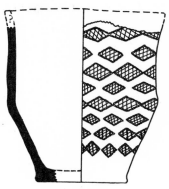

1005. S4 849,
Bawdsey, Suffolk.

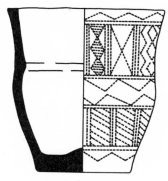

1006. S4 1762,
Brahan Castle?, Ross.

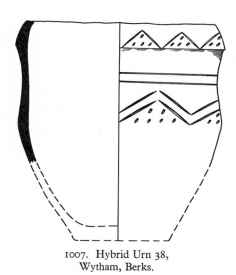

1007. Hybrid Urn 38,
Wytham, Berks.

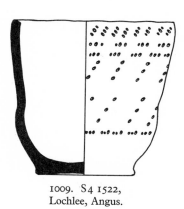

1008. S4 1720,
Urquhart, Moray.

1009. S4 1522,
Lochlee, Angus.

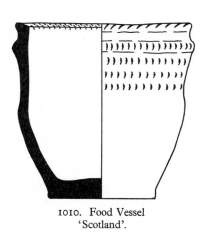

1010. Food Vessel
'Scotland'.

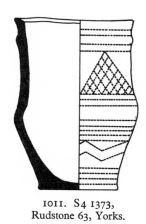

1011. S4 1373,
Rudstone 63, Yorks.

1012. Food Vessel
Dornoch, Sutherland.

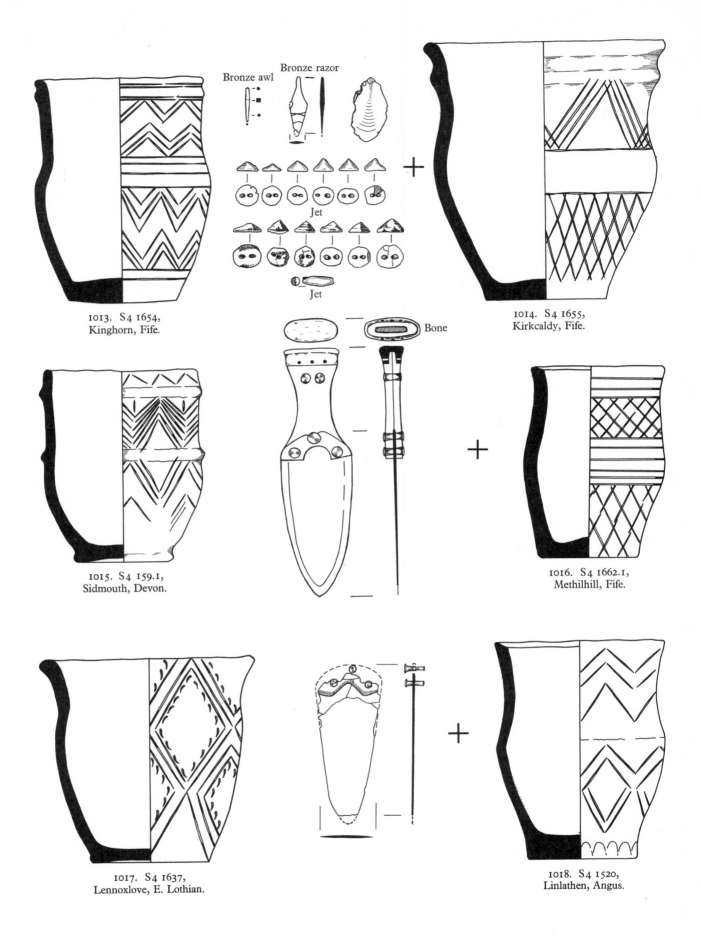

Bronze awl

Bronze razor

Jet

Jet

Bone

1013. S4 1654,
Kinghorn, Fife.

1014. S4 1655,
Kirkcaldy, Fife.

1015. S4 159.1,
Sidmouth, Devon.

1016. S4 1662.1,
Methilhill, Fife.

1017. S4 1637,
Lennoxlove, E. Lothian.

1018. S4 1520,
Linlathen, Angus.

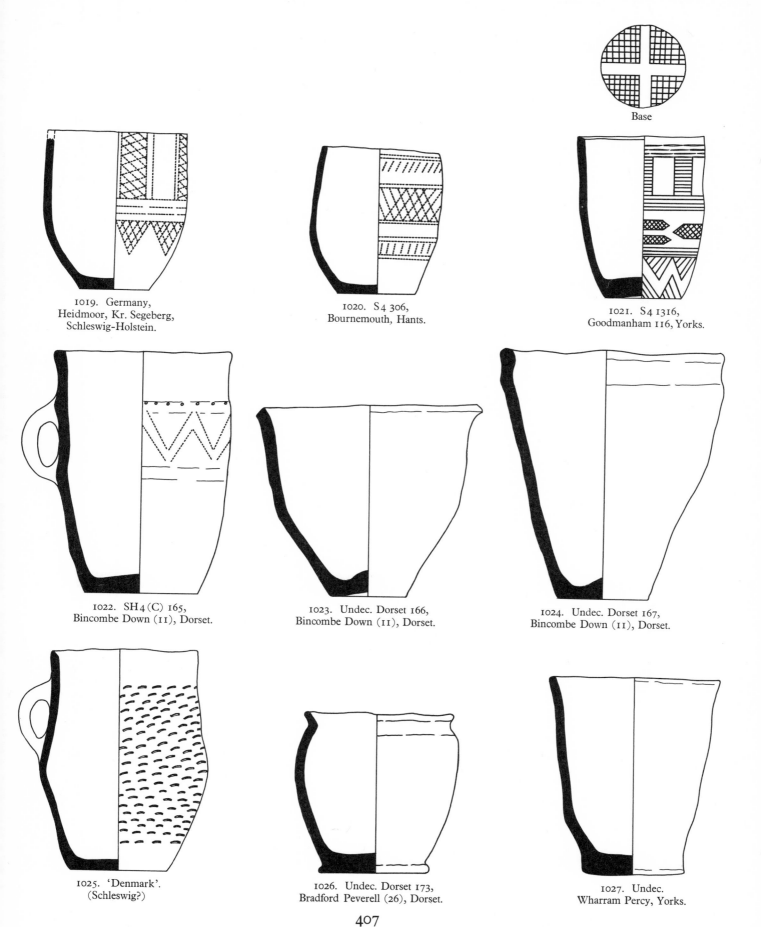

Base

1019. Germany,
Heidmoor, Kr. Segeberg,
Schleswig-Holstein.

1020. S4 306,
Bournemouth, Hants.

1021. S4 1316,
Goodmanham 116, Yorks.

1022. SH4(C) 165,
Bincombe Down (11), Dorset.

1023. Undec. Dorset 166,
Bincombe Down (11), Dorset.

1024. Undec. Dorset 167,
Bincombe Down (11), Dorset.

1025. 'Denmark'.
(Schleswig?)

1026. Undec. Dorset 173,
Bradford Peverell (26), Dorset.

1027. Undec.
Wharram Percy, Yorks.

407

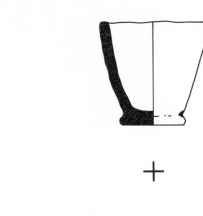

1029. Undec. Dorset
Martinstown, Dorset.

+

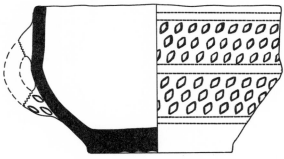

1028. Handled Bowl
Martinstown, Dorset.

1030. S4 1141,
Shrewton (5 K), Wilts.

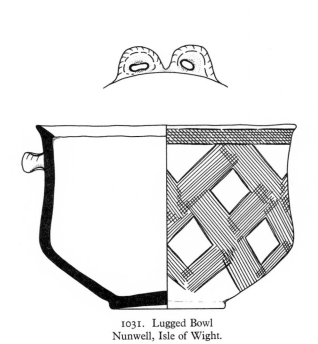

1031. Lugged Bowl
Nunwell, Isle of Wight.

1032. S4 1138,
Salisbury, Wilts.

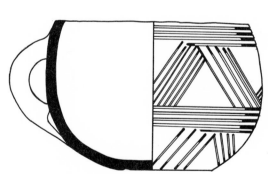

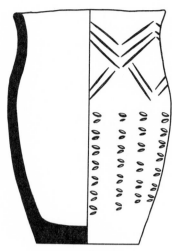

1033. Handled Bowl
Langton Matravers, Dorset.

1034. S4 218,
Worth Matravers, Dorset.

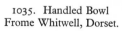
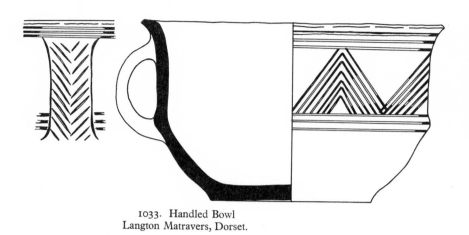

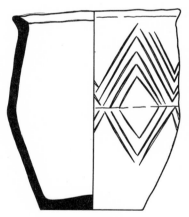

1035. Handled Bowl
Frome Whitwell, Dorset.

1036. S4 1177,
Wilsford (62) Wilts.

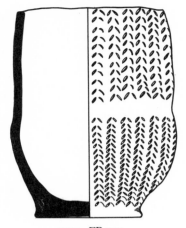

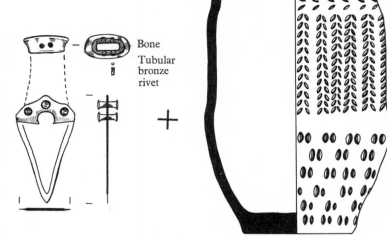

Bone
Tubular
bronze
rivet

1037. FP 307,
Bournemouth, Hants.

1038. FP 746,
Eynsham, Oxon.

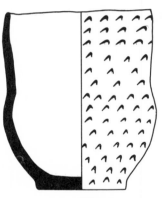

1039. FP 875,
Creeting St Mary, Suffolk.

1040. FP 216,
Winterbourne St Martin (32), Dorset.

1041. FP 116,
Ashford, Derby.

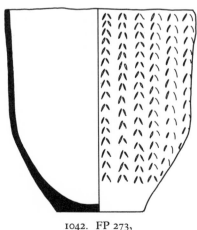

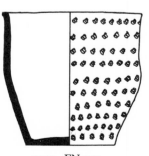

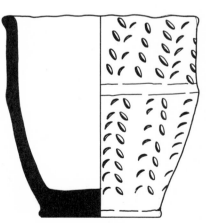

1042. FP 273,
'Essex'.

1043. FN 252,
Gt. Oakley, Essex.

1044. FP 668,
Dalton, Northumb.

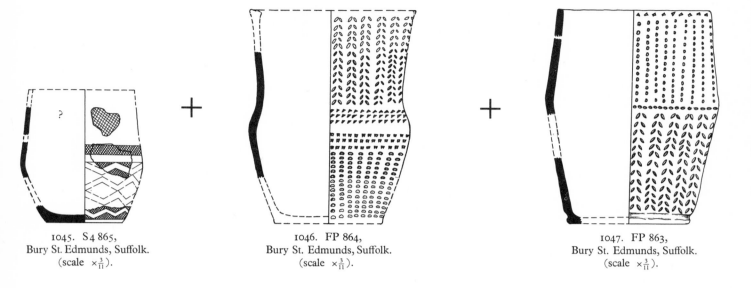

1045. S4 865,
Bury St. Edmunds, Suffolk.
(scale ×3/11).

1046. FP 864,
Bury St. Edmunds, Suffolk.
(scale ×3/11).

1047. FP 863,
Bury St. Edmunds, Suffolk.
(scale ×3/11).

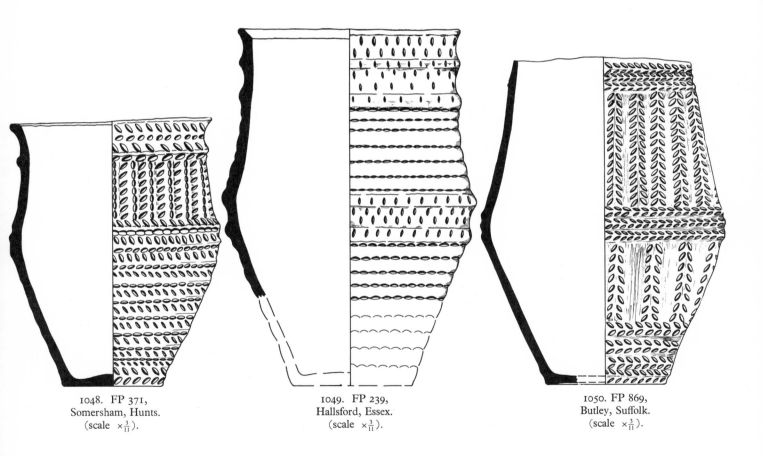

1048. FP 371,
Somersham, Hunts.
(scale ×3/11).

1049. FP 239,
Hallsford, Essex.
(scale ×3/11).

1050. FP 869,
Butley, Suffolk.
(scale ×3/11).

411

Handle
lost

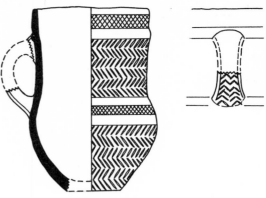

1051. SH2(A) 952,
Tuddenham, Suffolk.

1052. SH2(B) 13,
Abingdon, Berks.

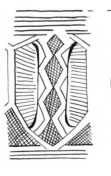

Base

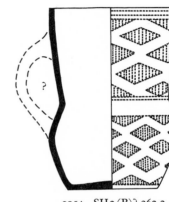

Handle
uncertain

1053. SH2(A) 262.1,
Sible Hedingham, Essex.

1054. SH2(B)? 262.2,
Sible Hedingham, Essex.

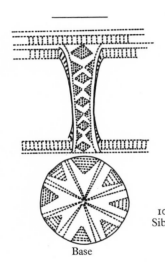

1055. SH2(B) 75,
March, Cambs.

1056. SH2(B) 740,
Eynsham, Oxon.

1057. SH3(A) 48,
Bottisham, Cambs.
(scale ×3/10).

Base

Handle
lost

1058. SH4(B) 1406,
Whitby area, Yorks.
(scale ×3/10).

1059. SH3(C) 446,
Denton, Lincs.
(scale ×3/10).

1060. SH3(C) 315,
Christchurch, Hants.
(scale ×3/10).

Base

1061. SH3(B) 71,
Fordham, Cambs.
(scale ×3/10).

1062. SH3(A) 510,
Bodney Hall, Norfolk.
(scale ×3/10).

413

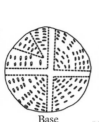

Base

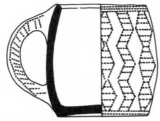

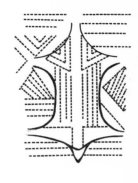

1063. SH3(C) 484.1,
South Willingham, Lincs.

1064. SH3(B) 638,
Newton-in-the-Willows, Northants.

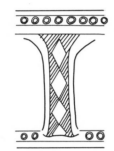

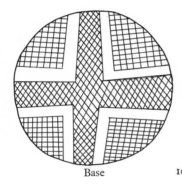

Base

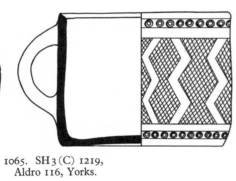

1065. SH3(C) 1219,
Aldro 116, Yorks.

1066. SH3(B) 632,
Brixworth, Northants.

Handle
lost

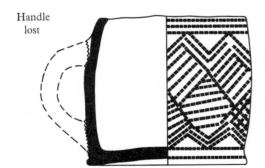

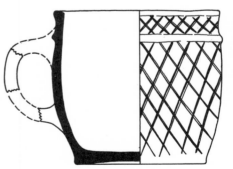

1067. SH3(C) 208,
Winterbourne St. Martin (346), Dorset.

1068. SH3(C) 1318,
Guisborough, Yorks.

1069. SH4 (B) 721,
Cassington, Oxon.

1070. SH4 (B) 571,
North Creake, Norfolk.

1071. SH4 (B) 1314,
Goodmanham 113, Yorks.

Handle
lost

1072. SH4 (B) 245,
Lion Point, Essex.

1073. SH4 (C) 106,
Try Menhir, Cornwall.

1074. Handled Food Vessel
Monquhitter, Aberdeen.

415

Handle lost

1075. SH4(B) 511,
Brancaster, Norfolk.

1076. SH4(B) 541,
Gresham, Norfolk.

1077. SH4(C) 1360,
Pickering, Yorks.

1078. SH4(B) 1839,
Cwm Du, Brecknock.

1079. SH4(B) 742,
Eynsham, Oxon.

1080. SH4(B) 475,
Risby Warren, Lincs.

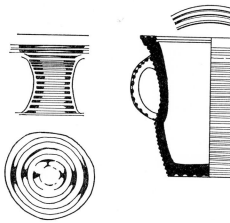

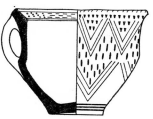

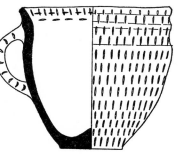

1082. Handled Food Vessel
Caythorpe, Lincs.
(scale ×$\frac{4}{15}$).

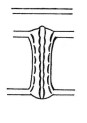

1081. Handled Food Vessel
Balmuick, Perth. (scale ×$\frac{4}{15}$)
(compare Rillaton cup).

1083. Handled Food Vessel
Garton Slack, Yorks.
(scale ×$\frac{4}{15}$).

1084. SH4(B) 451,
Grantham, Lincs.
(scale ×$\frac{4}{15}$).

1085. Handled Food Vessel
Snip Gill, Helmsley, Yorks.
(scale ×$\frac{4}{15}$).

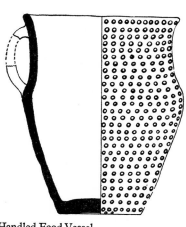

1086. Handled Food Vessel
Somersham?, Hunts.
(scale ×$\frac{4}{15}$).

1087. Handled Food Vessel
Huggate and Warterwold, Yorks.
(scale ×$\frac{4}{15}$).

CONCORDANCE LIST

Sequential beaker corpus numbers relate to the figure numbers of the illustrations as follows:

Corpus no.	Figure no.	Corpus no.	Figure no.	Corpus no.	Figure no.	Corpus no.	Figure no.
2	773	107	618	224	397	334	155
4	785	108	285	225	409	336	208
5	781	109	470	226	894	337	209
6	782	111	615	227	532	344	119
7	147	113	620	229	845	347	123
8	767	114	295	232	342	348	224
9	843	115	776	233	953	349	517
10	769	116	1041	234	924	350	98
13	1052	117	757	235	434	351	889
14	870	118	822	239	1049	352	222
19	168	119	823	241	440	353	223
21	518	120	819	242	565	354	244
22	87	122	910	243	357	355	243
25	205	128	934	244	909 and	356	960
26	204	130	775		915	358	848
27	892	132	913	245	1072	360	800
28	352	135	529	248	373	363	844
32	152	139	842	249	335	363.1	61(b)
33	63	140	568	250	414	364	577
34	81	143	818	252	1043	365	783
36	137	145	813	255	58	366	878
37	997	149	853	256	366	367	566
38	1007	153	824	257	367	368	438
39-40	192	155	880	258	362 and	370	779
41	199	156	356		365	371	1048
42	115	158	886	259	360-1	373	296
43	13	159	91	260	363	375	195
44	102	159.1	1015	262.1	1053	380	935
47	929	162	149	262.2	1054	385	92
48	1057	164	917	263	671	386	380
54	426	165	1022	264	172	387	774
57	480	166	1023	265	572	388	406
63	905	167	1024	273	1042	389	254
64	901-4	169	69	277	520	390	338
65	906	170	118	278	925	391	741
66	766	172	932	300	812	392	629
68	885	173	1026	302	161	393	70
69	564	176	1000	306	1020	394	101
70	994	177	187	307	1037	396	435
71	1061	180	225	308	1003	397	627
72	959	183	66	310	923	398	394
75	1055	184	65	311	884	399	403
76	911	191	218	313	78	400	336
77	93	192	48 a.	315	1060	401	633
86	791	193	97	318	104	406	423
87	498	201	215	323	129	407	38
92	751	203	801	327	921	408	73
93	632	204	998	328	849	409	389
94	561	208	1067	329	122	411	382
101	814	216	1040	330	84	413	350
104	961	217	75	331	575	414	391
105	820	218	1034	332	1001	420	211
106	1073	221	278	333	815	422	100

Corpus no.	Figure no.	Corpus no.	Figure no.	Corpus no.	Figure no.	Corpus no.	Figure no.
423	907	632	1066	722	991	857	68
424	955	633	146	729	995	860	759
425	762	634	860	730	14	862	116
426	854	635	987	731	996	863	1047
428	852	638	1064	735	128	864	1046
436	887	640	230	740	1056	865	1045
437	926	641	229	741	326	866	117
439	788	642	24	742	1079	869	1050
445	760	644	855–7;	743	986	870	567
446	1059		859	744	951	871	437
450	808	645	858	745	999	872	390
451	1084	646	937	746	1038	874	589
453.1	291	647	272	747	993	875	1039
457	46a.	647.1	299	748	220	876	340
463	784	647.2	300	749	193	877	941
475	1080	648	689	750	194	882	176
478	448	649	538	751	981	883	177
484.1	1063	650	330	755	164	884	175
493	930	651	3	756	938	885	641
495	970	652	700	758	931	886	431
496	411	655	695	759	263	888	372
497	370	656	684	760	246	889	346
499	376	657	653	761	216	890	393
501	747	658	512	762	217	891	408
503	214	659	513	764	509	892	413
504	786	660	872	765	433	893	57
505	425	664	594	766	221	894	838
507	798	665	447	767	85	895	916
508	636	668	1044	768	109	899	506
509	637	669	282	769	110	900	635
510	1062	671	319	770	64	902	343
511	1075	675	313	772	261	903	421
514	940	676	315	773	191	904	837
516	850	677	314	776	255	905	412
517	395	678	320	777	404	906	379
518	535	679	321	778	112	908	248
519	348	681	476	779	113	909	418
521	444	682	238	784	353	914	958
522	877	683	473	792	883	919	442
523	792	684	540	800	821	920	415
524	793	686	537	803	521	921	400
525	777	687	990	813	966	922	436
531.1	918	688	527	817	354	925	805
541	1076	690	816	818	54	926	804
545	628	691	550	820	830	929	879a–b.
547	212	692	699	821	957	930.1	920
550	989	693	297	822	478	931	879c.
559	752	694	253	825	862	933.1	489
560	523	695	654	826	754	941	787
563	560	696	655	827	742	942	479
569	439	697.1	41	832	150	948	624
571	1070	698	239	833	768	950	364
577	625	700	50a.	834	939	951	441
584	392	703	893	835	861	952	1051
585	933	705	307	841	339	953	795
586	402	707	866	842	634	954	796
587	936	710	510	844	86	960	803
588	422	711	869	847	432	961	401
589	368	712	644	848	417	967	753
595	623	713	984	849	1005	970	207
603	424	714	985	850	420	971	875
613	405	716	165	852	429	972	378
614	799	717	240	853	430	973	576
620	114	718	120	854	107	975	770
621	847	719	977	855	108	976	27
631	874	721	1069	856	106	979	649

Corpus no.	Figure no.	Corpus no.	Figure no.	Corpus no.	Figure no.	Corpus no.	Figure no.
980	12	1139	643	1282	559	1399	836
981	344	1140	549	1283	811	1400	828
982	345	1141	1030	1284	927	1402	533
983	111	1145	891	1291	652	1403	640
986	826	1146	851	1292	651	1405	524
987	827	1150	181	1293	817	1406	1058
988	562	1151	171	1296	778	1408	39
989	396	1155	67	1298	763	1409	601
990	385	1156	219	1299	290	1411	797
991	167	1157	138	1300	288	1412	369
992	351	1159	183	1303	555	1413.1	468
993	337	1160	182	1304	665	1413.2	1004
995	226	1162	156	1305	667	1414	5
996	427	1164	962	1306	666	1415	596
998	967	1168	794	1307	77	1417	474
1003	227	1171	159	1309	675	1418	247
1005	127	1172	971	1310	302	1419	582
1007	399	1173	60	1311	303	1420	588
1013	619	1177	1036	1314	1071	1421	499
1014	236	1185	898	1316	1021	1423	551
1018	604	1186	897	1317	30	1424	552
1019	306	1190	765	1318	1068	1425	645
1020	305	1194	749	1320	863	1429	722
1021	590	1195	900	1321	245	1430	281
1023	23	1197	1002	1322	507	1432	587
1027	105	1198	95	1323	873	1433	659
1034	809	1202	121	1324	835	1434	660
1036	162	1204	134	1326	964	1435	544
1037	846	1207	184	1327	650	1436	542
1039	890	1209.1	638	1328	758	1438	505
1045	103	1209.2	639	1331	868	1439	598
1046	840	1209.3	196	1332	772	1441	673
1051	233	1210	780	1334	531	1442	672
1063	347	1211	988	1335	508	1443	661
1067	76	1212	534	1343	71	1444	554
1070	62	1213	284	1344	136	1445	15
1071	515	1215	28	1347	876	1446	631
1072	982	1216	755	1350	744	1449	669
1073	516	1217	807	1351	810	1450	670
1075	133	1218	888	1352	789	1451	704
1076	153	1219	1065	1353	790	1454	694
1078	839	1221	539	1355	963	1455	668
1081	186	1223	32	1360	1077	1456	724
1082	185	1225	33	1361	267	1457	682
1083	978	1232	31	1362	88	1458	573
1084	170	1233	34	1365	334	1459	715
1085	11	1238	304	1366	511	1460	716
1087	834	1245	947	1367	530	1461	717
1088	965	1246	293	1368	536	1466	503
1101	829	1247	173	1369	298	1470	602
1102	99	1248	174	1370	705	1471	546
1103	864	1252	574	1371	386	1472	547
1105	228	1256.1	976	1373	1011	1473	548
1108	188	1256.2	974	1374	865	1475	487
1109	189	1256.3	973 b.	1375	526	1476	726
1111	259	1256.4	973 a.	1376	10	1477	691
1113	750	1256.5	975	1377	331	1478	721
1114	802	1259	18	1381	501	1480	495
1119	948	1265	553	1384	541	1482	500
1125	130	1269	89	1387	61	1483	605
1126	748	1272	928	1389	761	1484	471
1127	745	1273	806	1390	756	1485	585
1129	179	1275	764	1391	329	1486	522
1130	899	1279	328	1392	983	1487	449
1135	132	1280	979	1395	771	1488	664
1138	1032	1281	289	1397	871	1489	657

CONCORDANCE LIST

Corpus no.	Figure no.	Corpus no.	Figure no.	Corpus no.	Figure no.	Corpus no.	Figure no.
1490	658	1580	732	1686	256	1780	46b.
1491	277	1582	16	1688	458	1781	257
1492	72	1583	545	1689	241	1782	686
1493	545	1584	492	1692	718	1783	275
1494	462	1586	678	1693	586	1787	269
1496	273	1587	702	1698	662	1788	2
1497	486	1588	270	1700	712	1789	1
1498	481	1589	727	1702	674	1790	333
1499	7	1592	309	1703	713	1791	570
1500	600	1593	308	1704	460	1792	569
1501	493	1596	642	1705	607	1794	603
1502	630	1606	656	1706	952	1799	20
1503	725	1609	731	1707	595	1800	21
1504	622	1614	613	1708	729	1808	51a–b.
1505	683	1617	48b.	1710	710	1810.1	79
1506	477	1619	49b.	1713	490	1813	48c.
1507	317	1620	709	1715	280	1814	50c.
1508	318	1622	706–8	1718	563	1826	82
1509	580	1624	294	1719	494	1827	621
1510	4	1625	606	1720	1008	1828	908
1511	610	1627	49a.	1721	723	1838	242
1513	19	1630	450	1722	312	1839	1078
1515	646	1631	703	1723	311	1840.1	912
1516	445	1632	235	1727	491	1841	685
1519	485	1633	583	1728	496	1844	472
1520	1018	1635	525	1729	697	1845	616
1521	451	1636	581	1730	663	1846	972
1522	1009	1637	1017	1731	578	1849	867
1523	456	1638	949	1732	611	1849.1	617
1524	647	1642	50a.	1734	692	1850	497
1525	453	1643	35a.	1735	29	1852	158
1526	502	1645	519	1737	714	1853	969
1527	8	1646	558	1738	17	1854	896
1529	83	1648	648	1739	287	1855	895
1530	711	1649	457	1741	74	1856	833
1531	676	1650	488	1743	514	1857	359
1532	677	1651	557	1744	609	1858	825
1536	51c.	1652	459	1745	593	1860	954
1538	46c.	1653	483	1745.1	733	1861	956
1544	701	1654	1013	1746	276	1868	200
1545	980	1655	1014	1747	720	1869	355
1547	597	1656–7	36a–b.	1749	719	1870	832
1550	80	1659	9	1753	96	1875	831
1551	232	1661.1	35b.	1755	126	1876	950
1552	484	1662.1	1016	1756	528	1877	614
1558	231	1663	6	1761	327	1881	264
1562	914	1667	579	1762	1006	1882	250
1564	124	1672	968	1764	266	1909	202
1571	698	1673	680	1767	696	1910	206 and 251
1572	728	1674	679	1768	690		
1573	22	1675	730	1769	301	1911	206
1574	26	1676	584	1770	841	1912	206 and 251
1575	475	1681	571	1772	556		
1576	612	1682	504	1773	693	1922	125
1577	608	1683	324	1774	591	1932	687
1578	482	1684	323	1775	310	1933	688
1579	592	1685	322	1776	599		

APPENDIX 1

DEFINITIVE CHARACTERISTICS

Shape: 1. Beaker shape terminology; 2. British beaker shape variations. Styles: 3. Beaker decorative styles and their variation with time. Motifs: 4. Beaker motif catalogue and Motif Groups 1–5; 5. Beaker motif and style cross-correlation chart as a 45 by 45 matrix. Summary: 6. The integrated classification scheme, combining the variation patterns of shape, style and motifs.

1.1. Beaker shape terminology

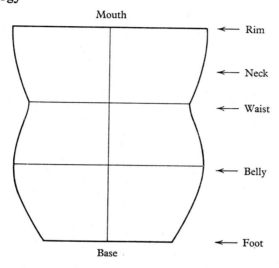

Mouth

← Rim

← Neck

← Waist

← Belly

← Foot

Base

1.2. British beaker shape variations

I — I   II — II   III — III

IV — IV

VI   V   VIII — VIII

VII — VII   IX — IX

1.3. Beaker decorative styles and their variation with time

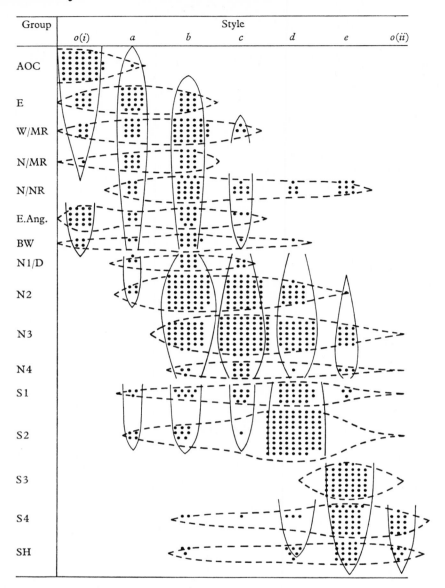

One dot = one restorable beaker.

1.4. Beaker motif catalogue

Basic European, Motif Group 1

Motif no.

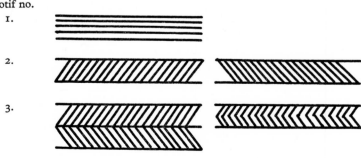

1.

2.

3.

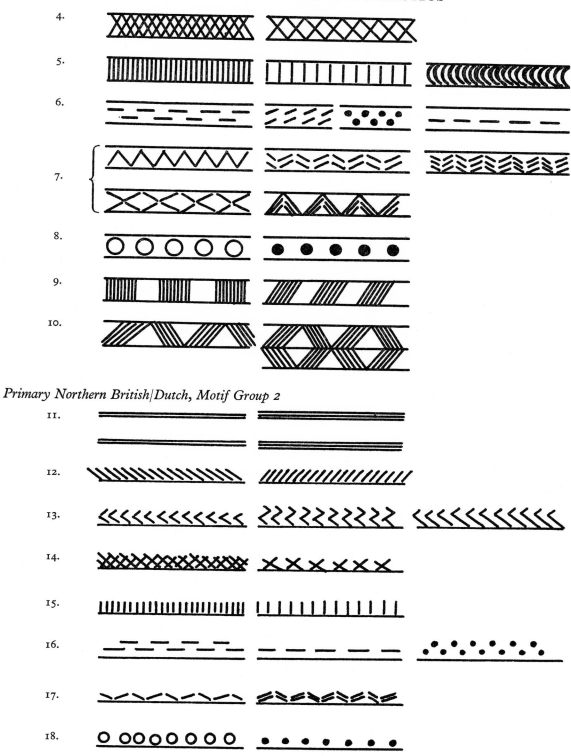

Primary Northern British/Dutch, Motif Group 2

Late Northern British, Motif Group 3

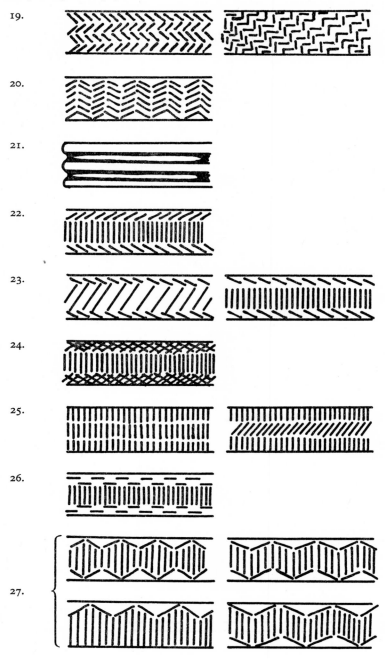

19.

20.

21.

22.

23.

24.

25.

26.

27.

Southern British, Motif Group 4

Panels and metopes, Motif Group 5

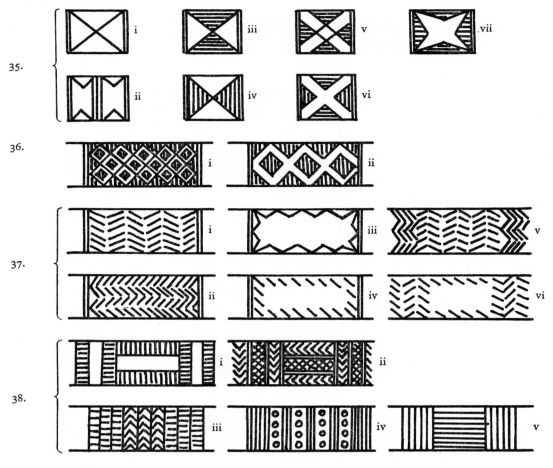

1.5. Beaker motif and style cross-correlation chart as a 45 by 45 matrix

The aim of this chart, an unsorted matrix, is to express succinctly the actual frequency of occurrence of individual motifs with one another on the same beakers and with the particular zonal styles. The sample of beaker data analysed on this chart includes 773 beakers, practically all the intact and restorable beakers from England, Scotland and Wales; the data was stored and the frequency of occurrence calculated by EDSAC II (Cambridge).

Key

Each entry in each square of the chart represents the number of times those two features occur together on the same beaker, in the sample of 773. The figure entries in bold type represent the total occurrence of each feature in the whole of the data sample tested; frequencies greater than ten have been tinted.

The numbers running along the axes bordering the chart, from 1–45, are code numbers for the following features: numbers 1–38 are equivalent to beaker motif nos. 1–38 in Appendix 1.4; so that motif no. 1 is trait no. 1, and so on. The thick outline indicates the change of motif preference with changing styles 39–44. Number 39 is decorative style *o* (see Fig. II); no. 40 is decorative style *a*; no. 41 is decorative style *b*; no. 42 is decorative style *c*; no. 43 is decorative style *d*; no. 44 is decorative style *e*; no. 45 indicates that the beaker is handled.

Correlation matrix of motif co-occurrences. Column groups across the top: Basic European Motif, Group 1 (cols 1–10); Primary Northern, Group 2 (cols 11–18); Late Northern, Group 3 (cols 19–27); Southern Motif, Group 4 (cols 28–34); Metope Group 5 (cols 35–38); Zonal Styles o (39), a (40), b (41), c (42), d (43), e (44); Handled, H (45). Row groups down the left side: Basic European Motif Group 1 (rows 1–10); Primary Northern and Dutch Motif Group 2 (rows 11–18); Late Northern British Motif Group 3 (rows 19–27); Southern British Motif Group 4 (rows 28–34); Panels and Metopes Motif Group 5 (rows 35–38); Zonal Styles o 39, a 40, b 41, c 42, d 43, e 44; Handled H 45.

Row	1	2	3	4	5	6	7	8	9	10	11	12	13	14	15	16	17	18	19	20	21	22	23	24	25	26	27	28	29	30	31	32	33	34	35	36	37	38	39 o	40 a	41 b	42 c	43 d	44 e	45 H
1	265	28	31	53	25	11	36	1	5	5	12	40	9	8	3	6	8	3	9	12	17	1	9	1	1	0	10	0	17	2	2	2	3	3	1	0	3	4	75	45	88	22	23	11	5
2		144	47	55	36	13	33	0	3	3	74	26	1	3	1	2	10	1	12	18	5	2	13	2	0	0	11	0	24	5	6	11	9	1	5	1	4	6	3	16	36	21	40	26	6
3			138	54	41	17	32	0	2	4	73	28	5	12	2	4	14	0	20	18	8	4	19	1	4	0	10	0	20	5	10	4	3	0	4	1	10	7	0	9	42	23	48	16	2
4				237	80	25	40	0	4	8	125	25	3	7	4	3	17	0	19	20	13	4	13	3	1	0	21	1	37	7	10	13	13	12	11	3	6	11	3	24	72	33	66	32	5
5					210	28	47	4	1	2	115	19	1	7	3	2	17	1	15	14	7	7	19	4	4	3	16	0	42	2	10	25	18	9	11	3	5	10	13	13	60	24	74	29	6
6						72	19	0	3	6	38	12	2	2	4	5	7	0	16	8	9	0	5	1	1	3	3	0	18	4	9	3	10	3	4	0	6	2	9	31	31	9	18	7	1
7							143	1	6	1	59	14	5	0	0	0	20	1	16	0	2	2	3	0	3	0	17	0	20	0	9	13	10	3	4	0	0	2	10	10	48	17	36	21	13
8								13	0	0	0	1	1	0	0	0	0	0	0	0	0	0	0	0	1	0	0	0	0	0	0	0	1	2	1	0	0	4	0	1	3	0	0	1	0
9																													0										0	0	0	0	0	1	0
10										11	22	11								5									2										1	7	0	2	8	4	2
11											287	39	5	12	4	4	34	1	33	13	6	4	21	4	5	0	25	2	60	7	19	33	25	5	15	5	10	16	4	6	65	47	115	44	7
12												95	9	7	2	3	9	0	9	14	13	0	2	0	0	7	7	2	14	3	1	2	5	1	2	1	5	6	2	8	30	19	26	8	0
13													17	1	0	2	2	0	4	3	1	6	6	1	1	0	0	0	6	0	0	0	0	0	0	0	1	0	2	6	3	3	4	4	0
14														29	0	2	4	0	4	1	0	0	6	6	1	1	3	0	2	3	3	3	5	1	0	0	1	0	1	13	13	3	4	1	0
15															12	0	2	0	7	0	0	0	2	0	2	0	0	0	0	0	0	0	0	0	0	0	0	0	0	0	0	3	4	4	0
16																12	0	1	3	3	3	0	1	0	0	0	0	1	1	0	3	0	0	0	0	0	0	0	0	4	6	2	4	4	0
17																	58	0	4	8	6	1	5	0	1	0	10	0	8	2	5	3	2	0	5	0	4	5	1	2	18	13	15	8	0
18																		5	0	0	0	1	1	0	0	0	0	0	0	0	0	0	0	0	0	0	0	0	2	1	1	2	1	0	0
19																			48	8	2	0	2	6	0	0	4	0	6	0	0	3	0	0	2	2	4	5	2	2	18	13	15	8	1
20																				66	7	0	8	0	0	4	0	0	6	2	7	4	0	2	2	1	3	3	2	1	12	12	16	5	1
21																					47	0	3	3	1	0	4	1	12	3	4	2	2	2	0	0	1	1	1	10	18	13	25	9	3
22																						8	0	1	1	0	0	0	5	0	0	1	0	0	0	0	0	2	0	2	2	2	7	2	0
23																							39	6	1	0	8	6	6	1	0	0	1	0	3	0	3	0	0	6	15	12	7	4	0
24																								7	0	0	0	0	1	1	0	0	0	0	0	0	0	0	0	1	1	1	5	0	0
25																									8	0	3	0	2	0	0	0	0	0	0	0	0	0	0	3	3	2	2	0	0
26																										0	0	0	1	0	0	0	0	0	0	0	0	4	1	0	1	0	0	0	0
27																											52	0	5	1	4	3	2	2	2	2	1	2	0	0	11	15	18	5	0
28																												4	2	0	0	0	0	2	0	0	1	4	2	0	1	1	2	1	1
29																													120	6	12	19	10	4	8	1	4	6	7	2	11	15	18	17	5
30																														24	7	7	1	0	0	0	0	1	1	1	2	9	7	4	0
31																															46	7	5	4	4	2	3	9	1	3	5	5	10	20	11
32																																72	16	6	6	3	4	4	0	4	5	0	31	31	6
33																																	59	5	4	5	0	2	7	3	0	23	26	10
34																																		26	0	0	0	0	0	2	0	0	9	13	4
35																																			26	0	0	3	0	0	2	0	15	6	1
36																																				7	0	1	0	0	0	0	6	1	0
37																																					20	0	0	0	6	6	3	0	0
38																																						26	0	0	3	3	12	0	1
39 o																																							94	0	0	0	0	0	8
40 a																																								67	0	0	0	0	1
41 b																																									202	0	0	0	0
42 c																																										82	0	0	0
43 d																																											191	0	3
44 e																																												125	16
45 H																																													29

1.6. The integrated classification scheme, combining the variation patterns of shape, style and motifs

The figure 1 in a particular row or column indicates that the beaker group makes use of that particular shape, style or motif group (see Fig. II; Appendix 1.2, 1.4). A ringed entry indicates the most frequent shape, style or motif group for that particular beaker group, i.e. the most typical.

	Style							Shape									Motif Group			
	o(i)	a	b	c	d	e	o(ii)	I	II	III	IV	V	VI	VII	VIII	IX	1	2	3	4
AOC	①	1						①	1	1							①			
E	1	①	①					①	1	1							①	1		1
W/MR	1	①	①	1				1	①	1							①	1		1
N/MR	1	①	①					1	①	1							①	1		
N/NR		1	①	①	1	1			1	①							①	①	1	
E.Ang.	①	1	①	1					1	①							①	①		
BW	1	1	①	1	1			1	1	①	1						①	①	1	
N1		1	①	1					1		①						1	①		
N2			①	①	1	1					①	①	1				1	①		
N3			1	①	①	1						1	①	①	1		1	1	①	
N4			1	①	1	1								1	①		1	1	①	
S1	1	1	1	①	1							1		①	1		1	1	1	①
S2	1	1	1	①	1									1	①		1	1		①
S3							①							①		1	1	1		①
S4			1	1	1	①	1							1		①	1	1		①

APPENDIX 2

MINOR CHARACTERISTICS

1. Cord defined zone beakers and beakers using cord decoration; 2. British Neolithic and beaker pottery with cardium shell impressions; 3. The length of the comb used to impress beaker decoration; 4. Variation in comb length with beaker group; 5. Beaker comb types; 6. The external colour of beaker fabric; 7. The grit used in beaker fabric; 8. Beakers with decoration on the inner rim surface; 9. Beakers with rim-top decoration; 10. Beakers with the lower half or third of the body undecorated; 11. Beakers with cordoned rims; 12. Beakers with collared rims; 13. Beakers with decorated bases; 14. The pattern of minor characteristic variation.

2.1. Cord defined zone beakers and beakers using cord decoration

British beakers with cord defined horizontal zones

These beakers have the horizontal zone boundaries cord impressed, whilst the motifs are comb impressed. The seven British beakers of this type can now be added to the map of the European examples (Gersbach (1957)).

Site	County	Corpus no.	Group
Brampton	Hunts.	363.1	E fig. 61(*b*)
West Keal, Hall Hill	Lincs.	491	E
Brean Down	Somerset	778	E fig. 112
Avebury, Windmill Hill	Wilts.	1057	E
Avebury, W. Kennet Avenue	Wilts.	1070	E fig. 62
Wilsford barrow (54)	Wilts.	1173	E fig. 60
Dalkey Island, Ireland	Co. Dublin	1893	E

British beakers with cord impressed external decoration, not AOC beakers, not cord zoned beakers (above) and not necessarily with cord within the rim (see Appendix 2.8)

Site	County	Corpus no.	Group
Hartington, Elk Low	Derby.	132	Mortlake hybrid fig. 913
Lesmurdie cist D.	Banff.	1588	N/NR? fig. 270
Kincardine Castle	Perth.	1743	N2 fig. 514
Ballyedmonduff, Ireland	Co. Dublin	1891	S2(W)?

2.2. British Neolithic and beaker pottery with cardium shell impressions

County	Site	Ceramic	Refs.
Anglesey	Lligwy	Neolithic	Piggott (1954), 179
Anglesey	Newborough Warren	E beaker	No. 1826, fig. 82
Argyll.	Ardnamurchan	E beaker	No. 1529, fig. 83
Argyll.	Islay	Neolithic	McInnes (1961), 67–84
Argyll.	Poltalloch	E beaker	No. 1550, fig. 80
East Lothian	Hedderwick	Neolithic	McInnes (1961), 67–84
Inverness.	Clettraval	N/NR beaker	No. 1668
Inverness.	Eilean an Tighe	Neolithic	McInnes (1961), 67–84
Inverness.	N. Uist, Clachan	Neolithic	*P.S.A.S.* LXXXVII, 198
Inverness.	N. Uist, Unival	Neolithic	McInnes (1961), 67–84
Kirkcud.	Bargrennan	Neolithic	McInnes (1961), 67–84
Lancashire	Walney, North End	Neolithic	*C.W.A.S.* NS., L, 15
Northumb.	Plessy Mill	Food Vessel	McInnes (1961), 67–84
Pembroke.	Caldey Island	N/NR? beaker	No. 1879
Suffolk	Pakenham	Neolithic	Smith (1956), Fig. 126, 7
Shetland	Ness of Gruting	Neolithic	McInnes (1961), 67–84
Shetland	Stanydale	Neolithic	McInnes (1961), 67–84
Wigtown.	Glenluce Sands	Neolithic	McInnes (1961), 67–84 Fig. 62
Wigtown.	Glenluce Sands	E beaker	No. 1810.1, fig. 79
Wigtown.	Portpatrick, Spittal	Food Vessel	McInnes (1961), 67–84

2.3. The length of the comb used to impress beaker decoration

The comb length, in mms, is given first, then the corpus number of the beaker in parentheses (summary in Appendix 2.4).

AOC
  10 (1788)

E
  30 (34)
  41 (77)
  25 (318)
  30 (770)
  35 (893)

W/MR
  26 (201)
  42 (348)
  40 (352)
  15 (547)
  48 (503)
  38 (633)
  30 (717)
  33 (1207)
  46 (1036)
  31 (1150)

N/MR
  42 (1418)

42 (1632)
37 (1781)
38 (501)
34 (647)

N/NR
  36 (1624)
  35 (1723)
  48 (1020)

E. Ang.
  43 (496)
  40 (586)
  47 (847)

BW
(Stamp length)
  36 (400)
  31 (390)
  47 (413)
  25 (902)
  48 (841)

N1/D
  20 (1494)

30 (1525)
42 (1521)
38 (1523)
37 (1649)

N2
  40 (1466)
  41 (1489)
  44 (1497)
  49 (1498)
  50 (1575)
  40 (1635)
  29 (1650)
  54 (57)
  49 (86)
  47 (109)
  15 (364)
  40 (688)
  40 (683)
  34 (649)
  40 (973)
  47 (1019)
  32 (1282)

N2(L)
  30 (1444)
  30 (1433)
  39 (1458)
  40 (1718)
  39 (1722)
  39 (69)
  40 (94)

N3
  35 (1420)
  28 (1419)
  41 (1425)
  32 (1434)
  37 (1485)
  35 (1488)
  40 (1470)
  34 (1509)
  35 (1577)
  40 (1579)
  37 (1586)
  40 (1606)
  53 (1625)
  47 (1636)

39 (1705)
36 (1767)
47 (1774)
41 (93)
30 (397)
30 (712)
33 (900)
15 (1021)
21 (1409)
34 (1304)

N3(L)
  40 (1587)
  30 (1710)

N4
  38 (1692)

S1
  15 (370)
  31 (833)

S2
  40 (9)
  47 (68)

45 (351)
40 (426)
33 (634)
40 (986)
35 (1195)
46 (1039)

S3
  38 (72)
  41 (233)
  48 (366)
  45 (877)
  40 (1347)

S4
  41 (1720)

SH
  —

2.4. Variation in comb length with beaker group

The single number entries represent the number of beakers in each group having comb impressions of a particular length (comb length in mms).

```
S4        .......... ......... ......... I........ .....
S3        .......... ......... ......I.II...I..I. .....
S2        .......... ......... ..I.I....3....III.. .....
S1        .....I.... ......... I........ ......... .....
N4        .......... ......... .......I. ......... .....
N3        .....I.... I.......I.3.112312.142.....2.. ..I..
N2        .....I.... I.......12.I.I....371..I..2.21...I.
N1        ..........I.........I......II. .I........ .....
BW        .......... ....I.... I....I... .....I.I. .....
E. Ang.   .......... ......... ......I..I..I... .....
N/NR      .......... ......... ...II... .......I. .....
N/MR      .......... ......... ...I..II. .2....... .....
W/MR      .....I.... .....I...II.I....I.I.I...I.I. .....
E         .......... ....I...2....I.... I........ .....
AOC       I........ ......... ......... ......... .....
          |         |         |         |         |
          10 mms    20        30        40        50
```

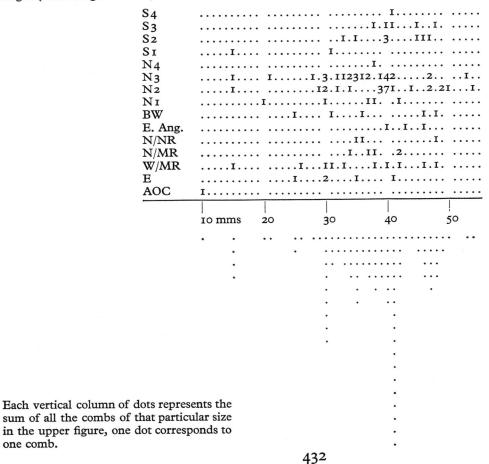

Each vertical column of dots represents the sum of all the combs of that particular size in the upper figure, one dot corresponds to one comb.

2.5. Beaker comb types

The types of comb used to impress beaker designs vary widely. The shape of the tooth varies from rectangular to square and the thickness of the comb can arbitrarily be divided into:

fine comb—less than 1 mm. in maximum breadth;
medium comb—more than 1 mm., less than 1·5 mms (approx.);
coarse comb—more than 1·5 mms in breadth.

All entries greater than 10% are set in bold type.

	Incised	Coarse Rect.	Coarse Sq.	Medium Rect.	Medium Sq.	Fine Rect.	Fine Sq.	Cord	100%
S4	**55·5%**	4·4%	4·4%	**31·1%**	4·4%	—	—	—	100%
	25	2	2	14	2	—	—	—	45
SH	**51·5%**	6·1%	3·0%	**27·3%**	3·0%	9·1%	—	—	
	17	2	1	9	1	3	—	—	33
S3	**14·1%**	4·7%	—	**53·5%**	**11·6%**	**16·3%**	—	—	
	6	2	—	23	5	7	—	—	43
S2	5·0%	1·3%	2·5%	**55·6%**	**13·9%**	**15·2%**	6·3%	1·3%	
	4	1	2	44	11	12	5	1	80
S1	8·2%	2·1%	2·1%	**51·1%**	**14·2%**	**18·3%**	4·1%	—	
	4	1	1	25	7	9	2	—	49
N4	**13·3%**	—	6·7%	**53·3%**	6·7%	**13·3%**	6·7%	—	
	2	—	1	8	1	2	1	—	15
N3	6·8%	0·8%	1·5%	**36·4%**	**19·7%**	**23·5%**	9·7%	—	
	9	1	2	48	26	31	12	—	129
N2	5·6%	—	0·8%	**34·4%**	**22·4%**	**27·2%**	8·8%	0·8%	
	7	—	1	43	28	34	11	1	125
N1	5·9%	—	—	**41·1%**	**11·8%**	**17·6%**	**23·5%**	—	
	1	—	—	7	2	3	4	—	17
BW	**100%**	—	—	—	—	—	—	—	
	BW	—	—	—	—	—	—	—	20
E. Ang.	**26·4%**	5·6%	7·6%	**18·9%**	7·6%	**13·2%**	1·9%	—	
	14	3	4	10	4	7	1	—	53
N/NR	**33·1%**	2·5%	—	**30·8%**	**22·1%**	7·7%	2·5%	—	
	13	1	—	12	9	3	1	—	39
N/MR	**18·5%**	—	—	**40·6%**	7·4%—	**25·9%**	3·7%	3·7%	
	5	—	—	11	2	7	1	1	27
W/MR	4·0%	4·0%	2·0%	**38·0%**	**10·0%**	**36·0%**	6·0%	—	
	2	2	1	19	5	18	3	—	50
E	9·1%	1·8%	3·6%	**25·5%**	**18·2%**	**23·6%**	9·1%	9·1%	
	5	1	2	14	10	13	5	5	55
AOC	—	—	—	—	—	—	—	**100%**	
	—	—	—	—	—	—	—	40	40

Comb type

2.6. The external colour of beaker fabric

An arbitrary notation of the overall colour of the exterior of the beakers was applied to the vessels studied, mainly complete or restorable beakers. The results of this rough analysis are set out below.

Entries higher than 14·0% have been set in bold type to illustrate the dark to light trend in preferred colouring.

	Dark brown	Wax red	Red buff	Yellow buff	Buff	100%
S4	4·4%	—	**26·6%**	**15·5%**	**53·2%**	100%
	2	—	12	7	24	45
SH	—	—	**39·4%**	**15·2%**	**45·5%**	
	—	—	13	5	15	33
S3	9·3%	—	**31·0%**	**16·3%**	**44·2%**	
	4	—	13	7	19	43
S2	7·6%	—	**34·2%**	**21·5%**	**34·2%**	
	6	—	27	17	27	77
S1	8·2%	—	**32·6%**	**16·3%**	**42·9%**	
	4	—	16	8	21	49
N4	—	—	13·5%	—	**86·5%**	
	—	—	2	—	13	15
N3	6·5%	—	**22·0%**	12·9%	**59·0%**	
	8	—	29	17	78	132
N2	8·0%	0·8%	**37·3%**	9·6%	**44·0%**	
	10	1	47	12	55	125
N1	11·8%	—	**41·1%**	5·9%	**41·1%**	
	2	—	7	1	7	17
BW	10·0%	—	**35·0%**	**15·0%**	**40·0%**	
	2	—	7	3	8	20
E. Ang.	11·3%	1·9%	**43·4%**	7·6%	**35·4%**	
	6	1	23	4	19	53
N/NR	5·1%	—	**15·4%**	10·2%	**69·2%**	
	2	—	6	4	27	39
N/MR	3·7%	3·7%	**37·0%**	11·1%	**44·5%**	
	1	1	10	3	12	27
W/MR	2·0%	**42·0%**	**28·0%**	8·0%	**20·0%**	
	1	21	14	4	10	50
E	**14·5%**	**18·2%**	**38·2%**	5·5%	**23·6%**	
	8	10	21	3	13	55
AOC	**30·0%**	2·5%	**40·0%**	—	**27·2%**	
	12	1	16	—	11	40

Dark colouring—Light colouring

2.7. The grit used in beaker fabric

The table below represents a superficial analysis of the grit added to beaker fabric. Several vessels have more than one additive, hence the percentages may sum to greater than 100%. Entries over 20% have been set in bold type.

	None	Pot	Flint	Stone	Shell	Chalk	River grit	100%
SH	12·0% 3	32·0% 8	44·0% 11	8·0% 2	4·0% 1	—	20·0% 5	100% 25
S4	3·0% 1	39·4% 13	42·4% 14	24·2% 8	6·1% 2	3·0% 1	12·1% 4	33
S3	13·3% 5	26·3% 10	26·3% 10	26·3% 10	—	7·9% 3	7·9% 3	38
S2	8·0% 6	10·6% 8	29·3% 22	38·7% 29	1·3% 1	6·7% 5	13·3% 10	75
S1	4·1% 2	14·2% 7	55·2% 27	20·4% 10	—	4·1% 2	14·2% 7	49
N4	— —	— —	— —	100% 12	— —	— —	— —	12
N3	1·7% 2	4·3% 5	11·1% 13	71·0% 83	—	2·6% 3	6·0% 7	117
N2	5·0% 5	5·0% 5	19·0% 19	70·0% 70	1·0% 1	4·0% 4	2·0% 2	100
N1	7·7% 1	— —	15·4% 2	69·3% 9	—	7·7% 1	—	13
BW	— —	27·8% 5	50·0% 9	22·2% 4	—	5·5% 1	—	18
E. Ang.	2·4% 1	21·9% 9	63·4% 26	9·8% 4	4·9% 2	2·4% 1	9·8% 4	41
N/NR	— —	8·8% 3	20·6% 7	73·5% 25	—	8·8% 3	—	34
N/MR	— —	22·2% 4	22·2% 4	50·0% 9	—	5·5% 1	22·2% 4	18
W/MR	14·3% 7	26·5% 13	42·9% 21	8·2% 4	4·1% 2	—	18·3% 9	49
E	10·8% 4	18·9% 7	18·9% 7	24·3% 9	—	—	27·0% 10	37
AOC	27·8% 10	11·1% 4	2·8% 1	44·4% 16	2·8% 1	2·8% 1	11·1% 4	36

Grit used

2.8. Beakers with decoration on the inner rim surface

c—corded internal decoration   d—comb impressed internal decoration

AOC			N/MR	N2	S1
697.1c	1228c	1629c	1551c	1212d	—
1663c	699c	1565c	1558d	518d	
1023c	1639c	1696d		1699d	S2
1235c	1808c	1817d	N/NR	1701d	—
1408c	732c	1893c	647.2	1518d	
980c	1617c	1906c	(grooved)		S3
1527c	1628c	1906d		N3	—
1659c	1695c	1921d	E. Ang.	1702d	
1754c	1892c	1926d	—		S4
1788c	1914c	1939d		N4	—
1789c	E	1918c	BW	1476d	
1259c	184c	W/MR	981d	1431d	SH
468c	1741d	—		1503d	—
444c	1307d		N1/D	1456d	
1222c	818c		1311c	1429d	

2-2

2.9. Beakers with rim-top decoration

This decoration is always comb impressed or incised, not cord.

AOC	BW	518	1531	S1	S3(W)
—	982	135	1576	953	821
	983	57	1577	1298	522
E	156	1436	1648	6	
—		1472	374	S2(W)	S3(E)
	N1/D	1498	1018	153	172
W/MR	1487	1699	1409	436	1164
—	1521	1728	1139	703	
		N3	648	690	S4
N/MR	N2	1631	652	1145	1545
—	822	1683	1845	1195	1720
	1252	1710	1877	1875	1762
N/NR	1718	1737		1841	687
693	1367	1419	N4	125	
1668	1368	1441	1460		SH
	1335	1452	1431	S2(E)	48
E. Ang.	942	1517		645	
—	683	1477		1849	

2.10. Beakers with the lower half or third of the body undecorated

Those beakers on which the lower body area has been blocked-in, or which have a few scattered marks but still display a 'decorated top/undecorated body' contrast, have an X against the corpus number below, thus—772X.

Corpus no.	Site	Group	
22X	Cholsey, Berks.	E	fig. 87
135X	Longstone, Blake Low, Derby.	N2	fig. 529
391	Capel-le-Ferne, Kent	S1	fig. 741
420	Glaston, Leics. and Rutland	W/MR	fig. 211
453.1	Kirkby-le-Bain	N/NR	fig. 291
469	Risby Warren, Lincs.	N/NR	—
503	Bardolph Fen, Norfolk	W/MR	fig. 214
640	Peterborough, Fengate, Northants.	W/MR	fig. 230
759	Oxford, Polestead Rd., Oxford.	N/MR	fig. 263
772X	Stanton Harcourt, Oxford.	N/MR	fig. 261
1111	Farleigh Wick, Wilts.	N/MR	fig. 259
1259	Cave S., Kettlethorpe, Yorks.	AOC	fig. 18
1350	Newton Mulgrave area, Yorks.	S1	fig. 744
1361	Pickering, Yorks.	N/NR	fig. 267
1362	Pickering, Raindale, Yorks.	E	fig. 88
1375	Rudstone 66, Yorks.	N2	fig. 526
1738X	Auchterarder, Perth.	AOC	fig. 17
1764	Urquhart, Findon, Ross and Cromarty	N/NR	fig. 266
1783	Dornoch, Sutherland.	N/NR	fig. 275
1808	Glenluce Sands, Wigtown.	AOC	fig. 51a

2.11. Beakers with cordoned rims

Cordoned rim—a pinched-up external ridge not changing the smooth internal profile of the beaker (see Fig. VI).

AOC	1445	33	W/MR	1558	1299
1023	460	159	337	1689	1391
1751	468	34	1162	1867	
1752	699	1569	970	1838	E. Ang.
1753	1639	1825	717		972
1259	1808	385	1110	N/NR	890
642		1128		108	496
1799	E	85	N/MR	373	414
1800	1362		354	469	989
1582	1269		355	1281	858

BW	N2(L)	S1	S3		
992	1265	—	—	1654	1314
993				962	1360
N1/D	N3	S2(W)	S4	956	721
—	—	1399	332	SH	571
	N4	S2(E)	1197	1318	511
	—	825	1534	632	245
			1655	13	

2.12. Beakers with collared rims

Collared rim—an applied clay ring luted to the neck at an angle, giving rise to a pronounced change in internal profile (see Fig. VI).

AOC	N/NR	N3	S2(E)	S4	956
457	—	652	229	37	38
1780			835	176	608
E	E. Ang.	S1	1103	204	579
77	—	—	645	713	743
1603	BW			731	
1201	—	S2(W)	S3	745	SH
W/MR	N1/D	894	834	753	952
—	—	971	877	635	742
N/MR	N2	929	522	1138	262
1882	—	931	1347	1413	541
			366	936	106
			472	910	

2.13. Beakers with decorated bases (complete vessels and sherds)

AOC	N/MR	BW	N3	S2	S4
—	—	—	1767	971 (S2(W))	1316
				301 (S2(E))	
E	N/NR	N1/D	N4	64	SH
1343	—	—	—	212	484.1 SH3(C)
				1059	1219 SH3(C)
W/MR	E. Ang.	N2	S1	1199	71 SH3(B)
773	—	—	—		48 SH3(A)
				S3	262.1 SH2(A)
				911	
				458	

2.14. The pattern of minor characteristic variation

The analysis of the spectrum of minor characteristics below suggests two major patterns—an early pattern of characteristics, within the thin outline, and a later pattern within the solid outline. The beaker groups then show three variations on these patterns: (1) *an early tradition*, using the early characteristic pattern; groups AOC, E, W/MR, N/MR; (2) *a Northern tradition*, combining the early and later characteristic pattern; groups N/NR, E. Ang., BW, N1, N2, N3, N4; (3) *a Southern tradition*, using the later characteristic pattern; groups S1, S2, S3, S4, SH.

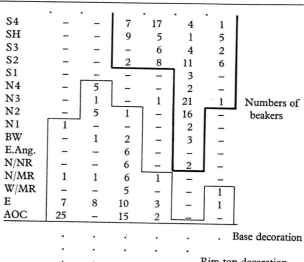

	Base decoration	Rim top decoration	Collared rims	Cordoned rims	Internal rim decoration in comb	Internal rim decoration in cord
S4	–	–	7	17	4	1
SH	–	–	9	5	1	5
S3	–	–	–	6	4	2
S2	–	–	2	8	11	6
S1	–	–	–	–	3	–
N4	–	5	–	–	2	–
N3	–	1	–	1	21	1
N2	–	5	1	–	16	–
N1	1	–	–	–	2	–
BW	–	1	2	–	3	–
E.Ang.	–	–	6	–	–	–
N/NR	–	–	6	–	2	–
N/MR	1	1	6	1	–	–
W/MR	–	–	5	–	–	1
E	7	8	10	3	–	1
AOC	25	–	15	2	–	–

Numbers of beakers

Base decoration
...Rim top decoration
....Collared rims
...Cordoned rims
...Internal rim decoration in comb
......Internal rim decoration in cord

APPENDIX 3

ASSOCIATIONS

1. Artefact association list; 2. Summary of beaker and artefact association pattern; 3. Analysis of grave associations by sex; 4. Associations between beakers and other pottery; 5. British beaker grave types; 6. British beakers certainly or possibly with cremation burials; 7. Position of the beaker relative to the skeleton in the grave; 8. Summary of beaker position relative to the skeleton; 9. Orientation of beaker skeletons; 10. Summary of beaker skeleton orientation.

3.1. Artefact association list

This list includes artefacts in closed association or certain association with beakers, arranged in sequence under the appropriate beaker groups. The term 'uncertain association' here signifies that some doubt about the actual association is possible but in these particular cases the weight of evidence still makes them probable.

Whenever the sex of the skeleton is known, it is recorded at the beginning of the entry.

The number of perforations recorded for the bracers in every case represents the *total* number of completed perforations; in brackets at the end is the Atkinson bracer class (Note 39).

A summary and abstract of the artefact association pattern, group by group and artefact by artefact, is in Appendix 3.2; an analysis by sexes is in Appendix 3.3.

AOC

651	Northumb.	Alston, Kirkhaugh: (fig. 3) 1 Gold earring 1 Barbed and tanged flint arrowhead
1317	Yorks.	Lea Green, Grassington: 1 Barbed and tanged flint arrowhead
1408	Yorks.	Willerby Wold 235: 3 Flint scrapers
1553	Argyll.	Salen, Mull: 2 Frags. bent bronze (?), indet. 1 Flint flake
1582	Banff.	Forglen: 1 Barbed and tanged flint arrowhead
1656	Fife	Leuchars, Brackmont Mill: (fig. 36) 1 AOC beaker, no. 1656 1 Bowl Undec., no. 1657, inverted over beaker

E

33	Berks.	Radley, Barrow 4(*a*): (fig. 63) Male 2 Gold earrings 3 Barbed and tanged flint arrowheads
159	Devon	Langcombe, Plym Valley: (fig. 91) 3 Barbed and tanged flint arrowheads
169	Dorset	Blackbush, Cranbourne Chase: ? Flint blades ? Flint cores
184	Dorset	Thickthorn Long Barrow, Gussage St Michael (163*a*): (fig. 65) Female 1 Bronze (?) awl
363.1	Hunts.	Brampton, barrow: (fig. 61(*b*)) Interment with 'maritime' beaker 1 Amber bead
739	Oxford.	Drayton St Leonard: 1 Stag's antler pick
768	Oxford.	Stanton Harcourt: (figs. 109–10) Female 1 E beaker, no. 768 1 E Undec. beaker, no. 769 1 Flint blade 1 Flint flake
778	Somerset	Brean Down: (figs. 112–13) 1 E beaker, no. 778 1 FN beaker, no. 779
829	Staffs.	Ilam Moor: Female (?) and child 1 E (?) beaker, no. 829 1 FN beaker, no. 830 1 Bronze (?) awl
854	Suffolk	Brantham Hall Farm: (figs. 106–8) Female and child 1 E beaker, no. 854 1 FN beaker, no. 855 1 E beaker, no. 856

1269 Yorks. Egton Bridge:
3 Frags. bronze (?)

1935 Co. Sligo Moytura:
1 Thin bronze (?) strip about 12 in long
Uncertain association

W/MR

25 Berks. Inkpen Hill: (figs. 204–5)
1 W/MR beaker, no. 25
1 Polypod bowl, no. 26

36 Berks. Sutton Courtenay:
1 Tanged copper dagger
Uncertain association

39 Bucks. Bledlow, Wain Hill: (fig. 192)
1 W/MR beaker, no. 39
1 Bowl Undec., no. 40
1 Frag. bronze (?) (possibly Saxon)

201 Dorset Tarrant Launceston (5):
1 Flint flake knife
1 Trephined disc from skull

352 Hants. Winchester, St James' Terrace:
(figs. 222–3)
1 W/MR beaker, no. 352
1 BW beaker, no. 353
Uncertain association

735 Oxford. Dorchester Site XII: (fig. 128)
Male
1 Tanged copper dagger
1 Knife, bronze with 3 rivets
1 Stone bracer, 4 perforations (C1)

749 Oxford. Eynsham: (figs. 193–4)
1 W/MR beaker, no. 749
1 Bowl, no. 750
1 Bronze (?) awl

761 Oxford. Summertown, Oxford: (figs. 216–17)
1 W/MR beaker, no. 761
1 FN beaker, no. 762
1 Barbed and tanged flint arrowhead

773 Oxford. Stanton Harcourt: (fig. 191)
1 W/MR beaker, no. 773 (with decorated base)
1 Bone spatula
1 Flint flake knife

882 Suffolk Fakenham: (figs. 175–7)
1 W/MR beaker, no. 882
1 W/MR beaker, no. 883
1 FN beaker, no. 884
1 Flint dagger
Uncertain association

991 Sussex Devil's Dyke, Beggars Haven:
(fig. 167)
3 Sheet bronze (?) tubular beads
14 Lignite disc beads

1081 Wilts. Boyton: (figs. 185–6)
1 W/MR beaker, no. 1081
1 W/MR beaker, no. 1082

1108 Wilts. Larkhill, Durrington: (figs. 188–9)
1 W/MR beaker, no. 1109
1 Undec. beaker, no. 1108

1125 Wilts. Mere, Barrow (6a): (fig. 130)
Male
1 Tanged copper dagger
2 Gold button caps (1 lost)
1 Bone spatula
1 Bracer, stone, 2 perforations (B1)

1129 Wilts. Overton West: (fig. 179)
Male
1 Flint dagger

1135 Wilts. Roundway, barrow (8): (fig. 132)
Male
1 Tanged copper dagger
1 Copper racquet (?) pin
1 Bracer, stone, 4 perforations (B2)
1 Barbed and tanged flint arrowhead

1143 Wilts. Sutton Veny, barrow (11a):
1 Bracer, stone, 6 perforations (B3)
2 Boar's tusks
Beaker type uncertain

1157 Wilts. Wilsford (G1): (fig. 138)
1 Bone belt ring
1 Perforated boar's tusk

1158 Wilts. Wilsford (G1):
Female
1 Stone plaque

1159 Wilts. Wilsford (G1): (fig. 183)
Female and child
1 W/MR beaker, no. 1159
1 Undec. beaker, no. 1160

1204 Wilts. Winterslow Hut (11): (fig. 134)
Male (?)
1 Tanged copper dagger
1 Bracer, stone, 6 perforations (B3)
2 Large barbed and tanged flint arrowheads (1 lost)

1247 Yorks. Broxa Moor, barrow 4: (figs. 173–4)
1 W/MR beaker, no. 1247
1 W/MR beaker, no. 1248
Uncertain association

N/MR

354 Hereford. Olchon: (fig. 244)
Male
1 Barbed and tanged flint arrowhead

355 Hereford. Olchon: (fig. 243)
1 Flint flake

717 Oxford. Cassington, Tolley's Pit: (fig. 240)
1 Jet belt ring

772 Oxford. Stanton Harcourt, Linch Hill: (fig. 261)
Male, in wooden coffin
1 Bone belt ring
7 Barbed and tanged flint arrowheads

1051 Wilts. Avebury, Longstone Cove:
1 Bronze (?) stain on the collar bone

1111 Wilts. Farleigh Wick, Jug's Grave: (fig. 259)
Male
1 N/MR beaker, no. 1111
1 W/MR beaker, no. 1112, frags.
1 Gold button cap
1 Bone belt ring
4 Barbed and tanged flint arrowheads
1 Flint blade

1838 Brecknock. Penderyn, Pant y Waen:
1 Stone pendant, central perforation

1867 Glamorgan. Sutton Llandow:
Male
7 Barbed and tanged flint arrowheads

1882 Pembroke. Talbenny, South Hill: (fig. 250)
1 Unfinished flint arrowhead
Palisade barrow

1910 Co. Limerick Knockadoon, Lough Gur: site D:
Frags. N/MR and W/MR beakers
1 Gold button cap (?)
Uncertain association

NN/R

221 Durham Offerton, Hasting Hill: (fig. 278)
Male
1 Bone awl
1 Antler pick end
1 Flint flake knife
Sea shells, fish and bird bones

669 Northumb. Doddington, Horton Castle:
1 N/NR beaker, no. 669
1 Indet. beaker, no. 670 (lost, N2?)

675 Northumb. Hexham, Dilston Park, (A): (figs. 313–15)
Cremation
1 N/NR beaker, no. 675
1 N/NR beaker, no. 677
1 N3 beaker, no. 676

678 Northumb. Hexham, Dilston Park, (B): (figs. 320–1)
Cremation
1 N/NR beaker, no. 678
1 N3 beaker, no. 679

1020 Westmorland Clifton, Penrith: (figs. 305–6)
Male
1 N/NR beaker, no. 1020
1 N2 beaker, no. 1019

1246 Yorks. Broxa, barrow 4: (fig. 293)
Cremation
1 Jet button

1310 Yorks. Goodmanham 99: (figs. 302–3)
1 N1/D beaker, no. 1311
1 N/NR beaker, no. 1310
Uncertain association

1369 Yorks. Rudstone 62: (fig. 298)
Cremation
1 Pebble hammerstone

1491 Aberdeen. Ruthven, Huntly: (fig. 277)
1 Slate disc, perforated and incised

1496 Aberdeen. Slap, Turriff: (fig. 273)
1 Flint flake

1507 Aberdeen. Whitestone, Skene: (figs. 317–18)
Male
1 N/NR beaker, no. 1507
1 N3 beaker, no. 1508
3 Flint scrapers

1593 Berwick. Cockburnspath, Hoprig: (figs. 308–9)
Cremation
1 N/NR beaker, no. 1593
1 N2 beaker, no. 1592

1685 Kincardine. Dunnottar: (figs. 322–4)
Female
1 N/NR beaker, no. 1685
1 N3(L) beaker, no. 1683
1 N3(L) beaker, no. 1684

1723 Nairn. Cawdor: (figs. 311–12)
1 N/NR beaker, no. 1723
1 N2(L) beaker, no. 1722

1784 Sutherland. Dunrobin:
Female
118 Shale disc beads, only 6 perforated
18 Imperforate quartz pebbles

E. Ang.

852 Suffolk Brandon Fields: (figs. 429–30)
1 E. Ang. beaker, no. 852
1 E. Ang. beaker, no. 853
1 Bracer, stone, 6 perforations (B3)

1371 Yorks. Rudstone 62: (fig. 386)
Female
2 Bronze awls
1 Flint flake knife
3 Flint flakes
Uncertain

BW

28 Berks. Lambourne Down 17: (fig. 352)
Male
1 Disc scraper
1 End scraper
6 Flint flakes

353	Hants.	Winchester, St James' Terrace: (figs. 222–3) 1 BW beaker, no. 353 1 W/MR beaker, no. 352 Uncertain association
817	Somerset	Stoford Barwick: 1 Deer antler pick
992	Sussex	Falmer, Ditchling Rd.: Male 1 Barbed and tanged flint arrowhead Heap of snail shells
993	Sussex	Findon, Church Hill: (fig. 337) 1 BW beaker, no. 993 and cremation 1 FP beaker, no. 994 2 Ovate flint axe roughouts
1857	Glamorgan.	Gelligher, Llancaiach-Isaf: Male 'Ornaments', now lost

N1/D

665	Northumb.	Bellingham, Sneep: (fig. 447) Female 8 Flint scrapers
1516	Angus	Monikie, Kingswells: 1 Rubbing stone ? Flint flakes
1521	Angus	Linlathen, Broughty Ferry: (fig. 451) 1 Flint end-scraper

N2

94	Cambs.	Wilburton Fen: (fig. 561) Male 1 Ox horn
134	Derby.	Kenslow, Knoll Fm.: 1 Bone crescent 2 Bone awls 1 Jet pulley-ring 2 Flint flake knives Uncertain association
135	Derby.	Longstone, Blake Low: (fig. 529) Female 1 Antler tine
140	Derby.	Minning Low: 1 Bronze awl 1 Flint flake knife
277	Gloucs.	Barnwood: (fig. 520) Male 1 Flint flake knife
349	Hants.	Stockbridge: (fig. 517) Female 1 Copper awl
367	Hunts.	Houghton; N2(L); (fig. 566) 1 Flint flake knife

684	Northumb.	Lesbury, Birney Knowe: 1 N2 beaker, no. 684 1 ? beaker, no. 685 (lost)
691	Northumb.	Lilburn Steads, W. Lilburn: (fig. 550) Female 1 Single-rivet copper (?) dagger 1 Jet button 1 Flint flake 1 Piece of chalk
695	Northumb.	North Sunderland: (figs. 654–5) Female 1 N2 beaker, no. 695 1 N3 beaker, no. 696 1 ? beaker, no. 697 (lost)
822	Somerset	Wincanton: N2(L): (fig. 478) 1 Flint scraper
1012	Warwick.	Baginton: 1 Flint flake knife
1073	Wilts.	Avebury, Beckhampton Grange: (fig. 516) Child 2 Flint flakes
1140	Wilts.	Shrewton, Nettdown (5k): (fig. 549) Male 1 Single-rivet copper (?) dagger 1 Bone tanged pommel
1187	Wilts.	Winterbourne Monkton (10): 2 Flint flake knives 1 Barbed and tanged flint arrowhead
1265	Yorks.	Driffield; N2(L): (fig. 553) Male 1 Single-rivet copper (?) dagger 2 Amber V bored oval buttons 1 Bracer, stone, 4 perforations (C1), with 4 gold-capped tubular copper rivets 1 Hawk's skull (?)
1303	Yorks.	Garton Slack 161; N2(L): (fig. 555) Male 1 Jet button 1 Flint flake knife
1322	Yorks.	Hanging Grimston 55: (fig. 507) Male 25 Flint flakes
1344	Yorks.	Huggate and Warterwold 254: 1 Bronze awl
1335	Yorks.	Huggate and Warterwold 254: (fig. 508) 1 Amber bracer (?) fragment Uncertain association
1366	Yorks.	Rudstone 61: (fig. 511) Female 1 Antler pick

1367	Yorks.	Rudstone 62: Male 1 Iron ore nodule
1368	Yorks.	Rudstone 62: (fig. 536) 2 Pebble-hammers, with chipped waists
1375	Yorks.	Rudstone 66: (fig. 526) 4 Flint scrapers 2 Flint flakes
1402	Yorks.	Towthorpe 211½: (fig. 533) Male 1 Flint flake
1423	Aberdeen.	Cruden, Ardifferry: (figs. 551–2) Male 1 N2 beaker, no. 1423 1 N2 beaker, no. 1424 1 Bracer, stone, 4 perforations (C1) 7 Flint barbed and tanged arrowheads 2 Flint flake knives
1433	Aberdeen.	Broomend, Inverurie: (figs. 659–60) 2 Males 1 N2(L) beaker, no. 1433 1 N3 beaker, no. 1434
1435	Aberdeen.	Broomend, Inverurie: (figs. 542–4) Male and child 1 N2 beaker, no. 1435 1 N2 beaker, no. 1436 1 Horn ladle 2 Flint flakes
1458	Aberdeen.	Johnstone, Leslie: N2(L): (fig. 573) 2 Flint scrapers
1472	Aberdeen.	Mains of Leslie, Premnay: (figs. 547–8) 1 N2 beaker, no. 1472 1 N2 beaker, no. 1473
1482	Aberdeen.	Parish of Leslie: (fig. 500) Male 3 Flint arrowheads (?) (lost)
1486	Aberdeen.	Persley Quarry: Male 1 Flint flake knife 1 Flint flake
1501	Aberdeen.	Tyrie, Upper Boyndlie: 1 Flint flake knife
1575	Banff.	Boharm, Achroisk: (fig. 475) 1 Copper (?) stained bone
1592	Berwick.	Cocksburnspath, Hoprig: (figs. 308–9) 1 N2 beaker, no. 1592 1 N/NR beaker, no. 1593
1646	E. Lothian	Nunraw, Garvald: Child 1 Flint flake

1651	Fife	Dairsie; N2(L): 4 Barbed and tanged flint arrowheads
1701	Lanark.	Carnwath, Wester Yird Houses: N2(L): Decorated capstone on cist Food Vessel sherds
1719	Moray.	Urquhart, Law Fm.: 5 Bone crescents perforated at one end, as a necklace
1722	Nairn.	Cawdor: (figs. 311–12) 1 N2(L) beaker, no. 1722 1 N/NR beaker, no. 1723
1772	Roxburgh.	Jedburgh, Lanton Tower: N2(L): (fig. 556) 1 Flint flake knife 2 Flint blades 11 Flint flakes

N3

648	Northumb.	Alnwick, Shipley Fm.: Female 2 Pieces of red ochre
652	Northumb.	Amble: (fig. 700) 1 N3 beaker, no. 652 1 ? beaker, no. 653 (lost) 1 Flint flake 1 Pebble-hammerstone
692	Northumb.	Norham: Copper (?) stain on beaker
1018	Westmorland	Clifton, Penrith Female (?) 1 Bone awl
1209	Worcs.	Pershore: ? Flint flakes 2 Boar's tusks
1291	Yorks.	Garrowby Wold 104: (figs. 651–2) Male (?) 1 N3 beaker, no. 1291 1 N3 beaker, no. 1292
1304	Yorks.	Garton Slack 163: 1 Flint flake knife
1305	Yorks.	Gardon Slack 163: (fig. 667) Male 1 Polished flint axe 3 Flint flakes 1 Bone awl 1 Flint flake knife
1306	Yorks.	Garton Slack 163: (fig. 666) Female 1 Bronze (?) awl 7 Flint flakes 1 Pebble-hammer
1327	Yorks.	Hempholme: 1 Flint flake knife

1370 Yorks.
Rudstone 62:
Female
1 Flint flake knife

1434 Aberdeen.
Broomend, Inverurie: (figs. 659–60)
2 Males
1 N3 beaker, no. 1434
1 N2(L) beaker, no. 1433
1 Bone pulley-ring
2 Flint scrapers
1 Flint flake

1441 Aberdeen.
Clashfarquhar, Banchory:
(figs. 672–3)
1 N3 beaker, no. 1441
1 N3 beaker, no. 1441

1443 Aberdeen.
Clinterty: (fig. 661)
Male
1 Polished schist axe
2 Barbed and tanged arrowheads
1 Flint flake knife
1 Topaz
1 Bone awl
1 Bone pulley-ring
1 Flint scraper
4 Flint flakes

1449 Aberdeen.
Ellon: (figs. 669–70)
1 N3 beaker, no. 1449
1 N3 beaker, no. 1450
4 Barbed and tanged arrowheads
Uncertain association

1451 Aberdeen.
Ellon, Hillhead; N3(L):
Male
1 Flint flake knife
1 Pebble-hammer
1 Charred fircone

1453 Aberdeen.
Freefield:
1 Flint strike-a-light (?)
1 Iron ore nodule
Uncertain association

1508 Aberdeen.
Skene, Whitestone: (figs. 317–18)
Male
1 N3 beaker, no. 1508
1 N/NR beaker, no. 1507
3 Flint scrapers

1531 Argyll.
Callachally, Mull: (figs. 676–7)
1 N3 beaker, no. 1531
1 S3(E) beaker, no. 1532
1 Bracer, stone, 2 perforations (A1)
1 Single-rivet copper (?) dagger

1533 Argyll.
Campbeltown, Balnabraid:
1 Flint flake knife
2 Disc shale beads

1586 Banff.
Lesmurdie:
1 Iron ore nodule
1 Flint strike-a-light
2 Flint scrapers

1591 Berwick.
Chirnside, Harelaw Hill:
1 Flint flake

1614 Dumfries.
Auchencairn, Closeburn:
1 Flint strike-a-light

1665 Inverness.
Corran Ferry:
1 Flint flake strike-a-light (?)

1667 Inverness.
Lochend:
Male
1 Flint scraper

1683 Kincardine.
Dunnottar: (figs. 322–4)
Female
1 N3(L) beaker, no. 1683
1 N3(L) beaker, no. 1684
1 N/NR beaker, no. 1685

1698 Kirkcud.
Mainsriddle: (fig. 662)
Male
1 Bone pulley-ring

1702 Lanark.
Crawfurd: (fig. 674)
1 Cremation?
1 Bronze arm-ring
2 Bronze spearheads (?)
Uncertain association

1730 Nairn.
Cawdor: (fig. 663)
2 Bone awls
1 Bone chisel

1744 Perth.
Tippermallo, Methven:
3 Flint scrapers

1768 Roxburgh.
Eckford: (fig. 690)
2 Flint flakes

N4

1460 Aberdeen.
Keir, Belhelvie: (figs. 715–17)
Female
1 N4 beaker, no. 1461
1 N4 beaker, no. 1460
1 N3(L) beaker, no. 1559

1478 Aberdeen.
Newlands, Oyne: (fig. 721)
Male
1 Bracer, stone, 4 perforations (C1)
1 Bracer, stone, 2 perforations (A2)
1 Barbed and tanged arrowhead
2 Flint flake knives
1 Flint scraper
2 Flint flakes

1609 Caithness
Heathfield, Glengolly: (fig. 731)
1 N4 beaker, no. 1609
1 ? beaker, no. 1610 (lost)
1 Cremation

1692 Kincardine.
Upper Mains Catterline: (fig. 718)
Male
1 Flint scraper
1 Re-used, decorated cist slab

1749 Ross.
Fyrish, Evantoun: (fig. 719)
Male
1 Bracer, stone, 4 perforations (C1)

S1

4	Beds.	Harrowden: (figs. 781–2, 785) 1 Flint dagger 1 Iron ore nodule Uncertain association
115	Derby.	Alsop. Green Low: (fig. 776) Male 3 Bone spatulae 1 Bone awl 1 Iron ore nodule 1 Flint dagger 3 Barbed and tanged arrowheads 4 Flint scrapers 1 Flint flake knife 2 Flint flakes
117	Derby.	Bakewell, Haddon Field: (fig. 757) Male 1 Barbed and tanged arrowhead 1 Antler spatula 1 Bronze awl (All above now lost)
129	Derby.	Elton Moor: 3 Coloured quartz pebbles 2 Iron ore nodules 1 Igneous stone polished axe fragment 1 Polished flint axe 1 Flint strike-a-light 1 Flint flake knife 21 Flint scrapers 17 Waste flakes Uncertain association
269	Essex	Thorpe Hall: 1 Flint dagger Heap of cockle shells
826	Staffs.	Stanshope, Ramscroft: (fig. 754) Child 1 Flint blade
827	Staffs.	Stanshope, Ramscroft: (fig. 742) Child 1 Flint scraper
941	Suffolk	Needham Market: 1 Flint axe (lost)
953	Suffolk	Undley, Lakenheath: (figs. 795–6) 1 S1 beaker, no. 953 1 FP beaker, no. 954
1210	Yorks.	Acklam Wold 124: (fig. 780) Male 1 Flint dagger 1 Flint flake knife 1 Flint strike-a-light 1 Iron ore nodule 1 Bone awl 1 Jet button 1 Jet pulley-ring 1 Oval amber button

1275	Yorks.	Ferry Fryston 161: 1 Bronze awl
1296	Yorks.	Garton Slack 37: (fig. 778) 1 Flint dagger 1 Flint strike-a-light (lost) 1 Iron ore nodule (lost) 1 Stone battle-axe 1 Jet button
1352	Yorks.	Painsthorpe 4: 1 Flint flake knife
1389	Yorks.	Staxton: Female 1 Flint blade
1390	Yorks.	Staxton 11: (fig. 756) Male 1 Iron ore nodule 1 Flint strike-a-light

S2(E)

123	Derby.	Cowdale, Gospel Hillock: ? Flint flakes
645	Northants.	Fengate, Peterborough: 1 Flint scraper
792	Somerset	Charmy Down 1: (fig. 883) 1 Two-rivet (?) bronze dagger 1 Incised shale barrel bead
825	Staffs.	Mouse Low, Deepdale: (fig. 862) Male 2 Bone spatulae 4 Barbed and tanged flint arrowheads 1 Flint flake knife
835	Staffs.	Castern, Wetton: 1 Flint flake (lost)
1037	Wilts.	Amesbury (51): (fig. 846) 1 Bronze awl 1 Flint scraper 2 Antler spatulae
1103	Wilts.	Durrington, Woodhenge 1: (fig. 864) Male 1 Tourmaline granite battle-axe
1323	Yorks.	Hanging Grimston 55: 1 Jet button 1 Flint flake knife
1374	Yorks.	Rudstone 66: Female 1 Flint flake knife
1849	Carmarthen.	Llannon, Cors-Y-Dre: 3 Flint flake knives

S2(W)

27 Berks. Lambourn Down 31: (fig. 892)
Male
6 Barbed and tanged flint arrowheads
1 Jet button
1 Flint end scraper
1 Flint strike-a-light
1 Flint flake knife
1 Flint burin-end knife

139 Derby. Smerrill Moor:
Male
1 Bone spatula
1 Flint flake knife (lost)
1 Flint flake knife
4 Flint flakes

145 Derby. Rusden Low:
Female and child
1 Flint flake knife

153 Derby. Youlgrave, Bee Low:
1 Serrated flint blade

158 Devon Fernworthy: (fig. 886)
1 Bronze dagger fragment
1 Jet button
1 Flint flake knife

226 Essex Berden: (fig. 894)
Female (?)
1 Bronze arm-ring (?) (lost)

690 Northumb. Lilburn Steads, Wooler:
1 Flint dagger

800 Somerset Corston:
Male
1 Black slate whetstone (?)
1 Flint strike-a-light
1 Iron ore nodule
3 Flint scrapers
1 Flint flake knife

802 Somerset Corston:
1 Flint flake knife
1 Flint flake

820 Somerset Wick, Stogursey:
4 Flint scrapers
1 Flint flake
1 Pebble-hammer

986 Sussex Brighton, Church Hill: (figs. 826–7)
Adult and child
1 S2(W) beaker, no. 986
1 S2(W) beaker, no. 987

1039 Wilts. Amesbury (54): (fig. 890)
1 Flint dagger
1 Polished, faceted hammerstone

1087 Wilts. Calne Without (2c):
1 Bronze dagger fragment (?)

1131 Wilts. West Overton (6B):
Male
1 Bronze awl
2 Slate whetstones (?)
1 Antler spatula
1 Flint strike-a-light
1 Iron ore nodule
1 Flint flake knife

1185 Wilts. Winterbourne Monkton:
(figs. 897–8)
1 S2(W) beaker, no. 1185
1 S2(W) beaker, no. 1186
1 Polished and faceted hammer-stone
1 Jet pulley-ring
2 Jet buttons
1 Flint flake knife
1 Soft stone disc

1195 Wilts. Winterbourne Stoke (54): (fig. 900)
2 Slate whetstones (?)
1 Flint blade
1 Jet button
1 Jet pulley-ring

1217 Yorks. Aldro 116:
Male
1 Bronze awl
1 Flint flake
Bones of small dog

1218 Yorks. Aldro 116: (fig. 888)
Male
1 Three-rivet bronze dagger

1293 Yorks. Garrowby Wold 104:
Male
1 Flint flake knife

1324 Yorks. Hanging Grimston 55:
1 Flint flake knife

1833 Brecknock. Cwm Car, Dolygaer:
1 Barbed and tanged flint arrowhead

1834 Brecknock. Llanelieu, Ty-du:
1 Flint dagger

1854 Denbigh. Ysgwennant, Llansilin:
1855 Barrow, two separate but coeval graves
Beaker no. 1 (1854)—fig. 896
Beaker no. 2 (1855)—fig. 895, with associations:
Traces of burnt bone
2 Jet buttons
2 Jet belt rings
2 Whetstones
1 Pyrites nodule
1 Flint striker

S2(E)?

486.1 Lincs. Tallington:
2 Bronze basket earrings, un-decorated

445

S2 (Hybrids)

366 Hunts.   Houghton: (fig. 878)
1 Flint flake knife

1347 Yorks.   Middleton-on-the-Wolds:
(fig. 876)
1 Flint dagger
1 Iron ore nodule
1 Flint strike-a-light
2 Jet buttons
1 Bone awl (lost)
1 Flint flake

S3(E)

72 Cambs.   Little Downham: (fig. 959)
1 Flint dagger
1 Flint flake knife
1 Jet button
1 Jet pulley-ring

128 Derby.   Brownedge, Dowel:
1 Jet button
1 Flint flake knife
1 Flint strike-a-light

233 Essex   Gt Chesterford: (fig. 953)
1 Flint dagger
Uncertain association

382 Isle of Wight   Nodgham, Carisbrooke:
1 Barbed and tanged flint arrowhead

828 Staffs.   Stanshope, Ramscroft:
1 Flint flake knife

834 Staffs.   Swinscoe, Top Low:
Male
? Flint flakes

1214 Yorks.   Aldro 54:
1 Barbed and tanged flint arrowhead
Uncertain association

1673 Inverness.   Kraiknish, Skye: (figs. 679–80)
1 S3(E) beaker, no. 1673
1 N3 beaker, no. 1674
1 Flint scraper

1861 Glamorgan.   Merthyr Mawr, Riley's Tumulus:
Male
1 Flint flake knife

1876 Montgomery.   Darowen, Cefn-Coch-Gwyllt:
(fig. 950)
2 Three-rivet bronze daggers
Uncertain association

S3(W)

104 Cornwall   St Buryan:
1 Flint scraper
Uncertain association

424 Leics.   Knipton: (fig. 955)
1 Bronze, decorated bracelet

821 Somerset   Wick, Stogursey:
Male
1 Flint dagger
1 Flint arrowhead roughout

1119 Wilts.   East Kennet (1C): (fig. 948)
1 Stone battle-axe
1 Three-rivet bronze dagger

S4

747 Oxford.   Eynsham, Foxley Fm.:
Female
1 Bronze awl

1083 Wilts.   Brigmerston:
1 Antler pick

1394 Yorks.   Thirsk, Sutton Bank:
Female
1 Jet disc bead
2 Flint flakes

1520 Angus   Linlathen, Cairn Gregg: (fig. 1018)
1 Three-rivet bronze dagger

1655 Fife   Kirkcaldy: (fig. 1014)
1 Tanged bronze razor, class 1B,
hazel haft
1 Bronze awl
12 Jet buttons
1 Jet fusiform bead
1 Flint flake

1662.1 Fife   Methilhill, Ashgrove Fm.:
(fig. 1016)
1 Three-rivet bronze dagger with
wooden haft and leather scabbard
1 Bone pommel

1803 Wigtown.   Glenluce, Stoneykirk:
188 Jet disc beads
1 jet triangular toggle

SH

262.1 Essex   Sible Hedingham: (figs. 1053–4)
1 SH2(A) beaker, no. 262.1
1 SH2(B)? beaker, no. 262.2
Uncertain association

721 Oxford.   Cassington, Tolley's Pit: SH4(B):
Female
1 Bronze awl

1314 Yorks.   Goodmanham 113; SH4(B):
Male
1 Flint flake

1360 Yorks.   Pickering; SH4(C):
1 Flint flake knife
4 Flint scrapers

FP

116 Derby.   Ashford, Shack Low:
1 Flint scraper

122 Derby.   Buxton, Stakor Hill: (fig. 910)
Female
2 Bronze basket earrings, undecorated (lost)
1 Flint flake knife

203 Dorset   Tarrant Launceston (8):
1 Bronze awl

218 Dorset   Worth Matravers:
? Flint scrapers

746 Oxford.   Eynsham, Foxley Fm.: (fig. 1038)
Male
1 Three-rivet bronze dagger
1 Bone pommel
2 Tubular bronze pommel-rivets

1114 Wilts.   Figheldean (25):
Male
1 Flint flake knife

1273 Yorks.   Elloughton:
Male
1 Bone awl

1333 Yorks.   Huggate Wold 216:
1 Flint flake knife

1353 Yorks.   Painsthorpe 4:
Child
1 Flint flake knife

1828 Anglesey   Pentraeth, Merddyn-Gwyn: (fig. 908)
1 Three-rivet bronze dagger
1 Jet button
1 Flint flake

FN

329 Hants.   Iford, Sheepwash:
2 Flint flakes

Beakers of unknown type

361 Herts.   Tring, The Grove:
2 Beakers (?)
1 Bracer, stone, 4 perforations (C1)
1 Bracer, stone, 2 perforations (C1 unfinished)
1 Jet pulley-ring, grooved rim
3 Barbed and tanged flint arrowheads

639 Northants.   Norton Hall:
4 Beakers (?)
1 Flint dagger
Uncertain association

823 Staffs.   Alstonefield, Steep Low:
1 Beaker (?)

1 Amber button
1 Iron ore nodule

1344 Yorks.   Melton Quarry: (fig. 136)
1 Undec. rim fragment (Bowl?)
1 Bone belt ring
1 Bracer, stone, 2 perforations (B1)

1840.1 Brecknock.   Ystradfellte:
1 Beaker (FP)
1 Flint dagger

3.2. Summary of beaker and artefact association pattern

The artefacts found associated with British beakers in the graves have been hand sorted to bring out the underlying correlation with the particular beaker groups. The resulting diagram is shown below.

The figures on the diagram represent the number of graves of each beaker group to contain that particular artefact. A question mark indicates an uncertain association, a plus sign indicates an additional probable association. The diagram suggests five main accretions of associations:

(1) *A basic beaker association range*, virtually a Neolithic assemblage barring the metal awls, held in common by all the beaker groups;

(2) *An early beaker association range*, which extends the basic range by the inclusion of decorated, gold basket earrings and possibly more copper artefacts;

(3) *The Middle Rhenish association range*, including a wealth of new objects introduced by the W/MR and N/MR groups, notably the cast copper daggers and stone bracers B1–3;

(4) *The Northern British association range*, including another new artefact range, differing from the last and apparently linked with the Northern British/Dutch groups N1–4;

(5) *The Southern British association range*, selectively integrating part of the Middle Rhenish and the Northern British association ranges. This range is linked with the Southern British beaker groups S1–4 and strikingly confirms the origin of that native assemblage as independently suggested on ceramic analysis.

These five groups can be seen outlined on the diagram (p. 448).

Associations	Beaker types																
	AOC	E	W/MR	N/MR	N/NR	E.Ang.	BW	N1/D	N2	N3	N4	S1	S2	S3	S4	SH	FP
Flint flakes	1	1	–	1	1	1	1	1	9	8	1	2	7	1	2	1	1
Flint blades	–	2	–	1	–	–	–	–	1	–	–	2	2	1	–	–	–
Flint scraper	1	–	–	≈	–	–	1	2	3	6	2	3	5	1	–	1	2
Flint arrowhead	3	2	3	5	–	–	1	–	4	2	1	2	3	2	–	–	–
Second vessel	1	4	9	–	8	1	2	–	8	8	1+	1+	2	2	–	+	–
Antler pick	–	1	–	–	1	–	1	–	2	–	–	–	–	–	1	–	–
Bronze (?) awl	–	2	1	–	–	2	–	–	3	1	–	2	3	–	2	1	1
Shale/jet beads	–	–	1	–	1	–	–	–	–	1	–	–	1	–	3	–	–
Gold earrings	1	1	–	–	–	–	–	–	–	–	–	–	–	–	–	–	–
Tanged copper dagger	?	?	5	–	–	–	–	–	–	–	–	–	–	–	–	–	–
B1 bracer	–	–	1	–	–	–	–	–	–	–	–	–	–	–	–	–	–
B2 bracer	–	–	1	–	–	–	–	–	–	–	–	–	–	–	–	–	–
B3 bracer	–	–	2	–	–	1	–	–	–	–	–	–	–	–	–	–	–
Bone belt ring	–	–	1	2+	–	–	–	–	–	–	–	–	–	–	–	–	–
Gold button cap	–	–	1	1+	–	–	–	–	–	–	–	–	–	–	–	–	–
Bone/antler spatulae	–	–	2	–	–	–	–	–	–	–	–	2	4	–	–	–	–
Flint dagger	–	–	2	+	–	–	–	–	–	–	–	5	3+	2+	–	–	–
Jet pulley-ring	–	–	–	1	–	–	–	–	?	–	–	1	4	1	–	–	–
Bronze dagger, class I	–	–	1	–	–	–	–	–	–	–	–	–	3+	–	–	–	1
Stone battle-axe	–	–	–	–	–	–	–	–	–	–	–	1	1	1	–	–	–
Slate whetstone (?)	–	–	–	–	–	–	–	–	–	–	–	–	5	–	–	–	–
Bronze (?) earrings	–	–	–	–	–	–	–	–	–	–	–	–	1	–	–	–	1
Bronze dagger II/III	–	–	–	–	–	–	–	–	–	–	–	–	–	2	2	–	1
Flint axe	–	–	–	–	–	1	–	–	–	1	–	2	1	–	–	–	–
Stone axe	–	–	–	–	–	–	–	–	1	1	–	1	–	–	–	–	–
Iron ore nodule	–	–	–	–	–	–	–	1	1+	–	–	5+	4	–	–	–	–
Flint strike-a-light	–	–	–	–	–	–	–	–	3+	–	–	4	5	1	–	–	–
Flint, flake knife	–	–	1	–	1	1	–	–	11	8+	1	4	16	5	–	1	4
Jet buttons	–	–	–	–	1	–	–	–	2	–	–	2	8	2	1	–	1
Amber buttons	–	–	–	–	–	–	–	–	1	–	–	1	–	–	–	–	–
Bone awl	–	–	–	–	1	–	–	–	1	4	–	2	1	–	–	–	1
Bronze arm-ring	–	–	–	–	–	–	–	–	–	1	–	–	?	–	–	–	–
Pebble-hammers	–	–	–	–	1	–	–	–	1	3	–	–	1	–	–	–	–
Bone pulley-rings	–	–	–	–	–	–	–	–	–	3	–	–	–	–	–	–	–
Bone crescents	–	–	–	–	–	–	–	–	2	–	–	–	–	–	–	–	–
Boars' tusks	–	–	2	–	–	–	–	–	–	1	–	–	–	–	–	–	–
1-Rivet bronze dagger	–	–	–	–	–	–	–	–	3	1	–	–	–	–	–	–	–
C1 bracer	–	–	1	–	–	–	–	–	2	–	2	–	–	–	–	–	–
A1 bracer	–	–	–	–	–	–	–	–	–	1	–	–	–	–	–	–	–
A2 bracer	–	–	–	–	–	–	–	–	–	–	1	–	–	–	–	–	–

3.3. Analysis of grave associations by sex

	Male graves	Female graves		Male graves	Female graves
	Total sexed graves	Total sexed graves		Total sexed graves	Total sexed graves
Male associations			Pyrites nodule	6/6	—
Flint arrowheads	16/16	—	Strike-a-light flint	5/5	—
Tanged copper daggers	4/4	—	Amber buttons	2/2	—
Bracers, all types	8/8	—			
Belt rings, all types	6/6	—			
Gold button caps	2/2	—	*Probably male associations*		
Antler spatulae	6/6	—	Flint scrapers	10/11	1/11
Flint dagger	4/4	—	Flint flakes	14/19	5/19
Bronze daggers, types I–III	3/3	—	Flint flake knives	19/23	4/23
Stone battle-axe	1/1	—	Jet buttons	3/4	1/4
Slate polishers	2/2	—	Bone awl/pin	6/7	1/7
Flint and stone axes	2/2	—	One-rivet bronze daggers	2/3	1/3

448

	Male graves	Female graves	Unsexed associations
	Total sexed graves	Total sexed graves	Bronze arm-rings
			Bone crescents
			Boars' tusks

Probably female associations

	Male graves	Female graves
Shale/jet beads	—	2/2
Second vessel with one body only	2/9	7/9*
Antler pick/hoe (?)	1/3	2/3
Bronze awls	3/11	8/11

Male or female associations

	Male graves	Female graves
Flint blades	2/4	2/4
Earrings gold/bronze	1/2	1/2
Pebble-hammers	1/2	1/2

Note. The appearance of a jet button and bronze single-rivet dagger in the female list are due to a single interment, rather disturbed, 691, Lilburn Steads, W. Lilburn, Northumberland.

* Most of the female graves with several vessels are with a young or newborn child: in four cases two beakers accompany double adult male burials.

3.4. Associations between beakers and other pottery

These associations represent closed, or probably closed finds, indicating the types of pottery contemporary to the beaker groups. Almost all the associations are in fact other accessory beakers, usually of the same group. Each site has been treated on its merits, all the available cases of valid association are included and the list has been prepared entirely independently to the beaker classification scheme. This association list therefore forms an important test of the general validity of the new scheme. In the text, references to particular cases of association evidence are noted by their corpus numbers for conciseness, thus nos. 25–6, refers to nos. 25–6 below, the beaker and bowl from Inkpen Hill, Berks.

Virtually all the sites quoted are either graves or sealed pits containing domestic rubbish; these are noted as 'grave' or 'pit'. Depending on the individual stratigraphy, the particular site is registered as a 'certain' closed find, 'probable' closed find, or 'dubious' if the stratigraphy is disturbed.

Name	Corpus no.	Beaker	Reliability	Site	
Inkpen Hill,	25	W/MR	certain	grave?	fig. 205
Berks.	26	Bowl			fig. 204
Bledlow,	39	W/MR	probable	grave?	fig. 192
Bucks.	40	Bowl			fig. 192
Burwell,	50	Lost	certain	grave	
Cambs.	51	Lost			
Snailwell,	86	FP	probable	grave?	fig. 791
Cambs.	87	N2			fig. 498
Dovercourt,	230	FN	probable	pit	
Essex	231	E. Ang.			
Great Clacton,	235	FN	dubious	grave?	
Essex	236	Lost			
	237	Lost			
	238	Lost			
Lion Point,	246	BW	probable	pit	
Essex	247	E. Ang.?			
	248	FN			
Little Holland,	249	BW	dubious	grave?	
Essex	250	E. Ang.			
Christchurch,	313	E	dubious	grave?	
Furzy, Hants.	314	AOC			
Southbourne,	346	E	probable	grave?	
Roebury, Hants.	347	FN			fig. 123
Winchester, Hants.	352	W/MR	probable	grave	fig. 222
Hants.	353	BW			fig. 223
Tring,	361	Lost	certain	grave	
Herts.	362	Lost			
Barham,	385	E	dubious	grave?	fig. 92
Kent	386	FN			fig. 380

Name	Corpus no.	Beaker	Reliability	Site	
East Tuddenham,	523	S 1	dubious	grave?	fig. 792
Norfolk	524	FP			fig. 793
Overa Heath,	573	FN	probable	pit	
Norfolk	574	BW			
	575	E. Ang.			
	576	E. Ang.			
Amble,	652	N3	probable	grave	fig. 700
Northumb.	653	Lost			
Doddington,	669	N/NR	probable	grave	
Northumb.	670	Lost			
Hexham, cist A,	675	N/NR	certain	grave	fig. 313
Northumb.	676	N3			fig. 315
	677	N/NR			fig. 314
Hexham, cist B,	678	N/NR	certain	grave	fig. 320
Northumb.	679	N3			fig. 321
Lesbury,	684	N2	certain	grave	
Northumb.	685	Lost			
North Sunderland,	695	N2	certain	grave	fig. 654
Northumb.	696	N3			fig. 655
	697	Lost			
Cassington,	724	FP	probable	pit	
Oxford.	725	S 4?			
Eynsham,	749	W/MR	certain	grave	fig. 193
Oxford.	750	Bowl			fig. 194
Summertown,	761	W/MR	certain	grave	fig. 216
Oxford.	762	FN			fig. 217
Stanton Harcourt,	768	E	certain	grave	fig. 109
Oxford.	769	Undec.			fig. 110
Brean Down,	778	E	certain	grave?	fig. 112
Somerset	779	FN			fig. 113
Chew Park,	796	E?	probable	pit	
Somerset	797	FN			
Compton Martin,	798	E	probable	pit	
Somerset	799	FN			
Stogursey,	818	E	probable	grave	fig. 54
Somerset	819	FN			
Ilam Moor,	829	E?	dubious	grave	
Staffs.	830	FN			
Brandon Fields,	852	E. Ang. FN	probable	grave?	fig. 429
Suffolk	853	E. Ang. FN			fig. 430
Brantham Hall,	854	E	certain	grave	fig. 107
Suffolk	855	FN			fig. 108
	856	E			fig. 106
Bury	863	FP	probable	pit	fig. 1047
St Edmunds,	864	FP			fig. 1046
Suffolk	865	S 4			fig. 1045
Butley,	867	S 4	probable	pit	
Neutral Fm.,	868	S 3(E)?			
Suffolk	869	FP			fig. 1050
Creeting	871	E. Ang. FN	probable	pit	
St Mary,	872	E. Ang.			
Suffolk	873	E. Ang.			
Felixstowe,	887	BW	probable	pit	
Suffolk	888	FN			fig. 372
Undley,	953	S 1	certain	grave	fig. 795
Suffolk	954	FP			fig. 796
Brighton,	986	S 2(W)	certain	grave	fig. 826
Sussex	987	S 2(W)			fig. 827

Name	Corpus no.	Beaker	Reliability	Site	
Findon, Sussex	993 994	BW FP	probable	grave	fig. 337
Brougham, Westmorland	1017	N3 Vase Food Vessel	dubious	grave	
Clifton, Penrith, Westmorland	1019 1020	N2 N/NR	certain	grave	fig. 306 fig. 305
Avebury, Beckhampton, Wilts.	1073 1074	N2 Indet.	dubious	grave	fig. 516
Boyton, Wilts.	1081 1082	W/MR W/MR	certain	grave	fig. 186 fig. 185
Durrington, Woodhenge, Wilts	1104 1105	W/MR W/MR	dubious	grave?	
Durrington, Larkhill, Wilts.	1108 1109	Undec. W/MR	certain	grave	fig. 188 fig. 189
Wilsford (G1), Wilts.	1159 1160	W/MR Undec.	certain	grave	fig. 183 fig. 182
Winterbourne Monkton, Wilts.	1185 1186	S2(W) S2(W)	certain	grave	fig. 898 fig. 897
Garrowby Wold 104, Yorks.	1291 1292	N3 N3	certain	grave	fig. 652 fig. 651
Garton Slack 163, Yorks.	1305 1306	N3(L) N3	certain	grave	fig. 667 fig. 666
Huggate and Warterwold 254, Yorks.	1334 1335	N2 N2	dubious	grave	fig. 508
Painsthorpe Wold 4, Yorks.	1351 1352	S2(W) S1	probable	grave	
Ardiffery, Cruden, Aberdeen.	1423 1424	N2 N2	certain	grave	fig. 551 fig. 552
Broomend, 1, Aberdeen.	1433 1434	N2(L) N3	probable	grave	fig. 659 fig. 660
Broomend, 2, Aberdeen.	1435 1436	N2 N2	probable	grave	fig. 544 fig. 542
Clashfarquhar, Aberdeen.	1441 1442	N3 N3	probable	grave	fig. 673 fig. 672
Ellon, Aberdeen.	1449 1450	N3 N3	dubious	grave	fig. 669 fig. 670
Keir, Belhelvie, Aberdeen.	1459 1460 1461	N3(L) N4 N4	probable	grave	fig. 715 fig. 716 fig. 717
Mains of Leslie, Aberdeen.	1472 1473	N2 N2	certain	grave	fig. 547 fig. 548
Pittodrie, Oyne, Aberdeen.	1489 1490	N2 N3	dubious higher level in cist	grave	
Whitestone, Aberdeen.	1507 1508	N/NR N3	probable	grave	fig. 317 fig. 318
Callachally, Mull, Argyll.	1531 1532	N3 S3(E)	probable	grave	fig. 676 fig. 677
Cockburnspath, Berwick.	1592 1593	N2 N/NR	certain	grave	fig. 309 fig. 308
Glecknabae, Bute	1603 1604	E FN	dubious	grave	fig. 94
Heathfield, Glengolly, Caithness	1609 1610	N4 Lost	dubious	grave	fig. 731
Leuchars, Brackmont Mill, Fife	1656 1657	AOC Bowl	certain	grave?	fig. 36a fig. 36b

Name	Corpus no.	Beaker	Reliability	Site	
Skye, Kraiknish,	1673	S3(E)	probable	grave	fig. 680
Inverness.	1674	N3			fig. 679
Balbridie, Durris,	1678	N3	probable	grave	
Kincardine.	1679	Lost			
Dunnottar,	1683	N3(L)	probable	grave	fig. 324
Nether-Criggie,	1684	N3(L)			fig. 323
Kincardine.	1685	N/NR			fig. 322
Cairnholy II,	1695	AOC	dubious	grave?	
Kirkcudbright.	1696	E			
	1696.1	E?			
	1696.2	FN			
Cawdor,	1722	N2(L)	probable	grave	fig. 312
Nairn.	1723	N/NR			fig. 311
Kilcoy,	1750	AOC	probable	grave?	
West Cairn,	1751	AOC			
Ross and Cromarty	1752	AOC			
	1753	E			fig. 16
	1754	AOC			
	1755	FN			fig. 126
Cairnpapple,	1791	N2(L)	certain	grave	
West Lothian	1792	N2(L)			
Knockdoon, Glenluce Sands,	1799	AOC	certain	grave?	fig. 21
Wigtown.	1800	AOC			fig. 20

3.5. British beaker grave types

British beaker graves can be arbitrarily divided into barrow and non-barrow graves, then further subdivided into the seven basic forms noted below. The term 'shaft' has here been employed to denote beaker graves cut into the old surface by more than 3 ft. The term '2ndy' indicates a secondary grave, in a barrow earlier than the beaker grave. Entries over 10% are set in bold type.

S4	8·3%	—	**16·7%**	**12·5%**	**12·5%**	**50·0%**	—	100%
	2	—	4	3	3	12	—	24
SH	**15·0%**	—	**10·0%**	**10·0%**	5·0%	**60·0%**	—	
	3	—	2	2	1	12	—	20
S3	**19·4%**	3·2%	**22·6%**	6·5%	**12·9%**	**35·4%**	—	
	6	1	7	2	4	11	—	31
S2	**22·0%**	**13·5%**	**11·9%**	**15·2%**	**11·9%**	**22·0%**	3·4%	
	13	8	7	9	7	13	2	59
S1	**35·7%**	7·1%	**10·7%**	—	—	**39·3%**	7·1%	
	10	2	3	—	—	11	2	28
N4	—	—	—	9·1%	**90·9%**	—	—	
	—	—	—	1	10	—	—	11
N3	—	2·1%	3·2%	**14·7%**	**66·4%**	**12·6%**	1·1%	
	—	2	3	14	63	12	1	95
N2	6·4%	7·5%	4·3%	9·6%	**52·0%**	**14·9%**	5·3%	
	6	7	4	9	49	14	5	94
N1	—	—	**11·1%**	**11·1%**	**44·4%**	**33·3%**	—	
	—	—	1	1	4	3	—	9
BW	9·1%	9·1%	—	**18·2%**	9·1%	**45·5%**	9·1%	
	1	1	—	2	1	5	1	11
E. Ang.	**26·7%**	—	—	—	—	**60·0%**	**13·3%**	
	4	—	—	—	—	9	2	15
N/NR	**13·8%**	6·9%	6·9%	**24·1%**	**34·4%**	**10·4%**	3·5%	
	4	2	2	7	10	3	1	29
N/MR	**14·3%**	7·1%	—	**21·4%**	**42·8%**	**14·3%**	—	
	2	1	—	3	6	2	—	14
W/MR	**25·0%**	8·3%	2·8%	—	—	**58·1%**	5·6%	
	9	3	1	—	—	21	2	36

	Barrow grave	Barrow and shaft	Barrow 2ndy grave	Barrow and cist	Cist grave	Flat grave	Shaft grave	
E	12·0% 3	—	8·0% 2	—	12·0% 3	64·0% 16	4·0% 1	25
AOC	47·2% 8	—	5·9% 1	—	17·6% 3	17·6% 3	11·8% 2	17 100%

Grave types

3.6. British beakers certainly or possibly with cremation burials

The number of 'certain' human cremations with British beakers is very small indeed. Many cases accepted as cremation burials are extremely suspect for the following reasons: charcoal and scorching are frequent features in beaker inhumation graves; so are calcined food bones; grey deposits of 'ash' in old reports are often clearly records of the decayed wooden cists common with beaker inhumations; secondary cremations have been inserted in several beaker cists with inhumations. It follows that some discrimination must be exercised, therefore I have noted certain/probable cremations as *probable* and possible/dubious cremations as *possible*. The cremations below are listed in sequence of the beaker groups and a summary of the overall pattern will be found at the end of this section.

Site	Corpus no.	Group	Reliability
Alston, Kirkhaugh I, Northumb.	651	AOC	possible
Cuning Hill, Inverurie, Aberdeen.	1445	AOC	possible
Forglen barrow, Banff.	1582	AOC	possible
Knockdoon,	1799	AOC	possible
Glenluce, Wigtown.	1800	AOC	
Mynydd-y-Bryn Llansilin, Denbigh.	1852	W/MR	possible
Buckieburn, Shankhead, Stirling.	1781	N/MR	possible
Hexham,	675	N/MR	probable
Dilston, A, Northumb.	677	N/NR	
Hexham, Dilston, B, Northumb.	678	N/NR	probable
Broxa Moor 4, Yorks.	1246	N/NR	probable
Rudstone barrow 62, Yorks.	1369	N/NR	probable
Cockburnspath, Hoprig, Berwick.	1593	N/NR	possible
Allan, Pendreich, Perth.	1739	N/NR	possible
Durval, Sancreed, Cornwall	98	BW?	probable
Cley-next-the-Sea, Norfolk	519	BW	probable
Burrington, Blackdown 5, Somerset	784	BW	possible
Felixstowe Golf Course, Suffolk	887	BW	possible
Findon, Church Hill, Sussex	993	BW	probable
Ty-Llwyd, Groeswen, Glamorgan.	1869	BW	possible
Rudstone, barrow 62, Yorks.	1368	with N/NR no. 1369 (N2	probable)
Cockburnspath, Hoprig, Berwick.	1592	with N/NR no. 1593 (N2	possible)
Hexham, Dilston, A, Northumb.	676	with N/NR no. 675-7 (N3	probable)
Hexham, Dilston, B, Northumb.	679	with N/NR no. 678 (N3	probable)
Tifty, Fyvie, Aberdeen.	1500	N3	possible
Buckie, Rathven, Banff.	1576	N3	probable
Crawfurd, Lanark.	1702	N3	possible
Heathfield, Glengolly, Caithness	1609	N4	possible
Worlington, Mildenhall, Suffolk	967	S1	possible
Broad Down, Honiton, Devon	155	S2(W)?	probable
Dolygaer, Cwm Car, Brecknock.	1833	S2(W)	possible
Bwlch-y-Gwrhyd Drum, Caernarvon.	1841	S2(W)	possible
Llanelltyd, Myndd, Merioneth.	1875	S2(W)	possible
Bury St Edmunds, Suffolk	865	S4	probable
Butley Neutral Fm., Suffolk	867	S4	possible
Stoneykirk, Glenluce, Wigtown.	1803	S4/hybrid	probable

Summary of beaker cremations

(Not including those Northern beakers which were found with N/NR beakers and cremations in closed finds.)

Group	Probables and possibles	Probables	Possibles
AOC	4	—	4
E	—	—	—
W/MR	1	—	1
N/MR	1	—	1
E. Ang.	—	—	—
N/NR	6	4	2
BW	6	3	3
N1	—	—	—
N2	—	—	—
N3	3	1	2
N4	1	—	1
S1	1	—	1
S2(W)	4	1	3
S2(E)	—	—	—
S3	—	—	—
S4	3	2	1
SH	—	—	—

Cremation appears to have been a burial rite employed by the Barbed-Wire and Northern/North Rhine groups. Otherwise the rite is only apparent in the final phases of the Northern and Southern beaker traditions (N4, S4), or in the westernmost fringe of the Developed Southern beakers (S2(W)): of the four cases, three are Welsh, one from Devon; the latter secondary to a Food Vessel cremation suggesting the influence responsible.

3.7. Position of the beaker relative to the skeleton in the grave

For convenience, the crouched burial is divided into four quadrants: (1) beaker in front of the skull, above knee level; (2) beaker in front of the feet, below knee level; (3) beaker behind the skull and shoulders, above the pelvis; (4) beaker behind the pelvis and feet, below pelvis level.

(M)—Male skeleton   (F)—Female skeleton
(X)—Indet. skeleton   (C)—Child skeleton

Thus 735(M)(2) represents beaker number 735 in the corpus with a male skeleton in position 2 above.

AOC
730(X)(4)
732(X)(1)
1408(X)(1)
1376(F)(3)
1215(X)(3)

E
33(M)(2)
183(F)(2)
184(F)(2)
770(F)(4)
768(F)(4)

818(M)(3)
854(F)(2)

W/MR
201(X)(2)
177(X)(1)
264(F)(1)

348(F)(2)
735(M)(2)
1076(X)(2)
1077(M)(2)
1204(M)(2)
1115(X)(2)
1081(X)(2)
1143(X)(2)
1162(M)(2)
1125(M)(1)
1036(X)(1)
1135(M)(2)
36(X)(2)
1151(X)(2)

N/MR
1496(X)(3)
354(M)(2)
772(M)(3)

N/NR
1624(X)(2)
1634(X)(1)?
1784(F)(3)
221(M)(1)
1279(F)(1)
1369(C)(1)
1310(F)(1)
1300(X)(3)
1299(M)(2)
1213(X)(2)

E. Ang.
1006(X)(2)
1371(F)(4)
1007(F)(1)

BW
28(M)(2)
992(M)(2)
1006(X)(2)
1063(M)(2)

N1/D
1523(M)(1)
1649(X)(1)?
665(F)(3)
1311(F)(1)

N2
1435(M)(4)
1436(C)(4)
1433(M)(3)
1594(M)(3)
1646(C)(3)
1635(C)(2 or 4)
1677(X)(1 or 3)
1651(X)(1 or 3)
135(F)(1 or 3)
140(X)(3)
691(F)(3)
667(X)(3)?
658(X)(3)
659(X)(1)
803(M)(1)
988(X)(1)
1073(C)(3)

1187(X)(3)
1384(X)(1)
1265(X)(4)
1366(X)(3)
1367(M)(3)
1375(X)(3)
1334(X)(2)
1402(M)(3)
1322(M)(1)
1303(M)(4)
1743(X)(1 or 3)

N3
1441(X)(2)
1463(X)(3)
1477(M)(1)
1454(X)(3)
1508(M)(3)
1470(M)(3)
1586(X)(1)
1606(M)(1 or 3)
1625(X)(1 or 3)
1631(M)(3)
1636(F)(4)
1666(M)(4)
1667(M)(3)
1710(M)(3)
1730(X)(3)
110(M)(3)
220(M)(3)
219(M)(3)
648(F)(3)
1018(F)(2)
1403(M)(3)
1370(F)(3)
1309(C)(1)
1304(X)(3)
1305(X)(2)
1306(X)(3)
1434(M)(3)

N4
1503(M)(1)
1692(M)(3)

S1
117(M)(4)
130(X)(1)
115(M)(3)
826(C)(1 or 3)
827(C)(4)
1194(M)(1)
1113(X)(4)
1395(M)(4)
1390(M)(3)
1275(X)(4)
1216(M)(1)
1352(X)(3)
1332(X)(3)
1298(M)(3)
1296(M)(3)
1210(M)(3)

S2
139(M)(3)
351(F)(1)

645(X)(4)
707(X)(3)
800(M)(1)
820(F)(2)
835(X)(3)
802(X)(4)
825(M)(1)
986(C)(1)
987(C)(1)
1103(M)(3)
1145(X)(3)
1195(X)(4)
1101(X)(4)
1078(X)(1)
1039(X)(4)
1037(X)(3)
1397(X)(4)
1374(F)(2)
1324(X)(4)
1323(F)(4)
1217(M)(3)
1351(X)(3)
1320(X)(4)
1404(M)(3)
1283(M)(3)
145(F)(1)
153(X)(1)
197(X)(3)

S3
756(C)(4)
821(M)(4)
834(M)(4)
1119(X)(4)
1164(X)(4)
1355(X)(3)
1284(C)(3)

S4
747(F)(2)
745(M)(4)
743(M)(4)
722(C)(1)
719(M)(1)
731(X)(4)
1280(C)(2)
1177(M)(1)
1373(C)(1)
1211(C)(2)

SH
165(M)(4)?
740(C)(1)
742(M)(1)
721(F)(1)
1360(X)(3)
1314(M)(3)

3.8. Summary of beaker position relative to the skeleton (based on data in Appendix 3.7)

Four main burial positions for the beaker—X—are coded 1–4 below. Entries over 20% are set in bold type.

	(1)	(2)	(3)	(4)	100%
S4	**40·0%** 4	30·0% 3	— —	30·0% 3	10
SH	**50·0%** 3	— —	**33·3%** 2	16·7% 1	6
S3	— —	— —	**28·3%** 2	**71·7%** 5	7
S2	**26·6%** 8	6·6% 2	**36·6%** 11	**30·0%** 9	30
S1	18·7% 3	— —	**50·0%** 8	**31·3%** 5	16
N4	**50·0%** 1	— —	**50·0%** 1	— —	2
N3	14·8% 4	11·1% 3	**66·6%** 18	7·4% 2	27
N2	**25·0%** 7	7·1% 2	**53·5%** 15	14·3% 4	28
N1	**75·0%** 3	— —	**25·0%** 1	— —	4
BW	— —	**100%** 4	— —	— —	4
E. Ang.	**33·3%** 1	**33·3%** 1	— —	**33·3%** 1	3
N/NR	**50·0%** 5	**30·0%** 3	20·0% 2	— —	10
N/MR	— —	**33·3%** 1	**66·6%** 2	— —	3
W/MR	**23·5%** 4	**76·5%** 13	— —	— —	17
E	— —	**57·1%** 4	14·3% 1	**28·6%** 2	7
AOC	**40·0%** 2	— —	**40·0%** 2	20·0% 1	5

(1)   (2)   (3)   (4)   100%

Position

3.9. Orientation of beaker skeletons—direction of the spine to skull axis

(M)—Male skeleton   (F)—Female skeleton
(X)—Indet. skeleton   (C)—Child skeleton

AOC
732(X) E.
730(X) N.E.
1408(X) N.
1376(F) N.W.
1215(X) N.E.

E
33(M) N.W.
183(F) S.E.

739(X) N.N.E.
768(F) S.W.
818(M) N.

W/MR
201(X) N.W.
348(F) S.W.
1076(M) N.
1077(M) N.
1204(M) N.
1115(X) N.
1081(X) E.
1145(X) N.
1162(M) N.
1151(X) N.
1125(M) E.
1036(X) N.
1150(X) N.E.
1135(M) N.
1129(M) N.

N/MR
354(M) N.
772(M) N.E.
1111(M) N.

N/NR
1624(X) W.
1634(X) W.
1784(F) N.W.
221(M) W.
1020(M) S.
1279(F) N.
1310(F) N.W.
1300(X) W.
1299(M) E.
1213(X) E.S.E.

E. Ang.
414(X) E.N.E.
1371(F) E.N.E.

BW
28(M) N.
992(M) N.E.
1063(M) S.

N1/D
1523(M) N.E.
1649(X) W.
665(F) N.W.
1311(F) N.W.

N2
1435(M) E.
1436(C) N.
1501(X) N.
1594(M) W.
1646(C) W.
1635(C) E.
1651(X) S.
1677(X) E.
1743(X) S.
140(X) N.
219(M) E.
349(F) S.

691(F) W.?
667(X) E.
658(X) E.
803(C) N.
1073(C) N.
1405(M) E.
1265(X) E.
1366(X) W.S.W.
1367(M) S.
1375(X) W.
1334(X) W.
1402(M) E.
1322(M) W.
1303(M) N.
659(X) E.

N3
1441(X) N.E.
1463(X) E.
1454(X) E.
1524(X) W.?
1586(X) N.N.E.
1599(X) E.?
1606(M) N.
1631(M) N.E.
1631(M) N.E.
1636(F) E.
1666(M) N.E.
1667(M) N.N.E.
1587(X) S.W.
1710(M) E.
1730(X) W.
1774(X) E.
110(M) N.E.
220(M) E.
648(F) W.
652(X) S.W.
1017(M) S.
1018(F) S.
1403(M) E.
1370(F) E.
1309(C) N.W.
1324(X) E.
1304(M) E.
1306(F) W.
1477(M) N.E.
1470(M) W.
1508(M) E.
1625(X) W.
1305(X) E.

N4
1478(M) N.E.
1503(M) S.E.
1692(M) N.E.

S1
117(M) W.S.W.
1194(M) N.
1395(M) E.
1390(M) E.
1275(X) S.W.
1216(M) N.E.
1352(X) N.
1332(X) W.
1298(M) W.

1296(M) N.E.
1210(M) N.N.E.
269(X) E.

S2
153(X) N.W.
139(M) N.E.
197(X) N.
351(F) S.W.
645(X) N.E.
707(X) W.
820(F) S.
800(M) W.
802(X) N.W.
1103(M) N.
1145(X) S.
1101(X) N.
1039(X) N.
1037(X) N.
1397(X) E.S.E.
1323(F) W.
1283(M) E.
1374(F) W.
1217(M) S.
1218(M) N.E.
1351(X) W.
1320(X) E.
792(X) S.
1324(X) E.

S3
278(F) S.
756(C) N.
821(M) N.
1119(X) E.
1355(X) E.N.E.
1347(X) E.
1284(C) E.

S4
747(F) N.
745(M) N.
743(M) E.
722(C) S.E.
719(M) N.W.
731(X) N.E.
1177(M) S.E.
1280(C) E.S.E.
1373(C) S.
1211(C) N.

SH
740(C) S.W.
721(F) N.E.
1360(X) N.
1314(M) N.E.
1219(M) N.E.
742(M) N.W.

3.10. Summary of beaker skeleton orientation, all groups

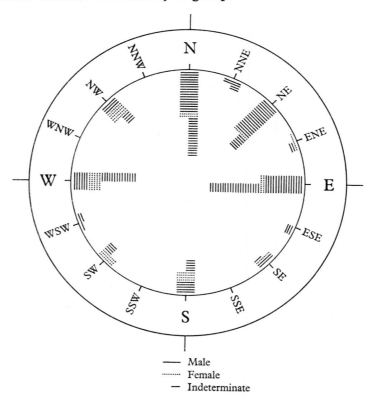

— Male
.... Female
— Indeterminate

Summary of beaker orientation, for selected groups:

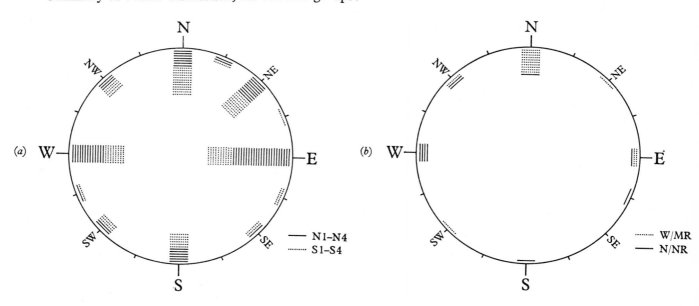

(a)

— N1–N4
.... S1–S4

(b)

.... W/MR
— N/NR

APPENDIX 4

STRATIGRAPHY

Relative stratigraphy—an abstract of sites yielding some stratigraphic information about beaker ceramics.

Relative stratigraphy

The sites in this appendix represent an attempt to collect every case of relative stratigraphies involving beaker pottery. Each site has been interpreted on its own merits, without reference to the implications of the beaker typology; thus providing an independent test for the classification. Sites on which no real stratigraphy exists have been excluded; sites where other interpretations are possible have been labelled *Uncertain* below.

This appendix is a synopsis of the full report on each beaker site, referenced by the corpus number and summarised in more detail in the typed sheets opposite each drawing in the original corpus volumes.

Under each site below, the sequence of stratigraphy and events is suggested by the numeration, 1. being the earliest. When under a single phase, or number, there are several entries, then the stratigraphy on the site is such that these events cannot be further separated; they take place after the preceding and before the succeeding phases but not necessarily contemporarily within the phase. Unless further qualified, the beakers mentioned were, or probably were, from inhumation burials.

12 Berks.   Abingdon Camp:
1. Causeway Camp with Abingdon Ware in ditch filling
2. Indet. beaker sherd, 7 ft above ditch bottom
Uncertain

28–9 Berks.   Lambourne 17:
1. BW, no. 28
2. Inhumation, flint dagger, strike-a-light and iron ore nodule
N2, no. 29

133 Derby.   Hartington, Parcelly Hay:
1. Indet. beaker, no. 133 (lost)
2. Inhumation, bronze three-rivet dagger and stone battle-axe

134 Derby.   Kenslow, Knoll Fm.:
1. N2, no. 134
2. Inhumation, bronze three-rivet dagger
Uncertain

145–8 Derby.   Rusden Low:
1. E, no. 146
N/NR?, no. 147, stacked and replaced by:
2. S2(W), no. 145 and S2(W)? no. 148
Uncertain

150–1 Derby.   Swarkeston:
1. Pre-barrow phase, Western Neolithic sherds
2. Pre-barrow phase, S2(?) and FP beaker domestic site, nos. 150–1; Bowl Food Vessel sherds same level
3. Barrow constructed for oak coffin burial with flint knife, Yorkshire Food Vessel types
4. Barrow enlarged for three cremations in Collared Urns

153–4 Derby.   Youlgrave, Bee Low:
1. N2, no. 154
2. S2(W), no. 153
Uncertain

155 Devon   Broad Down, Honiton:
1. Dorset Vase Food Vessel and cremation
2. S2(W)?, no. 155 and cremation

164–7 Dorset   Bincombe Down (11):
1. Beaker Bowl (S2?), no. 164
2. SH4(C), no. 165
Undec. Dorset Ware, no. 166
Undec. Dorset Ware, no. 167

180 Dorset   Frampton (4):
1. Undec. Dorset Ware, no. 180
2. 2 Collared Urns with pigmy cups
2 Biconical Urns

181 Dorset   Frampton (5):
1. S2(W), no. 181
2. Dorset Vase Food Vessel
3. Dorset Vase Food Vessel and 6 faience beads *(continued)*

Enlarged Vase Food Vessel
Collared Urn

183–6 Dorset Thickthorn long barrow (163*a*):
1. Windmill Hill Ware and long barrow erection
2. E, no. 183
   E, no. 184
FN and Indet. sherds, nos. 185–6 in ditch middle silt with Mortlake Ware sherds

209–12 Dorset Winterbourne St Martin; Maiden Castle:
1. Hembury and Windmill Hill Wares, Causeway Camp and primary silt
2. Cursus barrow construction
3. AOC and FN, nos. 209–10
   Mortlake Ware (e.g. site 'L')
   S2(?) and FP, nos. 211–12
   Grooved Ware

213–14 Dorset Winterbourne St Martin (46)
1. H(DO), no. 213, together with Undec. Dorset Ware, no. 214
2. Wessex II bronze dagger, Incense Cup and cremation

216–17 Dorset Winterbourne St Martin (32)
1. E, no. 217
2. FP, no. 216
Uncertain

221 Durham Hasting Hill:
1. N/NR-FN, no. 221
2. Yorkshire Vase Food Vessels
   Cordoned Urns
   Incense Cup and Collared Urns

264–7 Essex Thorpe Hall:
1. W/MR, no. 264
2. N2(L), no. 265
   S1, no. 266
   S1, no. 267

325–7 Hants. Holdenhurst:
1. Windmill Hill Ware and long barrow erection
2. Mortlake Ware in the middle silting in ditch
3. S2(W) and FP, nos. 325–7, higher than 2

339 Hants. Nutbane, Penton Grafton:
1. Windmill Hill Ware and long barrow erection
2. W/MR, no. 339, in latest ditch silt

349 Hants. Stockbridge Down 1:
1. N2, no. 349
2. Collared Urn, cremation, jet and faience beads, including annular faience type, bronze awl of tanged Wessex type

481–2 Lincs. Skendleby, Giants Hill:
1. Windmill Hill Ware and long barrow erection
   AOC, no. 481, sealed in final filling
2. Jet belt-slide of Peterborough type, in ditch middle silt (E/F)
3. S2(W), no. 482, around hearth in final silt

505 Norfolk Barton Bendish:
1. E. Ang., no. 505
2. Cremation (?) with two-rivet bronze dagger
Uncertain

643–6 Northants. Peterborough, Fengate No. 1:
1. Mortlake Ware
2. FP, no. 643
   S2(E), nos. 643–5
   S3(E), no. 646

659 Northumb. Bamburgh 197:
1. N2, no. 659
2. Cordoned and Encrusted Urn, cremation

730–1 Oxford. Cassington Site B:
1. AOC, no. 730
2. S4, no. 731

770–1 Oxford. Stanton Harcourt:
1. AOC, no. 771
2. E, no. 770
Uncertain

772 Oxford. Stanton Harcourt, Linch Hill:
1. Peterborough (?) burial with jet belt-slide and polished flint knife
2. N/MR, no. 772, with bone belt ring, etc.

784 Somerset Burrington T.5:
1. BW, no. 784, and cremation (?)
2. Food Vessel and Collared Urn
Uncertain

792 Somerset Charmy Down 1:
1. S2(E)?, no. 792 with Wessex I bead and bronze knife
2. Enlarged Food Vessel and cremation
Uncertain

826–8 Staffs. Deepdale, Ramscroft:
1. S1, no. 826
   S1, no. 827
2. S3(E), no. 828
3. Cremation, unaccompanied
   Inhumation and four-rivet bronze dagger

834 Staffs. Swinscoe, Top Low:
1. S3(E), no. 834
2. Collared Urn, cremation and bone spatula

858–9 Suffolk

Brantham Hall, Ring-Ditch:
1. E. Ang., no. 858
2. E. Ang., no. 859

1009–11 Sussex

Whitehawk:
1. Whitehawk and Ebbsfleet Ware, erection of Causewayed Camp, primary silting
2. E, no. 1009, in final ditch silting
   FN, no. 1010
   Undec. E., no. 1011

1018–20 Westmorland

Clifton, Penrith:
1. N/NR, no. 1020, in association with:
   N2, no. 1019, in one cist
2. N3, no. 1018, in second cist
Uncertain

1034–8 Wilts.

Amesbury (51)
1. W/MR, no. 1036
2. W/MR, no. 1038
3. S2(W), no. 1034
4. Indet., no. 1035 (lost)
5. S2(E), no. 1037
Uncertain

1039–40 Wilts.

Amesbury (54)
1. S2(W), no. 1039
2. Incense Cup (?) and 'many' faience beads

1042 Wilts.

Amesbury (56)
1. Inhumation with three-rivet bronze dagger and polished hammerstone
2. Beaker no. 1042 (lost)

1046 Wilts.

Amesbury, Fargo Plantation:
1. S2(W), no. 1046
2. Dorset Vase Food Vessel and cremation
Uncertain, 1 and 2 possibly contemporary

1053–4 Wilts.

Avebury Ditch:
1. Windmill Hill and Mortlake Ware, under bank and in primary silt of encircling henge
2. Middle silt of main ditch yielded Mortlake Ware
   E?, no. 1053
   FN, no. 1054

1055–60 Wilts.

Avebury, Windmill Hill:
1. Windmill Hill Ware pre-Causewayed Camp and in primary silt. C14 2850 ± 150 B.C.
2. Windmill Hill and Ebbsfleet Ware in middle silt of ditches
3. AOC, no. 1056, mixed, upper silt included:
   E, no. 1057, all types, no finer stratification
   Mortlake Ware
   FP, no. 1058

S2(W), no. 1059
SH4(C), no. 1060
Fengate and Grooved Ware, C14 1540 ± 150 B.C.
4. Primary Collared Urn, and cremation

1063–4 Wilts.

Avebury, The Sanctuary, Overton Hill:
1. Phase I, timber circles with Mortlake Ware in sockets
2. Phase II, stone circle erected simultaneously with the Avebury Avenue and Avebury stone circles
   AOC, no. 1064, in stone sockets, therefore contemporary or earlier than phase II
   E, no. 1070, in Avenue stone hole
3. Post-phase II
   BW, no. 1063, against stone 14, with burial
   N2, no. 1071, against stone 25b in Avenue

1094–5 Wilts.

Collingbourne Kingston III:
1. S2(?) and FP, nos. 1094–5, domestic site pre-barrow erection
2. Barrow construction with:
   2 Collared Urns and 2 Miniature Urns, with faience, jet and amber beads, cremations

1096–8 Wilts.

Downton, Pit 56:
1. Mortlake Ware, earlier than or contemporary with:
2. AOC, no. 1096
   FN, no. 1097
   Indet., no. 1098
Uncertain

1101 Wilts.

Durrington (36):
1. S2(W), no. 1101
2. Collared Urn, Incense Cup and cremation

1102 Wilts.

Durrington Walls, barrow:
1. W/MR(?)—Undec., no. 1102
2. Grooved Ware domestic debris

1103 Wilts.

Durrington, Woodhenge I:
1. S2(E), no. 1103
2. Grooved Ware domestic debris
Uncertain

1104–7 Wilts.

Durrington, Woodhenge:
1. Grooved Ware primary, under henge bank, in primary silt
2. AOC, no. 1107, on surface and high in silt of timber post holes
   W/MR, no. 1104, found with the remaining beakers
   W/MR? no. 1105
   E, no. 1106, in the middle ditch silt
Uncertain

1111–12 Wilts. Farleigh Wick:
1. W/MR?, no. 1111
2. N/MR, no. 1112, with gold
disc, etc.
Uncertain

1114 Wilts. Figheldean (25):
1. FP, no. 1114
2. Food Vessel (lost) and inhumations
3. Cremations, two bronze daggers
(lost) and boars' tusks
Uncertain

1131 Wilts. Overton G(6B):
1. S2(W), no. 1131
2. Primary Collared Urn, cremation
with Wessex I bead
Uncertain

1140–1 Wilts. Shrewton (5K):
1. N2, no. 1140
2. S4, no. 1141

1162–3 Wilts. Wilsford (2b):
1. Indet. (lost), no. 1163
2. W/MR, no. 1162

1164 Wilts. Wilsford (34)
1. Long Barrow
2. S3(W), no. 1164

1166–70 Wilts. Wilsford (51):
1. Ebbsfleet and Mortlake Wares
in pit
2. N/MR, no. 1169, from central
grave
Indet., no. 1170, from central
grave
3. FP, no. 1168, from central grave
Grooved Ware in silted ditch,
bucket vessel
Uncertain

1171 Wilts. Wilsford (52):
1. W/MR, no. 1171
2. Grooved Ware and cremation
3. FP, no. 1172
4. Cremation
Uncertain (2 possibly primary)

1173–6 Wilts. Wilsford (54):
1. AOC, no. 1174
E, no. 1173
W/MR, no. 1175, all tipped out
by:
2. Bluestone battle-axe and three-
rivet bronze dagger
Uncertain

1187–8 Wilts. Winterbourne Monkton (10):
1. N2, no. 1187
2. S3(W), no. 1188

1190 Wilts. Winterbourne Stoke (10):
1. S1, no. 1190
2. Collared Urn and cremation

1194 Wilts. Winterbourne Stoke (35):
1. Inhumation with bronze dagger
(lost) and polished hammerstone
2. S1, no. 1194

1204 Wilts. Winterslow Hut (11):
1. W/MR, no. 1204
2. Wessex Biconical Urn, cremation
and amber beads, Wessex bronze
awl, bronze razor

1211 Yorks. Acklam Wold 204:
1. Yorkshire Vase Food Vessel,
inhumation
2. S4, no. 1211, inhumation
Yorkshire Vase Food Vessel,
plano-convex flint knife, cremation
Uncertain

1212–14 Yorks. Aldro 54:
1. N2, no. 1212
2. N/NR, no. 1213
3. S3(E), no. 1214
4. Oak coffin burial (?)

1215–20 Yorks. Aldro 116:
1. AOC, no. 1215
2. S1, no. 1216
S2(W), no. 1217
S2(W), no. 1218
SH3(C), no. 1219
3. Yorkshire Vase Food Vessel,
with lid

1246–8 Yorks. Broxa Moor 4:
1. W/MR, no. 1247
W/MR, no. 1248, thrown out by:
2. N/NR, no. 1246, cremation and
jet button
Uncertain

1265 Yorks. Driffield:
1. N2(L), no. 1265
2. Yorkshire Vase Food Vessel,
inhumation and bone toggle

1275 Yorks. Ferry Friston 161:
1. S1, no. 1275
2. 2 Yorkshire Vase Food Vessels
and plano-convex flint knife
3. Collared Urns and cremations

1276–8 Yorks. Flamborough Head:
1. Heslerton and Ebbsfleet Ware
2. AOC, no. 1278, mixed together
with:
FN, no. 1277
E, no. 1276

1280 Yorks. Folkton 242:
1. S4, no. 1280
2. 2 Yorkshire Vase Food Vessels
with inhumations

1283–4 Yorks. Ganton 21:
1. Yorkshire Vase Food Vessel and
inhumations

2. S2(W), no. 1283
   S3(E), no. 1284
   4 Yorkshire Vase Food Vessels
   with inhumations and cremations
   Uncertain

1291–3 Yorks.   Garrowby Wold 104:
1. N3, no. 1291, associated with:
   N3, no. 1292
2. S2(W), no. 1293
3. Handled Food Vessel and plano-
convex flint knife

1298 Yorks.   Garton Slack 75:
1. S1, no. 1298
2. Yorkshire Vase Food Vessel,
inhumation and cremation, jet disc
bead necklace and toggle, bronze
awl
3. Yorkshire Vase Food Vessel and
cremation
4. 2 Yorkshire Vase Food Vessels,
one cremation, one inhumation

1299 Yorks.   Garton Slack 80:
1. N/NR, no. 1299, and inhumation
2. Barrow and cremation trench
with cremations, no associations but
Yorkshire Neolithic parallels, e.g.
no. 1300

1300 Yorks.   Garton Slack 81:
1. Neolithic Cremation trench,
cremations and Grimston Ware
sherds
2. N/NR, no. 1300, and inhumation
Indet., no. 1301
3. Inhumation with jet toggle

1304–6 Yorks.   Garton Slack 163:
1. N3, no. 1304
   N3(L), no. 1305, in actual
association with:
   N3, no. 1306

1307 Yorks.   Garton Slack, Craike Hill:
1. Grimston and Heslerton Ware
with hearth
2. Ebbsfleet and Mortlake Ware
from a pit, contemporary or earlier
than:
   E, no. 1307
Uncertain

1309–11 Yorks.   Goodmanham 99:
1. N/NR, no. 1311
   N1/D, no. 1310
2. N3, no. 1309

1320–1 Yorks.   Hanging Grimston 56:
1. N/MR, no. 1321
   S2(E), no. 1320
2. Collared Urn and cremation
Uncertain

1322–4 Yorks.   Hanging Grimston 55:
1. N2, no. 1322
2. S2(E), no. 1323
3. S2(W), no. 1324

1328 Yorks.   Heslerton 5:
1. S1, no. 1328, thrown out of
grave by:
2. Yorkshire Vase Food Vessel and
inhumation
Uncertain

1332–3 Yorks.   Huggate Wold 216:
1. S1, no. 1332
2. FP, no. 1333
3. Collared Urn, cremation, plano-
convex flint knife, jet toggle

1334–5 Yorks.   Huggate and Warterwold 254:
1. Cremation trench (?) with
Grimston Ware
2. N2, no. 1334, in same grave as:
   N2, no. 1335 (?)
Uncertain

1351–4 Yorks.   Painsthorpe Wold 4:
1. S1, no. 1351
   S2(W), no. 1352
2. S2(W), no. 1354
   FP, no. 1353
3. 2 Yorkshire Vase Food Vessels,
one with cremation, one inhumation

1355 Yorks.   Painsthorpe Wold 83:
1. Yorkshire Vase Food Vessel and
cremation
2. Inhumation and plano-convex
flint knife
   S3(W), no. 1355, and inhumation
3. Collared Urn and cremation
Uncertain

1366 Yorks.   Rudstone 61:
1. Neolithic cremation area (?) with
Grimston Ware and leaf flint
arrowheads
2. N2, no. 1366
   Male inhumation and jet pulley-
ring and button

1367–72 Yorks.   Rudstone 62:
1. N/NR, no. 1369, and cremation
   N2, no. 1367, and inhumation
   N2, no. 1368, and cremation
2. N3(L), no. 1370, and inhumation
3. S2(W), no. 1372, and inhumation, scattered by:
4. E. Ang.?, no. 1371, inhumation
and 2 bronze awls, probably a Food
Vessel/beaker hybrid convergent to
E. Ang. form

1374–5 Yorks.   Rudstone 66:
1. N2, no. 1375
2. S2(E), no. 1374

1376–8 Yorks.

Rudstone 67:
1. AOC, no. 1376
2. W/MR, no. 1378
   N/NR, no. 1377, in uncertain
   relationship
3. 4 Yorkshire Vase Food Vessels
   with inhumations

1384 Yorks.

Sherburn 7:
1. Neolithic barrow over com-
   munal burials with Grimston and
   Heslerton Ware
2. N2, no. 1384

1395–6 Yorks.

Thornton Dale:
1. Mortlake Ware
   N2, no. 1396
2. S1, no. 1395

1397–8 Yorks.

Thwing 60:
1. Indet., no. 1398 (S?)
2. Inhumation with jet button and
   pulley-ring, the latter radially and
   the former with cruciform incised
   design S2(E), no. 1397, and another
   inhumation

1400–1 Yorks.

Towthorpe 21:
1. S2(W), no. 1400
2. S2(W), no. 1401, scattered by:
3. Food Vessel and inhumation
   Incense Cup (?) and cremation

1403–4 Yorks.

Weaverthorpe 42:
1. Neolithic barrow and multiple
   inhumations with Grimston and
   Heslerton Ware
2. N3, no. 1403
   S2(W), no. 1404

1405 Yorks.

Weaverthorpe 297:
1. N2, no. 1405
2. Yorkshire Vase Food Vessel,
   inhumation and 2 plano-convex
   flint knives

1408 Yorks.

Willerby 235:
1. 2 Unaccompanied inhumations
   in grave cut through a burnt area
2. Another, as above
3. AOC, no. 1408, this beaker
   approaches corded food vessel
   forms
   In unknown relationship to the
   above sequence was a hoard of 3
   decorated and 1 undecorated flat
   bronze axes, buried in upper
   mound

1518 Angus

Kirkbuddo, Gallows Hill:
1. N2, no. 1518
2. Food Vessel
Uncertain

1533 Argyll.

Campbeltown:
1. Clyde-Carlingford long cairn

2. N3, no. 1533
   2 Cordoned Food Vessels
   1 Cordoned Urn, cremation and
   bronze fragment

1541 Argyll.

Cragabus Cists, Islay:
1. Clyde-Carlingford long cairn,
   inhumations and Western Neolithic
   Ware
2. AOC, no. 1541
   Undec., no. 1541.1

1551 Argyll.

Poltalloch, Largie:
1. Clyde-Carlingford long cairn,
   cremations and Beacharra Ware
2. AOC, no. 1548
   E, no. 1550 (cardium), sherds of
   these two beakers may be the ones
   in original report
   N/MR, no. 1551

1582–4 Banff.

Forglen:
1. AOC, no. 1582
2. N1/D, no. 1583
3. N2, no. 1584

1590 Berwick.

Chirnside, Edington Mill:
1. N2, no. 1590, disturbed by:
2. Vase Food Vessel
Uncertain

1592–3 Berwick.

Cockburnspath, Hoprig:
1. N/NR, no. 1593, in same cist as:
   N2, no. 1592
2. Inhumation with flint scraper,
   strike-a-light and iron ore nodule
   2 peripheral cremations in
   inverted enlarged Food Vessels

1601–2 Bute

Giant's Graves, Arran:
1. Clyde-Carlingford long cairn,
   with cremations and Western
   Neolithic Ware
2. Indet., no. 1601 and
   N2?, no. 1602

1603–4 Bute

Glecknabae:
1. Clyde-Carlingford long cairn,
   with cremations and Western
   Neolithic Ware
2. E, no. 1603 together with:
   FN, no. 1604

1611–12 Caithness

Lower Dounreay:
1. Horned long cairn with inhumations, and Western Neolithic
   Ware
2. AOC, no. 1611, together with:
   Undec., no. 1612
3. Indet., no. 1612.1 (N2?)

1613 Caithness

Tulach an T'sionnaich:
1. Horned long cairn, inhumations
   and a cremation
2. Indet., no. 1613

1649–50 Fife.
Collessie:
1. N1/D, no. 1649
2. N2, no. 1650
3. Cremation with gold pommeled, riveted bronze dagger

1668 Inverness.
North Uist, Clettraval:
1. Clyde-Carlingford long cairn, with cremations and Beacharra and Unstan Ware
2. Neolithic vessels as above, amidst roof-fall and beaker sherds: N/NR (cardium), no. 1668
3 Sterile and Iron Age strata

1669 Inverness.
North Uist, Geirsclett:
1. Clyde-Carlingford long cairn
2. AOC, no. 1669

1670 Inverness.
North Uist, Langass Barp:
1. Passage Grave, with cremations
2. Indet., no. 1670 (N4?)

1671 Inverness.
North Uist, Unival:
1. Passage Grave/long cairn hybrid Unstan Ware and Rinyo I bowl, inhumations
2. Over 12 in. sterile silt and roof-fall
3. Undec., no. 1671 (Undec. E), and frags. of small bowl

1672 Inverness.
Skye, Kilmarie:
1. Clyde-Carlingford long cairn
2. S3(E), no. 1672

1675 Inverness.
Skye, Rudh'an Dunain:
1. Passage Grave, with Western Neolithic Ware
2. 2 ft of sterile roof-fall
3. N4, no. 1675

1694 Kirkcud.
Cairnholy I:
1. Clyde-Carlingford long cairn, with Western Neolithic Ware
2. E, no. 1694
Peterborough Ware
3. Food Vessel burial

1695–6 Kirkcud.
Cairnholy II:
1. Clyde-Carlingford long cairn, with Western Neolithic Ware
2. AOC, no. 1695
E, no. 1696
E?, no. 1696.1
FN, no. 1696.2

1701 Lanark.
Carnwath, Wester Yird Houses:
1. Food Vessel and cist with decorated capstone
2. N2(L)?, no. 1701
Uncertain

1734 Orkney
Rousay, Rinyo:
1. Rinyo I—Neolithic village of stone houses, with flat base, grooved and cordoned pottery

('B and C' wares), some Unstan sherds
2. Rinyo II—continued rebuilding and gradual dominance of coarse, undecorated bucket vases and plastic cordoned ware
3. N3, no. 1734 beaker buried in closing phases of Rinyo II; 6 in above doorway of house 'A', itself overlying house 'E', but earlier than house 'C' overlying the beaker

1750–6 Ross.
Kilcoy, West Cairn:
1. Horned long cairn, charcoal deposits and cremations
2. Sterile layer of 6–9 in. clean sand
3. AOC, no. 1750
AOC, no. 1751
AOC, no. 1752
E, no. 1753
AOC, no. 1754
FN, no. 1755
4. N2, no. 1756, secondary to the main beaker deposit, separated by roof-fall

1757–9 Ross.
Kilcoy, Cairn Glas
1. Horned long cairn, cremation and flint leaf arrowhead
2. E, no. 1757
FN, no. 1758
Indet., no. 1759

1778 Shetland
Stanydale, Sandsting:
1. AOC?, no. 1778, sherds from packing at bottom of main roof post hole
2. Horned, heel-shaped stone house with internal buttresses, clearly related to the same cairn forms, pottery allied to Rinyo I
Uncertain

1786 Sutherland.
Embo:
1. AOC, no. 1786.2
Indet, no. 1786.1
2. Food Vessel, shale beads and flint knife

1790–3 W. Lothian
Cairnpapple Circle:
1. Semi-circle of 7 stone-holes with cremations, bone pins, Western Neolithic Ware
2. Henge with large stone circle, enclosed by ditch and external bank, 2 opposed entrances
3. N/NR, no. 1790, buried against outer face of stone 8, in phase II circle
4. N2(L), no. 1791 in same grave with:
N2(L), no. 1792, the grave and cairn now destroying the centre of the circle
Indet., no. 1793 from henge ditch silt (*continued*)

5. Food Vessel inhumation, cairn enlarged
6. Collared Urn cremations, cairn enlarged
Uncertain

1799–1801 Wigtown. Knockdoon, Glenluce Sands:
1. AOC, no. 1799, in association with:
AOC, no. 1800, both in wooden cist of oak and oak bark buried in sand. Also in cist were:
E, no. 1801 in sherds Peterborough Ware (possibly giant FN)
Uncertain

1822 Anglesey Bedd Bronwen, Llanbabo:
1. S3(W), no. 1822
2. Collared Urn and cremation

1827 Anglesey Pant-y-Saer:
1. Megalithic tomb (passage grave?)
2. N3, no. 1827, in inserted cist

1828 Anglesey Pentraeth, Merddyn-Gwyn:
1. FP, no. 1828, with three-rivet bronze dagger, jet button, etc.
2. Bowl Food Vessel, false-relief decorated
Enlarged Food Vessel, cremation and bone pommel
2 Collared Urns and cremations

1829–30 Anglesey Porth Dafarch, Holyhead:
1. S2(W), no. 1829
Indet., no. 1830
2. Collared Urns
Incense Cups and cremations

1832 Anglesey Ty-Newydd, Llanfaelog:
1. Passage grave
2. AOC?, no. 1832

1835 Brecknock. Llanigon, Pen-y-Wyrlod
1. Severn-Cotswold long barrow
2. FN, no. 1835

1840 Brecknock. Talgarth, Ty-Isaf:
1. Megalithic tomb in long cairn, inhumations and Western Neolithic Ware
2. Indet., no. 1840

1851 Denbigh. Capel Garmon:
1. Megalithic tomb in long cairn, inhumations and Western Neolithic Ware
2. Indet., no. 1851

1853 Denbigh. Plas Heaton, Henllan:
1. FP, no. 1853
2. Collared Urn and cremation

1860–3 Glamorgan. Merthyr Mawr, Riley's Tumulus:
1. Primary cist and barrow, inhumations but no associations
2. S3(E), no. 1860
S3(E), no. 1861
S3(E)?, no. 1862
Indet., no. 1863 (lost)

1867 Glamorgan. Sutton, Llandow:
1. N/MR, no. 1867
2. Incense Cup, bronze dagger, bone bead
3. Collared Urns and cremations

1868 Glamorgan. Tinkinswood, St Nicholas:
1. Severn-Cotswold long barrow, inhumations and Western Neolithic Ware
2. Beaker Bowl(?), no. 1868

1880 Pembroke. Castlemartin, Linney Burrows:
1. S4/hybrid, no. 1880, almost Food Vessel in form
2. Collared Urn and cremation

1882 Pembroke. Talbenny, South Hill:
1. N/MR, no. 1882, barrow with stake circle and stone revetment
2. 2 Collared Urns, cremations
Incense Cup and bronze dagger

1. All-Over-Cord beaker from Bathgate, W. Lothian, no. 1788. The inset shows smudged area redecorated before firing with a point-tooth comb (fig. 2). Beaker height, 14 cms

2. European Bell beaker from Cholsey, Berks., no. 22 (fig. 87). Beaker height, 16 cms

3. Wessex/Middle Rhine beaker from Sewell, Totternhoe, Beds. (see Note 57), from a male burial with bracer, bone belt toggle, and European spiral-top 8 % tin bronze pin; a new find (1968). Restored beaker height, 18 cms

4. Barbed-Wire beaker from Lambourne, Berks., no. 28 (fig. 352). Beaker height, 14·5 cms

5. Primary Northern British beaker from Goodmanham, Yorks., no. 1311 (fig. 303). Beaker height, 17 cms

6. Late Southern British beaker probably from Eriswell, Suffolk, no. 877 (fig. 941). Beaker height, 19 cms

7. Above: Late Southern British handled beaker from Fordham, Cambs., no. 71 (fig. 1061). Beaker height, 13 cms.
Below: Developed or Late Southern British handled beaker from Bottisham, Cambs., no. 48 (fig. 1057). Beaker height,
16·5 cms. Compare these vessels and their designs with those of wooden vessels on Plate 8

8. Wooden handled vessels from the Kasai district of the Congo. Vessel heights: above, 13 cms; below, 15 cms

APPENDIX 5

MATRIX ANALYSIS AND BRITISH BEAKERS

1. Histograms of the five basic beaker shape ratios and their breakdown into ranges; 2. Key to the thirty-nine variable traits sorted in the matrix; 3. The unsorted matrix; 4. The sorted matrix; 5. Interpretation of the sorted matrix and key to groups; 6. Calculation of the range of shape of the groups interpreted from the sorted matrix; 7. Diagrammatic representation of the beaker groups suggested by the matrix pattern; 8. A note on the computer programs written in connection with the matrix analysis of archaeological material by Dr J. Grant; 9. Short bibliography of matrix analysis and related techniques.

5.1. Histograms of the five basic beaker shape ratios and their breakdown into ranges

In the attempt to express the variations in beaker shape proportions as a series of ranges or multistate traits, the five main proportion ratios were plotted for the sample of 760 complete or restorable English and Scottish beakers. The resulting histograms of these beaker proportions can be found in the sequence of five graphs below.

The histograms were prepared for the: rim/waist diameter ratio (see Appendix 1.1); belly/waist diameter ratio; foot/waist diameter ratio; rim height/waist height ratio; rim height/waist diameter ratio. All the measurements are diameters apart from the heights, all of which were measured from the base upwards.

When the histograms had been plotted, the next step was to break the total range of each proportion ratio into sensible sub-ranges. In this way, given beakers could be said to fall within this or that particular range which could then be treated as a matrix attribute in the normal way (Appendix 5.2). This process of isolating these minor ranges proceeded by examining the histogram and then approximately isolating the 'peaks' with their standard deviations, in the hope of picking up submerged populations. The resulting ranges are marked on the histograms that follow by thick lines, the range then being numbered for use as a trait in the matrix. These ranges are defined in Appendix 5.2 and divide rim/waist diameter ratio into traits 1, 2, 3; belly/waist diameter ratio into traits 4, 5, 6; foot/waist diameter ratio into traits 7, 8, 9; rim height/waist height ratio into traits 10, 11, 12, 32; rim height/waist diameter ratio into traits 37, 38, 39.

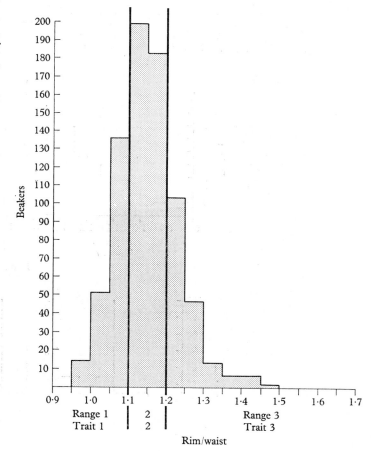

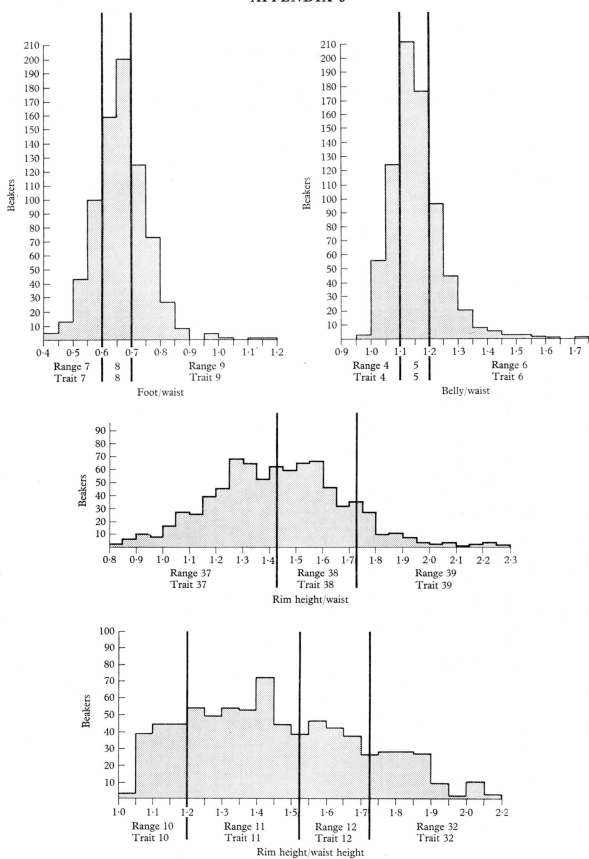

Beakers

Range 7   8   Range 9
Trait 7   8   Trait 9

Foot/waist

Beakers

Range 4   5   Range 6
Trait 4   5   Trait 6

Belly/waist

Beakers

Range 37   Range 38   Range 39
Trait 37   Trait 38   Trait 39

Rim height/waist

Beakers

Range 10   Range 11   Range 12   Range 32
Trait 10   Trait 11   Trait 12   Trait 32

Rim height/waist height

5.2. Key to the thirty-nine variable traits sorted in the matrix

This key and the matrix details that follow are a slightly more extensive account of the experiment described in Clarke (1962). The thirty-nine variables, arbitrarily selected in the attempt to code beaker characteristics, are as follows (the irregular trait numeration is due to changes made as the work proceeded):

Shape and size

Trait no.
1. Rim/waist diameter ratio, range 0·90–1·10
2. Rim/waist diameter ratio, range 1·10–1·20
3. Rim/waist diameter ratio, range 1·20–1·40 plus
4. Belly/waist diameter ratio, range 0·90–1·10
5. Belly/waist diameter ratio, range 1·10–1·20
6. Belly/waist diameter ratio, range 1·20–1·50 plus
7. Foot/waist diameter ratio, range 0·40–0·60
8. Foot/waist diameter ratio, range 0·60–0·70
9. Foot/waist diameter ratio, range 0·70–0·90 plus
10. Rim height/waist height ratio, range 1·00–1·20
11. Rim height/waist height ratio, range 1·20–1·52
12. Rim height/waist height ratio, range 1·52–1·72
32. Rim height/waist height ratio, range 1·72–2·00 plus
13. Extremely recurved, or rolled-over rim
14. Externally straight/concave neck and rim
15. Externally straight/convex neck and rim
33. Stand-ring base
34. Dished base
35. Squeezed-out foot
36. Prominent internal boss within the base
37. Rim height/waist diameter, range 0·80–1·42
38. Rim height/waist diameter, range 1·42–1·72
39. Rim height/waist diameter, range 1·72–2·35 plus

Position of decoration, i.e. style

Trait no.
16. Style *o*, Fig. II, all-over decoration, no zones
17. Style *a*, Fig. II, multiple equal-width zones
18. Style *b*, Fig. II, broad zones, often paired/trebled narrow zones
19. Style *c*, Fig. II, fully contracted zones, sometimes with filling bridging the zones
20. Style *d*, Fig. II, filled neck area, belly alternately zoned
21. Style *e*, Fig. II, filled neck area, median zone, filled belly area

Decorative motifs

Trait no.
22. Motif Group 2—fringe decoration pendant from the zones
23. Motif Group 3—complex hatching between fringes
26. Motif Group 4—positive/negative contrast designs
25. Motif Group 5—panels or metopes
24. All-over ribbed and grooved neck
27. Internal rim decoration
28. Decoration on the rim surface
29. Cord impressed decoration
30. Barbed-Wire, thread-wound stamp impressions
31. Finger-pinched rustication

Total number of traits—39.

Total trait frequency of occurrence (i.e. the total occurrence of each trait in the sample of 760 complete or restorable vessels)

Trait no.	Occurrences	Trait no.	Occurrences
1	206	20	155
2	389	21	106
3	167	22	190
4	192	23	351
5	392	24	105
6	176	25	64
7	169	26	134
8	360	27	28
9	231	28	60
10	137	29	37
11	346	30	18
12	151	31	49
13	124	32	127
14	225	33	43
15	410	34	298
16	132	35	147
17	39	36	156
18	185	37	310
19	135	38	329
		39	121

The sample used

This experiment was carried out on 760 complete or completely restorable beakers from England and Scotland, corpus nos. 1–1821, excluding the fragmentary examples.

Procedure

The procedure was that outlined in Clarke (1962). The 760 beakers were coded for the 39 traits above, describing their shape, style and decoration. The computer EDSAC II then calculated the cross-correlation of each trait with every other trait and this was printed out in the unsorted matrix in Appendix 5.3 (also Clarke (1962), 376, Fig. 3).

A program for the data was devised by Dr J. Grant with advice from Dr R. Needham, Dr Wheeler and Mr W. Easterbrook, of the Mathematical Laboratory, Cambridge. The aim of this program was to sort the data in such a manner as to best isolate clumps of characteristics occurring frequently and simultaneously search for the underlying chronological pattern predicted by Brainerd and Robinson (1951). The suggested program is outlined in Appendix 5.8.

The beaker data was then re-sorted many times employing the new program. The resulting sorted matrix is printed out in Appendix 5.4. Minor modifications and corrections to printing errors present in the original publication are dealt with below.

Modifications

In the matrices that follow, the two kinds of zero have been distinguished—the 'significant' zero where the two traits could occur together but never do so, is noted; the 'false' zero where the two traits are mutually exclusive, e.g. parts of the same shape range, has been filled in in black.

More accurate calculations have very slightly modified the range of shape proportions as shown in the diagram in Appendix 5.7.

More recent analyses of the beaker data

These original experiments in the analysis of the data were carried out between 1960–3 using the numerical frequencies of the joint occurrences of the pairs of beaker attributes in the matrices (Appendix 1.5 and Appendices 5.3, 5.4). With the publication of Sokal and Sneath's *Principles of Numerical Taxonomy* (1963), a number of more sophisticated statistical procedures for multifactorial analysis were made available. Therefore, since the completion of this initial series of analyses a second series of experiments has been nearly completed, 1963–8, using the more powerful techniques now widely available for the first time.

The recent series of analyses have included a multidimensional cluster analysis clustering actual vessels into groups, product–moment correlation matrices between the attributes, and multiple factor analysis. Besides a more accurate analysis of the data, the recent series of tests have been designed to compare and contrast the results achieved by the analysis of a single set of data by several different techniques—each with its own most effective domain. It is hoped to publish this recent set of experiments as a separate monograph as soon as the series is completed. Nevertheless, it has still seemed desirable to publish more fully the original background of the early matrix analyses, however primitive these may now seem. At least, perhaps, they may now provide some simple data for analysis by students taking practical courses in computing and analytical archaeology.

5.3. The unsorted matrix, showing the frequency correlation of traits in British beaker pottery. (For key to thirty-nine traits, see Appendix 5.2.)

	1	2	3	4	5	6	7	8	9	10	11	12	13	14	15	16	17	18	19	20	21	22	23	24	25	26	27	28	29	30	31	32	33	34	35	36	37	38	39
1		•	•	79	85	42	53	101	52	84	44	41	80	25	101	63	8	49	13	34	38	26	60	14	13	46	2	13	7	8	22	37	14	67	45	35	106	79	21
2	•		•	84	224	81	87	189	113	50	223	64	44	138	206	57	18	101	86	80	45	119	204	62	30	57	16	28	19	8	23	53	24	151	86	85	160	173	56
3	•	•		29	85	53	29	71	67	3	81	46	0	62	105	12	13	36	37	41	23	46	87	29	21	31	10	19	11	2	4	37	5	81	17	36	44	78	45
4	79	84	29		•	•	58	96	38	24	83	38	20	74	97	60	10	35	24	22	40	32	65	13	11	35	7	14	16	1	22	47	7	61	35	42	149	41	2
5	85	224	85	•		•	81	187	124	57	193	83	50	123	219	45	25	98	73	93	54	112	191	53	36	75	15	35	20	9	20	60	22	163	76	85	141	205	46
6	42	81	53	•	•		30	77	69	56	70	30	54	28	94	27	4	52	38	40	12	46	95	39	17	24	6	11	1	8	7	20	14	74	36	29	20	83	73
7	53	87	29	58	81	30		•	•	43	80	23	37	74	57	49	13	53	15	22	15	28	55	19	10	25	8	9	9	8	17	23	12	55	21	19	74	73	22
8	101	189	71	96	187	77	•		•	57	174	75	53	108	199	54	17	85	74	80	48	97	178	48	32	71	11	30	20	7	22	55	23	149	61	72	153	146	61
9	52	113	67	38	124	69	•	•		37	92	53	34	43	154	29	9	47	46	53	43	65	118	38	22	39	9	21	8	3	10	49	8	94	65	65	83	110	38
10	84	50	3	24	57	56	43	57	37		•	•	112	21	4	55	6	54	15	3	3	23	36	19	1	5	3	4	3	14	9	•	22	43	46	17	69	49	19
11	44	223	81	83	193	70	80	174	92	•		•	11	175	159	49	22	103	94	53	18	130	185	72	23	25	22	30	27	4	11	•	8	142	71	83	149	141	56
12	41	64	46	38	83	30	23	75	53	•	•		1	19	131	17	10	15	20	50	39	25	72	8	20	47	3	17	5	0	14	•	8	66	14	37	52	76	21
13	80	44	0	20	50	54	37	53	34	112	11	1		•	•	51	6	51	14	0	2	21	32	14	2	4	1	5	3	14	8	0	23	36	47	15	61	45	18
14	25	138	62	74	123	28	74	108	43	21	175	19	•		•	63	23	76	37	14	7	59	75	39	5	14	23	6	33	3	10	11	6	98	30	36	123	81	21
15	101	206	105	97	219	94	57	199	154	4	159	131	•	•		17	10	58	84	141	97	110	244	52	57	116	4	49	1	1	30	116	14	163	70	105	125	203	82
16	63	57	12	60	45	27	49	54	29	55	49	17	51	63	17		•	•	•	•	•	2	2	10	0	9	7	3	28	4	24	11	12	45	31	9	94	31	7
17	8	18	13	10	25	4	13	17	9	6	22	10	6	23	10	•		•	•	•	•	5	7	0	0	2	3	1	3	1	1	1	0	24	5	5	18	17	4
18	49	101	36	35	98	52	53	85	47	54	103	15	51	76	58	•	•		•	•	•	63	106	35	4	5	10	8	4	11	5	14	12	74	37	38	70	74	41
19	13	86	37	24	73	38	15	74	46	15	94	20	14	37	84	•	•	•		•	•	63	97	18	15	3	5	15	2	2	2	6	6	48	29	42	51	60	24
20	34	80	41	22	93	40	22	80	53	3	53	50	0	14	141	•	•	•	•		•	36	101	33	28	61	3	20	0	0	5	49	8	65	21	37	36	84	35
21	38	45	23	40	54	12	15	48	43	3	18	39	2	7	97	•	•	•	•	•		18	33	5	16	54	0	12	0	0	12	46	5	38	45	25	41	56	9
22	26	119	46	32	112	46	28	97	65	23	130	25	21	59	110	2	5	63	63	36	18		104	53	22	6	•	19	4	1	0	12	6	85	69	60	73	88	29
23	60	204	87	65	191	95	55	178	118	36	185	72	32	75	244	2	7	106	97	101	33	104		62	40	17	17	39	5	5	8	59	17	143	27	98	119	159	73
24	14	62	29	13	53	39	19	48	38	19	72	8	14	39	52	10	0	35	18	33	5	53	62		4	3	7	9	1	2	2	6	5	41	8	23	37	43	25
25	13	30	21	11	36	17	10	32	22	1	23	20	2	5	57	0	0	4	15	28	16	22	40	4		•	0	6	0	0	0	20	4	26	11	16	18	30	16
26	46	57	31	35	75	24	25	71	39	5	25	47	4	14	116	9	2	5	3	61	54	6	17	3	•		4	20	6	0	4	57	5	53	4	19	40	72	22
27	2	16	10	7	15	6	8	11	9	3	22	3	1	23	4	7	3	10	5	3	0	•	17	7	0	4		4	11	0	0	0	0	13	9	9	17	8	3
28	13	28	19	14	35	11	9	30	21	4	30	17	5	6	49	3	1	8	15	20	12	19	39	9	6	20	4		1	1	1	9	2	23	6	20	24	29	7
29	7	19	11	16	20	1	9	20	8	3	27	5	3	33	1	28	3	4	2	0	0	4	5	1	0	6	11	1		0	0	2	1	25	9	2	32	5	0
30	8	8	2	1	9	8	8	7	3	14	4	0	14	3	1	4	1	11	2	0	0	1	5	2	0	0	0	1	0		1	0	6	1	9	0	8	7	3
31	22	23	4	22	20	7	17	22	10	9	11	14	8	10	30	24	1	5	2	5	12	0	8	2	0	4	0	1	0	1		15	5	11	17	1	26	19	4
32	37	53	37	47	60	20	23	55	49	•	•	•	0	11	116	11	1	14	6	49	46	12	59	6	20	57	0	9	2	0	15		5	48	13	19	41	63	23
33	14	24	5	7	22	14	12	23	8	22	8	8	23	6	14	12	0	12	6	8	5	6	17	5	4	5	0	2	1	6	5	5		•	49	3	22	15	6
34	67	151	81	61	163	74	55	149	94	43	142	66	36	98	163	45	24	74	48	65	38	85	143	41	26	53	13	23	25	1	11	48	•		•	71	118	130	50
35	45	86	17	35	76	36	21	61	65	46	71	14	47	30	70	31	5	37	29	21	45	69	27	8	11	4	9	6	9	9	17	13	49	•		48	69	57	21
36	35	85	36	42	85	29	19	72	65	17	83	37	15	36	105	9	5	38	42	37	25	60	98	23	16	19	9	20	2	0	1	19	3	71	48		69	68	19
37	106	160	44	149	141	20	74	153	83	69	149	52	61	123	125	94	18	70	51	36	41	73	119	37	18	40	17	24	32	8	26	41	22	118	69	69		•	•
38	79	173	78	41	205	83	73	146	110	49	141	76	45	81	203	31	17	74	60	84	56	88	159	43	30	72	8	29	5	7	19	63	15	130	57	68	•		•
39	21	56	45	2	46	73	22	61	38	19	56	21	18	21	82	7	4	41	24	35	9	29	73	25	16	22	3	7	0	3	4	23	6	50	21	19	•	•	

5.4. The sorted matrix

This shows the clumping of high frequency traits into significant groups, which have been outlined with contours and numbered. For the content of these groups, see interpretative diagram, Appendix 5.7.

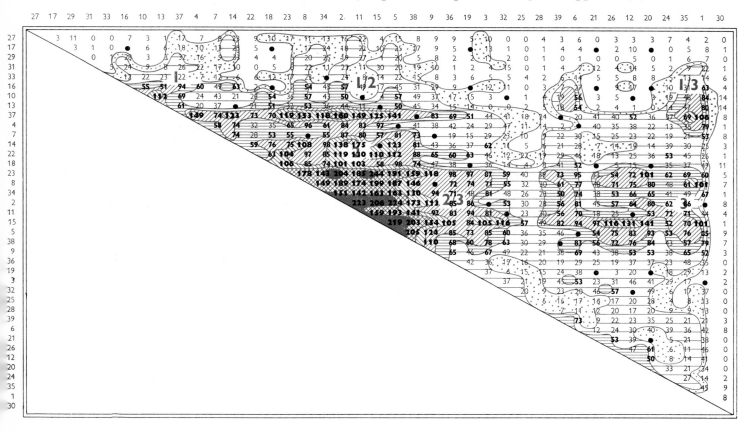

469

5.5. Interpretation of the sorted matrix (Appendix 5.4) and key to groups

The problems and procedure involved in attempting to produce a valid interpretation of the sorted matrix have been discussed in Chapter 3.

A tentative attribution of traits—X represents the presence of the trait—to the general clusters 1, 1/2, 1/3, 2, 2/3, 3, outlined on the sorted matrix, is given below. In Appendix 5.6 there is an attempt to reconstruct the range of shape these clusters imply, and in Appendix 5.7, a schematic illustration of the situation indicated by the sorted matrix, with tentative beaker groupings.

	Matrix groups					
Trait no.	I	1/2	1/3	2	2/3	3
1			X			X
2	X	X		X	X	X
3				X	X	
4	X		X	X		
5		X	X	X	X	X
6			X			X
7	X		X	X		
8		X		X	X	X
9		X		X	X	X
10	X	X	X			
11		X		X	X	X
12						X
13	X	X	X			
14	X	X	X	X		
15		X		X	X	X
16	X	X	X			
17	X	X	X			
18		X	X	X		
19				X	X	
20						X
21						X
22		X	X	X		
23		X		X	X	X
24			X			X
25					X	
26						X
27	X	X				
28					X	X
29	X	X				
30			X			
31	X	X	X			
32					X	
33	X	X	X			
34		X		X	X	X
35			X			X
36		X		X	X	X
37	X	X	X	X		
38		X		X	X	X
39						X

5.6. Calculation of the range of shape of the groups interpreted from the sorted matrix

In an attempt to visualise the groups of traits isolated in the sorted matrix (Appendix 5.5), the first step is to express the shape ratios as ranges of shapes which exhibit the ranges of decoration.

To express the range of shape proportions the individual ratios are evaluated for a unit, common waist diameter. When one of the matrix groups has two ranges from the same shape ratio then the total range is taken as possible. If the waist diameter is taken as unity, then the shape components can be evaluated as follows:

H – Total height of beaker from rim to base
h—Height of waist or point of inflexion, from the base

W—Waist diameter   R—Rim diameter
B—Belly diameter   F—Base diameter

Group 1

H/W—trait 37 = 0·80–1·42 = 1·11 ± 0·31
  given W = 1·00, therefore H = 1·11 ± 0·31
H/h—trait 10 = 1·00–1·20 = 1·10 ± 0·10
  Therefore $h = \dfrac{1·11 + 0·31}{1·10 + 0·10} = 1·05 ± 0·38$
R/W—trait 2 = 1·10–1·20 R = 1·15 ± 0·05
B/W—trait 4 = 0·90–1·10 B = 1·00 ± 0·10
F/W—trait 7 = 0·40–0·60 F = 0·50 ± 0·10

Group 1/2

H/W—traits 37 and 38—therefore H = 1·26 ± 0·46
H/h—traits 10 and 11—therefore h = 1·12 ± 0·60
R/W—trait 2—therefore R = 1·15 ± 0·05
B/W—trait 5—therefore B = 1·15 ± 0·05
F/W—traits 8 and 9—therefore F = 0·75 ± 0·15

Group 1/3

H/W—trait 37—therefore H = 1·11 ± 0·31
H/h—trait 10—therefore h = 1·05 ± 0·38
R/W—trait 1—therefore R = 1·00 ± 0·10
B/W—traits 4–6—B = 1·20 ± 0·30
F/W—trait 7—therefore F = 0·50 ± 0·10

Group 2

H/W—traits 37–8—therefore H = 1·26 ± 0·46
H/h—trait 11—therefore h = 0·98 ± 0·45
R/W—traits 2 and 3—therefore R = 1·25 ± 0·15
B/W—traits 4 and 5—therefore B = 1·05 ± 0·15
F/W—traits 7–9—therefore F = 0·65 ± 0·25

Group 2/3

H/W—trait 38—therefore H = 1.57 ± 0.15
H/h—traits 11–32—therefore h = 1.07 ± 0.36
R/W – traits 2–3—therefore R = 1.25 ± 0.15
B/W—trait 5—therefore B = 1.15 ± 0.05
F/W—traits 8–9—therefore F = 0.75 ± 0.15

Group 3

H/W—traits 38–9—therefore H = 1.88 ± 0.47
H/h—traits 11–12—therefore h = 1.40 ± 0.57
R/W—traits 1–2—therefore R = 1.05 ± 0.15
B/W—traits 5–6—therefore B = 1.30 ± 0.20
F/W—traits 8–9   therefore F = 0.75 ± 0.15

5.7. Diagrammatic representation of the beaker groups suggested by the matrix pattern

The short lines represent the average limits within which the group is defined; the decoration shows only one format of the group ranges.

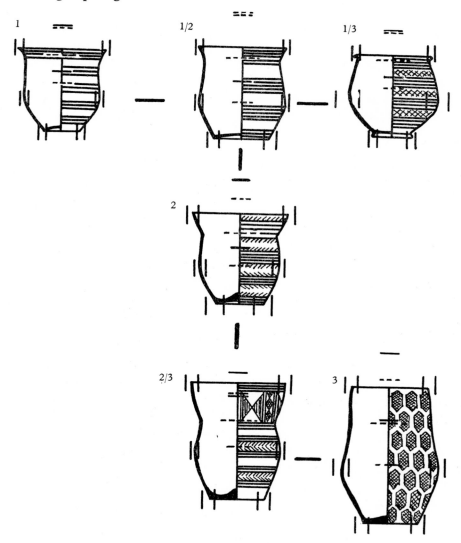

5.8. A note on the computer programs written in connection with the matrix analysis of archaeological material by Dr J. Grant, Cambridge Mathematical Laboratory

Preliminary note

Throughout, we shall be referring to a matrix of numbers of n rows and columns, denoting the element common to the ith row and jth column by a_{ij}.

Theoretical background

Robinson showed how it is possible to arrive at a matrix of coincidence and the problem is then the adoption of some criterion for rearranging the rows and columns in order to produce the desired pattern where possible. One approach is to take the half of the matrix above the diagonal (that is, the a_{ij} with $j \geqslant i+1$, i taking values between 1 and $n-1$, inclusive) and, working out from the diagonal along the rows and columns form all the differences of the forms $a_{i,j} - a_{i,j+1}$ and $a_{i,j} - a_{i-1,j}$. We then try to rearrange the matrix in order to minimise the ratio

$$\frac{-\,(\text{sum of negative differences})}{(\text{sum of positive differences}) - (\text{sum of negative differences})}.$$

W. D. Easterbrook in the preliminary investigation (described in a dissertation submitted in partial fulfilment of the regulations governing the Diploma in Numerical Analysis and Automatic Computing in the University of Cambridge), found that it was desirable to give extra weight to large differences, and suggested that this could be done most simply by considering the ratio

$$F = \frac{\text{sum of the squares of the negative differences}}{\text{sum of the squares of all the differences}}$$

and this ratio was adopted for the subsequent work.

We now move on to describe in outline the programs written for the computer EDSAC II.

Build-up of the matrix

We assume that initially all elements of the matrix are set to zero.

A data-tape consisting of a set of data for each pot is provided for the computer. Each set consists of a string of numbers corresponding to the properties possessed by an individual pot, and is terminated by some unique, recognisable symbol; the whole tape is terminated by another such symbol. The tape is read set by set, and each is dealt with in turn. From each list every possible combination (i, j) of property i and property j appearing in the list is formed and one is added into the element $a_{i,j}$ of the matrix.

The most recent version of this program also counts the number of pots and also the number of times that the individual properties occur. This enables us to replace the absolute values $a_{i,j}$ by the ratios

$$a_{i,j}/(N_i + N_j - a_{i,j})$$

where N_i is the number of times that property i occurs etc.

Finally, $a_{i,i}$ which is not used, is put equal to i to serve as a flag during the subsequent interchanges.

The matrix is then punched out on paper-tape to serve as input for the second program.

Sorting the matrix

The program reads in the matrix produced by the program just described, storing it, and then attempts the rearrangement of the rows and columns (keeping the matrix symmetric) in such a way as to minimise the ratio defined above.

The value of F for the initial matrix is calculated, and we then try interchanges of pairs of rows and columns—say the ith and the jth—and check whether F is decreased or not. All possible interchanges are tried, starting with $(n, n-1)$, $(n, n-2)$, ..., $(n, 1)$ and then $(n-1, n-2)$, ..., $(n-1, 1)$ and finishing with $(2, 1)$.

The re-evaluation of F at each stage was found to be costly in time, and so we keep track only of those differences dependent on the elements of the ith and jth rows and columns, seeing how these vary with the inter-change, and adjusting F appropriately. If the inter-change does not produce a decrease in F, it is reversed. Otherwise, the new value is printed out—to serve as an indication of how the minimisation is proceeding—and we move on to the next combination.

When the iteration is completed, there is the option of starting a fresh one or of printing out the matrix for examination.

Additional features

The elements of the matrix are printed out in blocks of n numbers corresponding to the individual rows, and before any overall picture of the matrix can be obtained, these have to be transferred manually to another diagram. To avoid this labour, it is possible to obtain a rough 'map' of the matrix consisting of single digits giving an indication of the size of the elements.

5.9. Short bibliography of matrix analysis and related techniques

The literature on experimental numerical taxonomy in all fields is growing daily. This short reference list is intended to give the background necessary for a proper understanding of the scope of the techniques.

Fortunately, for the first time, a balanced, expert definitive work is now available—see Sokal and Sneath (1963), below.

ASCHER, M. 'A mathematical rationale for graphical seriation.' *American Antiquity* 25 (1959), 212–14.

BELOUS, R. E. 'The central California chronological sequence re-examined.' *American Antiquity* 18 (1953), 341–53.

BRAINERD, G. W. 'The place of chronological ordering in archaeological analysis.' *American Antiquity* 16 (1951), 301–13.

Clarke, D. L. 'Matrix analysis and archaeology with particular reference to British Beaker pottery.' *P.P.S.* XXVIII (1962), 371–83.

'Matrix analysis and archaeology—a reply.' *Nature* 199 (1963), 790–2.

KROEBER, A. L. 'Statistical Classification.' *American Antiquity* 6 (1940–1), 29–44.

LEHMER, D. J. 'Robinson's coefficient of agreement—a critique.' *American Antiquity* 17 (1952), 151.

MATTHEWS, J. 'Application of matrix analysis to archaeological problems.' *Nature* 198 (1963), 930; *Nature* 199 (1963), 792.

MEIGHAN, C. W. 'A new method for the seriation of archaeological collections.' *American Antiquity* 25 (1959), 203–11.

NEEDHAM, R. M. *A method for using computers in information classification.* The International Congress on Information Processing. Munich, 1962.

ROBINSON, W. S. 'A method for chronologically ordering archaeological deposits.' *American Antiquity* 16 (1951), 293–301.

'Robinson's coefficient of agreement—a rejoinder.' *American Antiquity* 18 (1952), 60–1.

SMITH, W. 'George Walton Brainerd—1909–1956. Bibliography.' *American Antiquity* 22 (1956), 165–8.

SOKAL, R. R. and MICHENER, C. D. *A statistical method for evaluating systematic relationships.* University of Kansas, Science Bulletin 38 (1958), 2, 1409–38.

SOKAL, R. R. and SNEATH, P. H. A. *Principles of numerical taxonomy* (1963). Matrix Analysis, pp. 207–9, 284.

SPAULDING, A. C. 'Statistical techniques for the discovery of artefact types.' *American Antiquity* 18 (1953), 305–13.

TUGBY, D. J. 'A typological analysis of axes and choppers from Southeast Australia.' *American Antiquity* 24 (1958), 24–34.

WILLIAMS, W. T. and DALE, M. B. 'Partition correlation matrices for heterogeneous quantitative data.' *Nature* 196 (1962), 602.

473

APPENDIX 6

A CORPUS LIST OF BRITISH BEAKERS

A corpus list of the beaker pottery of England, Scotland, Wales and Ireland, complete vessels and sherds; giving the museum holding the beaker, the beaker group and references to the beaker's detailed history.

In the corpus that follows, the beakers and sherds are arranged in alphabetical order, under counties also in alphabetical sequence. The counties are arranged internally within the arbitrary sequence—England, Scotland, Wales, Ireland—used throughout this work. The overall sequence is then numbered continuously, from Bedfordshire to County Waterford, from nos. 1–1944. Alterations and corrections have made necessary a few decimalised entries, thus Shoebury, nos. 260.1 and 260.2. All references are given by the corpus number, which by itself will supply the site name, county and country, if necessary. All site names are those that are entered in the museum registers and inscribed on the vessels, the prime aim being to identify a particular beaker and site by the name. Barrow numbers are entered after the site name, when in brackets these represent the standardised Grinsell barrow number for Wessex barrows, thus: Wilsford (40); without brackets the barrow number is that of the excavator thus: Weaverthorpe 297.

Each corpus number and entry represents a single beaker or sherd, except where the site has yielded hundreds of sherds, in which case the site is shown in capitals and one entry equals the presence of a minimum of one such type on the site.

The label 'Indet.' indicates that the sherd or beaker is of indeterminate grouping. A blank — represents the loss or destruction of the beaker, which now remains unclassifiable. The suffix F following the corpus number means that the entry is in fragments; without the suffix F the beaker is complete or completely restorable.

The entries are arranged under five columns, thus: *Corpus no., Site name, Museum, Beaker group, References.*

ENGLAND

Bedfordshire

Corpus no.	Site	Museum	Beaker group	References
1 F	Bedford District	Bedford	FP	Unpub.
2	Clifton	Bedford A.2.3431	S 1	*Ant. J.* XVIII, 285, Pl. LIX, Fig. 2; *Beds. Mag.* (1949), 106–9
3 F	Dunstable, Five Knolls barrow 2	Luton 7.1925	Indet.	*Man*, no. 12 (1927), 21
	Harrowden, Eastcotts	Bedford		*Beds. Mag.* 2 (1949/50),
4 F		(1)	S 1	no. 11 (winter),
5 F		(2)	S 1	103–6
6 F		(3)	S 1	*Ibid.*
7	Kempston	Bedford BMS.A/3	W/MR	*Ant. J.* XVIII, 284–5; *Beds. Mag.* 2 (1949/50), no. 11, 106
8	Kempston	B.M. 1929 4–10 1	S 1	*Ibid.* 105; *Ant. J.* XVIII, 284, Pl. LVIII
9	Shefford	Cambridge 59.D.1	S 2(E)	*Ant. J.* XVIII, 285, Pl. LIX; *A.C.R.* App. 1, XX
10	Turvey Abbey	Bedford BMS.A/1	S 1	*Ant. J.* XVIII, 284, Pl. LVIII (2)

Berkshire

Corpus no.	Site	Museum	Beaker group	References
11	Abingdon	Ashmolean 1887.3021	N2	A. 43; Berks. 1
12 F	Abingdon Camp	Ibid.	Indet.	Ant. J. XXXVI, 16; Ox. XXI, 10 (I); Berks. 13 and 15
13	Abingdon, Appleford	B.M. 1862 7-2 21	SH2(B)	A. 292; Berks. 3; Ox. XXI, 12
14	Abingdon, Northcourt	Ashmolean 1937.616	S2(E)	Berks. 3; Ox. III, 26, Pl. IIIF
15 F	Blewbury,	Newbury.	FP	N.F.C. VII, no. 3,
16 F	Churn Plain,	Pitt-Rivers	S?	170, Fig. 35
17 F	Barrow B	Oxford	Indet.	
18 F	Barrow C	Ibid.	Ibid.	
19	Brightwell, Slade End	Reading	W/MR	Unpub.
20 F	Caversham	Reading	S3(W)?	Unpub.
21 F	Chieveley, Curridge	Reading OA. 271	N2?	N.F.C. VI, no. 4, 218
22	Cholsey	B.M. 1893 4-26 8	E.	A. 22; Ox. III, 26, Pl. IIIG; Berks. 4
23 F	FARNCOMBE DOWN	M.O.W.	FN	Unpub.
24 F	BARROW		E.?	
	Inkpen Hill	Newbury		Ant. J. XVI, 97,
25		(1) OA·273	W/MR	Pl. XXII
26		(2) OA.272	Bowl	Ibid.
27	Lambourne Barrow 31	B.M. 1862 7-7 5	S2(W)	A. 7; Berks. 5; N.F.C. (1870-1), 178; B.A.J. 55, 22-3, Fig. 5
28	Lambourne Barrow 17	B.M. (1) 1862 7-7 4	BW	B.A.J. 55, 23-5, Fig. 6-7; A. 41; Berks. 6
29 F		(2) Unreg.	N2	B.A.J. 55, 23-5, Fig. 7
30 F	Little Wittenham	Ashmolean 1950.3	Indet.	Ox. XXI, 10; Berks. 14
31 F	Long Wittenham	Ibid. 1936.330	E.	Ox. II, 1; Berks. 7
32	Radley	Ibid. 1933.1618	W/MR	Ant. J. XV, 38, Pl. VII, 2; Berks. 8
33	Radley (4a)	Ibid. 1944.121	E.	Ox. XIII, 1-9; Berks. 12; Invent. G.B. 2
34	Sutton Courtenay	Ashmolean 1933.1200	E.	Berks. 9; Ox. XXI, Fig. 4; Ant. J. XIV, 267, Pl. xxx
35	Sutton Courtenay	Reading University	FN	Berks. 10; Arch. LXXVI, 62, Pl. v, 1
36 F	Sutton Courtenay	Lost	W/MR?	Berks. 16; Ox. XXI, 11, Fig. 5
37	Theale	Reading 73.52	S4	P.S.A.L. 2s. XXI, 313
38 F	Wytham	Ashmolean Rolleston Coll.	S4/Hybrid	Berks. 11

Buckinghamshire

Corpus no.	Site	Museum	Beaker group	References
	Bledlow,	Aylesbury		Records of Bucks.
39 F	Cop Barrow,	(1)	W/MR	Vol. 13, 332, Pl. 7;
40 F	Wain Hill	(2)	Bowl	E.M.S.Bucks. 51, Fig. 11
41	Chesham?	Aylesbury L.36	W/MR?	Unpub.
	Hitcham,	B.M.		M.N.F.C. 8th Rep.
42	Win Hill	(1) 94 12-10 42	FN	(1890-1), 46;
43		(2) 94 12-10 43	AOC	E.M.S.Bucks. 51,
44		(3) 94 12-10 44	E.	Fig. 10, 1-3
	Saunderton,	Aylesbury		E.M.S.Bucks., 51-2,
45 F	Lodge Hill	139.57	E.?	Fig. 13
46 F	Barrow	140.57	FN	Ibid.

Cambridgeshire

Corpus no.	Site	Museum	Beaker group	References
47	Barnwell	Cambridge 98.62	S3(E)	A.C.R. App. I, I; A. 69
48	Bottisham Lode	Cambridge Z.11491	SH3(A)	C.A.S. XXXI, 350, Pl. IX; Ant. IX, 348, Pl. VII
49 F	Bottisham Lode	Cambridge Z.14826A–D	FP	Unpub.
50	Burwell,	Lost (1)	—	C.A.S. XLV, xxii;
51	Newmarket	Lost (2)	—	A.C.R. 326, App. III
52 F	Cambridgeshire	Cambridge 48.341	S?	Unpub. Braybrooke Coll.
	Cambridgeshire	Cambridge 27.613 (1)	N/MR	Unpub. Ridgeway Coll.
53 F				
54 F		(2)	E. Ang.	Ibid.
55 F	Cherry Hinton, War Ditches	Cambridge	FP	C.A.S. XLII, Pl. 23, Fig. 3
56 F	Chesterton	Ibid.	Indet.	A.C.R. App. I, VIII
57	Chippenham Park	Ibid. 44.14	N2	Unpub.
58 F	Chippenham barrow I	Cambridge 36.855–6	S?	C.A.S. XXXVI, 140, Fig. 5
59 F			FP	
60 F	Barrow 2	36.66	S?	Ibid. 145, Fig. 7
61 F	Barrow 3	49.272	S?	C.A.S. XXXIX, 30, Fig. 4
62 F		49.280	FP	
63 F	BARROW 5	49.269	SH2(?)	Ibid. 49, Figs.
64 F		49.271	S2(W)	
65 F			FP	
66	Doddington	Cambridge 98.598	S1	A.C.R. App. I, IX
67 F	Ely	Ibid. 22.587	Indet.	A.C.R. App. I, X; P.P.S.E.A. VI, 48
68	Ely, New Barns Lane	Ibid. 58.35	S2(W)	C.A.S. LII, I, Pl. I
	Ely, Springhead Lane	Ibid.		C.A.S. XXIX, 106
69		(1) 27.1681	N2(L)	
70		(2) 27.1678	S4	
71	Fordham	Ibid. A.1903.204	SH3(B)	A.C.R. Pl. I, App. I, XII; A. 296 (in error); Ant. IX, 348, Pl. VII
72	Little Downham	Cambridge Z.11490	S3(W)	C.A.S. XXXV, 145
73 F	Little Downham	Ibid. Z.14987 (1)	S?	Unpub.
74 F		(2)	FP	
75	March	Ibid. 22.572	SH3(B)	Arch. XLIII, 397; Arch. J. XIX, 364–5
76	Milton	Ibid. Z.14812	FP	Unpub.
	Shippea Hill, Burnt Fen	Ibid.		
77		(1) 44.16	E.	Unpub.
78		(2) 33.62	N2	Unpub.
	Shippea Hill, Peacocks Fm.	Ibid.		Ant. J. XV, 284
79 F		34.1202	Indet.	
80 F	Ibid.	London Inst. 60.875	AOC	Ibid.
81 F	SHIPPEA HILL, Plantation Fm.	Cambridge	FP	Ant. J. XIII, 268
82 F		31.237	S4	
83 F		33.622	S2(W)	
84 F			BW	
85 F			E.	
	Snailwell	Cambridge		
86		(1) 1896.183	FP	A. 65; A.C.R. App. I, XXI;
87		(2) 1896.184	N2	A. 89; A.C.R. App. I, XXII
	Snailwell	Cambridge		P.S.A.S. XLIII, 33
88 F	Barrow C	53.105	S?	

Corpus no.	Site	Museum	Beaker group	References
89 F	Barrow E	53.107	Indet.	
90 F	Barrow I	53.108	Indet.	
91 F	Barrow J	53.111	Indet.	
92	Soham	Ashmolean 1922.268	S1	*A.C.R.* App. I, xxix
93	Whittlesford	Cambridge 36.471	N3	*C.A.S.* xxxvii, 74, Pl. I
94	Wilburton Fen	*Ibid.*	N2(L)	*A.C.R.* Pl. I, 1, App. I, xxv

Cornwall

	Cataclews Bay, Harlyn	B.M.		*Arch. J.* CI, 23,
95 F	Harlyn	(1) Unreg.	E?	Table I A1, Fig. 3,
96 F		(2) Unreg.	FN?	Table I A2
97	Davidstow Moor barrow XXIV	C. K. Croft-Andrew	—	*W.C.F.C.* 2, no. 2 (1957–8), 21; *Arch. J.* CI, Table I A9
98	Durval, Sancreed	Lost	Indet.	Borlase (1872), 171, *Naenia Cornubiae*
99 F	GWITHIAN	C. Thomas	E.?	*W.C.F.C.* II, no. 5, 202
100 F			Undec.	
101 F	Prah Sands, Gernoe	Truro	S2(W)	*Arch. J.* CI, Table I A3, Fig. 3
102 F	St Juliot, Lousey barrow	(1) Lost	S?	*Arch. J.* CI,
103 F		(2) Lost	S?	Table I A7
104	Tregiffian Fm., St Buryan	St Buryan Church	S3(W)	*Arch. J.* CVII, 46, Table I A10, Fig. I
105	Trevedra, St Just in Penwith	Truro	S2(W)	*W.C.F.C.* 2, no. 5 (1960–1), Fig. 17; *W.C.F.C.* I, no. 2 (1954)
106	Try Menhir, Gulval	Truro	SH4(C)	*W.C.F.C.* 2, no. 5 (1960), 4

Cumberland

107	Ainstable	Carlisle 69.1948	N3	H.M.C. 49, no. 13; *C.W.A.S.* NS. XLVIII, 215, Fig. I
108	Ainstable, Broomrigg	Carlisle 1960	N/NR	Unpub.
109	Carlisle, Garlands Pit	Carlisle 10–78	N2	*C.W.A.S.* LVI, 7, H.M.C. 44–5, Pl. IIC
110	Castle Carrock 163	B.M. 79 12–9 1349	N3(L)	*B.B.* 379; A. 161
111	Cumberland, Unprovenanced	Carlisle Om.264–139	N3	*J.R.A.I.* XXXII, 41, Pl. XXIX; H.M.C. 46, Pl. II*b*
112 F	Mecklin Park, Irton Pike, Santon Bridge	Carlisle 61.1955	AOC	*C.W.A.S.* XXXVII, 104, Pl.
113	Nether Moor, Hunsonby	Carlisle no. 263	N3	*J.R.A.I.* XXXII, 383, no. 41, Pl. XXIX; A. 175; H.M.C. 45, Pl. I*d*
114	Newton, Penrith	Carlisle 27–26.434	N/NR	H.M.C. 44–6, Pl. II*d*; Skirwith Moor in Error in above ref.

Derbyshire

115	Alsop Moor, Green Low	Sheffield J.55.6	S1	*Vest.* 59; *Ten Yrs*, 286; *Reliquary* III, 176–8; *Arch. J.* XVIII, 415, Figs.
116	Ashford, Shacklow	*Ibid.* J.1956.37	FP	Unpub.
117	Bakewell, Haddon Field	*Ibid.* J.93.867	S1	*Ten Yrs*, 106; A. 51; *J.D.A.S.* LXXV, 105
118	Bradwell, Hazelbadge Hills	*Ibid.* (1) J.1956.86	S2(W)	Bagshawe Coll. Unpub.
119	Hills	(2) J.1957.26	S2(W)	Unpub.

Corpus no.	Site	Museum	Beaker group	References
120	Brassington, Sliper Lowe	*Ibid.* J.93.872	S2(W)	*Vest.* 52; A. 53; *Arch.* J. I, 247, Fig.
121 F	Brownslow	Lost	Indet.	*Ten Yrs,* 168; *J.D.A.S.* LXXV, 104
122	Buxton, Stakor Hill	*Ibid.* J.93.873	FP	*Ten Yrs,* 80–1; A. 62; *J.D.A.S.* LXXV, Fig. 3
123 F	Cow Dale, Gospel Hillock	B.M. 75 4–3 136	S2(E)	*Reliquary* VIII, 85–90
124		Lost	FN	A. 88
125 F	Crakendale Pasture	Sheffield J.1851	S2(W)	*Ten Yrs,* 71; *J.D.A.S.* LXXV, 104
126 F	Dovedale, Stoop Highedge	Lost	Indet.	Turner, 102, Pl. XXIII, 3
127 F	Dovedale, Thorpe Cloud	Sheffield N.83	Indet.	*Ten Yrs,* 27–8
128	Dowel, Sterndale	*Ibid.* J.93.859	S3(E)	*Ten Yrs,* 38; A. 63; *J.D.A.S.* LXXV, 104; *Y.A.J.* 31, 41
129 F	Elton Moor	Lost	Indet.	*J.D.A.S.* LXXV, 104, Fig. 4; *Vest.* 53; *Arch.* J. I, 248
130	Grindlow, Long Lowe	Sheffield J.1956.8	S1	*Reliquary* III, 206. Fig. A. 50; Jewitt, Fig. 109
131 F	Harborough Rocks, Cave	Birchover	Indet.	*J.D.A.S.* LXXV, 105; *J.D.A.S.* XXXI, 99
132	Hartington, Elk Low	B.M. 73 6–2 30	Hybrid	Jewitt, 73, Fig. 110; A. Pl. XLI, no. 204
133 F	Hartington, Parcelly Hay	Lost	Indet.	*Ten Yrs,* 22; *J.D.A.S.* LXXV, Fig. 7
134 F	Kenslow, Knoll Fm.	Sheffield N.80	N2	*Ten Yrs,* 20; *J.D.A.S.* LXXV, 105, Fig. 5
135	Longstone, Blake Low	Sheffield J.93.864	N2	*Ten Yrs,* 41; A. 90 *bis*; *J.D.A.S.* LXXV, Fig. 1
	Middleton, Calling Lowe Farm	*Ibid.*		
136 F		(1) N.69	E.	*Vest.* 98–9;
137 F		(2) N.69	S2(W)?	*J.D.A.S.* LXXV, 78, Fig. 7
138	Middleton, One Ash Fm.	Lost	Indet.	*Vest.* 54
139	Middleton, Smerrill Moor	Sheffield J.93.860	S2(W)	*Ten Yrs,* 102–3; A. 49
140	Minning Low	*Ibid.* J.93.861	N2(L)	*Vest.* 41; A. 68; *Arch.* 61, 103
141 F	Minninglow Fm, Ryestone Grange	*Ibid.* J.93.699	FP	*Ten Yrs,* 61
	Monsal Dale, Hay Top Hill	*Ibid.*		*Ten Yrs,* 74–6;
142 F		(1) Unreg.	S4	*J.D.A.S.* LXXV, 105;
143		(2) J.93.868	S2(W)	A. 54; Jewitt, Fig. 108
144 F	Ravenscliffe Cave	B.M. Unreg.	FP	*J.D.A.S.* XXXII, 141–6
	Rusden Low	Sheffield		*Ten Yrs,* 43–4;
145		(1) J.93.863	S2(W)	A. 57;
146 F		(2) N.98	E.	*J.D.A.S.* LXXV, 106
147 F		(3) N.98	N/NR?	
148 F		(4) N.98	S2(W)?	
149	Stoney-Middleton Dale	Derby 71.1927	S2(E)	*J.D.A.S.* (1926–7), 372
150 F	SWARKESTON	Derby	S2?	*J.D.A.S.* LXXX, 11–48
151 F	BARROW 4		FP	
152 F	Wardlow, Rolley Low	Lost	Indet.	*Vest.* 55; *Arc. Camb.* 7 s. V, 26
	Youlgrave, Bee Low	Sheffield		*Ten Yrs,* 72;
153		(1) J.93.866	S2(W)	A. 52; *Vest.* 35;
154 F		(2) Lost	N2	*J.D.A.S.* LXXV, 104; Jewitt MSS
154.1		(3) Bingley Coll. of Ed.	AOC	Unpub. (1967)

Devon

Corpus no.	Site	Museum	Beaker group	References
155 F	Broad Down, Farway, nr. Honiton	Exeter	S2(W)?	*D.A.E.S.* 4, 7; A. 16; *D.A.* II, 641, Pl. VIII; *Arch. J.* XXV, 307
156	Chagford Common, Dartmoor	Plymouth	BW	*D.A.* XXIX, 66–71 (1897); *V.C.H. Devon*, I, 360, Fig. 14; A. 40
157 F	Devon Unprovenanced	Torquay	Indet.	Unpub.
158	Fernworthy, Dartmoor	Plymouth	S2(W)	*D.A.* XXX, 108, Pl. III (1898); *V.C.H. Devon*, I, 358; A. 13
159	Langcombe, Plym Valley	Lost	E.	*D.A.* XXXII, 50, Pl. IX; A. 42a
159.1	Sidmouth, Burnt Common	Exeter 1967	S4	Unpub.
160 F	Torquay, Kents Cavern	Torquay	Indet.	*D.A.* II, 521
161 F	Woodbury Common	Lost	E.?	*D.A.E.S.* 2, 292, Pl. LXXXIII

Dorset

Corpus no.	Site	Museum	Beaker group	References
162	Almer, Stag Lodge	Farnham	W/MR	*P.S.A.S.* XXXVIII, 334, No. 59, Pl.; A. 26
163 F	Badbury Rings Barrow (?)	Poole	Indet.	*Arch. J.* III, 350
	Bincombe Down, Ridgeway Hill,	Dorchester		*D.N.A.S.* 65, 38, Pl.
164	Barrow (1)	(1) Bowl	Bowl	Pl. IXA; *Arc. Camb.* 7s. V, 19;
165		(2)	SH4(C)	*D.N.A.S.* 65, 38 Pl. IXB
166		(3) Undec.	⌠Undec.	*D.N.A.S.* 65, 38, Pl. IXC (not Iron Age)
167		(4) Undec.	⌡Dorset	*D.N.A.S.* 65, 38, Pl. IXD
168	Bincombe Down barrow (52), Ridgeway 4	Dorchester 105	⌠Undec. ⌡Dorset	*D.N.A.S.* XXXVII, 44, No. 32
169	Blackbush Down, Cranbourne	Farnham	E.	*C.C.* III, 240, P. CCXIV; A. 23
170	Bloxworth Down barrow (1)	B.M. 92 9–12 52	FN	*B.A.P.* 32; Hutchins, I, 184
171	Bradford Peverell (24a), Frome 10	Dorchester	H(DO)	*D.N.A.S.* XXXVII, 42, No. 10; A. 298
172	Bradford Peverell (30), Frome 8	*Ibid.* 1884.9.54	S3(E)	*D.N.A.S.* XXXVII, 41, no. 8; *D.N.A.S.* XXIX, 139, no. 92
173	Bradford Peverell (26), Frome 12	*Ibid.* 1884.9.99	⌠Undec. ⌡Dorset	*D.N.A.S.* XXXVII, 42, no. 12; *D.N.A.S.* XXIX, 140, no. 94
174 F		1884.9.98a	Indet.	Unpub. Sherd
175	Dewlish (6) barrow 33	Lost	—	Warne, 48 (1866)
176	Dorchester, Colliton Park	Dorchester 1940.28.1	S4	Unpub.
177	Dorchester barrow (5) Masonic Hall	*Ibid.*	W/MR	*D.N.A.S.* XXIX, 141; A. 30; *D.B.* 105
	'Dorset'	B.M.		Durden Coll.
178 F		92 9–1 339	S2(W)	Unpub.
179 F		92 9–1 350	S2(W)	Unpub.
180	Frampton barrow 1 (4)	Dorchester 1937.82.4	⌠Undec. ⌡Dorset	*D.N.A.S.* 80, 111–32
181 F	Frampton barrow 2 (5)	Dorchester	S2(W)	*D.N.A.S.* 80, 117–32
182 F	Gussage St Michael, Thickthorn Banks	*Ibid.*	Indet.	*D.N.A.S.* 81, 112, Fig.
	Gussage St Michael (163a),	Dorchester		*P.P.S.* I, 121;
183	Thickthorn Down	(1) 1936.67.1	E.	*P.P.S.* II, 80–4, Fig. 1;
184	Long barrow	(2) 1936.67.2	E.	*Ibid.* Fig. 2
185 F		(3) 1936.67.3	FN	*Ibid.*
186 F		(4) 1936.67.4/6	Indet.	*Ibid.*
187 F	Handley Down, Angle Ditch	Farnham	Indet.	*C.C.* IV, 112,
188 F			FP	Pl. 264, no. 14
189 F	Handley Down barrow (26)	Farnham	Indet.	*C.C.* IV, 140–1, Pl. 294, 6
190 F	Handley Down barrow (27)	Farnham	Indet.	*C.C.* IV, 138, Pl. 294, 11
191	Handley Down, nr. Wor barrow	Farnham	FN	A. 31; *C.C.* IV, 114, Pl. 265
192 F	Hilton (2), Melcombe Bingham	Dorchester 1916.3.6	AOC	*D.N.A.S.* XXXVIII, 80

Corpus no.	Site	Museum	Beaker group	References
193	Little Canford	Farnham 1934 M.O.W.	Undec. E.	*Ant. J.* XXXIV, 172; *S.E.U.S.S.* XL, 22 *P.P.S.* XXVI, 343
194 F	Long Crichel, Launceston Down, barrow	(1)	Indet.	
195 F		(2)	Indet.	
196 F	Long Crichel barrow (4)	Dorchester	Indet.	*D.B.* 118
197	Tarrant Hinton (20b), Racedown, Blandford	Lost	S2(W)	A. 15; *D.B.* 134
	TARRANT	Dorchester		*P.P.S.* VI, 112, Fig. 1;
198 F	LAUNCESTON (1), Crichel Down	(1)	FN	*Arch.* 90, 48–77, Fig. 2
199 F	barrow 11	(2)	AOC	*Ibid.*
200 F		(3)	E.?	*Ibid.*
201	Tarrant Launceston (5), Crichel 14	*Ibid.* 1945.23.3	W/MR	*Arch.* 90, 48–77, Fig. 25, left
202	Tarrant Launceston (7), Crichel 16	Dorchester	S3(W)	*Arch.* 90, 48–77, Fig. 3
203	Tarrant Launceston (8), Crichel 17	*Ibid.*	FP	*Arch.* 90, 48–77, Fig. 25 right
204	Weymouth, near	Ashmolean 1927.2673	S4	*Arc. Camb.* 7s. V, 26, Evans Coll.
205	Weymouth, Ridgeway (5), Waddon 12	Lost?	—	*D.N.A.S.* XXXVII, 45, no. 40; *D.B.* 141
206	Wimborne St Giles (9), Woodyates 9	Lost	—	*A.W.* 235; *W.A.M.* XLIII, 268, note
207 F	Winterbourne Kingston	Lost	S?	Warne, 9 (1866), Ex Friends
208	Winterbourne St Martin (34b), Maiden Castle 7	Dorchester	SH3(C)	*Arch.* XXX, 332, Pl. XVII, 7; *D.N.A.S.* XXIX, 134, 24
209 F	WINTERBOURNE	Dorchester	AOC	Wheeler, 143–64;
210 F	ST MARTIN,	and	FN	*Ibid.* Figs.
211 F	Maiden Castle	Lon. Inst.	FP	*Ibid.* Figs.
212 F	Ditches		S2?	*Ibid.* Figs.
213	Winterbourne St Martin (46),	Dorchester 1907.3.2	H(DO)	*D.N.A.S.* XXVI, 7–22, Pl. IV, 31; A. 299, Pl. III, 5
214	Martinstown I.	*Ibid.*	Undec.	
214.1 F		*Ibid.*	Indet.	
215 F	Winterbourne St Martin (44), Martinstown III	*Ibid.*	Indet.	*D.N.A.S.* XXVI, 23–35, Pl. VI, 21
216	Winterbourne St Martin (32),	*Ibid.* (1)	FP	A. 17; *D.B.*, 153;
217 F	Clansdown	(2)	E.	*D.N.A.S.* XXIX, 140, no. 93 for (1)
218	Worth Matravers, Sheepsleighs, nr. Swanage	B.M. Unreg. 1962	FP S4	*D.N.A.S.* 81, 117

Durham

Corpus no.	Site	Museum	Beaker group	References
219	Brandon Hill, Brancepeth, Tally-Ho Gate	Unknown	N2	*P.S.A.New.* 3s. I, 140; *Arch. Ael.* 3s. XI, 131, Fig.
220	Clara Vale, Ryton	Unknown	N3	*Arch. Ael.* 3s. XI, 132, Fig. 6; *P.S.A.New* 3s. V, 18–19
221	Hasting Hill, nr. Offerton	Sunderland	N/NR-FN?	*Antiquary*, XLVIII, 75; *Arch. Ael.* 3s. XI, 135, Fig. 15
222 F	Kellow Law	Barnard Castle	Indet.	*Arch. Ael.* 4s. XXIX, 213
223	Sacriston	B.M. Lost	N2	*Arch. Ael.* 3s. XI, 134, Fig. A. 177

Essex

Corpus no.	Site	Museum	Beaker group	References
224	Alresford Pit	Colchester 168.42	E. Ang.	*Ant. J.* XXVI, 67, Pl. IX, 3
225	Ardleigh, Martell's Fm.	*Ibid.* 63.44	E. Ang.	*Ibid.* 4
226 F	Berden	Saffron Walden	S2(W)?	*E.A.S.* NS. XV, 282, Fig. 1B; *E.A.S.* NS. XVI, 144
227	Colchester district?	Colchester 195.01	N2(L)	*Ant. J.* II, 338, Fig. 1

Corpus no.	Site	Museum	Beaker group	References
228 F	Colchester, Chitts Hill	*Ibid.* 808.04	E.	Unpub.
229	Colchester, Flagstaff Rd.	*Ibid.* 85.30	S2(E)	*Ant. J.* XXVI, 67–8, Pl. IX, 5
230 F	DOVERCOURT, MILL BAY	B.M.	FN	*J.R.A.I.* XLII, 119;
231 F		Unreg.	E. Ang.?	*P.P.S.* II, 182–90
232	Fingringhoe	Colchester 350.97	BW	*E.A.S.* XV, 290; A. 87
233	Great Chesterford, Borough Field	Cambridge (1) 48.342	S3(E)	*A.C.R.* App. I, no. VI; *P.S.A.L.* XXXII, 15
234	*Ibid.* ?	(2) 48.341	S3(E)	*A.C.R.* App. I, VII
	Great Clacton, Bull Hill	Colchester		*Ant. J.* IX, 251,
235		(1) 104.92	FN	Fig. 2; A. 85;
236		(2) Lost	—	*E.A.S.* XIII, 289;
237		(3) Lost	—	*V.C.H. Essex* I,
238		(4) Lost	—	255–65, Fig. 14 for (1), Fig. 15 incorrect
239 F	Hallsford	B.M. LV.1938	FP	Unpub.
240 F	Sand Pit	*Ibid.*	FN	*Ibid.*
241	Halstead, Piercy's	Colchester 719.57	E. Ang. FN.	*Ant. J.* XXVI, 67, Pl. IX, 1
242	Langham	*Ibid.* 2019.10	N2(L)	*E.A.S.* NS. XV, 287–9, Fig. 2; *Ant. J.* II, 330
243	Linford, Hall's Pit	Grays Thurrock	Bowl	*E.A.S.* XXV, Pt. III, 385; Thurrock Library Rep. 1958/9, 16, Pl.
244 F	LION POINT, JAYWICK, CLACTON	B.M.	FP	*P.P.S.* II, 178–90;
245 F		79 8–1 1	SH4(B)	*Lon. Inst. Rep.* II, 29;
246 F		*Ibid.*	BW	*J.R.A.I.* XLII, 119
247 F		*Ibid.*	E. Ang.?	*Ibid.*
248 F		*Ibid.*	FN	*Ibid.*
	Little Holland	Colchester		*Ant. J.* IX, 251,
249		(1) 1929	BW	Fig. 1, 1,
250		(2) 1929	E. Ang.	Fig. 1, 2
251	Manningtree, Furze Hill	Lost	E. Ang. FN	Unpub. MSS Ipswich Mus.
252	Oakley, Great	Colchester 137.93	FN	*V.C.H. Essex*, I, 265, Fig. 16
253 F	Pledgdon Sand Pit	B.M. Unreg.	FN	Unpub. Hazzledine-Warren
254	Rainham	Lost	S2(E)	*Arch.* 96, 159–62, Pl. LXIIA
255	St Osyth	Colchester 1931	E.	*Ant. J.* XXVI, 67–8, Pl. IX, 2
	SHOEBURY I (1909)	*Ibid.*		*Arc. Camb.* 7s. V, 26
256 F		(1) 1824.09B	E. Ang. FN	*E.A.S.* XV, 289, no. 1
257 F		(2) 1824.09C	E. Ang. FN	*Ibid.* no. 2
258 F		(3) 1824.09A	BW	Pollitt, Pl. XVI
259 F		(4) 1824.09D	E. Ang.?	Unpub.
260		(5) 1824.09	BW	Unpub.
260.1 F			{ FN	
260.2 F	SHOEBURY II	*Ibid.*	{ Undec.	Unpub.
261 F	(1904)	480.A.12.04	{ E.	*Ibid.*
262 F	Nr. Southchurch	*Ibid.*	E. Ang.	*Ibid.*
	Sible Hedingham	Colchester		*Ant. J.* IX, 252, Fig. 3
262.1	Hedingham	(1) 3.29.1	SH2(A)	*Ibid.*
262.2		(2) 3.29.2	?SH2(B)	*Ibid.*
263	Thorpe Hall, Southchurch	Prittlewell 375.1	N3?	*E.A.S.* XIX, 312–13, Fig. 3
	Thorpe Hall, Southchurch	*Ibid.*		*E.A.S.* XXV Pt. III,
264		(1) 859.1	W/MR	388
265		(2) 859.2	N2(L)	*Ibid.*
266 F		(3) 859.3	S1	*Ibid.*
267 F		(4) 859.4	S1	*Ibid.*
268	Thorpe Hall, Southchurch	*Ibid.* 189.1	E. Ang. Undec.	*Southend before the Conquest*, 63 (Iron Age)
269 F	Thorpe Hall, Southchurch	*Ibid.* 198.3	S1?	*E.A.S.* XIX, 311–13

Corpus no.	Site	Museum	Beaker group	References
270 F	SOUTHMINSTER CUTTING	Colchester	S4	Unpub.
271 F		34.89	FP	
272 F	Ulting, Gravel Pit	*Ibid.* 416.54	N3?	Unpub.
273	Essex, Unprovenanced	*Ibid.* 349.97	FP	Unpub.
274 F	WALTON-ON-THE-NAZE,	B.M.	FN	*P.P.S.* II, 182, Fig. 3, 1
275 F	STONE POINT	HW.15106	Indet.	
276	West Mersea	Colchester 2912.14	FN	*E.A.S.* XIII, Mus. Rep. 7, Pl. 2, 2; *E.A.S.* XV, 289

Gloucestershire

Corpus no.	Site	Museum	Beaker group	References
277	Barnwood	Cheltenham	N2	*P.P.S.* III, 160, Pl. XI(E); *B. and G.A.S.* LII, 218
278	Bourton-on-the-Water	Cheltenham	S3(E)	*P.P.S.* III, 163, Pl. XI(A)
279 F	Bourton-on-the-Water	Cheltenham	Indet.	*Ant. J.* XII, 284, Fig. 2, no. 3
280 F	Frampton on Severn,	Prof. R. J. C. Atkinson		*B. and G.A.S.* LXXIX, 24 and 114
	Barrow	(1)	—	
281 F		(2)	—	
282 F	Lechmore, Nailsworth	Gloucester A.3088	Indet.	*P.P.S.* III, 159, Pl. XI(B)
283 F	Leckhampton Camp	Cheltenham	Indet.	*P.P.S.* III, 159, Pl. XI(C); *B. and G.A.S.* XLVIII, 105
284 F	Notgrove Long barrow	*Ibid.*	Indet.	*P.P.S.* III, 162(J); *Arch.* 86, 146–7
285	Prestbury	Unknown	N/NR	*B. and G.A.S.* LX, 348, Fig.
286 F	Great Rissington, Long barrow	Gloucester	Indet.	*P.P.S.* III, 162(H)
287 F	Shenbarrow Camp, Stanton	*Ibid.*	Indet.	*P.P.S.* III, 162(G); *B. and G.A.S.* LXXX, 5, Fig. 8
288 F	Shurdington	Mrs N. Clifford	Indet.	*P.P.S.* III, 162(I)
	Swell	Ashmolean		*P.P.S.* III, 161,
289 F	Long barrows	VI 1936.11*a*	E.	Fig. 2(F)
290 F		VIII 1936.11*b*	Indet.	*P.P.S.* III, 161
300	Woodchester barrow	Stroud	S2(W)	*P.P.S.* III, 160, Pl. XI(D); *B. and G.A.S.* XLVIII, 304

Hampshire

Corpus no.	Site	Museum	Beaker group	References
301	Alton, Lower Farringdon	Alton	S2(E)	*Ant. J.* XXVII, 80, Fig.
	Boscombe Cemetery	B.M.		*S.E.U.S.S.* 40, 26,
302		1940 7–1 719	W/MR	Fig. 2;
303 F		Birmingham	W/MR	*B.N.S.S.* XXVIII, Table 1
304 F		*Ibid.* 40.36	AOC	*Ibid.*
305 F	Boscombe, Thistlebarrow	Christchurch	Indet.	*D.N.A.S.* 73, 62, Pl. 1C, 9
	Bournemouth, Glenferness Av.	B.M.		*S.E.U.S.S.* 40, 27, Fig. 4;
306		(1) 1940 7–1 720	S4	*P.P.S.E.A.* VII, 133;
307	Talbot Woods	(2) 1940 7–1 721	FP	*D.N.A.S.* 73, 60, Pl. IIIA
308		(3) 1940 7–1 722	S4	*Ibid.*
309 F	Bournemouth	Christchurch	W/MR	Unpub.
310	Bournemouth, Nursery Rd.	B.M.	FP Bowl	*S.E.U.S.S.* XL, 31, Fig. 10; *D.N.A.S.* 73, 60, Pl. 1B
	Brown Candover	Basingstoke		*H.F.C.* XII, 88;
311		(1) OC.701	S2(E)	*H.F.C.* XVIII, 61,
312 F		(2) OC.701	FN	Pl. XIII, 5; Unpub.
	Christchurch, Latch Fm., Furzy	Christchurch		*D.N.A.S.* 73, 61,
313		(1) FLF.4	E.	Pl. IIA
314 F		(2) Unreg.	AOC	Unpub.
315	Christchurch, Latch Fm, Furzy	*Ibid.* FLF.1	SH3(C)	*B.N.S.S.* 28, 51, Fig. 5; *D.N.A.S.* 73, 51, Fig. 1A
316 F	Christchurch, Latch Fm., Furzy	*Ibid.* FLF.7	FP	*D.N.A.S.* 73, 51, Fig. 1A
	Christchurch, Latch Fm.,	*Ibid.*		*D.N.A.S.* 73, 46, 60, 62,
317 F	Lower Close	LCLF 1–5	FP	Pl. 1D,
318 F			E.	Fig. 1D,
319 F		B.M. Unreg.	S2?	Fig. 1E

Corpus no.	Site	Museum	Beaker group	References
320 F	Christchurch, Latch Fm. barrow	B.M. 1940 7–1 717	FP	*P.P.S.* III, 442; *P.P.S.* IV, 172, Fig. 3
321 F	Christchurch, Wick Fm.	Christchurch	W/MR	*D.N.A.S.* 73, 62, Pl. IC, 7
322 F	Danebury West	Winchester	FP	*H.F.C.* XIV, 199
323	Fordingbridge	Salisbury 176	W/MR	*Arc. Camb.* 7s. V, 27
324 F	Hengistbury Head	Christchurch Hes. I	FP	*D.N.A.S.* 73, 62, Pl. IC, no. 8
325 F	Holdenhurst	*Ibid.*	FP	*P.P.S.* II, 20, Pl. XI;
326 F	Long barrow		S2(W)	*P.P.S.* III, 11–12
327 F			FP Bowl	*Ibid.*
	Iford, Castle Lane, Sheepwash	B.M.		*S.E.U.S.S.* 40, 28, Fig. 5;
328		(1) 1940 7–1 723	S2(E)	*D.N.A.S.* 73, 60,
329		(2) 1940 7–1 724	FN	Pl. IIIB
330		(3) 1940 7–1 725	E	*Ibid.*
331	Kinson, Broadway	Poole	N2(L)	*B.N.S.S.* XXVIII, 52–3, Fig. 7; *D.N.A.S.* 73, 43, Fig. IB
332	Kinson, Horsham Av.	B.M. 1940 7–1 718	S4	*S.E.U.S.S.* XL, 26, Fig. 3; *B.N.S.S.* XXVIII, 48, Fig. 2
333	Lymore, nr. Lymington	Christchurch	S2(W)	*Ant. J.* VIII, 95, Fig. 2
334	Martin	Salisbury 176	W/MR	*Arc. Camb.* 7s. V, 27
335	Michelmarsh, Broom Hill	Private Winchester	E	*Ant. J.* XIV, 251, Pl. XXIV Unpub.
336 F	Otterbourne-Silkstead, Poles Lane Pit	(1)	W/MR	*Ibid.*
337 F		(2)	W/MR	*Ibid.*
338 F	Over Wallop	Southampton (Lost)	Indet.	*H.F.C.* XIV, 270
339 F	Penton Grafton, Nutbane Long barrow	Andover	W/MR	*P.P.S.* XXV, 42, Fig. 8
340 F	Penton Mewsey, Mark Lane	Winchester	Indet.	*H.F.C.* VIII, Pt. III, 356
341 F	Purbrook, Gob's barrow	Lost	Indet.	*P.P.S.E.A.* VI, 355, App. II, no. 44
342 F	Rockbourne Down, barrow 1	Salisbury 1940	Indet.	*H.F.C.* XVI, Pt. 2, 157, Fig. 3
343 F	Roundwood, nr. Micheldever	Winchester	W/MR	*H.F.C.* IX, Pt. 2, 194–5, Pl. II, no. 62
344	Southborne, Whitepits	Christchurch SFDD–1	FN	*D.N.A.S.* 73, 60–1, Fig. IC; *B.N.S.S.* XXVIII, 52, Fig. 6
345 F	Southbourne, Heatherlea	Christchurch	FN	*D.N.A.S.* 73, 60–2, Pl. IC, 3 and 4
346 F	Southbourne, Roebury	*Ibid.*	E.	*D.N.A.S.* 73, 62,
347 F			FN	Pl. IC, 1, 2, 5, 6
348	Stockbridge Down	B.M. 1939 5–6 12	W/MR	*Ant. J.* XXVIII, 149, Pl. XVIIA
349	Stockbridge Down, no. 1	Unknown	N2	*Ant. J.* XX, 41, Pl. III
350	Warsash, Newbury Pit	Winchester	Undec. W/MR	*H.F.C.* XVI, 190–3
351	Weeke, nr. Winchester	*Ibid.*	S2(W)	*H.F.C.* XIX, Pt. 3, 276, Fig. I
	Winchester, St James' Terrace			*Antiquary*, XXVI, 233
352		⎰(1) *Ibid.*	⎰W/MR	*Ibid.*
353		⎱(2) Portsmouth	⎱BW	*Ibid.*

Herefordshire

	Olchon Valley	Hereford		*W.N.F.C.* (1930–2),
354		(1)	N/MR	147–53
355		(2)	N/MR	*B.B.C.S.* VI, 378–80
356 F	Mathon, Southend Fm.	Hereford	S3(W)	*W.N.F.C.* (1936–8), 127, Fig. 6
357 F	Ross-on-Wye, Merlins Cave	Bristol Spelaeo	Indet.	*B.U.S.S.* 2, no. 2, 151, Fig. 3

Hertfordshire

358	Hitchin?	B.M. 1915 12–8 206	S2(E)	*E.A.S.* NS. XV, 285, Fig. IA

Corpus no.	Site	Museum	Beaker group	References
359 F	Royston Heath, Long barrow	Cambridge 35.181	S2(W)	*P.P.S.* I, 106, Fig. 5
360	Tewin Chalkpit	Letchworth 29.59	FP	*E. Herts.A.S.* News Letter no. 8
361	Tring, The Grove	(1) Lost	—	*P.S.A.L.* 2s. V, 272;
362		(2) Lost	—	*Arch.* VIII, 429
363	Ware, Watton Rd	Hertford	S2(E)	*E. Herts.A.S.* X, Pt. III, 327, Fig.

Huntingdonshire

363.1 F	Brampton, barrow	M.O.W.	E.	M.O.W. excavation (1966), Unpub.
	Eynesbury, St Neots	Cambridge		*Ant. J.* X, 384–5,
364		(1) Z11486A	N2(L)	Pl. LVIA,
365		(2) Z11486B	S1	Pl. LVIB
	Houghton	St Ives		*Camb. and Hunts.A.S.*
366		(1) 30.659	S2/Hybrid	V, 248, Figs. 1, 2, 3;
367		(2) D55.8	N2(L)	*Ant. J.* X, 385
368		(3) D55.9	E. Ang. FN	
369 F	Orton Longueville	Cambridge Unreg.	Indet.	Unpub.
370	Ramsey St Mary	Peterborough	S1	*Arch.* LXII, 339; *V.C.H.Hunts.* I, 203
371	Somersham	Cambridge 1883.183	FP	A. 76; *P.P.S.* II, Pl. XII; *A.C.R.* App. I, XXIII
372	Somersham?	*Ibid.* 23.1215	H(FV)	*A.C.R.* App. I, no. XXX; *Ant. J.* IV, 131–3, Fig.
373	Stanground	Peterborough	N/NR	*V.C.H.Hunts.* I, 202, Note 2, Pl. 3

Isle of Man

374	Lonan, nr. Baroose	Unknown	N3	*C.A.S.* XXIV, 83 *P.P.S.* I, 83, Pl. IV, 1

Isle of Wight

375	Afton, nr. Freshwater	S. H. Warren Coll. B.M.?	Bowl	*I.O.W.N.H.A.S.* (1933), 293, Pl. I, Fig. 3
376 F	Arreton Down barrow	Carisbrooke	E.?	*P.P.S.* XXVI, 276,
377 F			Indet.	Fig. 7, nos. 47–9
378 F	Bonchurch, nr. Ventnor	*Ibid.*	S2(W)?	*I.O.W.N.H.A.S.* (1933), Pl. I, Fig. 6
379 F	Chale, Gore Down	Private	S2(W)?	*I.O.W.N.H.A.S.* (1933), 294, Pl. I, Fig. 4 a–f
380 F	Freshwater	Lost	S3(E)	*I.O.W.N.H.A.S.* (1933), 293, Pl. II
381 F	Niton Down barrow 2	Carisbrooke	Indet.	*I.O.W.N.H.A.S.* (1933), 294
382	Nodgham, Carisbrooke	Carisbrooke	S3(E)	*I.O.W.N.H.A.S.* (1933), 292, Pl. I, Fig. 1; *Arch.* LXXVI, 92, Fig. 22
383 F	St Johns, Ryde	*Ibid.*	Indet.	*I.O.W.N.H.A.S.* (1933), 295, Fig. 7 a–b

Kent

384 F	Allington	Lost	—	Jessup, 94; *Arc. Camb.* 7s. V, 27
385	Barham	Canterbury	E.	*A.C.* XLV, 175, Fig.
386	Barham	Newbury	E. Ang. FN	*Ant. J.* XIV, 183–4, Fig.
387	Brendly	Taunton	S1	A. 6; Jessup, 91

Corpus no.	Site	Museum	Beaker group	References
388	Bromley	Canterbury	E. Ang.	*A.C.* XLV, 174–5, Fig. *Arch. Assoc.* XXXIX, 407
389	Canterbury	B.M. 1910 12–10 32	N/MR	*V.C.H.Kent*, I, 324; Jessup, 93
390	Canterbury, Littlebourne	Canterbury 2687	BW	*P.S.A.L.* 2s. XVIII, 279
	Capel-le-Ferne, Folkestone	B.M.		
391		(1) 1955 7–3 1	S 1	Unpub.
392		(2) 1955 10–8 1	N 3	Unpub.
	Chislet, Highstead	B.M.		Jessup, 91;
393		(1) 1903 11–15 216	E.	A. 34;
394		(2) 1903 11–15 217	E.	A. 35
395	Dover, Connaught Park, Maison Dieu Fields	Dover, Destroyed	E. Ang.	*A.C.* XLV, 175
396	Dover Aerodrome	Deal	E. Ang. FP	*Ant. J.* XVI, 469, Pl. LXXXVIII right
397	Dover, St Margaret's Bay	Deal	N 3	*A.C.* LXX, 267
	Erith	London		Jessup, 90;
398		(1) A. 17459	E. Ang.	A. 36;
399		(2) A. 17460	E. Ang.	A. 37
400	Folkestone District	Folkestone	BW	*Ant. J.* XX, 487, Pl. LXXXIX, right
401	Folkestone Golf Links	*Ibid.*	N 3	*Ant. J.* XX, 487, Pl. LXXXIX, left
	Gravesend District?	Gravesend Hist. Soc.		Unpub.
402 F		(1)	BW	*Ibid.*
403 F		(2)	BW	*Ibid.*
404 F		(3)	E. Ang.	*Ibid.*
405 F		(4)	FP	*Ibid.*
406	Great Mongeham, Ripple	Deal	E. Ang.	*Ant. J.* XVI, 469, Pl. LXXXVIII, 2, left
407	Ightham	B.M. 1931 12–14 1	E. Ang.	*A.C.* XLV, 174, Fig. *Ant. J.* XII, 169, Fig. 2a
	Ightham? Reidentified, see Rayheugh, Northumberland	Maidstone		*A.C.* XLV, 174; *B.B.* 413–15
408	Maidstone, Lower Fant	Maidstone	E.	Jessup, 91, Fig. 14
409	Preston, nr. Ash	Canterbury	E. Ang.	Unpub.
410 F	Seasalter at Sea	Canterbury 7242	Indet.	Unpub.
411 F	Sturry Vicarage	Maidstone		
412		(1)	BW	*A.C.* XLV, 175–6, Fig.
		(2) Lost	—	*Ibid.*
413	Tovil	Maidstone	BW	Jessup, 91, Fig. 14
414	Upper Deal, Mongeham Lane	Deal	E. Ang.	*A.C.* LXIV, 150

Lancashire

Corpus no.	Site	Museum	Beaker group	References
415 F	WALNEY NORTH END	Barrow in Furness	AOC	*C.W.A.S.* NS. L, 15;
416 F			FN	*C.W.A.S.* NS. LV, 1
417 F			Undec.	*Ibid.*
	Warton Crag, Dogs Hole Cave, nr. Carnforth	Lancaster		Jackson, 102, 99, Fig.
418 F		(1)	AOC	*C.W.A.S.* NS. XIII, 56;
419 F		(2)	Indet.	H.M.C. 46–7

Leicestershire and Rutland

Corpus no.	Site	Museum	Beaker group	References
	Glaston Sand Pit	Oakham School		Unpub.
420		(1)	W/MR	ex Wymann-Abott
421 F		(2)	S 1?	Coll.
422	Glaston Sand Pit	London Inst.	E. (Undec.)	*Ibid.*

485

Corpus no.	Site	Museum	Beaker group	References
423	Harston	Ashmolean 1927.620	FP	*Ox.* III, 19, Pl. IVD
424	Knipton	Belvoir Castle	S3(W)	*Ant. J.* XV, 61, Figs. *Invent.G.B.* 20
425	Melton Mowbray?	Leicester	S1	*Ant. J.* XVII, 71, Fig.
	North Kilworth	Leicester		*Leics.A.S.* III, 111
426		(1) *Ibid.*	S2(E)	*Ibid.*
427		(2) Lost	—	*Ibid.*
428	Noseley	Leicester	S2(E)	*Ant. J.* XXI, 232, Fig.

Lincolnshire

Corpus no.	Site	Museum	Beaker group	References
429 F	Ashby Corner	Scunthorpe	N2	*N.W.Lincs.* 62
430 F	ASHBY PUERORUM, STAINSBY	Lincoln	FP	Unpub.
431 F			S4	Several hundred
432 F			SH4(C)	Sherds.
433 F	Bagmoor Mine	Scunthorpe	S2(W)	*N.W.Lincs.* 62
434 F	Barrowby	Grantham	FP	Unpub.
435 F	Barrowby	Lost	SH?	Unpub.
436	Billinghay	Lincoln 311.08	S2(W)	*Arch. J.* XCI, 159; *Arch. J.* CIII, Pl. IIC; 'Sleaford', Trollope (1860), 30, Pi. I, Fig. 4
437	Broughton	Scunthorpe 8.56	S3(E)	Unpub.
438 F	Burton Stather	D. N. Riley	S2(W)	*Arch. J.* XCI, 162
439	Gaythorpe	Grantham	FP	*Arch. J.* CIII, 6, Pl. IIE; *Arch. J.* XCI, 163
440 F	Conesby Mine	Scunthorpe	FP	*Arch. J.* XCI, 162; *N.W.Lincs.* 62
441 F	CROSBY WARREN	B.M.	FP	*Arch. J.* XCI, 175;
442 F		1935 2–5 86–90	Indet.	*P.P.S.* XXIII, 46
443 F		Scunthorpe	FN	*Ibid.*
444 F		*Ibid.*	AOC	*Ibid.*
445	Denton	B.M. WG.2282	S1	A. 58
446	Denton	Lincoln 1940.18	SH3(C)	*Arch. J.* XC, 125, Pl. IV
447 F	Denton	Grantham EBP.8	S2(W)	*Arch. J.* XCI, 165
448 F	FLIXBOROUGH	Scunthorpe	FN	*Arch. J.* XCI, 167; *N.W.Lincs.* 62
449 F	Grainthorpe, Beacon Hill	Private	S?	Unpub.
450	Grantham, Harlaxton Rd.	Grantham	S2(W)	*A.A.S.R.* 38, 207; *Arch. J.* CIII, 6, Pl. IID
451	Grantham, Harrowby Lane	Grantham EBP.18	SH4(B)	*Arch. J.* CIII, 6, Pl. IIF; *A.A.S.R.* 38, 207
	Grantham, Wyndham Park	*Ibid.*		Unpub.
452 F		(1) EBP.40	FP	*Ibid.*
453 F		(2) EBP.41	S2(W)	*Ibid.*
453.1	Kirkby-on-Bain, Tattershall Thorpe	Lincoln	N/NR	*Lincs. History and Arch.* 1, no. 1 (1964–5)
454 F	MANTON WARREN	B.M.	AOC	*Arch. J.* XCI, 175;
455 F		1935 2–5 97–102	FN	*P.P.S.* XXIII, 46
456 F		Scunthorpe	AOC and FN	*Ibid.*
457 F		Lincoln	AOC and FN	*Ibid.*
458 F		*Ibid.*	E. and S3(?)	*Ibid.*
459 F	NORMANBY PARK	Scunthorpe	Undec.	*Arch. J.* CIII, 5–6;
460 F			AOC	*P.P.S.* XXIII, 44
461 F	Osgodby	Lincoln	S2(W)	Unpub.
462 F	Ponton	Grantham DN.2871	Indet.	Unpub.

Corpus no.	Site	Museum	Beaker group	References
463	Revesby Abbey	Lincoln 107.11	S 1	*Arch. J.* LXXXIX, 179; *A.A.S.R.* 38, 207
464 F	RISBY WARREN	Cambridge 35.1242–3	FP	*Arch. J.* XC, 129;
465 F			Indet.	*P.P.S.* XXIII, 40, Figs.
466 F		B.M.	*Ibid.*	*Ibid.*
467 F		1935 2–5	S?	*Ibid.*
468 F		Scunthorpe	AOC	*Ibid.* Fig. 7, no. 2;
469 F		*Ibid.*	N/NR	*Ibid.* Fig. 7, no. 1;
470 F		*Ibid.*	N 2	*Ibid.*
471 F		*Ibid.*	FP	*Ibid.* Pl. IX, 3;
472 F		*Ibid.*	S 3(E)	*Ibid.* Pl. IX, 1 and 2
473 F		*Ibid.*	S 4	*Ibid.*
474 F		*Ibid.*	SH 4(C)	*Ibid.*
475 F		*Ibid.* SM.2	SH 4(B)	*Ibid.* Fig. 4, no. 9
476 F	Roxby, Ryecliffe	Private	N 2?	Unpub.
477 F	Roxby, Sheffields Hill	Private	Indet.	*N.W.Lincs.* 63
478	Salmonby	Lincoln 12.54	N 1/D	Unpub.
479 F	Salmonby, New England	Lincoln	S 4	Unpub.
480 F	Scotton	Private	Indet.	*N.W.Lincs.* 63
481 F	Skendleby, Giant's Hill	B.M.	AOC	*Arch.* 85, 53, Fig. 22
482 F		1935 4–12	S 2(W)	*Ibid.* 67 Figs.
483 F	SOUTH KELSEY	Lincoln	S 4	Unpub.
484 F			FP	
484.1	South Willingham	Lincoln	SH 3(C)	Unpub.
484.2		1966	S 2(E)	Unpub.
485 F	Stenigot, Louth	Private	S?	Unpub.
486 F	Sudbrook	Grantham	S 2(W)	*Arch. J.* XCI, 182
486.1 F	Tallington	Cambridge	S 2(E)?	Unpub. 1963
487 F	Thealby Mine	Scunthorpe	S 3(E)?	Unpub.
488	Thornton, nr. Horncastle	Lost	S 4	*Arch. J.* XIII, 86, Fig. A. 60a
489 F	West Keal, Bunkers Gorse	Lincoln	Indet.	*Arch. J.* XCI, 170
490 F			FP	
491 F	WEST KEAL, HALL HILL	Lincoln	E.	*Arch. J.* LXXXIX, 180
492 F			FN	
493	Woolsthorpe?	York 1006.47	S 3(E)	*Arch. J.* XCI, 163; A. 67
494	Wooton, Howe Hill Barrow	Lost	—	*Arch. J.* XCI, 187

Middlesex and London

	Brentford, Old England	London		Vulliamy, 87;
495		(1) P.16	FP	*Arch.* 69, 11, Fig. 8, 2;
496		(2) P.20	E. Ang.	*Ibid.* Fig. 8, 1
497 F	Bow, Victoria Park	B.M. 64 2–12 1	FN	*P.S.A.L.* 2s. II, 350
498 F	Hammersmith, Crabtree	*Ibid.* 1906 7–2 10	FP	*Arch. J.* LXXXVI, 84
499	Hammersmith	London P.15.1865	E. Ang. FN	Vulliamy, 87; *Arch.* 69, 11
500 F	Hammersmith, Thames	Guildhall A.19481	FP	Unpub.
501	Leadenhall St., Midland Bank	Guildhall	S 1?	Unpub. Dubious authenticity

Norfolk

502 F	Arminghall Henge	Norwich	FP	*P.P.S.* II, 18, Fig. 9
503	Bardolph Fen	Wisbech 6.11.1835	W/MR	*Arc. Camb.* 7s. V, 26
504	Barton Bendish	Cambridge 36.105	S 1	*C.A.S.* XXXVII, 74, Pl. IIb

Corpus no.	Site	Museum	Beaker group	References
505 F	Barton Bendish, Marham Airfield	Norwich 169.953	E. Ang.	N.A.S. XXXI, 397, 224–30
506 F	Barwick	Norwich 151.957	S2(W)?	Unpub.
507	Bergh Apton	*Ibid.* 34.14	FP	*C.A.S.* XXXIX, 50
	Blakeney, Gallows Hill	Nottingham University		N.A.S. XXVIII (1942), Pt. I, 25
508		(1)	N3	
509		(2)	N3	Unpub.
510	Bodney Hall	Norwich 185.930	SH3(A)	*P.P.S.E.A.* VI, Pl. XIX; *P.P.S.E.A.* VII, 107–10
511	Brancaster	*Ibid.* 230.960	SH4(B)	Unpub.
512 F	Bridgham	*Ibid.* 20.953	S?	Unpub.
513 F	Caldecote	*Ibid.* 413.960	Indet.	Unpub.
	Castle Acre	Norwich		*C.A.S.* (1895), 85;
514		(1) 66.29	S3(E)	A. 44
515 F		(2) 25.90	S3(E)?	Unpub.
516 F		(3) 25.90	S2(E)	Unpub.
517	Chedgrave	*Ibid.* 395.960	E. Ang.	Unpub.
518	Cley Churchyard	*Ibid.* 44.06	N2	N.A.S. XXII (1925), 208; *Nor. Mus. Cat.* (1909), no. 321
519	Cley-next-the-Sea	*Ibid.* 56.925	BW	N.A.S. XXII, Pt. II, 206 (1925)
520 F	Coltishall	Lost	S1	Rolfe Coll. MSS. F1084 Norwich
521	Cromer, Central Rd	Norwich 151.940	N1/D	N.A.S. XXVIII Pt. I, 25; *Ant. J.* XVI, Pl. 203–4
522	East Harling	*Ibid.* 174.929	S2/Hybrid	Unpub.
	East Tuddenham	*Ibid.*		*P.P.S.E.A.* VII, 424,
523		(1) 71.935	S1	Pl. XIX
524		(2) 71.935	FP	*Ibid.*
525	East Winch	*Ibid.* 607.76.94	S1	A. 91
526 F	EDINGTHORPE	*Ibid.*	FP	N.A.S. XXXI, Pt. IV.
527 F		177.952	FN	(Several hundred sherds)
528 F			SH4(C)	
529 F			S4	
530 F			E. Ang.	
531 F			E.	
531.1 F			Bowl?	
532 F	Feltwell	Kings Lynn	S3(E)	Unpub.
533 F	Frettenham	Norwich 222.960	E. Ang.	Unpub.
534	Gayton-Thorpe	Private	S4	Unpub.
535 F	Great Bircham, Boiler Common	Norwich	Indet.	Unpub.
536 F		1.32.958	FN	
537 F	Great Bircham, Hurm Covert	*Ibid.*	Indet.	Unpub.
538 F		1.32.9582	FN	
539 F	Great Massingham	*Ibid.* 35.954	S?	Unpub.
540 F		7.164.946	S?	*Ibid.*
541	Gresham, East Beckham	*Ibid.* 80.940	SH4(B)	*P.P.S.E.A.* I, 381, Fig. N.A.S. XXVIII, Pl. I, 1; *P.P.S.* VII, 144
542 F	Grimston	23.177.953	E.?	Unpub.
543 F	Grimston, Bell Inn	Lost	—	Unpub.
544 F	Grimston Heath	Sandringham?	FP	Unpub.
545	Halvergate	Norwich 376.959	N3	Unpub.
546 F	Harpley Common	Norwich 10.939	FP	Unpub.
547	Heacham	Kings Lynn	W/MR	N.A.S. XXXI, Pt. 4 (1957), 396
548 F	Heacham	Norwich 197.950	FN	*Ibid.*

Corpus no.	Site	Museum	Beaker group	References
549 F	Hilborough	Private	FP	Unpub.
550	Hilgay, Wood Hall	Cambridge 34.129	S4	*C.A.S.* XXXVII, Pl. II*a*, 75
551 F	HOE, EAST DEREHAM	Norwich	E. Ang.	*P.P.S.EA.*VI, 365–8
552 F		42.932A	FN	
553 F	HOCKWOLD-CUM-WILTON	*Ibid.*	FP	Unpub.
554 F		121.960	SH?	
555 F		43.953	S?	
556 F		11.32.958	FN	
557 F	*Ibid.*	Mr F. Curtiss	FP	Unpub. (Several hundred
558 F		*Ibid.*	S4	sherds)
559	Hockwold-cum-Wilton	Mr P. Salway Cambridge	S1	Rep. pending Camboritum
560	Kelling Heath	Norwich 1608.76.94	N2	A. 90
561 F	KINGS LYNN, S. WOOTON LANE	Kings Lynn	S4	Unpub.
562			FP	
563	Massingham Heath (Little)	*Ibid.*	N2(L)	*V.C.H.Norfolk*, I, 277; *Arc. Camb.* 7s. V, 27
564 F	Massingham	B.M.	FP	Unpub.
565 F	Heath	8.7.37	S4	
566 F	*Ibid.*	Norwich 4.164.946	*Ibid.*	*Ibid.*
567 F	METHWOLD, WHITEPOT DROVE	Norwich	E.	Unpub.
568 F		204.957	FN	
569	Methwold	B.M. 85 12–12 I	E. Ang. FN	*A.C.R.* App. I, XVIII; A. 80
570 F	Methwold, Hythe	Private 1957	—	Unpub.
571	North Creake	Norwich 370.957	SH4(B)	*N.R.C.B.* (1955), no. 8
572 F	Norwich, The Avenue	Norwich 154.948	Indet.	Unpub.
573 F	OVERA HEATH, ECCLES	*Ibid.* 43.932	FN	*P.P.S.E.A.* VI, 368
574 F			BW	
575 F			E. Ang.	
576 F			E. Ang.	
577	Rackheath, Dobbs Beck	*Ibid.* 98.35	N3	A. 92
578 F	REFFLEY, GAYWOOD, KINGS LYNN	*Ibid.*	FP	(Small sample)
579 F		11.164.946	S4?	
580 F		B.M.	FP	(Several hundred sherds)
581 F		1938 12–2	S4	B.M. 'Later Prehistoric
582 F			SH4(C)	Antiquities' (1953), 40, Fig.
583 F	Ringland	Norwich	Indet.	Unpub.
584	Rollesby	*Ibid.* 481.960	E. Ang.	Unpub.
	Runcton Holme	Cambridge		*P.P.S.E.A.* VII, 200;
585		(1) 32.6	S3(E)	*C.A.S.* XXXVIII, 164
586		(2) 31.344	E. Ang.	*Ibid.*
587		(3) 32.563	S3(E)	*Ibid.*
588 F		(4) 37.8	E. Ang.	*Ibid.*
589		(5) 37.9	E. Ang. FN	*Ibid.*
590		(6) 37.9A	E. Ang. FN	*Ibid.*
591 F		(7) 32.564	N2?	*Ibid.*
592 F		(8) 32.566A	N2?	*Ibid.*
593 F		(9) 32.566B	Indet.	*Ibid.*
594 F		(10) 37.11	FN	*Ibid.*
595	Salthouse	Norwich 197.955	N3	*N.R.C.B.* (1955), no. 8
596 F	Santon Warren	*Ibid.*	E. Ang.	Unpub.
597 F	East,	178.955	S2(W)	
598 F	West,	179.955	Indet.	Unpub.
599 F	*Ibid.*	*Ibid.*	FP	*Ibid.*

Corpus no.	Site	Museum	Beaker group	References
600 F	Santon Firebreak	*Ibid.* 311.962	FP	Unpub.
601 F	Snarehill, Great and Little	*Ibid.* 195.959	S?	Unpub.
602 F	Snettisham, Ken Hill	Norwich 219.950	Indet.	N.A.S. XXXI, Pt. IV, 396; *P.P.S.* XX, 34
603	Stalham, Devils Ditch	*Ibid.* 4.50	E. Ang.	A. 51
604 F	STOKE FERRY, RIVER WISSEY	Cambridge	FP	Unpub.
605 F		27.1260	FN	
606 F		28.7980	SH3(C)	
607 F		*Ibid.*	SH4(C)	
608 F		*Ibid.*	S4	
609 F		*Ibid.*	S2(W)	
610 F		*Ibid.*	N2	
611 F	Stowbridge, Luddington Pit	B.M.	FP	Unpub.
612 F		1937 5–4 16	S3(E)	
613	Stowbridge, Wallington	Norwich 18.164.946	E. Ang.	Unpub.
614	Sutton, Ingham Mill	*Ibid.* 106.945	FP	N.A.S. XVIII, Pt. II, Pl. XLIV
615 F	Swaffham, Castle Arch.	*Ibid.* 494.960	Indet.	Unpub.
616	Syderstone, Sculthorpe Airfield	*Ibid.* 138.950	E. Ang.	N.A.S. XXXI, 397
617 F	Taverham	*Ibid.* 291.959	N3	Unpub.
618 F	Thetford District	Thetford	S?	Unpub. W. G. Clarke Gift
619 F	Thetford Castle	Norwich 514.962	Indet.	Unpub.
620	Tottenhill Church	B.M. 1923.1–12.1	FN	K. and H. (1932), 101, Pl. VIII, 3
621	Trowse with Newton	Norwich 203.958	S2(E)	*P.P.S.* XXV, 270
622 F	WALLINGTON, STOWBRIDGE	B.M.	FP	*B.M.Quarterly*, 11, 192
623 F		1937 54–1 15	S4?	
624 F	Weeting	Norwich 10.939	Indet.	Unpub.
625 F	Weeting, Grimes Graves	Norwich 163.948	FP	Unpub.
626 F	WEETING, FENGATE FM.	Private	FP	Unpub.
627 F			S?	
628 F	West Rudham Long barrow	Norwich	Indet.	N.A.S. XXVI, Pt. 3 (1930), 328
629 F	West Runton	*Ibid.* 153.948	Indet.	*Ant. J.* XXIX, 81
630 F	Wormegay	Lost	Indet.	Unpub. (1938)
631 F	Wortwell	Norwich 167.950	S2(E)	N.A.S. XXXI, Pt. IV, 396

Northamptonshire

632	Brixworth	Northants 138/1954–5	SH3(B)	*P.S.A.L.* 2s. XIII, 301, Fig.; A. 295
633	Brixworth	*Ibid.* D 139/1954–5	W/MR	Unpub.
634	Brixworth	*Ibid.* 240/1954–5	S2(E)	Unpub.
635	Loddington, nr. Kettering	*Ibid.* D.39/1954–5	S4	*P.S.A.L.* 2s. XIX, 313; *Antiquary*, XXXIX (1903), 164; A. 66
636 F	NEWARK, AMERICA FM.	Peterborough	S2(W)	Unpub.
637 F			FP	Wymann Abbott Coll.
637.1 F			S3?	
638	Newton-in-the-Willows	B.M. 1925 7–8 1	SH3(B)	*Ant. J.* V, 430, Fig.
639 F	Norton Hall Gravel Pits	Lost	—	A. p. 56; *P.S.A.L.* 2s. II, 186; *P.S.A.L.* 2s. XIX, 313
	Peterborough, Fengate	London Inst.		
640		(1) Giant Bkr	W/MR	*Ant. J.* II, 226, Fig. 5
641		(2) Giant Bkr	W/MR	Unpub.

Corpus no.	Site	Museum	Beaker group	References
642		(3)	AOC	Unpub.
643 F	PETERBOROUGH, FENGATE	London Inst.	FP	*Arch.* 62, 334, Figs. 4–6
644 F	PIT No. 1	*Ibid.*	S2(E)	*Ibid.*
645		Northants Z12	S2(E)	*Ant. J.* II, 235, Fig. 14;
646		*Ibid.* 1907	S3(E)	*Arch.* 62, 336, Fig. 1, Pl. XXXVII

Northumberland

647	Akeld, nr. Wooler	Newcastle 1932.86	N/NR	*P.S.A.New.* 4s. 5 (1932), 333
647.1	Alnwick, Chatton	Newcastle	N/NR	Unpub. with
647.2		1967	N/NR	C. 14 date.
647.3			S4/FV	G. Jobey
648	Alnwick, Shipley Fm.	Alnwick 1958	N3	*Arch. Ael.* 4s. XXXVIII, 244 Fig.
649	Alnwick, Whitehouse	Alnwick, no. 20	N2	*Alnwick Cat.* Pl. XI, 13; A. 173*a*
650	Alwinton, nr. Harbottle	B.M. 79 12–9 1764	N/NR	A. 162
651 F	Alston, Kirkhaugh I	Newcastle 1936.13	AOC	*Arch. Ael.* 4s. XIII, 207–16
	Amble	Alnwick		*Arch. J.* XIV, 282, Fig.
652		(1) No. 19	N3	*Alnwick Cat.* Pl. XIV*a*, 1;
653		(2) Lost	—	A. 161*a* for (1)
654 F	Amble	Lost	—	*P.S.A.New.* VI (1893–4), 72
655	Amble	Newcastle 1923.2.1	N3	*P.S.A.New.* I, 4s. 8, Pl. *P.S.A.New.* NS. VI, 32 (1893–4)
656	Ancroft, Cursed Field	B.M. WG.2286	N3	A. 180
657 F	Bamburgh, Rayheugh Fm.	Maidstone, Kent	N3	*B.B.* 415; *A.C.* XLV, 174. In error as Ightham
658 F	Bamburgh 193, Rayheugh Fm.	Maidstone, Kent	N2	*B.B.* 413–14; *A.C.* XLV, 174. In error as Ightham
659	Bamburgh, Rosborough barrow 197	B.M. 79 12–9 1427	N2	*V.C.H.North.* I, 257–9; *B.B.* 415–16, Fig. 158; A. 181
660	Beanley Moor, Broomridge	Alnwick, no. 22	S2(W)	*Alnwick Cat.* Pl. XII, left, 14, no. 22; A. 159*a*
661	Bedlington, Mill Field	Hancock Mus. Newcastle	N3	*P.S.A.New.* 4s. X, 322, Pl. IV, 3
	Belford, Edmond Castle	Lost		*C.W.A.S.* VI (1883),
662		(1) *Ibid.*	—	470, Note
663		(2) *Ibid.*	—	*Ibid.*
664	Bellingham, Smalesmouth	B.M. 79 12–9 1770	N3	*B.B.* 436; A. 174; *N.D.N.H.* I(2), 153, P. XV, Fig. I
665	Bellingham, Sneep, Tarret Burn	Newcastle	N1/D	*P.S.A.New.* 3s. IV, 173; *Arch. Ael.* 2s. XV, 49, Fig. 2; A. 173
666	Black Heddon	Lost	N3	*Arch. Ael.* I, 5, Note *P.S.A.New.* 4s. XI, 270, Pl. IV
667	Blaydon, Summerhill	Sunderland	N2	*Arch. Ael.* 4s. XVI, 263, Fig.
668	Dalton, Huntlaw	Newcastle 1927.2A	FP	*Ant. J.* XIII, 262, Pl. XLI, Fig. 1; *P.S.A.New.* 4s. III, 19, Pl.
	Doddington, Horton Castle	Newcastle		*Arch. Ael.* 4s. VIII,
669		(1) 1830.3	N/NR	162
670		(2) Lost	—	
671	Ford, Etall Moor	B.M. 79 12–9 1740	N/NR	*B.B.* 404; A. 164
672 F	Ford, Etall Moor barrow 184	B.M. 79 12–9 1379	S4?	*B.N.C.* V, 197, Pl. XIII, Figs. 5 and 6

Corpus no.	Site	Museum	Beaker group	References
	Fowberry	B.M.		*Arch. Camb.* 7s. v, 28
673 F		(1) Unreg.	N2	*Ibid.*
674 F		(2) Unreg.	N2	*Ibid.*
	Hexham, Dilston Park, Cist (A)	Newcastle		*Arch. Ael.* 3s. II, 136–46;
675		(1) 1931.30	N/NR	*Ibid.* Fig. 1; A. 167;
676		(2) 1931.31	N3	*Ibid.* Fig. 2; A. 168;
677		(3) 1931.32	N/NR	*Ibid.* Fig. 3; A. 169;
678	*Ibid.* Cist (B)	(1) 1931.33	N/NR	*Ibid* A 170;
679		(2) 1931.34	N3	*Ibid.* A. 171
680	Hexham, Howford	Lost	—	*Arch. Ael.* 3s. II, 129
681	High Buston	Alnwick, no. 6A	N2	*Arch. Ael.* 3s. XI, 44, Pl. *P.S.A.New.* 3s. V, 243
682	Ilderton	Newcastle 1910.9	N/MR	*P.S.A.New.* 3s. IV, 198, Pl.
683	Jesmond	Newcastle 1814.14	N2	*Arch. Ael.* 4s. V, 19, Pl. V, 2
	Lesbury, Birney Knowe	Alnwick		*Alnwick Cat.* 12,
684		(1) No. 18	N2	Pl. XII, right; A. 172*a*
685		(2) Lost	—	
686	Lesbury, Hawkhill	Newcastle 1850.18	N2	*P.S.A.New.* 4s. XI, 274; *B.N.C.* III, 63, Fig.
	Lilburn Hill, Cairnfold Field	Newcastle		*Arch. Ael.* XIII, 352;
687		(1) 1888.22.1	S4	Pl. XXII, Fig. B; A. 166;
688		(2) 1889.22.1	N2	*P.S.A.New.* 2s. IV, 162
689 F		(3) *Ibid.* sherds	Indet.	*Ibid.*
690	Lilburn Steads	Kelvingrove 94.188	S2(W)	*P.S.A.L.* XXXII, 15; A. 159
691	Lilburn, West Lilburn	Newcastle Lost	N2	*Arch. Ael.* 4s. XXIV, 217, Fig.
692	Norham	B.M. 79 12–9 1738	N3	A. 183
693	Norham Castle Estate	B.M. 1936 10–14 1	N/NR	*P.S.A.New.* 4s. XI. 193
694	Norham, Gryndan	N.M.A. E.G. 34	N/MR	*P.S.A.S.* XXXVIII, 339, no. 110; A. 184
	North Sunderland, Blue Bell Inn	B.M.		*Arch. Ael.* 4s. XV, 150;
695		(1) WG.2283	N2	A. 179;
696		(2) WG.2284	N3	A. 178;
697 F		(3) Lost	—	*B.N.C.* IV, 428, Pl. XIII
697.1	Ponteland	Newcastle 1965	AOC Bowl	Unpub.
698	Rock, Ellsneuk barrow	Newcastle 1933.8	N/MR	*Ant. J.* II, 258; *P.S.A.New.* 4s. VI, 146–9
699 F	ROSS LINKS	Newcastle	AOC	*Arch. Ael.* 4s. V, 13, Pl.
700 F			FN	*P.S.A.New.* 4s. III, 75
701 F			Undec.	*Ibid.*
702 F			Indet.	*Ibid.*
703	Rothbury, Old	B.M. 79 12–9 1736	S2(W)	A. 158; *B.B.* 433
704 F	Rothbury	Alnwick Mechanics Inst.	N?	*P.S.A.New.* VII (1935), 33
	Scremerston, Borewell Fm.	Newcastle		*P.S.A.New.* 4s. XI, 264
705		(1) 1948.8(?)	N/NR	*Ibid.*
706		(2) Lost	—	*Ibid.*
707	Seahouses, Cist, 8, North Sunderland	Newcastle 1910.11	S2(E)	*P.S.A.New.* 3s. II, 194–5, Pl.
	Trewhitt Hall, barrow	Trewhitt Hall		*Antiquary*, XLVIII, 32;
708		(1) Restored	N3	*P.S.A.S.* XLVI, 21, Fig. 3;
709 F		(2) Sherds	Indet.	*Ibid.* Fig. 5
710	West Wharmley	Newcastle 1928.16	N2	*P.S.A.New.* 4s. III, 176, 187–9, Pl.
711	Woodhorn	B.M. 79 12–9 1753	S2(E)	A. 160
712	Unknown loc. Alnwick area?	Alnwick, no. 21	N3	*Alnwick Cat.* 13, no. 21, Pl. XIII; A. 174*a*

Nottinghamshire

Corpus no.	Site	Museum	Beaker group	References
	Clumber Park, The Dukeries,	Worksop		Unpub.
713	Worksop	(1)	S4	*Ibid.*
714		(2)	S4	*Ibid.*
715 F	Cromwell, Round barrow	Newark 104.50	Indet.	Unpub.

Oxfordshire

Corpus no.	Site	Museum	Beaker group	References
716	Cassington	Ashmolean 1931.526	W/MR	*Ant. J.* XIV, 268, Pl. XXX, 2; Oxon. 1
717	Cassington	*Ibid.* 1932.43	N/MR	*Ibid.*; Oxon. 2, Pl. XXXI, 1
718	Cassington Grave 1	*Ibid.* 1933.1619	FN	*Ibid.* 271; Oxon. 3, Pl. XXXI, 2
719	Cassington Grave 5	*Ibid.* 1933.1620	S4	*Ibid.*; Oxon. 4, Pl. XXXIII, 1
720 F	Cassington Grave 6	*Ibid.* 1933.1747	S4?	*Ibid.* 272; Oxon. 5
721	Cassington Grave 10	*Ibid.* 1933.1621	SH4(B)	*Ibid.* 273; Oxon. 6, Pl. XXXIII, 2
722	Cassington Grave 11	*Ibid.* 1933.1622	S4	*Ibid.* 274; Oxon. 7, Fig. 2
723 F	Cassington Grave 12	*Ibid.* 1933.1744	S?	*Ibid.* 274; Oxon. 8
724 F	CASSINGTON DOMESTIC PIT	*Ibid.*	FP	*Ox.* III, Pl. VB, 15,
725 F		1935.63*a*	S4?	30, App. III;
726 F		1935.66	Indet.	Oxon. 9–10
727 F	Cassington	*Ibid.* 1943.13	Indet.	Oxon. 35*a*
728 F	Cassington	*Ibid.* 1939.497	Indet.	*Ox.* V, 5; Oxon. 35
729	Cassington Pit II	*Ibid.* 1943.10	S4	*Ox.* VIII/IX, 193; Oxon. 36
730 F	Cassington (B)	*Ibid.* 1947.305	AOC	*Ox.* XVI, 1–4, Fig. 2*b*; Oxon. 37
731	Cassington (B)	*Ibid.* 1947.306	S4	*Ox.* XVI, 1–4, Fig. 2*a*; Oxon. 38
732 F	Clifton Hampden	*Ibid.* Pr. 75 (1896–1908)	AOC	*P.S.A.L.* 2s. III, 21; *Ox.* XXI, Fig. 2; Oxon. 11
733 F	Culham Fields	Lost	—	*Ox.* XXI, 11 Fig. 5; Oxon. 52
734 F	Dorchester	Unreg.	SH3(B)	*Ox.* III, 28; Oxon. 12
735	Dorchester Site XII	Ashmolean 1950.395	W/MR	*Ox.* XV, 106; Oxon. 50; *Invent. G.B.* 1
736 F	Dorchester	*Ibid.*	E.?	*Ox.* XVII, 216;
737 F	Site XIII		S?	*Ox.* XVI, 80; Oxon. 53
738	Dorchester	*Ibid.* 1962.245	S3(E)	Unpub. Oxon. 58(?)
739	Drayton St Leonard	Lost	E.?	Oxon. 13; *P.S.A.L.* 2s. II, 204
740	Eynsham, Foxley Fm.	Ashmolean 1930.761	SH2(B)	*Ant. J.* XI, 280, Pl. XXXIX, Oxon. 14
741	Eynsham	*Ibid.* 1937.617	N/NR	*Ox.* III, 28, P. IIID; Oxon. 15
742	Eynsham	*Ibid.* 1937.1618	SH4(B)	*Ibid.* Pl. IVA; Oxon. 16
743	Eynsham	*Ibid.* 1937.1619	S4	*Ibid.* Pl. IVB; Oxon. 17
744	Eynsham	*Ibid.* 1937.886	S3(E)	*Ibid.* Pl. IIIE; Oxon. 18
745	Eynsham	*Ibid.* 1938.405	S4	*Ibid.* App. I, no. 14; Oxon. 19
746	Eynsham	*Ibid.* 1953.IIIA	FP	*Ibid.* Pl. IVC, 15; *Invent. G.B.* 14; Oxon. 20
747	Eynsham	*Ibid.* 1938.406	S4	*Ox.* III, App. I, 18; Oxon. 21
748	Eynsham	*Ibid.* 1941.13	FN	*Ox.* XXI, 4, Fig. 1; *Ox.* VI, 85; Oxon. 39
	Eynsham	*Ibid.*		*Ox.* XXI, 4, Fig. 1;
749		(1) 1941.14	W/MR	Oxon. 40;
750		(2) 1941.15	Bowl	Oxon. 41
751	Eynsham	*Ibid.* 1941.12	S4	*Ox.* XXI, 5, Fig. 2; *Ox.* VI, 85; Oxon. 42
752 F	Eynsham, City Fm.	Unreg.	BW	Rep. pending
753	Hardwick	Banbury	S4	*Ox.* XXI, 10–11, Fig. 2; *P.S.A.L.* VII, 100, Fig. Oxon. 22
754 F	Langford Downs, Lechlade	Ashmolean 1952.563	Indet.	*Ox.* XI/XII, 63; Oxon. 49

Corpus no.	Site	Museum	Beaker group	References
755	Little Rollright	*Ibid.* 1951.379	W/MR	*Ox.* XVI, 80, Pl. IXB; *Ox.* XXI, 2, Fig.; Oxon. 34
756	North Stoke barrow	*Ibid.* (1) 1957.110	S3(E)	*Ox.* XXIX, 1–12, Fig. 4; Oxon. 51
757 F		(2) 1959.251	FP	
758	Oxford, Polstead Rd	*Ibid.* 1888.758	S3(E)	*P.S.A.S.* XXXVIII, 381, Fig. 51; Oxon. 23; A. 64
759	Oxford, Polstead Rd	*Ibid.* 1889.7	N/MR	*Ox.* III, 29, App. II; Oxon. 24
760	Oxford, Summertown	*Ibid.* 1886.1452	N/MR	*Ox.* XXI, Fig. 4; Oxon. 25 Mislabelled Oxon. 32
761	Oxford, Summertown	*Ibid.* (1) WG.1788	W/MR	*P.S.A.S.* XXXVIII, 306; A. 75; Oxon. 26;
762		(2) WG.1789	FN	Oxon. 27; *Arch.* LXXVI, 93–7
763 F	Standlake	*Ibid.* 1940.219	FP	*Ox.* VI, 88; Oxon. 48; *Ox.* XXI, 8
764	Stanton Harcourt	*Ibid.* 1930.647	N2	*Ox.* III, Pl. IIIC; *Ant. J.* XI, 59, Fig. 2; Oxon. 28
765	Stanton Harcourt	*Ibid.* 1930, 648	E. Ang.	*Ant. J.* XI, 59, Fig. 1; Oxon. 29
766	Stanton Harcourt	*Ibid.* 1930.649	FN	*Ant. J.* XI, 59, Fig. 3; Oxon. 30
767	Stanton Harcourt	*Ibid.* 1935.20	E.	*Ox.* III, 30, App. II; Oxon. 31
768	Stanton Harcourt	*Ibid.* (1) 1953.110a	E.	*Ox.* XVII/XVIII, 218; *Ox.* XXI, 5–6, Fig. 2; Oxon. 43;
769		(2) 1953.110b	E. Undec.	*Ibid.* Oxon. 44
770	Stanton Harcourt, Beard Mill	H. J. Case	E.	*Ox.* XXI, 6, Fig. 2; Oxon. 45
771 F	Stanton Harcourt, Beard Mill	H. J. Case	AOC	*Ox.* XXI, 6, Fig. 2; Oxon. 46
772	Stanton Harcourt, Linch Hill	Ashmolean 1945.100–2	N/MR	*Ox.* VII/IX, 34–5; Oxon. 47
773	Stanton Harcourt	*Ibid.* 1961.496	W/MR	*Ox.* XXVIII, 21; Oxon. 54
774	Stanton Harcourt	*Ibid.* 1962.72	AOC	Unpub. Oxon. 56(?)
775 F	Taynton, South Lawn	*Ibid.*	Indet.	*P.P.S.* III, 162
776	Yarnton	*Ibid.* 1886.1413	N/MR	*P.S.A.S.* XXXVIII, 384, Fig. 65; Oxon. 32; A. 77
777	Yarnton	B.M. 79 12–9 1784	E. Ang.	Oxon. 33; A. 79

Somerset

Corpus no.	Site	Museum	Beaker group	References
778 F	Brean Down	Bristol Spelaeo (1) Destroyed	E.	*Ant. J.* XVIII, 172, Pl. XLVII; *B.U.S.S.* no. 1,
779 F		(2) *Ibid.*	FN	88, Figs.; ApSimon (1961)
780 F	BREAN DOWN	Bristol	AOC	ApSimon (1961);
781 F		Spelaeo	FN	*B.U.S.S.* Rep. Figs.
782 F			FP	*Ibid.*
783 F			S?	*Ibid.*
784	Burrington, Blackdown, barrow T. 5	*Ibid.*	BW	*B.U.S.S.* 7, no. 1, 45; *B.U.S.S.* 2, no. 1, 67, Pl. V; *B.U.S.S.* 2, no. 2, 132, Pl. X
785 F	BURRINGTON, BOS SWALLET	*Ibid.*	SH(?)	*B.U.S.S.* 7, no. 1, 45,
786 F		*Ibid.*	S3(W)	Note
787 F		*Ibid.*	S2(W)	*Ibid.*
788 F		*Ibid.*	FP	*Ibid.*
789 F	CANNINGTON, BRIDGWATER	M.O.W. (1)	Indet.	Unpub. From Dark Age
790 F		(2)	Indet.	Cemetery (1962)
791 F		(3)	FP	
792 F	Charmy Down barrow 1	Unknown	S2(E)?	*Ant. J.* XXX, 34, Fig. 4, no. 2
793 F	Cheddar, Chelms Combe	Wells	S?	*S.A.S.* LXXII, 106–13; Dobson, 43

Corpus no.	Site	Museum	Beaker group	References
794 F	Cheddar, Soldier's Hole	Bristol Spelaeo	FP	*Ant. J.* VIII, 204
795 F	Cheddar, Sun Hole	*Ibid.*	FP	*B.U.S.S.* 3, no. 2, 91, Pl. IVA, nos. 5, 6, 7
796 F	CHEW PARK	ApSimmon	E.?	Unpub.
797 F			FN	
798 F	Compton Martin, Benbridge	*Ibid.*	E.	Unpub. dom. pit
799 F		*Ibid.*	FN	about 8–12 vessels
	Corston, nr. Bath	Bristol Spelaeo		*B.U.S.S.* 4, no. 2, 130,
800		(1) Restored	S2(W)	Fig.
801 F		(2) Sherds	Indet.	*Ibid.*; *Ant. J.* XXI, 151;
802 F		(3) Destroyed	S2(W)	*B.U.S.S.* 5, no. 2, 142, pl. 17
803	Culbone, nr. Porlock	Taunton A.917	N2	*S.A.S.* XLII, 56–66, Pl. A. 39
804 F	Ebbor Gorge, Bridged Pot	Wells	FP	*Ant. J.* VIII, 198; Dobson, 43
805 F	Ebbor Gorge, Rock Shelter	Wookey Hole Mus. 1953	Indet.	Unpub.
806 F	GORSEY BIGBURY, Mendip	Bristol	FP	*B.U.S.S.* 5, no. 1,
807 F		Spelaeo	SH(?)	3–56, Figs.
808 F		Half Coll.	S2(W)	*B.U.S.S.* 6, no. 2,
809 F		destroyed	S3(W)?	185–99
810 F	Meare East, Lake Village	Taunton	Indet.	Unpub.
811 F			Indet.	*Ibid.*
812 F	Middlezoy Quarry	Taunton A.938	Indet.	Unpub.
	NETTLEBRIDGE, COCKLES WOOD CAVE, SHELTER E	Taunton		*S.A.S.* XCVI, 193,
813 F		(1) Restorable	S3(W)	Fig. 1;
814 F		(2) Sherds	FP	*S.A.S.* LXXII, 106–13
	For (2) see:	Wells Mus.		
815 F	Rowberrow Cavern	Bristol Spelaeo	S?	*B.U.S.S.* 2, no. 3, 190–209; Dobson, 42
816 F	Sigwell barrow III	Ashmolean 1482.1806	Indet.	*J.R.A.I.* VIII, 189
817	Stoford Barwick	Taunton A.911	BW	A. 42 *bis*; Dobson, 40; *S.A.S.* XXXII (1), 14; *S.A.S.* IV, 8; *S.A.S.* LIV, 67
	Stogursey, Wick barrow	Taunton		*S.A.S.* LIV(II), 1–67;
818		(1)	E.	*Ibid.* Pl. VII, 1; A. 20;
819 F		(2) Sherd	FN	
820		(3)	S2(W)	*Ibid.* Pl. VIII; A. 11;
821		(4)	S3(W)	*Ibid.* Pl. VIII; A. 12
822	Wincanton	Taunton	N2(L)	*S.A.S.* XLII, 62, Note A. 42

Staffordshire

823 F	Alstonefield, Steep Low	Lost	Indet.	*Vest.* 76–7
824 F	Deepdale, nr. Wetton	Lost	Indet.	*J.D.A.S.* LXXV, 104, Fig. 7a(c); *Vest.* 85
825	Deepdale, Mouse Low	Sheffield J.93.862	S2(E)	*Ten Yrs*, 115–16; A. 60
	Deepdale, Ramscroft, Stanshope	*Ibid.*		*Ten Yrs*, 158–9;
826		(1) J.93.871	S1	A. 56;
827		(2) J.93.856	S1	A. 71;
828		(3) Lost	S3(E)	Jewitt MSS Sheffield
	Ilam Moor	*Ibid.*		*Vest.* 82;
829 F		(1) No. 50	E.?	*J.D.A.S.* LXXV, 105,
830 F		(2) Lost	FN	Fig. 2
831 F	Manifold Dale, Thors Cave	Buxton	Indet.	*J.D.A.S.* LXXV, 107
832	Normacott Sandpit	Stoke on Trent	W/MR	*J.D.A.S.* LXXV, 106
833	Rocester	Stoke on Trent	S1	*J.D.A.S.* LXXV, 76, Fig. 6
834	Swinscoe, Top Low	Sheffield J.93.858	S3(E)	*Ten Yrs*, 136; A. 59
835	Wetton, Castern	*Ibid.* J.93.865	S2(E)	*Vest.* 87–8; A. 55 *Reliquary* NS. VII, 125, Fig.

Corpus no.	Site	Museum	Beaker group	References
836 F	Wetton, Elder Bush Cave	Buxton	Indet.	*J.D.A.S.* LXXV, 104
837 F	Wetton, Gratton Hill	Sheffield, no. 60	S 4	*Vest.* 79
	Wetton, Three Lowes	Lost		Jewitt MSS Sheffield,
838 F		(1) *Ibid.*	S 4	Figs.
839 F		(2) *Ibid.*	S 3	*Vest.* 69–70
840 F		(3) *Ibid.*	Indet.	

Suffolk

841	Badwell Ash, Bury St Edmunds	Peterborough	BW	*Lon.Inst.Rep.* no. 11, 35
842	Barnham Cross	Ipswich R.1944.15	N 3	*Ant. J.* XXIV, 147
843 F	Barnham Heath	*Ibid.* 1948.74	FP	Unpub.
844	Barton Hill, Mildenhall	Colchester 351.97	E.	A. 93 and p. 26
845 F	Barton Mills	Cambridge 26.493	Indet.	Unpub.
846 F	Barton Mills, Beacon Hill	*Ibid.* 23.1634	Indet.	*C.A.S.* XXVI, 46, Fig. 11
847	Bawdsey	Ipswich 1927.47	E. Ang.	*P.P.S.E.A.* VI, 358, no. 18
848	Bawdsey	B.M. 56 6–27 4	E. Ang.	Unpub.
849	Bawdsey Cliff	Ipswich 1949.141	S 4	*Arch. Inst.* (1846), 3(?)
850	Boyton	Ipswich 1920.526	E. Ang.	*P.P.S.E.A.* VI, 358, no. 19
851 F	Brandon, Palmers Heath	Mildenhall	BW	Unpub.
	Brandon Fields	B.M.		*P.S.A.L.* 2s. V, 271;
852		(1)	E. Ang. FN	A. 82;
853		(2)	E. Ang. FN	A. 83
	Brantham Hall, womans grave	Ipswich		*P.P.S.E.A.* VI, 356,
854		(1) 1925.1.2	E.	Pl. XXVIII, Fig. 3;
855		(2) 1925.1.3	FN	*Ibid.* Fig. 4;
856		(3) 1925.1.4	E.	*Ibid.* Fig. 5
	Brantham Hall, Adjacent Grave	Ipswich		*P.P.S.E.A.* VI, 356,
857		1925.1.1	E.	Pl. XXVIII, Fig. 6
	Brantham Hall, Ring Ditch	*Ibid.*		*P.P.S.E.A.* VI, 356
858 F		(1) 1925.4	E. Ang.	*Ibid.*
859 F		(2) 1925.4	E. Ang.	*Ibid.*
860	Brantham Hall, Gravel Pit	*Ibid.* A.1931.222	S 1	*P.P.S.E.A.* VI, 360, Pl. XXX, Fig. 8
861 F	Brightwell Heath	Ipswich	Indet.	*Nature* (1921), 273
862	Bury St Edmunds, District	Lost	FN	*A.C.R.* 26, Pl. I, no. 4
	Bury St Edmunds,	Bury St Edmunds		*P.S.I.A.* XXVII,
863 F	Gainsborough Road	(1)	FP	Pt. 2, 90
864 F		(2)	FP	*Ibid.*
865 F		(3)	S 4	*Ibid.*
866	Butley	Ipswich 1930.176.40	FN	*P.P.S.E.A.* VI, 358, no. 20
867 F	BUTLEY, NEUTRAL FM.	*Ibid.*	S 4	*P.S.I.A.* XXV,
868 F		R.1949.158	S 3(E)?	Pt. 2, 207–8
869		Restored	FP	*Ibid.*
870	Coddenham, Rectory Garden	*Ibid.* Unreg.	N 2(L)	Unpub.
	Creeting St Mary	*Ibid.*		*P.P.S.E.A.* VI, 360,
871		(1) 1931.232.1	E. Ang. FN	Pl. XXIX, no. 12;
872		(2) 1931.232.2	E. Ang.	*Ibid.* no. 11;
873 F		(3) 1931.232.3	E. Ang.	*P.S.I.A.* XXV, Pt. 2, 209
874	Creeting St Mary	*Ibid.* 1932.127	N 3	Unpub.
875	Creeting St Mary	*Ibid.* 1938.45.47	FN	Unpub.
876	Eriswell, Foxhole Heath	Elveden Estate	BW	Unpub.
877	Eriswell, Curdle Head	Cambridge 1897.181	S 3(E)	A. 45; *A.C.R.* App. I, no. XI (Barton Mills?)
878 F	Eriswell, Fox Hill	*Ibid.* 23.1361	S?	Unpub.

Corpus no.	Site	Museum	Beaker group	References
879 F	Eriswell, Foxhole Heath	*Ibid.* 48.227	Indet.	*P.P.S.E.A.* II, 39
880 F	ERISWELL, BLACKSMITH PIT	Mildenhall	E. Ang.	*P.S.I.A.* XXVII,
881 F			FN	Pt. I, 43
	Fakenham	Ipswich		Unpub.
882 F		(1) 1951.36.4	W/MR	*Ibid.*
883 F		(2) 1951.36.5	W/MR	*Ibid.*
884 F		(3) 1951.36.6	FN	*Ibid.*
885	Felixstowe, Bath Rd	Ipswich 1930.211	N3	*P.P.S.E.A.* VI, 358, Pl. xxx, Fig. 7
886	Felixstowe, Chepstowe Rd	*Ibid.* 1947.60	E. Ang.	Unpub.
887 F	FELIXSTOWE, GOLF COURSE	*Ibid.*	BW	*P.P.S.E.A.* VI, 358
888 F		1921.60	FN	
889	Felixstowe Area	Ashmolean 1927.2674	BW	Unpub.
890	Felixstowe	B.M. 53 8–15 1	E. Ang.	*B.M. Guide* (1920), 68; A. 78
891	Felixstowe	B.M. 94 12–15 1	E. Ang.	*Ant.* V, 426, Pl. A. 86
892	Felixstowe Cliffs	B.M. 72 5–20 2	E. Ang.	Unpub.
893	Glevering, Framlingham	Cambridge 44.15	E.	Unpub.
894	Gravel, West Row	Private	S2(W)	Unpub.
895	Great Barton	Bury St Edmunds F11	FP	*A.C.R.* 26, Pl. II, no. 3
896 F	Great Bealings	Ipswich Unreg.	E. Ang.	Unpub.
897 F	Great Fakenham	Thetford	S?	Unpub.
898 F	Honnington Tumulus	Ipswich 1945.75	FP	Unpub.
899	Icklingham, Bernersfield Fm.	Elveden Estate	N2	Unpub.
900	Icklingham, Mitchell's Hill	Bury St Edmunds 775.725	N3	*P.S.I.A.* XI, 59
901	Icklingham Tumulus	Lost	—	*Arch. Assoc.* XXX, 195
902	Ipswich	Ipswich 1920.52.5	BW	*P.P.S.E.A.* VI, 358, Pl. XXXI, no. 14
903	Ipswich	*Ibid.* 1920.52.4	E. Ang.	*Ibid.* no. 15
904	Ipswich?	*Ibid.* 1920.52.1	S2(E)	*P.P.S.E.A.* VI, 358, Pl. XXVIII, no. 2
	Ipswich, Dales Rd, Boltons Pit	*Ibid.*		*P.P.S.E.A.* VI, 356,
905		(1) 1923.32	E. Ang.	Pl. xxx, no. 9;
906		(2) 1929.13	E. Ang. FN	*Ibid.* no. 10
907 F		(3) Unreg.	FP	
908	Ipswich District	*Ibid.* 1920.52.19	N/MR	*P.P.S.E.A.* VI, 356, Pl. XXXI, no. 13
909	Ipswich, Grimwoods Pit	*Ibid.* 1923–33	E. Ang.	*Ibid.*
909.1	Ipswich, Norwich Rd,	*Ibid.* 1923.33	S2(E)	*Ibid.* no. 16
909.2 F	Grimwoods Pit	Unreg.	E.	Unpub.
910 F	Ipswich, Violet Close	*Ibid.* 1951.171	S4	Unpub.
911 F	ISLEHAM, FIFTY FM	Cambridge	FP and S3	*C.A.S.* XXXV, 117–75
912 F		36.17–60	SH4(C)	*Ibid.*
913 F		B.M.	S4	*Ibid.*
914 F		1939 5–11 1 1939 5–11 16	S3(W)	*Ibid.* *Ibid.*
915 F	ISLEHAM, HAYLANDS HOUSE	Cambridge	FP	*C.A.S.* XXXV, 107–15
916 F		36.2	S?	
917 F	Ixworth, Newports Pit	Cambridge Z.14996	E. Ang.	Unpub.
918 F	Kennyhill, Burnt Fen	*Ibid.* 49.438	Indet.	Unpub.
919	Kersey	Ipswich 1920.52.3	E. Ang. FN	*P.P.S.E.A.* VI, 358, no. 21
920	Kettleburgh, Brandeston Pit	Ipswich R.1948.183	E. Ang.	Unpub.

Corpus no.	Site	Museum	Beaker group	References
921	Kirton, nr. Ipswich	*Ibid.* 1920.52.2	E. Ang.	*P.P.S.E.A.* VI, 358, no. 17; A. 84
922	Lakenheath	Cambridge 1912.282	E. Ang. FP	*A.C.R.* Pl. I, no. 3, App. I, no. XV
923 F	LAKENHEATH, NEW FEN,	Mildenhall	S2(W)	Unpub.
924 F	RIGHT UP DROVE		FP	
925 F	LAKENHEATH, JOIST FEN	Mildenhall	S1?	Unpub.
926 F			FP	*Ibid.*
927 F			FN	*Ibid.*
928 F			E. Ang.	*Ibid.*
929 F	LAKENHEATH, RABBIT HILL	Mildenhall	S2(W)	*C.A.S.* LIII, I, Figs.
930 F			FP	*P.S.I.A.* XXVIII, Pt. 1, 93
930.1 F			Bowl?	
931 F	LAKENHEATH, SAHARA	Mildenhall	S2(W)	*C.A.S.* XLII, 101
932 F		*Ibid.*	SH4(C)	*Ibid.*
933 F		*Ibid.*	FP	*Ibid.*
933.1		Restored	N2	*Ibid.*
934 F	Martlesham Heath	Ipswich Unreg.	FP	*P.S.I.A.* XXIV, Pt. 1, 36
935 F	MARTLESHAM PLANTATION	*Ibid.*	FP	*Ibid.*
936 F		1951.156	S4	
937 F	Mildenhall Fen	Cambridge 36.13 and 38.464	S2(W)	Unpub.
938 F	Mildenhall, Wild Street	*Ibid.*	FP	Unpub.
939 F	NEEDHAM MARKET	Ipswich	FP	Unpub.
940 F		R.1941.7	S?	
941	Needham Market	B.M. 56 6–27 2	S1	A. 47
942	Ousden	Bury St Edmunds	N2	Unpub.
943 F	Pakenham, Grimstone End	Ipswich 1958	N2?	Unpub.
944 F	Rickinghall Superior	*Ibid.* Unreg.	Indet.	*P.S.I.A.* XXVII, Pt. 3, 184
945 F	Rushmere	*Ibid.* 1950.136	E. Ang.	Unpub.
946 F	Santon Downham	B.M. Unreg.	S?	Unpub.
947 F	Santon Downham	Thetford	S?	Unpub.
948	Sicklesmere	Bury St Edmunds	N3	Unpub.
949 F	Sproughton	Ipswich	Indet.	*P.P.S.* XXV, 275
950	Stutton	B.M. 58 3–26 1	BW?	Unpub.
951	Sudbury	Cambridge 1914.339	FN	Unpub.
952	Tuddenham barrow	B.M. 79 12–9 1900	SH2(A)	A. 46 (Handle missing)
	Undley barrow, Lakenheath	B.M.		*V.C.H. Suffolk* I, 266;
953		(1) 79 12–9 1895	S1	A. 61; *A.C.R.* App. I, XVI;
954		(2) 12–9 1896	FP	*A.C.R.* App. I, no. XVII
955 F	WATTISFIELD, COTTAGE FIELD	Ipswich 1956.125	FP	*Arch. News Letter*
956 F			S4	(1961), 7, no. 5, 102;
957 F			SH4(C)	*P.S.I.A.* XXVII, 117
958 F	WEST STOW barrow	Bury St Edmunds	FP	*P.S.I.A.* (1963),
959 F			S?	pending
960	Wherstead, Thorington Hall	Ipswich 1920.527	FP	*P.P.S.E.A.* VI, 356, Fig. *Man* XVI, 97, Fig. 2
961	Woolpit, Seamans Pit	*Ibid.* R.1938.196	E. Ang.	Unpub.
	WOOLVERSTONE PARK	*Ibid.*		*P.P.S.E.A.* VI, 361,
962 F		(1) 1947.42.1	S4	no. 22/23
963 F		(2) 1947.42.2	S4	
964 F		(3) *Ibid.* 2–16	N2	
965 F		(4) *Ibid.*	FP	
966 F	WORDWELL	Unknown	Indet.	*P.S.I.A.* XXI, Pt. 3, 263
967	Worlington	B.M. 83 7–2 1	S1	*A.C.R.* App. I, no. XXVI; A. 70; *P.S.A.S.* XXXVIII, 329
968 F	Worlington, Swales Tumulus	Mildenhall	E.?	*C.A.S.* L, 107–12

Surrey

Corpus no.	Site	Museum	Beaker group	References
969	Chiddingfold, Gostrode Fm.	Lost	—	*Nenia Britannica* (1798) 162, J. Douglas
970	Ham, Earl Dysart's Pit	London S.3.119	W/MR	Unpub.
971	Kew, Thames	*Ibid.* P.19	S2(W)	*Arch.* LXIX, 9–10, Fig. 8, 3
972	Kew Gardens, West Hall Rd	Guildford	E. Ang. FN	*Ant. J.* XII, 170, Pl. XXXIII, 2*b*
973	Limpsfield, West Heath, (Titsey in error)	Guildford (1)	N2(L)	*P.S.A.L.* 2s. (1893–5), XV, 51;
974 F		(2) Lost	—	*Surrey A.C.* XXXV, 4–5, Pl. IA for (1)
975	Mortlake, Thames	London A.13471	S1	*Arch. J.* LXXXVI, 84, Pl. VII, left
976	Mortlake, Red House	*Ibid.* 28.37	AOC	*Arch. J.* LXXXVI, 84, Pl. VII, right
977 F	Mortlake, Thames	*Ibid.* A.13672	Indet.	*Arch. J.* LXXXVI, 84
978 F	Mortlake, Thames	*Ibid.* A.13660	S?	Unpub.
979	Mortlake, Thames	B.M. 1909 5–18 13	N3	Vulliamy, 87, Pl. IV
980	Mortlake, Thames	B.M. 1909 5–18 14	AOC	*Arch. J.* LXXXVI, 82
981	Mortlake, Thames	B.M. 72.3–29 11	BW Bowl	*Ant. J.* IV, 149, Pl. XXVIII, 1; A. Pl. XXX, No. 21
982	Putney, Thames	London	BW Bowl	*Ant. J.* IV, 150, Pl. XXVIII, 2
983 F	Walton-on-Thames, Oatlands Park	Weybridge	Bowl	*Surrey A.C.* XXXV, 5, Pl. IB

Sussex

Corpus no.	Site	Museum	Beaker group	References
984 F	Beltout Camp, Beachy Head	Lewes	Indet.	*S.A.C.* LV, 51
985 F	Blackpatch, Flint Mines	Worthing	Indet.	*S.E.Nat. and Ant.* XXXIV, 28; *S.A.C.* LXV, 69
986	Brighton Church, Hill	Lewes (1) 34.8	S2(W)	*S.A.C.* LXXVI, 1, Fig. 1; Sx. 000;
987		(2) 34.8	S2(W)	Sx. 010; *S.A.C.* XCII, 108, Fig.
988	Burpham	Worthing	N2(L)	*S.A.C.* 98, 15, Fig. 2
989	Cissbury barrow	B.M. 79 12–9 2099	E. Ang.	Sx. 071; *S.A.C.* LXII, 39; *S.A.C.* XCII, 108, Fig. 1
990	Cissbury barrow	B.M. 39 10–29 156	Undec.	*S.A.C.* LXVIII, 277; Sx. 073; *S.A.C.* LXXII, 39
991 F	Devil's Dyke, Beggars Haven	B.M. 90 6–22 1 Lewes	W/MR	*S.A.C.* LXXII, 39; A. 38; Sx. 051
992	Falmer, Ditchling Rd	Brighton	BW	*S.A.C.* LXXII, 39; Sx. 070; *Arch.* LXXVI, 93
993	Findon, Church Hill	Worthing (1)	BW	Curwen, 122 and 158; Sx. 072;
994		(2)	FP	Sx. 100; *P.P.S.* II, Fig. 11
995	Hassocks Sand Pit	Lewes	W/MR Undec.	*S.A.C.* XCII, 108; Sx. 080
996	Kingston Buci	Lewes	E. Ang. FN	*S.A.C.* LXII, 188; Sx. 061
997 F	Littlehampton, Thorncroft Rd	Littlehampton	Indet.	Unpub.
998	Park Brow, Sompting	Worthing L.12	S3(E)	*Sussex Notes and Queries,* VII, 59; Sx. 020
999 F	Park Brow, Sompting	Lewes	S2(W)?	*S.A.C.* LXIV, 35
1000 F	Patcham, Ladies Mile	Lewes	Indet.	*S.A.C.* 98, 137–9
1001 F	Pippering, The Burgh	Lewes	Indet.	*S.A.C.* LXXII, 38; *S.A.C.* LXIII, 10, Pl. 3, no. 4
1002 F	Plumpton Plain	Lewes	Indet.	*S.A.C.* LXXII, 40

Corpus no.	Site	Museum	Beaker group	References
1003	Rodmell, Heath Brow	Lewes	W/MR? Undec.	*S.A.C.* LXXII, 40; Sx. 081; *S.A.C.* LXXV, 232
1004 F	Selmeston	Lewes	Indet.	*Ant. J.* XIV, 139, Fig. 3, no. 1
1005	Selsey	Chichester	W/MR	*S.A.C.* XCII, 108, Fig. 1; Sx. 050
1006 F	Shoreham, Slonk Hill	Brighton	E. Ang. FN	*S.A.C.* LXXII, 39; Sx. 060
1007	Shoreham by Sea	Shoreham Marlepins	E. Ang.	Unpub.
1008	Telscombe Tye, barrow	Lost	S2(E)	*S.A.C.* LXXII, 37; Curwen, 160, Pl. XII, 3; Sx. 001
1009 F	WHITEHAWK CAMP	Brighton	E.	*Ant. J.* XIV, 119–21,
1010 F			FN	Figs. 41–71
1011 F			Undec.	*Ibid.*

Warwickshire

1012	Baginton	Coventry	N2	*T.B.A.S.* LIV, 65, Fig. 2; *Ant. J.* XII, 170–1, Fig.
1013	Lillington?	Warwick A.59	N3	*Warwick F.C.* (1901), 11; *Ibid.* (1903), 45
1014	Meriden?	Warwick A.44	N/MR	*Ibid.* *Ibid.*
1015 F	Nuneaton, Ryton Grange	Northants D.59/1954.5	N3?	Unpub.
1016	Warwickshire	Warwick	E.	Unpub. School Loan Coll.

Westmorland

1017	Brougham, Moorhouse Fm.	Coll. Soc. Ant. Lond.	N3	*Arch.* XLV, 414; A. 166*a*; H.M.C. 44, Pl. 11*a*
1018	Clifton, Penrith, Cist I	Ashmolean 1451.1886	N3	*C.W.A.S.* V, 83, Fig. 1; A. 165
1019	Clifton, Penrith, Cist II	Carlisle		*C.W.A.S.* V, 83;
1020		(1) OM.262 (2) OM.259	N2 N/NR	*Ibid.* Fig. 2; A. 176; *Ibid.* Fig. 3; A. 163
1021	Crosby Fell	Cambridge 47.83	N3	*Ant. J.* VI, 176, Pl. XXVIII
1022 F	Crosby Garrett 175	B.M. Lost	—	*B.B.* 391, no. 175; H.M.C. 43
1023	Sizergh Fell, nr. Kendal	Sizergh Castle	AOC	*C.W.A.S.* NS. LIII, 1, Fig. *C.W.A.S.* NS. IV, 71, Fig.

Wiltshire

1024 F	Aldbourne (1), Warren Fm.	B.M. Unreg.	Indet.	*W.A.M.* XLIII, 283; C. 1; *Arch.* LII, 48, CCLXXVI
1025 F	Aldbourne (3), Warren Fm.	*Ibid.* Unreg.	Indet.	*Arch.* LII, 48–9, CCLXXVIII; C. 2
1026 F	Aldbourne (5)	*Ibid.* Unreg.	Indet.	*Arch.* LII, 53, CCLXXX, C. 3
1027	Alderbury, nr. Whaddon	Salisbury 199	E.	*P.P.S.* IV, 96
1028 F	Alton Priors, Knap Hill Camp	Devizes DM.1594	AOC	*W.A.M.* XXXVII, 60, Note; C. 3A
1029 F	Alton Priors, Knap Hill Camp	*Ibid.* 1960	S3?	Unpub. 1960 excavations
1030	Amesbury (15), Normanton barrow 164	Lost Incense cup?	—	*A.W.* 205; C. 4; *D.M.C.* Pt. 1, no. 126
1031	Amesbury (19), barrow 132	Lost (1)	—	*A.W.* 199; C. 5 and 6;
1032		Lost (2)	—	*D.M.C.* Pt. 1, no. 123
1033	Amesbury (22), barrow 130	Lost Incense cup?	—	*A.W.* 199; C. 7
	Amesbury (51), 'Stonehenge' barrow	Devizes		C. 9 and 10 for (1) and (2);

Corpus no.	Site	Museum	Beaker group	References
1034		(1) DM.483	S2(W)	A. 2;
1035		(2) Lost	—	*A.W.* 163
1036	*Ibid.* M.O.W. (1960)	(3) M.O.W.	W/MR	Rep. pending;
1037		(4) M.O.W.	S2(E)	*W.A.M.* 58, 31
1038 F		(5) M.O.W.	W/MR?	*Ibid.*
	Amesbury (54), 'Stonehenge'	Devizes		C. 11 and 12
1039	barrow 39	(1) DM.477	S2(W)	A. 3
1040		(2) Lost	—	*A.W.* 173, Pl. XVII
1041	Amesbury (56), 'Stonehenge' barrow 25	Lost	—	*A.W.* 159; C. 8
1042	Amesbury (56), 'Stonehenge' barrow 43	Lost Devizes Assoc. nos. 89–90	—	*A.W.* 165; *D.M.C.* Pt. I, 89–90; C. 13
1043 F	Amesbury (61), Earls Farm Down	London Inst.	Indet.	*W.A.M.* LVI, 238
1044 F	Amesbury barrow (78 or 81)	Salisbury	S2(W)	Unpub. ex. L. V. Grinsell
1045	Amesbury (89?)	*Ibid.* 198	E.	*P.P.S.* IV, 96
1046	Amesbury, Fargo Plantation	*Ibid.*	S2(W)	*W.A.M.* XLVIII, 357
	Amesbury, 'Stonehenge'	*Ibid.*		*Ant. J.* III, 20;
1047 F		(1) 1716.173	S2(W)	*Ant. J.* VIII, 150;
1048 F		(2) 1752.85	W/MR	Atkinson, 82
1049 F	Avebury (10)	Ashmolean 1955.160V	Indet.	*W.A.M.* XLIII, 283; C. 15a
1050 F	Avebury (4)	*Ibid.* 1955.160U	Indet.	Unpub. ex. Passmore
	Avebury, Longstone Cove	Devizes		C. 15 and 16
1051		(1) DM.451	N/MR	*Man.* XII (1912), 200, Fig. 2;
1052 F		(2) *Ibid.*	Indet.	*W.A.M.* XXXVIII, 3–5, Fig.
1053 F	Avebury Ditch	Avebury	E.?	C. 16a;
1054 F			FN	*Arch.* 84, 138, Fig. 7
	AVEBURY, WINDMILL HILL DITCH	Devizes		*W.A.M.* XLIII, 283;
1055 F		(1) 1923	Indet.	C. 16b;
1056 F		(2) 1959	*AOC*	*W.A.M.* LVII, 154
1057 F			E.	*Ibid.*
1058 F			FP	*Ibid.*
1059 F			S2(W)	*Ibid.*
1060 F			SH4(C)	*Ibid.*
1061 F	Avebury, Windmill Hill Longbarrow Ditch	Dr I. Smith	Indet.	*W.A.M.* LVII, 392
1062	Avebury, Overton Hill	Lost	—	*W.A.M.* XX, 347; C. 17; Smith, 164, VIb
	Avebury, Sanctuary, Overton Hill	Devizes		*W.A.M.* XLV, 313, Pls. VII,
1063		(1) DM.488	BW	VIII and IX
1064 F		(2) DM.487	AOC	
1065 F	Avebury (22)	B.M. Unreg.	FP	Cunnington (1927),
1066 F	West Kennet Long barrow	(1) 1859	S2(W)?	Pl. X, XI;
1067 F		Devizes	E.	Piggott (1962), 44,
1068 F		(2) 1956	AOC	Fig. 14
1069 F		DM.1250–60	FN	*Ibid.*
	Avebury, West Kennet Avenue	Avebury		*Ant.* X, 423, Figs. 2 and 3;
1070		(1) Stone 18	E.	*P.P.S.E.A.* VII, 407
1071		(2) Stone 25b	N2	*Ibid.*
1072	Avebury, Beckhampton	Devizes DM.481	S4	*W.A.M.* XLIII, 399; C. 18
	Avebury, Beckhampton Grange	Avebury		*W.A.M.* LIII, 311,
1073		(1) GP.3	N2	Pl. III, Fig. 3
1074 F		(2) GP.3b	Indet.	
1075	Berwick St John (12) XX	Farnham	W/MR	C. 19; A. 25; *C.C.* II, 19–26, Pl. 77
1076	Berwick, St John, Rotherly	*Ibid.*	W/MR	C. 20; A. 27; *C.C.* II, 50, Pl. 92
1077 F	Berwick St John, South Lodge Camp, Rushmore	*Ibid.*	Indet.	*C.C.* II, 36–7, Figs. 6–9; C. 20a
1078	Bishops Cannings (54),	Devizes	S2(W)	*A.W.* II, 93; C. 21;

Corpus no.	Site	Museum	Beaker group	References
	Beckhampton 4	DM.183		*Arch. Inst.* (1849), 109, Fig. 10; *W.A.M.* VI, 321
1079 F	BOSCOMBE DOWN EAST	Salisbury	E.?	*P.P.S.* II, 216 note;
1080 F			FN	*W.A.M.* XLVII, 474
	Boyton	Lost		*Arch.* XV, 343, Pl. XVII;
1081	(1)	{ W/MR	{ W/MR	A. 23*a*, 23*b*; C. 22, 23;
1082	(2)	{	{ W/MR	*A.W.* 102
1083	Brigmerston barrow	Devizes DM.468	S4	A. 13*b*; C. 24; *D.M.C.* Pt. II, X 10, Fig. *W.A.M.* XXXV, 177
1084	Bulford	Salisbury 11.15	W/MR	*W.A.M.* XLIII, 350; C. 25; *W.A.M.* XXXVIII, 217(?)
1085	Bulford Camp	*Ibid.* 110.39	AOC	*W.A.M.* LI, 382, Fig. 3
1086 F	Bulford Down barrow 65	*Ibid.* 133.48	S2(W)	Unpub.
1087	Calne Without (2*c*), Oldbury	Devizes DM.480	S2(W)	*W.A.M.* XXIII, 215; C. 26; *W.A.M.* XLIII, 274
1088	Cherhill, nr. Calne	Salisbury	S3(W)	'Cherhill' (1941), 19, Fig. J. H. Blackford
	Codford St Mary, Lamb Down	M.O.W.		*P.P.S.* XXV, 273
1089 F		(1) Site F	AOC	misprinted Site E;
1090 F		(2) Site B	Indet.	Rep. pending
1091 F	Collingbourne Ducis (9?)	Devizes	Indet.	C. 27; *D.M.C.* II, X36; *W.A.M.* X, 91
	Collingbourne Kingston, Snail Down	Devizes and Birmingham		*W.A.M.* LVI, 127, 181 *Ibid.*
1092 F	Barrow XIV	*Ibid.*	AOC	*Ibid.*
1093 F	Barrow XIX	*Ibid.*	AOC	*Ibid.*
1094 F	BARROW III	*Ibid.*	S2?	*Ibid.*
1095 F	*Ibid.*	*Ibid.*	FP	*Ibid.*
1096 F	DOWNTON PIT 56	Salisbury	AOC	*W.A.M.* 58, CCX, 116;
1097 F			FN	*W.A.M.* 57, 13;
1098 F			Indet.	*W.A.M.* LVI, 248
1099	Durrington (8) barrow 66	Lost	—	*A.W.* 166; C. 28
1100	Durrington (25) barrow 84	Lost	—	*A.W.* 167; C. 29
1101	Durrington (36) barrow 93	Devizes DM.457	S2(W)	*W.A.M.* XVI, 171, Fig. C. 30; A. 4; *A.W.* 168, Pl. 18
1102	Durrington Walls, barrow	Salisbury 32.51	Undec. W/MR?	*Ant. J.* XXXIV, 164, 173
1103	Durrington, Woodhenge Circle I	Devizes DM.466–7	S2(E)	Cunnington (1929), 42, 151, Pl. 41, Figs.
	Durrington, Woodhenge	*Ibid.*		Cunnington (1929),
1104 F		(1) DM.1538	W/MR	Pl. 41, 4,
1105 F		(2) DM.1538	W/MR?	reconst. giant bkr,
1106 F		(3) DM.435	E.	Pl. 25, 3
1107 F		(4) DM.454	AOC	
	Durrington, Larkhill	Salisbury		*W.A.M.* LI, 381,
1108		{ (1) 136.46.1	{ W/MR Undec.	Fig. 1,
1109		{ (2) 136.46.2	{ W/MR	Fig. 2
1110 F	Durrington, Larkhill	Salisbury 322.45	W/MR?	Unpub.
	Farleigh Wick, Jug's Grave	Bristol		*W.A.M.* LII, 270
1111		(1) F.3594	N/MR	*Ibid.*
1112 F		(2) F.3618	W/MR?	*Ibid.*
1113	Figheldean (31) Long barrow 2	B.M. 73 12–19 6	S1	*Arch.* XLII, 180, 197–8, Fig. 6; C. 31; A. 5; *W.A.M.* XXXVIII, 390
1114	Figheldean (25) barrow 11	Devizes DM.485	FP	*W.A.M.* XXXVI, 623 *W.A.M.* XLIV, 118, Pl.
1115	Heytesbury, Imber Firs	Lost	W/MR	*W.A.M.* XXI, 259, Fig. *Arch.* XLIII, 393; C. 32; *A.W.* 86
1116	Heytesbury (4*f*) Tytherington	Lost	—	*A.W.* 104, C. 33

Corpus no.	Site	Museum	Beaker group	References
1117 F	Hilmarton, Goatacre	Devizes DM.275	W/MR	*D.M.C.* II, x89; C. 34
1118	Imber, Wadmans Coppice	Lost	—	*A.W.* 87; C. 35
1119	East Kennet (1c)	Hull 97.42 Associations Lost	S3(W)	*Arch. J.* XXIV, 28; *Ant. J.* I (1921), 128–9; *Arch. Inst.* (1849), no. 12, Figs. 12–14; C. 36; A. 4*a* and 10 in error
1120 F	Kilmington (3), Whitesheet Hill, barrow 4	Devizes DM.317	S2(W)	*A.W.* 423; C. 37; *D.M.C.* I, no. 368
1121 F	Kingston Deverill (2)	Devizes 11.55.216	Indet.	*W.A.M.* LVI, 182
1122 F	Little Bedwyn, Bath Rd	Ashmolean 1955.162	S2(W)	Unpub.
1123 F	Martindown Camp	Farnham	Indet.	*C.C.* IV, 202,
1124 F			FP	plates
1125	Mere (6*a*) barrow	Devizes DM.446	W/MR	*A.W.* 44, Pl. II; C. 38; Arch. XLIII, 527, Fig. 218; A. 19; *W.A.M.* XXI, 257; *Arch.* XLIII, 527, Fig. 218; *W.A.M.* XXXVII, 98; *D.M.C.* I, no. 81
	Netheravon	Devizes		*W.A.M.* XLIII, 490,
1126		(1) DM.458	S1	Fig. 1,
1127		(2) DM.459	S1	Fig. 2
1128 F	Ogbourne Down, Smeathe Ridge	Ashmolean 1955.161	E.?	*W.A.M.* XXXVIII, 587–8, Fig. 11
1129	Overton, West Lockeridge	Devizes DM.455	W/MR	*W.A.M.* XLI, 187; C. 39; *W.A.M.* XLIII, 395, Figs.
1130	Overton, West Lockeridge	Devizes DM.482	S2(W)	*D.M.C.* X151
1131	Overton, West barrow G (6B)	Dr I. Smith	S2(W)	*Ant.* XXXVIII (1964), 60
1132 F	Porton Down	Salisbury 38.1936	E.	Unpub.
1133 F	Rollestone Field 24	M.O.W.	—	*P.P.S.* XXV, 274
1134 F	Roundway (5) Oval barrow 6	Devizes DM.X70	Indet.	C. 40; *D.M.C.* II, x70; *W.A.M.* VI, 162
1135	Roundway (8)	Devizes DM.441–5 X70–50	W/MR	C. 41; A. 21; *W.A.M.* III, 185; *Arch.* XLIII, 392; *Reliquary* III, 178
1136 F	Roundway (9) barrow 4	Devizes DM.272	Indet.	*W.A.M.* VI, 161; C. 42; *D.M.C.* II X52
1137	Roundway Down	Lost	W/MR	*Arch. Inst.* 1849, 109, Fig. 9; C. 43
1138	Salisbury, Ashley Hill	Salisbury 111/57	S4	*W.A.M.* LI, 384, Fig. 4
1139	Shrewton, Nettdown barrow (5A)	Salisbury	N3	*P.P.S.* XXV, 274
	Shrewton, Nettdown barrow (5K)	Salisbury		*P.P.S.* XXV, 274
1140		(1)	N2	*Ibid.*
1141		(2)	S4	*Ibid.*
1142 F	Savernake Column	Devizes DM.279	W/MR	Unpub.
1143	Sutton Veny (11*a*)	Lost	W/MR?	*A.W.* 103, Pl. XII; *W.A.M.* X, 111, Fig. *D.M.C.* I, no. 63–4; C. 44
1144	Sutton Veny (11*b*)	Lost	—	*A.W.* 103; C. 45
	Swindon, Okus.	Ashmolean		*W.A.M.* XXXVIII, 42;
1145		(1) 1955.126	S2(W)	*Ibid.* Fig. 1; C. 46;
1146		(2) 1955.125	S2(E)	*Ibid.* Fig. 2; C. 47;
1147 F		(3) 1955.163	S3(E)	*Ibid.* Fig. 3; C. 48
	Swindon, Goddard Arms	Ashmolean		Unpub.
1148 F		(1) 1955.164	Indet.	*Ibid.*
1149 F		(2) 1957.129	Indet.	*Ibid.*

Corpus no.	Site	Museum	Beaker group	References
1150	Upavon Flying School	Devizes DM.456	W/MR	*W.A.M.* XL, 6; C. 49
1151	Upton Lovell (2*c*)	*Ibid.* DM.452	W/MR	*A.W.* 75, Pl. IX; A. 29; C. 50
1152 F	Wanborough barrow (1)	Ashmolean 1955.209	FP	*W.A.M.* XXVIII, 262; C. 51;
1153 F			Indet.	*W.A.M.* XXXVIII, 337
1154	Wilsford (G 1) Normanton 166	Lost See below	—	*A.W.* 206; C. 52
	Wilsford barrow (G 1)	M.O.W.		Rep. Pending
1155		(1) Restored	E.	Central Grave
1156		(2) *Ibid.*	W/MR	no. 9 *Ibid.*;
1157		(3) *Ibid.*	W/MR	no. 10 *Ibid.*;
1158 F		(4) *Ibid.*	W/MR	no. 11 *Ibid.*;
1159		{(5) *Ibid.* {	W/MR	no. 7 *Ibid.*;
1160		{(6) *Ibid.* {Undec.	W/MR	no. 8 *Ibid.*;
1161		(7) *Ibid.* Undec.	W/MR	no. 5 now lost; *W.A.M.* 58, 30
	Wilsford (2*b*), 'Normanton'	Devizes		*A.W.* 205; C. 53–4;
1162	barrow 161	(1) DM.453	W/MR	A. 28;
1163		(2) Lost	—	*D.M.C.* I, no. 147
1164	Wilsford (34), 'Normanton' 170 Long barrow	B.M. 73 12–19 5	S 3(W)	*W.A.M.* XXXVIII, 405; *Arch.* XLII, 196–8; A. 8; C. 55
1165	Wilsford (40), 'Lake 6'	Lost	—	C. 56; *A.W.* 210 *D.M.C.* no. I, 174*b*
1166	Wilsford (51), 'Lake 22'	Lost	—	*A.W.* 211; C. 57
1167		Lost	—	*Ibid.* C. 58–9;
1168		Devizes DM.184	FP	*Ibid.* Pl. 28, no. 8;
1169 F	*Ibid.*	(1) M.O.W.	N/MR	Unpub. 1960
1170 F	*Ibid.*	(2) M.O.W.	Indet.	*Ibid.*
	Wilsford (52), 'Lake 24'	M.O.W.		*P.P.S.* XXV, 275
1171		(1)	W/MR	*Ibid.*
1172		(2)	FP	*Ibid.*
	Wilsford (54), 'Lake 21'	M.O.W.		*P.P.S.* XXV, 275
1173 F		(1)	E.	*Ibid.*
1174 F		(2)	AOC	*Ibid.*
1175 F		(3)	W/MR	*Ibid.*
1176		(4) Lost	—	*A.W.* 211; C. 61
1177	Wilsford (62), barrow 13	Devizes DM.245	S 4	*A.W.* 208, Pl. 28, 3; C. 62; A. 33
1178	Wilsford (70) barrow 7	Lost	—	*Arch.* XLIII, 294; *A.W.* 208; C. 63
	Wilsford barrows, unknown	B.M.		C. 64–7;
1179 F	barrows in Lake Group	(1) 95 7–23 7	S 2(W)	*W.A.M.* XXV, 584
1180 F		(2) 96 7–23 9	S 2(W)	*Ibid.*
1181 F		(3) 95 7–23 10	W/MR	*Ibid.*
1182 F		(4) 95 7–23 11	E.?	*Ibid.*
1183 F	Winterbourne Dauntsey, Figsbury Rings	Devizes	Indet.	*W.A.M.* XLIII, 54*a*, 55*c* C. 67*a*
1184 F	Winterbourne Gunner	Salisbury 1963	AOC	Unpub. from Saxon cemetery
	Winterbourne Monkton	Devizes		*D.M.C.* II, X83–7*a*
1185		{(1) DM.470	{S 2(W)	A. 4*b*; C. 68
1186		{(2) DM.471	{S 2(W)	A. 4*t*; C. 69
	Winterbourne Monkton (10)	Lost		*Arch. Inst.* 1849, 105;
1187		(1) *Ibid.*	N 2	*Ibid.* Fig. aa; C. 70;
1188		(2) *Ibid.*	S 3(W)	*Ibid.* Fig. x; C. 71
1189 F	Winterbourne Monkton (16)	Ashmolean 1955.160	Indet.	C. 72
1190	Winterbourne Stoke (10), 27	Devizes DM.484	S 1	*A.W.* 125; A. 14; C. 73
1191 F	Winterbourne Stoke (12)	Ashmolean 1955.160*y*	AOC	C. 74
1192	Winterbourne Stoke (17) 8	Lost	—	*A.W.* 121; C. 75

Corpus no.	Site	Museum	Beaker group	References
1193	Winterbourne Stoke (20) 7	Lost	—	*A.W.* 121; C. 76
1194	Winterbourne Stoke (35) 4*a*	B.M.	S1	*W.A.M.* XI, 42;
		75 12–9 3		*W.A.M.* X, 23;
				A.W. 165; C. 77
1195	Winterbourne Stoke (54) barrow 5	Devizes	S2(W)	*A.W.* 118, Pl. XIV; C. 78;
		DM.461		*Arch.* XLIII, 425; A. 1;
				D.M.C. I, nos. 39, 72, 178, 210
1196	Winterbourne Stoke (56) 7	Lost	—	*A.W.* 115; C. 79; *D.M.C.* 71*a*
1197	Winterbourne Stoke? Stoke Rd	Devizes	S4	*D.M.C.* I, no. 164;
		DM.486		C. 80; A. 18*b*
1198 F	WINTERSLOW, EASTON DOWN	Salisbury	FN	*W.A.M.* XLV, 350;
1199 F		322.45	S2(W)	*W.A.M.* XLVI, 233;
1200 F		*Ibid.*	W/MR and	*W.A.M.* XLVII, 68
			N/MR	
1201 F		*Ibid.*	E.	*Ibid.*
1202		*Ibid.* Reconst.	FN	*Ibid.*
1203 F		B.M.	*Ibid.*	*Ibid.* A few sherds of all
		1936 3–12 32–35		types present
1204	Winterslow Hut (11), 3	Ashmolean	W/MR	*W.A.M.* XLVIII, 174, Pl. V;
		NC.507		*Arch.* XLIII, 361 and 449;
				C. 81; A. 24
1205 F	Wylye barrow (2)	Ashmolean	SH?	*W.A.M.* XLIX, 117,
1206 F		1955.162*ab*	Indet.	Pl. II
1207	Unknown, Wiltshire	Devizes	W/MR	Probably ex Colt Hoare.
				Labelled in error 'Upavon'

Worcestershire

Corpus no.	Site	Museum	Beaker group	References
1208	Draycott, Kempsey	Private	SH2(B)	*Ant. J.* XV, 276, Pl. XI
	Hill and Moor, Pershore	Worcester		*T.W.A.S.* NS.
1209.1	Pershore	(1)	N3	XXXIV, 20
1209.2		(2)	N3	*T.W.N.C.* IX, 53
1209.3		(3)	Bowl	*Ibid.*

Yorkshire

Corpus no.	Site	Museum	Beaker group	References
1210 F	Acklam Wold barrow 124	Hull 221.42	S1	*Forty Yrs*, 91–2,
				Pl. XXVII, Fig. 210–17
1211	Acklam Wold barrow 204	Hull 213.42	S4	*Forty Yrs*, 86–7; A. 110 *bis*
	Aldro barrow 54	Hull		*Forty Yrs*, 63–6;
1212		(1) 184.42	N2	*Ibid.* Fig. 134; A. 140;
1213		(2) 188.42	N/NR	*Ibid.* Fig. 131; A. 141;
1214 F		(3) 223.42	S3(E)	*Ibid.*
	Aldro barrow 116	Hull		*Forty Yrs*, 54–6;
1215		(1) 180.42	AOC	Fig. 100; A. 120;
1216		(2) 197.42	S1	Fig. 104; A. 119;
1217		(3) 203.42	S2(W)	Fig. 95; A. 121;
1218		(4) 209.42	S2(W)	Fig. 99; A. 118;
1219		(5) 216.42	SH3(C)	Fig. 101; A. 295 *bis*;
1220 F		(6) 242.42	AOC	*Ibid.* 56
1221 F	Amotherby	B.M.	N2	*Y.A.J.* 39, 398,
		76 2–10 5		Fig. B
	ANTOFTS WINDYPIT, HELMSLEY	Scarborough		*Dalesman* 18, no. 2,
1222 F		(1) 38.56	AOC	May 1956
1223 F		(2) 199.55	AOC	*Ibid.*
1224 F		(3) 200.55	AOC	*Ibid.*
1225 F		(4) 201.55	Undec.	*Ibid.*
1226 F		(5) 202.55	AOC	*Ibid.*
1227 F		(6) 203.55	Undec.	*Ibid.*
	ASHBERRY WINDYPIT, HELMSLEY	Scarborough		*Ibid.*
1228 F		(1) 213.55	AOC	*Ibid.*
1229 F		(2) 214.55	AOC	*Ibid.*
1230 F		(3) 215.55	AOC	*Ibid.*
1231 F		(4) 216.55	AOC	*Ibid.*
1232 F		(5) 217.55	E.?	*Ibid.*

Corpus no.	Site	Museum	Beaker group	References
1233		(6) 218.55	Bowl	Unpub.
1234 F		R. Hayes no. 14 Whitby	AOC	Unpub.
	Barnby Howes barrow II,			Y.A.J. 39, 22–6,
1235 F	E. Cleveland	(1) Restored	AOC	Fig. 8, 1;
1236 F		(2) Sherds	FN	Fig. 8, 2, 3
1237 F	Barningham Moor, How Tallon	Barnard Castle	Indet.	Unpub.
1238	Beverley, Market Weighton	Scarborough 842.38	N/NR	Unpub.
1239 F	Bishops Burton, Littlewood barrow 256	B.M. 79 12–9 1674	Indet.	Arch. LII, 32
1240 F	Bishops Burton, Littlewood barrow 257	B.M. 79 12–9 179	Indet.	Arch. LII, 34
1241 F	Bishops Burton, Littlewood 255	B.M. 79 12–9 1601	H(FV)? Undec.	Arch. LII, 30
1242	Boltby, Hesketh Moor barrow	(1) Destroyed	S2(E)?	Elgee, 55–6, Fig. 14e,
1243		(2) Ibid.	S2(E)?	Fig. 14f;
1244 F		(3) Leeds G. 5	S1	P.Y.G.P.S. IV (1865), 491–3
1245	Brantingham, Spout Hill	Hull	S3(W)	Arch. News Letter, 3, no. 5, 79
	Broxa Moor barrow 4	Mr Lamplough		Arch. News Letter, 3,
1246		(1)	N/NR	no. 5, 79
1247		(2)	W/MR	
1248		(3)	W/MR	
1249 F	Broxa Moor barrow	Mr Lamplough	E.?	Unpub.
1250 F	Broxa Moor barrow	Ibid.	S?	Unpub.
1251 F	BUCKLAND'S WINDYPIT, HELMSLEY	Ibid.	AOC	Unpub.
1252	Burstwick, Gravel Pit	Hull 23.55	N2(L)	Unpub.
	Calais Wold, barrow 100	Hull		Forty Yrs, 159
1253 F		(1) 230.42a	S2(W)	Ibid.
1254 F		(2) 230.42b	S?	Ibid.
1255 F		(3) 230.42c	FP	Ibid.
1256 F	Calais Wold barrow 86	Hull 227.42	Indet.	Forty Yrs, 168
1256.1 F	CASTLESHAW, ROMAN FORT	B.M. 1967	FP giant	Unpub.
1256.2 F			FP	pit
1256.3 F			S3 (W)	assemblage
1256.4 F			S3?	
1256.5 F			S3?	
	Cave, South Sandpit	Hull		E.R.A.S. xxv, 169
1257		(1) Lost	FP	Ibid.
1258 F		(2)	N2	Ibid.
1259	Cave, South Kettlethorpe	Hull 85.59	AOC	Unpub.
1260	Coates Moor, Nanny Howe	Mr R. Close	N2	Unpub.
1261 F	COTTAM WARREN,	Mr Grantham	S4	Unpub.
1262 F	OLD SLEDMERE		FP	
1263 F	Cowlam barrow 57	B.M. Unreg. WG.	S?	B.B. LVII; P.P.S. III, Pl. XIV, 9, 10
1264 F	Deighton North, Bank House Fm., Green Howe	Harrogate	AOC	P.P.S. v, 251
1265	Driffield	B.M. 79 12–9 1984	N2(L)	Arch. XXXIV, 251–5, Pl. XX, Fig. 6; A. 149
1266 F	Driffield, Old Show Field	Mr Grantham	Indet.	Y.A.J. 39, 169, Fig. 2, 1
1267 F	Driffield Area, Wolds	Mr Grantham	S4	Unpub.
1268 F			FP	Ibid.
1269	Egton Bridge, Orchard Hills	B.M. 79 12–9 1232	E.	B.B. 333, 53; Elgee, 57, Fig. 16; Arch. J. XXII, 261, Fig. 18
	Elloughton, Mill Hill Pit	Hull		
1270 F		(1) 1929	N?	Unpub.
1271 F		(2) 1929	N?	Unpub.
1272		(3) 207.42	S3(E)	Antiquary, XXXVIII, 82;
1273		(4) Lost	FP	E.R.A.S. xxv, 166, Fig. 1
1274 F	Eston Nab, Mount Pleasant	Private	S3(E)	Unpub. from barrow
1275	Ferry Friston barrow 161	B.M. 79 12–9 1347	S1	B.B. 371–3; A. 109

Corpus no.	Site	Museum	Beaker group	References
	FLAMBOROUGH HD. BEACON HILL	Scarborough		*Ant. J.* XXXVIII, 234;
1276 F		(1) 1222.51	E.	*Y.A.J.* 39, 1, n.
1277 F		(2) 1230.51	FN	
1278 F		(3) 1749.51	AOC	
1279	Flixton, Silver Bay, Filey Road	Scarborough 843.38.1	N/NR	*Ant. J.* XIII, 53–4
1280	Folkton barrow 242	B.M. 89 2–2 24	S 4	*Arch.* LII, 11, Fig. 3; A. 108
1281	Folkton barrow 245	B.M. 93 12–28 19	N/NR	*Arch.* LII, 16, Fig. 5; A. 152
1282	Fraisthorpe, Crossham Hills	Hull 95.42	N2(L)	Unpub.
	Ganton barrow 21	B.M.		*B.B.* 162–6, XXI;
1283		(1) 79 12–9 118	S2(W)	A. 130;
1284		(2) 79 12–9 122	S3(E)	A. 131
1285 F	Ganton barrow 22	B.M. 79 12–9 272	N2	*B.B.* 167, XXII
1286 F	Ganton barrow 27/28?	B.M. 79 12–9 319	Indet.	*B.B.* 173–5, XXVII–XXVIII
1287 F	GARROWBY WOLD BARROW 32	Hull	S2(W)	*Forty Yrs*, 146
1288 F		226.42	FP	
1289 F	Garrowby Wold barrow 39	Hull 125.42	AOC	*Forty Yrs*, 140
1290 F	Garrowby Wold barrow 42	Hull 224.42	S2(W)	*Forty Yrs*, 143, Fig. 383
	Garrowby Wold barrow 104	Hull		*Forty Yrs*, 134–6;
1291		(1) 190.42	N3	A. 122;
1292		(2) 191.42	N3	A. 123;
1293		(3) 199.42	S2(W)	A. 124
1294 F	GARROWBY WOLD BARROW 143	Hull	S2?	*Forty Yrs*, 148
1295 F		233.42	FP	
	Garton Slack barrow 37	Hull		*Forty Yrs*, 209,
1296		(1) 200.42	S 1	Pl. LXVIII; A. 98;
1297		(2) Lost	—	*P.S.A.L.* XXXII, 9
1298	Garton Slack barrow 75	Hull 204.42	S 1	*Forty Yrs*, 222–4; A. 103
1299	Garton Slack barrow 80	Hull 192.42	N/NR	*Forty Yrs*, 235.7; A. 146
	Garton Slack barrow 81	Hull		*Forty Yrs*, 238–41;
1300		(1) 186.42	N/NR	A. 156
1301 F		(2) 239.42	Indet.	
1302	Garton Slack barrow 141	Hull	H(FV)	*Forty Yrs*, 259, Fig. 725
1303	Garton Slack barrow 161	Hull 205.42	N2(L)	*Forty Yrs*, 211–12; A. 102
	Garton Slack barrow 163	Hull		*Forty Yrs*, 214–15;
1304		(1) 183.42	N3	A. 115;
1305		(2) 196.42	N3(L)	A. 116;
1306		(3) 189.42	N3	A. 117
1307	GARTON SLACK, CRAIKE HILL	Mr Grantham restored	E.	*Ant. J.* XXXVIII, 231, Fig. 6
1308 F	Gilling barrow, Howardian Hills	York	Indet.	Unpub.
	Goodmanham barrow 99	B.M.		*B.B.* 308–9;
1309		(1) 79 12–9 1200	N3	A. 132;
1310		(2) 79 12–9 1199	N/NR	A. 133;
1311		(3) 79 12–9 1201	N1/D	A. 134
1312 F	Goodmanham barrow 111	B.M. 79 12–9 1213	S2(W)	*B.B.* 319
	Goodmanham barrow 113	B.M.		*B.B.* 321–2;
1313 F		(1) 79 12–9 1217	S2(W)	*C.A.S.* XXXIX, 50, Fig. 15;
1314		(2) 79 12–9 1215	SH4(B)	A. 293
1315 F		(3) 79 12–9 1186	AOC	
1316	Goodmanham barrow 116	B.M. 79 12–9 1224	S 4	*B.B.* 325–6; A. 111
1317	Grassington, Lea Green barrow	Skipton	AOC	*Antiquary*, XXVI, 147–9; *Y.A.J.* 29, 361, Fig. 8 *d*
1318	Guisborough, Highcliff	Middlesborough	SH3(C)	Elgee, 70, Fig. 23 *e*
1319 F	Halton East	Skipton	S2(W)	*Antiquary*, XXVII, 122
	Hanging Grimston, barrow 56	Hull		*Forty Yrs*, 98–9;

Corpus no.	Site	Museum	Beaker group	References
1320		(1) 206.42	S2(E)	A. 104;
1321		(2) 217.42	N/MR	uncertain this barrow
	Hanging Grimston, barrow 55	Hull		*Forty Yrs*, 100–2;
1322		(1) 182.42	N2	*Ibid.* Fig. 246; A. 125;
1323		(2) 214.42	S2(E)	A. 126;
1324		(3) 201.42	S2(W)	A. 127
1325 F	Hanging Grimston barrow 131	Hull 236.42	Indet.	*Forty Yrs*, 112
1326	Hedon Howe barrow 281	Hull 198.42	S3(W)	*Forty Yrs*, 346–50; A. 99
1327	Hempholme in Holderness, nr. Brandesburton	Mr Grantham	N3	Unpub.
1328	Heslerton barrow 5	B.M. 79 12–9 43	S1	*B.B.* 142; A. 105
1329 F	Heslerton barrow 6	B.M. 79 12–9 45	S2(E)?	*B.B.* 144
1330 F	Heslerton East	Lost	—	*Y.P.S.* (1951), 15
1331	Huggate and Warterwold barrow 3	B.M. 79 12–9 1996	S2(E)	*Forty Yrs*, 311; A. 107
	Huggate Wold barrow 216	Hull		*Forty Yrs*, 309–10;
1332	Barrow 216	(1) 195.42	S1	A. 106
1333 F		(2) 240.42	FP	
	Huggate and Warterwold barrow 254	Hull		*Forty Yrs*, 320–1;
1334		(1) 185.42	N2	A. 147;
1335		(2) 220.42?	N2	reconstructed
1336 F	Huggate and Warterwold barrow 263	Hull 238.42	Indet.	*Forty Yrs*, 312
	Huggate and Warterwold barrow 264	Hull		*Forty Yrs*, 317–19;
1337		(1) 215.42	H(FV)	A. 296*a*
1338		(2) Lost	—	
1339 F	Hunmanby barrow 251	B.M. Lost	—	*Arch.* 52, 21–2; base sherd
1340 F	KILHAM, GALLOWS HILL	Mr Grantham	S?	Unpub.
1341 F			FP	Unpub.
1342 F	Kity Hill barrow 199	Hull	Indet.	*Forty Yrs*, 149
1343 F	Malton, West Lodge Gate	B.M. 53 11–15 18	E.	*Y.A.J.* 39, 397, Fig. 1*a*
1344 F	Melton Quarry	Hull 68.60.1	Indet.	Unpub. shred with bracer and bone ring
1345 F	MELTON QUARRY,	Hull	AOC	Unpub.
1346 F	'Hut Circles'		FN	
1346.1 F			Undec.	
1347	Middleton-on-the-Wolds	Hull	S2/Hybrid	Hull Mus. Pub. 55, 6, Pl. 1; A. 153; *E.R.A.S.* xv, 103, Pl. II
1348	Middleton-on-the-Wolds	Middleton Hall	N2(L)	*Forty Yrs*, 354; A. 100
	Newton Mulgrave, Area	Liverpool		Elgee, 56–7,
1349		(1) Destroyed	S4	Fig. 14*c*
1350		(2) *Ibid.*	S1	Fig. 14*d*
	Painsthorpe Wold, barrow 4	Hull		*Forty Yrs*, 113–17;
1351		(1) 202.42	S2(W)	A. 112;
1352		(2) 210.42	S1	A. 113;
1353		(3) 211.42	FP	A. 114
1354 F		(4) 222.42	S2(W)	
1355 F	Painsthorpe barrow 83	Hull 208/237.42	S3(W)	*Forty Yrs*, 119
1356 F	Painsthorpe barrow 98	Hull 229.42	S?	*Forty Yrs*, 130
	Painsthorpe Wold barrow 118	Hull		*Forty Yrs*, 128
1357 F		(1) 231.42*a*	AOC	*Ibid.*
1358 F		(2) 231.42*b*	S4	*Ibid.*
1359 F		(3) 231.42*c*	N2	*Ibid.*
1360	Pickering	Sheffield J.93.869	SH4(C)	*Ten Yrs*, 209, Fig. A. 294; *Arch. J.* XVIII, 415
1361	Pickering	Sheffield J.93.870	N/NR	*Ten Yrs*, 231; A. 157

Corpus no.	Site	Museum	Beaker group	References
1362	Pickering, Raindale, No Man's Land	York 1001.47	E.	Horne, 50, Fig.
	Riggs, barrow 36	Hull		*Forty Yrs*, 174
1363 F		(1)	S?	*Ibid.*
1364 F		(2)	FP	*Ibid.*
1365	Rossington	Doncaster	N/NR	Unpub. Giant beaker
1366	Rudstone barrow 61	B.M.	N2	*B.B.* 231;
		79 12–9 665		A. 144
	Rudstone barrow 62	B.M.		*B.B.* 235–44;
1367		(1) 79 12–9 699	N2	A. 135;
1368		(2) 79 12–9 700	N2	A. 136;
1369		(3) 79 12–9 701	N/NR	A. 137;
1370		(4) 79 12–9 698	N3(L)	A. 138;
1371		(5) 79 12–9 697	E. Ang.?	A. 139;
1372 F		(6) 79 12–9 702	S2(W)	*Arch. J.* XXVII, 71
1373	Rudstone barrow 63	B.M.	S4	*B.B.* 247;
		79 12–9 730		A. 110
	Rudstone barrow 66	B.M.		*B.B.* 253–5;
1374		(1) 79 12–9 902	S2(E)	A. 128;
1375		(2) 79 12–9 903	N2	A. 129
	Rudstone barrow 67	B.M.		*B.B.* 259–6;
1376		(1) 79 12–9 926	AOC	A. 143;
1377		(2) 79 12–9 927	N/NR	A. 142
1378 F		(3) Unreg.	W/MR	
1379 F	RUDSTON WOLDGATE	Mr Grantham	AOC	Unpub.
1380 F		Site 2	E.	*Ibid.*
1381	Scampston Park	York 1005.47	N2	Unpub.
1382 F	Scarborough, Castle Hill	Scarborough	S2(W)	Unpub.
		850.53 1–2		
1383 F	Settle, Sewell's Cave	Settle	AOC	*U.D.P.S.* IX (1936),
				201, Fig. 5
1384	Sherburn barrow 7	B.M.	N2	*B.B.* 146;
		79 12–9 46		A. 154
1385 F	Sherburn barrow 13	B.M.	Indet.	*B.B.* 154
		79 12–9 97		
1386 F	Sherburn barrow 14	B.M.	AOC	*B.B.* 155
		79 12–9 95		
1387	Skipsea Peat, Whithow Bog	York	E.	*P.P.S.* II, 230, Fig.
1388	Snip Gill, Windypit,	Scarborough	H(FV)	*Ant. J.* XXXV, 223,
	nr. Helmsley	652.53		Fig. 1, Pl. XXXVIA
	Staxton	Scarborough		*Y.A.J.* 40, 129–44,
1389		(1) 322.58	S1	Fig. 7(1)
1390		(2) 321.58	S1	Fig. 7(2)
		York		
1391		(3) C1.1951	N/NR	*Y.P.S.* (1951), 13–15;
1392		(4) C1.1947	S4	*Y.A.J.* 40, 144, Fig. 8
1393 F	Stuffield, barrow nr.	Mr Lamplough	Indet.	Unpub.
1394	Sutton Bank, nr. Thirsk	Unknown	S4	*Y.A.J.* 33, 419, Fig. 5
1395	Thornton Dale, Monklands	York		Elgee, 56, Fig. 14*a*;
		(1) 1002.47	S1	*Y.P.S.* (1911), 57–62, Pl. I;
1396 F	Monklands	(2) 1948.8.7	N2	*Ibid.* Pl. III, no. 2
	Thwing, barrow 60	B.M.		*B.B.* 226–8;
1397		(1) 79 12–9 657	S2(E)	A. 150;
1398 F		(2) 79 12–9 1557	Indet.	*Y.A.J.* 39, 3
1399	Tinshill, Leeds	Leeds	S2(W)	Unpub.
	Towthorpe barrow 21	Hull		*Forty Yrs*, 10–12;
1400		(1) 194.42	S2(W)	A. 101
1401 F		(2) 243.42	S2(W)	
1402	Towthorpe barrow 211½	Hull 193.42	N2	*Forty Yrs*, 19; A. 145
	Weaverthorpe barrow 42	B.M.		*B.B.* 193;
1403		(1) 79 12–9 435	N3	A. 155
1404 F		(2) 79 12–9 1545	S2(W)	
1405	Weaverthorpe, Barrow Nook 297	Hull 187.42	N2	*Y.A.J.* XXI, 214–16, Fig. 5
1406	Whitby Area	Liverpool	SH4(B)	Elgee, 57, Pl. VII, Fig. 2;
		Destroyed		*Arc. Camb.* 7s. V, 19, Fig. 6

Corpus no.	Site	Museum	Beaker group	References
1407	Whitwell Hill	Private	S4	*Y.A.J.* 33, 119, Fig.
1408	Willerby barrow 235	B.M. 93 12–28 1	AOC	*Arch.* LII, 2–4; A. 151
1409	York, Bootham Bridge	York 1000.47	N3	A. 148
1410 F	Yorkshire Wolds	Hull 234.42	FP	Uncertain barrow Mortimer College
	Yorkshire?	Hull		Bought at Fentons
1411		(1) 98.42	FP	Sale, Unprovenanced
1412		(2) 99.42	E. Ang. FN	*Ibid.*

SCOTLAND

1413.1	Scotland?	N.M.A. Unreg.	FP	Unpub. ex. Prof. Dunn Coll. Mistakenly thought to be a fake
1413.2	Scotland	N.M.A. E.G.10	S4	Unpub.

Aberdeenshire

1414	Aberdeenshire	N.M.A. E.G.39	AOC	*P.S.A.S.* XL, 313; A. 225; CM. 1
1415	Aberdeenshire	Aberdeen City Mus. Restored	N3	Unpub.
1416	Aberdeenshire	N.M.A. EA.136	Undec.	Unpub. ex. Rae Coll.
1417	Aberdeenshire	B.M. 56 11–4 1	N2	A. 251; CM. 27
1418	Aberdeenshire	B.M. 56 11–4 2	N/MR	A. 263; CM. 29
1419	Aberdeenshire	N.M.A. E.G.21	N3	A. 258; CM. 28
1420	Aberdeenshire	Kelvingrove 110–406	N3	Unpub.
1421	Aberdeen, King Street	N.M.A. E.G.35	N2	*P.S.A.S.* XXIV, 446; CM. 30
1422	Aberdeen, nr.	Unknown	N2?	A. 261; CM. 31
	Ardiffney? (Ardiffery), Cruden	Peterhead		*P.S.A.S.* XXII, 366;
1423		⌠(1)	⌠N2	Wilson, 175; Cat. Ant.
1424		⌡(2)	⌡N2	Edin. II; A. 228, 229; CM. 8, 9
1425	Ardoe, Bridge of Dee	Aberdeen 240.23	N3	Unpub.
1426 F	Atherb Fm., Buchan	N.M.A. EO 917–21	AOC	Unpub.
1427 F			Undec.	
1428 F	Atherb Fm., Powsode Cairn	N.M.A. EO 916	AOC	Unpub.
1429	Auchrynie	Aberdeen 240.15	N4	Unpub.
1430	Blackhills, Tyrie,	N.M.A. E.G.48	N/NR?	*P.S.A.S.* XLIII, 87; CM. 43
1431	Blackhills, Tyrie	Aberdeen	N4/FV	*P.S.A.S.* XLIII, 91
1432	Blairmore House, nr. Huntly	*Ibid.* 240.19	N3	Unpub.
	Broomend, Inverurie Cist. 1	N.M.A.		*P.S.A.S.* VII, 110;
1433		⌠(1) E.Q.23	⌠N2(L)	XVII, 455; XL, 27; LIV, 155;
1434		⌡(2) E.Q.24	⌡N3	A. 226, 227; CM. 3, 4
	Cist 2	Inverurie		*P.S.A.S.* VII, 115;
1435		⌠(1) E.Q.1	⌠N2	XVII, 455; XL, 27; LIV, 155;
1436		⌡(2) E.Q.2	⌡N2	A. 249; CM. 5, 6
1437 F	Cist 3	Inverurie	Indet.	*P.S.A.S.* VII, 115; LIV, 155; CM. 7
1438	Broomhill, Tough	N.M.A. E.G.58	N2	*P.S.A.S.* LX, 18; CM. 44

Corpus no.	Site	Museum	Beaker group	References
1439	Bruckleseat, Fyvie	N.M.A. E.G.59	N3	*P.S.A.S.* LX, 98; CM. 45
1440	Cairnie, Huntly	Elgin	N1/D	*P.S.A.S.* XXII, 342; A. 255; CM. 33
	Clashfarquhar, Banchory	Aberdeen		Wilson, I, 419;
1441	Banchory	(1)	N3	*P.S.A.S.* XXII, 363
1442		(2) Lost	N3	(1), CM. 23
1443	Clinterty, Kinellar	Aberdeen	N3	*J.R.A.I.* (1902), 383; *P.A.A.S.A.U.* (1902–4), 15; *Cat.M.Coll.* no. 10; A. 243; CM. 21
1444	Cruden, Aldie	N.M.A. E.G. 20	N2(L)	*P.S.A.S.* XI, 408; A. 237; CM. 16
1445	Cuning Hill, Inverurie	Inverurie	AOC	*P.S.A.S.* XXXVII, 230; CM. 68
	Drimdollo, District of	Aberdeen		Unpub.
1446	Ythan Wells	(1) 240.4	N3	
1447 F		(2) Sherd	Indet.	*Ibid.*
1448 F	East Finnercy, Dunecht	Prof. Atkinson	AOC	Piggott *et alia* (1962) 'Prehistoric Peoples of Scotland', 18
	Ellon	N.M.A.		*P.S.A.S.* XXVI, 262;
1449		(1) E.G.36	N3	A. 230; CM. 10;
1450		(2) E.G.37	N3	A. 231; CM. 11
1451	Ellon, Hillhead	Aberdeen	N3(L)	*Cat.M.Coll.* no. 8; CM. 55
1452	Elrick, Newhills	Aberdeen	N3	*P.S.A.S.* LIX, 208; *Cat.M.Coll.* no. 29; CM. 49
1453	Freefield	Unknown	N3	*P.S.A.S.* XV, 193; A. 241; CM. 20
1454	Glasterberry, Peterculter	Aberdeen	N3	*P.S.A.S.* XXXVI, 627; A. 259*a*; CM. 36, also CM. 60 in error
1455	Hill of Foulzie, King Edward	Banff	N3	*B.F.C.* 1901–5, April 1902, 25; CM. 70
1456	Insch?	Inverurie	N4	Unpub.
1457	Inveramsay, Chapel of Garioch	N.M.A. E.G.16	N3	*P.S.A.S.* IV, 165; A. 244; CM. 22
1458	Johnstone, Leslie	Aberdeen	N2(L)	*P.S.A.S.* LXIV, 218; CM. 50.
	Keir Belhelvie, Belhelvie	Aberdeen		*Cat.M.Coll.* no. 5;
1459		(1)	N3(L)	*Ibid.*; CM. 57;
1460		(2)	N4	CM. 56;
1461		(3)	N4	CM. 58
1462 F	Kemnay, nr.	N.M.A.	N2	*P.S.A.S.* LXXI, 367
1463 F	Kinaldy, Dyce	N.M.A. E.G.29	N3	*Cat.Ant.Soc.Scot.* 36; *C.B.* II, 25; CM. 46
1464 F	Kinaldy, Dyce	N.M.A. E.G.28	N3	*C.B.* II, 25; CM. 47
1465	Kintore	Kintore House Haliburton	AOC	'Scotland before the Scots', 101, Childe
1466	Leggats Den, Chapel of Garioch	N.M.A. E.G.57	N2	*P.S.A.S.* LX, 17; CM. 63
	Loanhead of Daviot	N.M.A.		*P.S.A.S.* LXIX, 168;
1467 F		(1) EP 60–76	AOC	*P.S.A.S.* LXX, 291
1468 F		(2) *Ibid.*	Indet.	*Ibid.*
1469 F		(3) *Ibid.*	Indet.	*Ibid.*
1470	Mains of Leslie, Premnay	Aberdeen	N3	*P.S.A.S.* XLI, 116; *P.A.A.S.A.U.* (1906–8), 54; A. 256; CM. 34
1471	Mains of Leslie, Premnay	Aberdeen 240.6A	N2	*P.S.A.S.* XLIII, 76; CM. 51
	Mains of Leslie, Premnay	Inverurie		*P.S.A.S.* XLVI, 344;
1472		(1) no. 5	N2	CM. 52;
1473		(2) no. 6	N2	CM. 53
1474	Memsie, Upper Cairn Fm.	Aberdeen	N3	*P.S.A.S.* LXXXVIII, 10, Fig. 5

Corpus no.	Site	Museum	Beaker group	References
1475	Mid Clova, Kildrummy	N.M.A. E.G.72	N2	*P.S.A.S.* LXVIII, 177; CM. 69
1476	Mill Farm, Rathen, nr. Fraserburgh	Aberdeen 240.16	N4	*P.S.A.S.* LXIX, 382
1477	Newlands, Oyne. Cist 1	N.M.A. E.G.65	N3	*P.S.A.S.* LXVII, 228; CM. 65
1478	Newlands, Oyne. Cist 2	Aberdeen	N4	*P.S.A.S.* LXX, 326
1479 F	Old Keig, Alford	N.M.A.	Indet.	*P.S.A.S.* LXVII, 37, 45; CM. 67
1480	Ord, Auchendoir	Aberdeen	N2	*P.A.A.S.A.U.* (1902–4), 17 *Cat.M.Coll.* no. 7; A. 239; CM. 19
1481 F	Parish of Glass	N.M.A. E.G. 42	N2	*P.S.A.S.* XXXVI, 67; CM. 48
1482	Parish of Leslie	B.M. 1911 7–19 1	N2	*Reliquary*, NS. III, 49; A. 248; CM. 26
1483	Parish of Strichen	Aberdeen	N3	*Cat.M.Coll.* no. 27; CM. 54
1484	Parkhill	Aberdeen	N2	*P.A.A.S.A.U.* (1902–4), 9; *Cat.M.Coll.* no. 4; A. 238; CM. 17
1485	Parkhill	N.M.A. E.G.2	N3	*P.S.A.S.* XVI, 70; *P.A.A.S.U.* 1902–4, 11 *Cat.M.Coll.* no. 14; A. 253; CM. 18
1486	Persley Quarry, Old Machar	Aberdeen	N2	*P.A.A.S.A.U.* (1902–4), 13; *Cat.M.Coll.* no. 12; A. 247; CM. 25
1487	Pitsligo, Bankhead	Peterhead	N1/D	*P.S.A.S.* XXII, 366; A. 260; CM. 37
1488	Pitsligo, Boghead Fm.	N.M.A. E.G.77	N3	*P.S.A.S.* LXXVII, 187
	Pittodrie, Oyne	Aberdeen		*P.S.A.S.* XL, 23;
1489		(1) 240.8	N3	A. 233*a*; CM. 14
1490		(2) 240.7	N2	A. 233*b*; CM. 15
1491	Ruthven, Huntly	Aberdeen	N/NR	Unpub.
1492	Savoch, Longside	Peterhead	E.?	*P.S.A.S.* XXII, 366; *Cat.Ant.Edin.* II; A. 246; CM. 24
1493	Skene, Blackhills	N.M.A. E.G. 67	N2	*P.S.A.S.* LXIX, 7; *Ibid.* LXVIII, 413–16
1494	Skene, Newhills	N.M.A. E.G.68	N1/D	*P.S.A.S.* LXVIII, 413–16
1495 F	Skillimarino, Old Deer	Peterhead	E.	Unpub.
1496	Slap, Turrif	N.M.A. E.Q.140	N/NR Undec.	*P.S.A.S.* X, 740; CM. 38
1497	Stoneywood	Aberdeen 233.7	N2	*P.A.A.S.A.U.* (1902–4), 12; *Cat.M.Coll.* no. 9; A. 254; CM. 32
1498	Stoneywood	Aberdeen 230.25	N2	*Cat.M.Coll.* no. 25; CM. 59
1499	Sundayswells Hill, Torphins	N.M.A. E.Q.566	AOC	*P.S.A.S.* XL, 312; A. 225*a*; CM. 2
1500	Tifty, Fyvie	Aberdeen	N3	*Cat.M.Coll.* no. 26; A. 257; CM. 35
1501	Upper Boyndlie Tyrie	N.M.A. E.Q.295	N2	*P.S.A.S.* XLIII, 79; CM. 40
1502	*Ibid.*	E.Q.296	N3(L)	*P.S.A.S.* XLIII, 79; CM. 41
1503	*Ibid.*	Aberdeen	N4	CM. 42 *Ibid.*
1504	Upper Boyndlie, Tyrie. Cist IV	Aberdeen 229.79	N3	*P.S.A.S.* LXVII, 176; CM. 66
1505	Upper Mains of Muiresk, Turriff	N.M.A. E.G.31	N3	*P.S.A.S.* XX, 98; CM. 39
1506	Westside of Brux, Mossat, Alford	Aberdeen 240.2	N2	Unpub.

Corpus no.	Site	Museum	Beaker group	References
	Whitestone, Skene	Aberdeen		*P.S.A.S.* XL, 28;
1507		⎰(1)	⎰N/NR	*P.A.A.S.A.U.* (1904–6), 128;
1508		⎱(2)	⎱N3	*Cat.M.Coll.* no. 3;
				A. 232, 233; CM. 12, 13

Angus

1509	Bandoch, Inverkeilor	N.M.A. E.G.94	N3	*P.S.A.S.* LXXXVI, 214
1510	Castle Huntly	Dundee	AOC	*P.S.A.S.* XXII, 346; CM. 71
1511	Colliston Mill, Arbroath	N.M.A. E.G.49	N3	*P.S.A.S.* XLIX, 15; CM. 79
1512	Fletcherfield	Fletcherfield	N2	*P.S.A.S.* LXV, 418; CM. 80
1513	Forfarshire	Dundee	AOC	Unpub.
1514 F	Greenlaw, Farnell	Montrose	N2	Unpub.
1515	Kame Hillock, Hill of Tealing	Dundee	N3	*P.S.A.S.* XXII, 346; CM. 81
1516	Kingswells, Fallows, Monikie	N.M.A. E.G.17	N1/D	A. 259; CM. 76
1517	Kirkbuddo	Coll. Soc. Ant. Lond.	N3	*Arch.* XLIII, Pt. II, 395, Pl. XXXI, Fig. 6; A. 236; CM. 72
1518 F	Kirkbuddo Gallows Hill	N.M.A. E.G.80	N2	*P.S.A.S.* LXXIX, 176
1519	Kirkbuddo, Roman Camp	N.M.A. E.G.79	N2	*P.S.A.S.* LXXIX, 175
1520	Linlathen, Cairn Gregg	Dundee	S4	*P.S.A.S.* VI, 98; XII, 449; A. 262; Anderson I.10; CM. 77
1521	Linlathen, Broughty Ferry	Dundee N.26	N1/D	Malcolm's 'Parish of Monifieth', 202; *P.S.A.S.* XXI, 316
1522	Lochlee, Milton Hill	N.M.A. EE.55	S4	*P.S.A.S.* XVIII, 364
1523	Lunanhead, Pitscandly	N.M.A. E.G.76	N1/D	*P.S.A.S.* LXXVI, 128
1524	Noranside, Fern	N.M.A. E.G.61	N3	*P.S.A.S.* XXVII, 66; A. 240; CM. 73
1525	Priest-Town, Edzell	N.M.A. E.G.5	N1/D	A. 242; CM. 74
1526	Wellgrove, Lochee	N.M.A. E.G.46	N2(L)	*P.S.A.S.* XL, 40; A. 250; CM. 75

Argyll

	ARDNAMURCHAN, SANA BAY	Cambridge		Man (1927), nos. 115,
1527		Restored	AOC	173; CM. 94;
1528 F		26.502	AOC	*Ibid.*; CM. 96
1529 F		26.501 Cardium	E.	Unpub.
1530	Ballymenach, Kilmartin	B.M. 79 12–9 1913	N3(L)	*P.S.A.S.* VI, 348; LXV, 278; A. 185; CM. 82
	Callachally, Glenforsa, Mull	N.M.A.		*P.S.A.S.* IX, 537;
1531		⎰(1) E.Q. 137	⎰N3	XI, 586; A. 217; CM. 89;
1532		⎱(2) E.Q.135	⎱S3(E)	CM. 90
1533	Campbeltown, Balnabraid	Hunterian	N3	*P.S.A.S.* LIV, 172; CM. 92
1534	Campbeltown, Glebe Street	Campbeltown	N/NR	*P.S.A.S.* LXVIII, 179; CM. 98
1535 F	COLL, TORASTAIN CORNAIG	Kelvingrove	AOC	*P.S.A.S.* LXII, 25;
1536 F		Robertson-	AOC	*P.S.A.S.* LIV, 172;
1537 F		MacKay (M.O.W.)	E.	CM. 94. Most of the material in about 200 sherds
1538 F		*Ibid.*	FN	
1539 F		*Ibid.*	Undec.	
1540 F	*Ibid.*	N.M.A. B.N.14–18	E.	*P.S.A.S.* XLIII, 328; CM. 97; *P.S.A.S.* LXVIII, 146
1541 F	Cragabus Cists, Islay	N.M.A. EO.255	AOC	*P.S.A.S.* XXXVI, 110
1541.1 F			Undec.	

Corpus no.	Site	Museum	Beaker group	References
1542 F	Gallanach, Oban	Unknown	Indet.	*P.S.A.S.* XXXI, 238
1543 F	Killelan Farm	Private	AOC	*Disc. and Exc. Scot.* (1961), 22–3
1544	Kilmory Knap, Lochgilphead	N.M.A. L.1956.14	N3(L)	*P.S.A.S.* XC, 228
1545 F	Kerrera Island, nr. Oban	N.M.A. L.1931.1	S4	*P.S.A.S.* LXVI, 407, Fig. 5
1546 F	Knoc-Riabhech	Hunterian D.1951.1813	N?	Unpub.
1547	Poltalloch Estate	N.M.A. H.P.O.13	N3	*P.S.A.S.* XXXIX, 242; A. 191; CM. 83
1548 F	*Ibid.* (Largie?)	H.P.O.15	AOC	*P.S.A.S.* XXXIX, 242; CM. 84 and 87 (?)
1549 F	*Ibid.* (Largie?)	H.P.O.16	N3	CM. 85, with above from chambered cairn (?);
1550 F		H.P.O.17 Cardium	E.	C.M. 88 (?)
1551	Poltalloch, Largie	B.M. 79 12–9 1925	N/MR	*P.S.A.S.* VI, 344; A. 198; CM. 86
1552	Poltalloch	N.M.A. Loan 1961	N2	*Disc. and Exc.Scot.* (1961), 11–12
1553 F	Salen, Mull	N.M.A. E.Q.269	AOC	*P.S.A.S.* XVII, 84; CM. 91
1554 F	Tiree	Kelvingrove	AOC	*P.S.A.S.* XLII, 328; CM. 93; *P.S.A.S.* LXVIII, 146

Ayrshire

Corpus no.	Site	Museum	Beaker group	References
1555 F	Ayr, Loudon Hill	N.M.A. E.G.95	AOC	Unpub.
1556 F	Borland Castle, Cumnock	Kilmarnock	Indet.	*P.S.A.S.* LXXIV, 136
1557 F	Dalmellington, Cairn Beoch	Unknown	Indet.	*P.S.A.S.* LXXII, 235
1558	Dalry, Court Hill	N.M.A. E.G.11	N/MR	*P.S.A.S.* X, 281; *Arch. Hist. Coll., Ayr and Wigton*, I, 53, 55; A. 199; CM. 99
1559 F	Haylee, Largs.	Unknown	—	*Proc.R.S.E.* XXVI, 279; *Arch.* 62, Pt. I, 246; A. 37; CM. 110
1560 F	Merkland Knowe	N.M.A. Unreg.1898	FN	Unpub.
	Muirkirk	N.M.A.		*P.S.A.S.* XLVIII, 373
1561 F	Circle 1;	E.G.A.2–14	Indet.	*Ibid.*; CM. 106
1562	*Ibid.* Circle 2;	E.G.A.1	FN/FV	*Ibid.*; CM. 100;
1563 F		E.G.A.2–14	AOC	*P.S.A.S.* XLVIII, 373;
1564 F		*Ibid.*	FN	LXI, 269; CM. 101–5
1565 F		*Ibid.*	E.	*Ibid.*
1566 F	*Ibid.* Circle 3;	*Ibid.*	Indet.	*P.S.A.S.* LIV, 210; CM. 107; *P.S.A.S.* LXIX, 379
1567 F	Muirkirk, Wellwood	N.M.A. E.G.A.106	N2	*P.S.A.S.* LVI, 131; CM. 109
1568 F	Shewalton	Greenock	AOC	Unpub.;
1569 F	Sands,	N.M.A. E.G.84	E.	CM. 111;
1570 F	*Ibid.* Moor	Kilmarnock	AOC	Unpub.

Banffshire

Corpus no.	Site	Museum	Beaker group	References
1571	Aberchirdir, Burnside of Whitefield	Forglen House	N3	*P.S.A.S.* XL, 306; A. 276; CM. 116
1572	Afforsk, Gardenstown	B.M. 1911 7–19 4	N4	*Reliquary*, NS. II, 178; A. 283; CM. 124
1573	Banffshire	Banff	AOC	*P.S.A.S.* XXII, 369
1574	Banffshire, Hill of Scatterty?	Banff	AOC	*P.S.A.S.* XXII, 370
1575	Boharm, Achroisk	N.M.A. E.G.1	N2	*P.S.A.S.* VIII, 341; A. 272; CM. 114

Corpus no.	Site	Museum	Beaker group	References
1576	Buckie, Rathven	B.M. 1911 7–19 2	N3	*Reliquary*, NS. I, 229; A. 267; CM. 112
1577	Buckie, St Peter's	N.M.A. E.G.4	N3	*P.S.A.S.* XVI, 415; A. 287; CM. 125
1578	Buckie, Easter Gollachy	B.M. 1911 7–19 5	N2	*P.S.A.S.* LXX, 357; CM. 128
1579	Carestown, Deskford	Banff	N3	*P.S.A.S.* XXII, 369; A. 270; CM. 113
1580	Cullen	Banff	N4	*P.S.A.S.* XXII, 369; A. 274; CM. 115
1581	Findlater Castle	Unknown	Possibly an Urn	Cordiner, III; CM. 127
	Forglen	Forglen House		*P.S.A.S.* XL, 279;
1582		(1)	AOC	A. 277; CM. 117;
1583		(2)	N1/D	A. 278; CM. 118;
1584		(3)	N2	A. 279; CM. 119
1585 F	Lesmurdie	N.M.A. Unreg. in E.Q.31	Indet.	*P.S.A.S.* I, 205; *C.B.* II, 16; CM. 120
1586	*Ibid.*	*Ibid.* E.Q.30	N3	*P.S.A.S.* I, 205; *C.B.* II, 16; A. 280; CM. 121
1587	*Ibid.*	*Ibid.* E.Q.32	N3(L)	*P.S.A.S.* I, 205; *C.B.* II, 16; A. 281; CM. 122
1588	*Ibid.*	*Ibid.* E.Q.31	N/NR?	*P.S.A.S.* I, 205; *C.B.* II, 16; A. 282; CM. 123
1589	Portsoy, Auchmore	Banff	N4	*P.S.A.S.* XXII, 369; A. 291; CM. 126

Berwickshire

1590 F	Chirnside, Edington Mill	N.M.A. E.Q.324	N2	*P.S.A.S.* XLVIII, 330; CM. 135
1591	Chirnside, Harelaw Hill	Mr Mitchell Innes, Whitehall	N3(L)	*B.N.C.* XIX, 340, Pl. XVIII; CM. 136
	Cockburnspath, Hoprig	N.M.A.		*B.N.C.* XII, 131; XXIV, 163;
1592		(1) E.Q.599	N2	A. 210; CM. 130;
1593		(2) E.Q.600	N/NR	A. 211; CM. 131
1594 F	Duns, Grueldykes	N.M.A. E.G.27 and 56	N2	*B.N.C.* V, 60; XXIV, 184; *P.S.A.S.* LVIII, 19; CM. 133
1595	Edrom, Broomdykes	Unknown	Indet.	*B.N.C.* XXIV, 185; CM. 134; *P.S.A.S.* XLVII, 172
1596	Gordon, Macksmill	N.M.A. E.G.86	N3	*B.N.C.* XI, 194; CM. 132; *Ibid.* XXIV, 186; A. 212a; *P.S.A.S.* XX, 100
1597 F	Gordon Moss	N.M.A. E.G.82	AOC	Unpub.
1598 F	Lauder, Hill House	N.M.A. E.G.83	Indet.	Unpub.
1599	Manderston	Unknown	N3(L)	*B.N.C.* X, 305; CM. 129; *Ibid.* XXIV, 184; A. 187

Bute

1600 F	Dunan Beg, Lamlash, Arran	N.M.A. E.O.309	N3/FV	*P.S.A.S.* XLIII, 343; CM. 137
1601 F	Giant's Graves, Whiting Bay,	N.M.A.	Indet.	*P.S.A.S.* XXXVII, 44;
1602 F		E.O.265–7	N2?	LXIII, 29; CM. 138–40
	Glecknabae, Bute	N.M.A.		*P.S.A.S.* XXXVIII, 37;
1603 F		(1) E.P.283–4	E.	CM. 141;
1604 F		(2) E.P.286–7	FN	CM. 142–4
1605 F	Great Cumbrae	Paisley	N2	Unpub.

Caithness

Corpus no.	Site	Museum	Beaker group	References
1606	Acherole, West Watten	N.M.A. E.G.43	N3	*P.S.A.S.* XXXIX, 418; A. 286 *bis*; CM. 145
1607 F	Freswick Bay	N.M.A.	AOC	*P.S.A.S.* LIX, 89;
1608 F		H.R.1019–24	Indet.	*P.S.A.S.* LXIX, 246
	Heathfield, Glengolly, nr. Thurso	Thurso		*P.S.A.S.* LXVIII, 115
1609		(1)	N4	
1610		(2) Lost	—	
1611 F	Lower Dounreay	N.M.A.	AOC	*P.S.A.S.* LXIII, 140;
1612 F		E.O.357–61	Undec.	LXIV, 12; CM. 146–8
1612.1 F			Indet.	
1613 F	Tulach an T'Sionnaich, Loch Calder	Insp. Ancient Mons. Scot.	Indet.	*Disc. and Exc.Scot.* (1961), 52
	Note			
	Garrywhin, Bruan and	Lost	—	*P.S.A.S.* VII, 503; CM. 149
	Yarrows II	Lost	—	CM. 149 a; *Ibid.* 497

The above vessels described as cord decorated are omitted from this list since it cannot be shown that they are beakers not food vessels or urns.

Dumfriesshire

Corpus no.	Site	Museum	Beaker group	References
1614	Auchencairn, Closeburn	N.M.A. E.G.51	N3	*P.S.A.S.* L, 152; *Cat.Ant.Soc.Scot.* (1863); CM. 151
1615 F	KIRKBURN, LOCKERBIE	R. B. K.	AOC	Unpub.
1616 F		Stevenson	FN	
1616.1 F			Undec.	

East Lothian

Corpus no.	Site	Museum	Beaker group	References
1617 F	ARCHERFIELD, GULLANE	N.M.A.	AOC	A. 220;
1618 F		H.R.552.569	E.	*P.S.A.S.* XLII, 308;
1619 F			FN	CM. 156–61
1620 F	*Ibid.*	*Ibid.*	S2(W)?	A. 219–21 (except
1621 F			N3	corded sherds);
1622 F			N3(L)?	*P.S.A.S.* XLII, 308
1623 F	Broxmouth, Waird, Oxwell Mains, Dunbar	N.M.A. E.G.44	N2	*P.S.A.S.* LXVIII, 183; CM. 188
1624	Drem	N.M.A. E.G.14	N/NR	*P.S.A.S.* XVI, 236, 299; CM. 190
1625	Drem, West Fenton	N.M.A. E.G.78	N3	*P.S.A.S.* LXXVIII, 114
1626 F	Dunbar	N.M.A. E.G.81	E.	Unpub.
1627 F	DUNBAR, HEDDERWICK	N.M.A.	FN	*P.S.A.S.* LXIII, 29;
1628 F		BM. 12–91	AOC	CM. 192
1629 F			E.	*Ibid.*
1630	Dunbar, Kirkhill Braes	N.M.A. E.G.93	N1/D	*P.S.A.S.* LXXXV, 179
1631	Dunbar, West Little Pinkerton	N.M.A. E.G.75	N3(L)	*P.S.A.S.* LXXIII, 231
1632	East Barns	N.M.A. E.G.41	N/MR	*P.S.A.S.* XXXV, 277; A. 197; CM. 152
1633	Humbie, Windy Mains	N.M.A. E.G.8	N3	*P.S.A.S.* III, 51; A. 216; CM. 153
1634 F	*Ibid.*	E.G.9	N/NR	*P.S.A.S.* III, 51; CM. 154
1635	Innerwick, Thornton	N.M.A. E.G.74	N2	*P.S.A.S.* LXXIII, 318
1636	Innerwick, Thurston Mains	N.M.A. E.Q.479	N3	*P.S.A.S.* LXXIV, 138

Corpus no.	Site	Museum	Beaker group	References
1637	Lennoxlove, Abbey Mains	N.M.A. 1906	S4	Unpub.
1638	Longniddry, Boglehillwood	N.M.A. E.G.50	S3(E)	*P.S.A.S.* L, 150; CM. 189
1639 F	NORTH BERWICK, TUSCULUM	N.M.A.	AOC	*P.S.A.S.* XLII, 270;
1640 F	SITE I	E.G.23–64	Undec.	A. 222 (now in sherds); *P.S.A.S.* XLII, 270; CM. 183–4
1641 F	*Ibid.*	N.M.A.	AOC	CM. 185–7; *Ibid.*
1642 F	SITE II	E.G. 64–101	FN	*Ibid.*
1643 F	*Ibid.*		Undec.	*Ibid.*
1644 F	*Ibid.*		E?	*Ibid.*
1645 F	North Berwick, West Links	N.M.A. E.G.91	N2	*P.S.A.S.* XXXIV, 123; A. 218; CM. 155
1646	Nunraw, Garvald	N.M.A. L.1944.1	N2(L)	*P.S.A.S.* LXXVIII, 116
1647	Skateraw, Innerwick	N.M.A.	S4	*P.S.A.S.* LXXIV, 141
1648	Skateraw	N.M.A. Loan M.O.W.	N3	*Disc. and Exc. Scot.* (1958), 39

Fife

	Collessie	N.M.A.		*J.R.A.I.* (1902), 382;
1649		(1) E.Q.50	N1/D	*P.S.A.S.* XII, 439;
1650		(2) E.Q.58	N2	A. 205; CM. 199 (1); A. 204; CM. 200 (2)
1651	Dairsie	N.M.A. E.G.193	N2(L)	*P.S.A.S.* XXI, 132; A. 190; CM. 193
1652	Denbeath	N.M.A. E.Q.587	N1/D	*P.S.A.S.* LXXXIII, 242; *P.S.A.S.* LXXXIV, 226; *Reliquary*, NS. III, 191–3
1653	Dunshelt Fort, Auchtermuchty	N.M.A. E.G.64	N2	*P.S.A.S.* LXVI, 14; CM. 201
1654	Kinghorn, Grangehill Fm.	N.M.A. E.G.24	S4	*P.S.A.S.* VIII, 143; CM. 202
1655	Kirkcaldy	Kirkcaldy	S4	*P.S.A.S.* LXXVIII, 110 *Invent.G.B.* no. 32
	Leuchars, Brackmont Mill	N.M.A.		Unpub.
1656		(1) Loan 1961	AOC	*Ibid.*
1657		(2) *Ibid.*	Bowl	*Ibid.* (Undec.)
1658 F	LEUCHARS, BRACKMONT MILL	St Andrews University	AOC	*P.S.A.S.* LXXVI, 86
1659	Leuchars, Tents Muir	St Andrews University	AOC	*P.S.A.S.* XVII, 384; A. 201; CM. 196
1660 F	*Ibid.* GARPIT	N.M.A.? (Not Perth)	AOC	*T.P.P.S.* VIII, 257; CM. 197–8
1661 F	LEUCHARS, TENTSMUIR	St Andrews	AOC	*P.S.A.S.* LXXXIV, 230
1661.1 F			FN	
1662 F	LEUCHARS, TENTSMUIR, MORTON LOCH FM. TAYPORT	Abertay Hist. Soc.	AOC	*Disc. and Exc. Scot.* (1956), 16
1662.1	Methilhill, Ashgrove Fm.	N.M.A. L.1963	S4	Unpub.
	St Andrews, Balnacarron, Parklaw	St Andrews University		*P.S.A.S.* XLI, 401;
1663		(1) U.51	AOC	A. 196 (for no. 194);
1664 F		(2) Sherds	AOC	Unpub. CM. 194–5

Invernesshire

1665	Corran Ferry	Ardgour House	N3	*P.S.A.S.* XXIV, 437; A. 288; CM. 203
1666	Kiltarlity, Kirkhill	Aberdeen	N3	*P.S.A.S.* LXVIII, 128, Fig. 2; CM. 210
1667	Lochend	Inverness	N3	*P.S.A.S.* LXXVIII, 106

Corpus no.	Site	Museum	Beaker group	References
1668 F	North Uist, Clettraval	N.M.A. Cardium HD.122	N/NR	*P.S.A.S.* LXIX, 500, Fig.
1669 F	North Uist, Geirisclett	N.M.A.; G.T.49 51–3 231	AOC	*P.S.A.S.* LXIII, 96; *N.U.* 255; CM. 207–8
1670 F	North Uist, Langass Barp	N.M.A.; E.O.348–350	Indet.	*P.S.A.S.* LXIII, 96; *N.U.* 247; CM. 206
1671	North Uist, Unival	N.M.A.?	Undec.	*P.S.A.S.* LXXXII, 23, Fig. 7
1672	Skye, Kilmarie, Loch Slapin	N.M.A. E.G.60	S3(E)	*P.S.A.S.* LXII, 22; CM. 209
	Skye, Kraiknish, Loch Eynort	N.M.A.		Man. (October 1929), no. 126;
1673		(1) E.G.62	S3(E)	CM. 204;
1674		(2) E.G.63	N3	CM. 205
1675	Skye, Rudh' An Dunain	N.M.A. E.O.382	N4	*P.S.A.S.* LXVI, 183; CM. 211
1676 F	Skye, Cave of Rudh' An Dunain	N.M.A.	N3	*P.S.A.S.* LXVIII, 200

Kincardineshire

1677	Balbridie, Durris	Durris House	N/NR	*P.S.A.S.* XL, 304; *P.A.A.S.A.U.* (1902–4), 22; *Cat.M.Coll.* no. 20; A. 234; CM. 212
1678 F	*Ibid.*	(1) N.M.A. E.G.45	N3	CM. 213; refs. as above;
1679		(2) Lost	—	CM. 214
1680	*Ibid.*	Durris	N2	CM. 215; refs. as above; A. 235
1681	Banchory-Ternan	Aberdeen	N2(L)	*Cat.M.Coll.* no. 24; CM. 219
1682	Dunnottar, Kernoon Fm.	N.M.A. E.G.54	N2	*P.S.A.S.* LVI, 17; CM. 216
	Dunnottar, Nether-Criggie	Aberdeen		*P.S.A.S.* LXXXVIII, 1
1683		(1) A	N3(L)	*Ibid.*
1684		(2) B	N3(L)	*Ibid.*
1685		(3) C	N/NR	*Ibid.*
1686	Dunnottar, Resting Hill	N.M.A. E.G.15	N/MR? Undec.	*P.S.A.S.* VI, 89; CM. 217
1687 F	Hill of Canterland	Montrose	N2	*P.S.A.S.* XXI, 403
1688	Parish of Kinneff and Catterline	Aberdeen	N1/D	*Cat.M.Coll.* no. 28; CM. 221
1689	Pityot, Fetteresso	Aberdeen	N/MR	*Cat.M.Coll.* no. 11; CM. 220
1690	Porthlethen, Longhillock	Unknown	Indet.	*P.S.A.S.* X, 195; CM. 222
1691	Stonehaven	B.M.	S4/FV	*P.S.A.S.* LXX, 357, Fig. 2
1692	Upper Mains of Catterline	Aberdeen	N4	*P.S.A.S.* LVIII, 27; *Cat.M.Coll.* no. 1; CM. 218

Kinross-shire

1693	Tillyochie	N.M.A. E.G.7	N3	A. 214; *Cat.Ant.Soc.Scot.* (1863); CM. 223, also CM. 64 in error; Wilson I, 426, II, 120

Kirkcudbrightshire

1694 F	Cairnholy I.	N.M.A. E.O.819–5	E.	*P.S.A.S.* LXXXIII, 109
1695 F	Cairnholy II	N.M.A.	AOC	*P.S.A.S.* LXXXIII, 109
1696 F		E.O.830–5	E.	
1696.1 F		*Ibid.*	E.?	
1696.2 F		*Ibid.*	FN	
1697 F	Castle Douglas, Mollence	Kirkcudbright	Indet.	Unpub.
1698 F	Mainsriddle	Dumfries	N3?	*P.S.A.S.* XC, 229

Corpus no.	Site	Museum	Beaker group	References
1699	Woodfield, Highbanks	Kirkcudbright 2185	N2	*P.S.A.S.* xxv, 24; *Proc.D.G.A.S.* (1926–8), 228; CM. 224

Lanarkshire

1700	Carluke, Mossplat	N.M.A. E.G.25	N3(L)	A. 186; *P.S.A.S.* iv, 551; CM. 225
1701 F	Carnwath, Wester Yird Houses	N.M.A. E.Q.	N2(L)?	Anderson, i, 88; CM. 229; *P.S.A.S.* x, 61
1702	Crawfurd	N.M.A. E.Q.138	N3	Anderson, i, 58; A. 213; *Arch. Assoc.* x, 7; xvii, 111; *J.R.A.I.* (1902), 383; CM. 228
1703	Glasgow, Victoria Park, Whiteinch	Glasgow Green Mus.	N3(L)	Unpub. (Misreconst. as two vessels)
	Lanarkmoor, Lanark	N.M.A.		*P.S.A.S.* v, 214;
1704		(1) E.G.18	N1/D	A. 208; CM. 226;
1705		(2) E.G.19	N3	A. 209; CM. 227
1706	Libberton, Drowsy Brae, Shieldhill	N.M.A. E.G.92	S3(E)	*P.S.A.S.* lxxxv, 183

Midlothian

	Borthwick, Cakemuir Hill	N.M.A.		*P.S.A.S.* ii, 482;
1707		(1) E.G.12	N3	A. 206; CM. 231
1708		(2) E.G.13	N4	A. 207; CM. 232
1709 F	Craigentinny	N.M.A. E.G.71	N2	*P.S.A.S.* lxxii, 6
1710	Juniper Green	N.M.A. E.G.3	N3(L)	*Arch.* iv, 50; A. 189; *C.B.* ii, 15; *P.S.A.S.* xxxix, 431; CM. 230

Morayshire

1711 F	Culbin Sands	Inverness	Indet.	*P.S.A.S.* xlv, 160, 167;
1712 F		N.M.A. Unreg.	Indet.	*Ibid.*
1713	Elgin, nr.	N.M.A. E.G.26	N2	A. 271; CM. 234
1714 F	Forres	Hunterian	N?	Unpub. (D.1951.1002)
1715	Gordonstown, Drainie	Elgin 1893.18	N/NR	A. 284; *P.S.A.S.* xxii, 343; CM. 236
1716 F	Hopeman, Duffus	Elgin X.60	N4?	Unpub.
1717	Knockando, Acres	Elgin-Lost 1870.1	N2	A. 268; *P.S.A.S.* xxii, 342; CM. 233
1718	Knockando, Lyne	N.M.A. E.G.96	N2(L)	*P.S.A.S.* lxxxviii, 232
1719	Urquhart, Law Farm	Elgin 1818.1	N2	*P.S.A.S.* xxii, 34; *P.S.A.S.* xxvi, 67
	Urquhart, Sleepie's Hill	Elgin		*P.S.A.S.* xxii, 343;
1720		(1) 1888.7	S4	A. 275; CM. 235;
1721		(2) 1853.1	Bowl	A. 285; CM. 237

Nairnshire

	Cawdor	Cambridge		*P.S.A.S.* lxix, 397;
1722		(1) 23.1316	N2(L)	CM. 243;
1723		(2) 23.1317	N/NR	CM. 244
	Cawdor?	Cawdor Castle loaned N.M.A.		G. Bain (1893), 12–13, 'History of Nairnshire';
1724 F		(1) L.1963	N/NR	*Ibid.* (?)
1725 F		(2) *Ibid.*	N3	*Ibid.* (?)
1726 F		(3) *Ibid.*	N2	*Ibid.* (?)

Corpus no.	Site	Museum	Beaker group	References
	Cawdor, Auchindoune	Inverness		*I.S.S.F.C.* I, 187;
1727		(1)	N2	CM. 240; *P.S.A.S.* LXVII;
1728		(2)	N2	CM. 241; 232
1729		(3)	N3	CM. 242; *Ibid.*
1730	Cawdor Castle, Inchnacaorach	B.M.	N3	A. 273; *P.S.A.L.* I
		61 6–27 4		(2nd series), 396; CM. 239
1731	Cuthbertown, Easter Delnies	Inverness	N3	Unpub.
1732	Nairn?	B.M.	N3	A. 266, CM. 238
		1911 7–19 3		

Orkney

1733	Birsay, Newhouse Mittens	N.M.A.	S4/Hybrid	*P.S.A.S.* LXXXIII, 240,
		E.G.89		P. XXXVII, no. 2
1734 F	Rousay, Rinyo	N.M.A.	N3	*P.S.A.S.* LXXIII, 26,
		HDA.99		Fig. 7; *P.S.A.S.* LXXXI, 16

Peeblesshire

1735	Drummelzier	N.M.A.	AOC	*P.S.A.S.* LXV, 357;
1736 F		E.Q.394	Indet.	CM. 246, 247
1737	Oliver, Tweedsmuir	N.M.A.	N3(L)	*P.S.A.S.* LVIII, 13
		E.G.55		CM. 245

Perthshire

1737.1	Aberfeldy, Lundin Farm	N.M.A. 1967	AOC	*P.S.A.S.* XCVIII, 126, Pl. XIX
1738	Auchterarder, Bailielands	N.M.A.	AOC	A. 200; *P.S.A.S.* XXXII,
		E.G. 40		314; CM. 249
	Bridge of Allan, Fairies Knowe,			*P.S.A.S.* VII, 519;
1739 F	Pendreich	(1) Lost	N/NR	*T.S.A.S.* (1926–7), 94;
1740 F		(2) Stirling	Indet.	A. 203, CM. 250 for (1)
1741	Fingask	N.M.A.	E.	*P.S.A.S.* LXXXVI, 208
		L.1952.3		
1742 F	Glencochil, Whitecairn	Perth	S2(W)?	*P.S.A.S.* XCII, 81, Fig. 7
1743	Kincardine Castle	N.M.A.	N2	*P.S.A.S.* XII, 682;
		E.G.6		A. 215; CM. 251
1744	Tippermallo, Methven	Stirling	N3	A. 192; *P.S.A.S.* XXXIII,
				145; CM. 248

Ross and Cromarty

1745	Achnasheen	N.M.A.	N3	Unpub.
		L.1962		
1745.1	Bruachaig	N.M.A.	N4	*P.S.A.S.* XCVII, 245, no. 2
	Dalmore, Alness Railway Cutting	Inverness		*P.S.A.S.* XIII, 258;
1746		(1)	N/NR	Anderson 1, 48
1747		(2)	N4	
1748	Eddertoun	Unknown	N3	Anderson, I, 90; *P.S.A.S.*
				VII, 268; A. 289; CM. 257
1749	Fyrish, Evanton	N.M.A.	N4	*P.S.A.S.* VI, 233; A. 269;
		E.Q.131		Anderson, I, 16; CM. 256
	Kilcoy V, West Cairn	N.M.A.		*Disc. and Exc.Scot.*
		L.1962		(1956), 23–4
1750 F		(1) *Ibid.*	AOC	Beakers (1)–(6)
1751 F		(2) *Ibid.*	AOC	associated in
1752 F		(3) *Ibid.*	AOC	secondary deposit
1753 F		(4) *Ibid.*	E.	(7) in final
1754 F		(5) Int. Dec.	AOC	tertiary deposit
1755 F		(6) Giant	FN	
1756 F		(7)	N2	
	Kilcoy, Cairn Glas.	N.M.A.		*P.S.A.S.* XC, 102;
1757 F		(1) E.O.959–60	E.	*P.S.A.S.* LIX, 71
1758 F		(2) E.O.961	FN	(3). Probably from

Corpus no.	Site	Museum	Beaker group	References
1759 F	*Ibid.*	(3) Unreg. (1906)	Indet.	Abercromby dig 1906; *P.S.A.S.* XC, 102
1760	Lochs, Lewis	Unknown	Indet.	*P.S.A.S.* LXII, 25; CM. 255
1761	Rosemarkie, Blackstand	N.M.A. E.G.90	N/NR	*P.S.A.S.* LXXXIII, 235
1762	Ross? Brahan Castle?	N.M.A. E.G.22	S4	A. 290; CM. 258
1763	Tarradale	Victoria and Albert 2009 1901	N3	*P.S.A.S.* XXVII, 358; CM. 259
1764	Urquhart, Findon Farm	N.M.A. E.G.69	N/NR	*P.S.A.S.* LXXI, 95, 248
1765 F	*Ibid.*	N.M.A. E.G.70	Indet.	*Ibid.*

Roxburghshire

1766 F	Bedrule	N.M.A. E.G.88	Indet.	Unpub.
1767	Eckford	N.M.A. E.G.38	N3	*P.S.A.S.* XXV, 29; *B.N.C.* XIV, 123; *J.R.A.I.* (1902), 379; A. 188; CM. 260
1768	Eckford, Wester Wooden	N.M.A. E.G.30	N3	*B.N.C.* XI, 186; CM. 262
1769	Edenmouth	N.M.A. L.1933	N/NR	*P.S.A.S.* LXVIII, 187; CM. 266
1770	Edgerston, Knock Hills	N.M.A. (1) E.G.85	S2(W)	*P.S.A.S.* LXXXI, 191;
1771 F		(2) E.Q.393	N2?	*P.S.A.S.* LXIII, 372; *P.S.A.S.* LXV, 13; CM. 263
1772	Jedburgh, Lanton Tower	N.M.A. E.Q.604	N2(L)	*Illus. L.N.* (14 January 1871); CM. 267
1773	Jedburgh, Temple Garden	Kelvingrove	N3	Unpub.
1774	Kelso, nr. Littleton Castle	N.M.A. E.G.23	N3	*P.S.A.S.* LXVIII, 187; CM. 261
1775	Kelso, Friars	N.M.A. L.1933.2166	N/NR	*P.S.A.S.* LXVIII, 187; CM. 265

Selkirkshire

1776	Ettrick	Hunterian A.128	N3	Unpub.

Shetland

1777 F	Fraga, Skatness	N.M.A.	Indet.	*P.S.A.S.* LXVII, 34; *P.S.A.S.* LXXXIV, 194; CM. 269
1778 F	Stanydale, Sandsting	Unknown	AOC?	*P.S.A.S.* LXXXIV, 194
1779 F	Unst.	N.M.A. E.G.33	N/NR?	*J.R.A.I.* (1902), 386; CM. 268

Stirlingshire

1780 F	Blaeberry Muir, Falkirk	Falkirk	AOC	Unpub.
1781	Buckieburn, Shankhead	Falkirk	N/MR	*Disc. and Exc.Scot.* (1960), 37
1782	Cambusbarron	Stirling	N3	A. 193; CM. 270
1783	Dornoch, Cambusmore	Inverness	N/NR	A. 265; CM. 271 mislabelled Alness, Dalmore

Sutherland

Corpus no.	Site	Museum	Beaker group	References
1784	Dunrobin Park	Dunrobin Castle	N/NR	A. 286; *J.R.A.I.* (1902), 380; *Reliquary* (1904), 61, NS. x; CM. 272
1785 F	Durness, Sarsgrum	N.M.A. E.G.97	Indet.	Unpub.
1786.1 F	Embo	N.M.A. E.Q.632	Indet.	*P.S.A.S.* xc, 225
1786.2 F			AOC	
1787	Strathnaver, Woodyknowe, Bettyhill	N.M.A. E.G.66	N/NR	A. p. 43, n. 2

West Lothian

Corpus no.	Site	Museum	Beaker group	References
1788	Bathgate	N.M.A. E.G.47	AOC	*P.S.A.S.* XL, 369, 371; A. 195; CM. 274
1789	Bathgate	N.M.A. E.G.53	AOC	*P.S.A.S.* LV, 12; CM. 275
	Cairnpapple Circle	N.M.A.		*P.S.A.S.* LXXXII, 88,
1790		(1) E.P.172	N/NR	Fig. 17, no. 3;
1791		(2) E.P.173	N2(L)	Fig. 17, no. 1;
1792		(3) E.P.174	N2(L)	Fig. 17, no. 2
1793 F		(4) E.P.175	Indet.	
1794	Tartraven	N.M.A. E.G.32	N3	*P.S.A.S.* XXI, 199; A. 202; CM. 276

Wigtownshire

Corpus no.	Site	Museum	Beaker group	References
1795 F	Burnt Dune, Glenluce Sands	E.U.C.	AOC	Unpub. Prof. R. J. C. Atkinson
1796 F	Clachsiant, Stoneykirk, Glenluce Sands	Lost	AOC	*P.S.A.S.* xv, 263, Fig. 1; *P.S.A.S.* XXI, 191; CM. 285–7
1797 F	*Ibid.*	N.M.A.	AOC	*P.S.A.S.* LXXXVI, 52;
1798 F		Unreg.	FN	*Ibid.*
	Knockdoon, Glenluce Sands	Kelvingrove		Palace of History II,
1799		(1) 55.96A	AOC	830, no. 21;
1800		(2) 55.96B	AOC	*P.S.A.S.* LXVIII, 189;
1801 F		(3) 55.96C	E	CM. 283 for (1 and 2)
1802 F	Pin Dune, Sites A and B Glenluce Sands	E.U.C.	AOC	Unpub. Prof. R. J. C. Atkinson
1803 F	Stoneykirk, Glenluce Sands	Private	S4/FV	*P.S.A.S.* XXXVI, 584; A. 36
1804 F	Torrs Warren, Dunragit,	N.M.A.	AOC	Unpub.;
1805 F	Glenluce Sands	Unreg. 1894	Undec.	*Ibid.*
1806 F		Cambridge	AOC	Unpub.;
1807 F		51.1043	FN	*Ibid.*
1807.1 F		51.1035	E.	*Ibid.*
1808 F	Glenluce Sands	N.M.A.	AOC	*P.S.A.S.* LXIV, 291;
1809 F		B.H.527	FN and E.	CM. 277, 278;
1810 F		*Ibid.*	Undec.	*Ibid.*
1810.1 F		B.H.A.75	Cardium E.	Unpub.
1811 F	Glenluce Sands	N.M.A.	AOC	*Cat. Nat. Mus. Scot.*
1812 F		E.E.49	FN	(1892), 173; CM. 279–82
1813 F	Glenluce Sands	N.M.A.	AOC	*P.S.A.S.* XI, 581;
1814 F		B.H.8614–	FN	*Cat. Nat. Mus. Scot.* (1892),
1815 F		8683	Undec.	90; CM. 288
1816 F	Glenluce Sands	Kelvingrove	AOC	*P.S.A.S.* LXVIII, 189;
1817 F		*Ibid.*	FN and E.	*P.S.A.S.* L, 219;
1818 F		Lost Ex. Mann	AOC	CM. 289–90
1819 F	Glenluce Sands	Dumfries	AOC	Unpub.
1820 F	Glenluce Sands	Hunterian B.1951.1754	AOC	Unpub.
1821 F	Glenluce Sands	Stranraer	AOC	Unpub.

WALES

Anglesey

Corpus no.	Site	Museum	Beaker group	References
1822 F	Bedd Bronwen, Llanbabo, Banks of Alau	B.M. Unreg. but with 81 7–6 3	S3(W)	W. 4, Fig. 4, 4; (C2); *Arc. Camb.* (1868), 238; R.C.A.M. Anglesey, LIV, 2
1823 F	NEWBOROUGH WARREN, Bryn Llwyd	Bangor	AOC	T.A.A.S. (1956),
1824 F		2845	FN	2–5; (1927), 23; (1929), 95;
1825 F		*Ibid.*	E.?	*P.P.S.* XXIII, 72;
1826 F		*Ibid.* Cardium	E.	*Arc. Camb.* (1927), 387
1826.1 F		*Ibid.*	Undec.	
1827 F	Pant-y-Saer, Llanfairmathafarneithaf	Cardiff 34.369.19	N3	W. 2, Fig. 5, 1; (B12); *Arc. Camb.* (1933), 185
1828	Pentraeth, Merddyn-Gwyn	Cardiff 39.579.6	FP	W. 1, Fig. 1, 1; (E4); *Arc. Camb.* (1908), 211, 297; (1940), 248; R.C.A.M. Anglesey, LIII, 10; LIV, 1; T.A.A.S. (1956), 5–8
	Porth Dafarch, Holyhead Island	B.M.		W. 6, Fig. 1, 7; (B10 and
1829 F		(1) 81 7–6 2	S2(W)	D5); *Arch. J.* XXXIII, 136,
1830 F		(2) 81 7–6 3	Indet.	139; *Arc. Camb.* (1868), 222; *Ibid.* (1878), 32–4; R.C.A.M. Anglesey, LIV, 3
1831	Rhosbeirio	Lost	S2(W)	W. 5, Fig. 3, 1; (C3); *Arch. J.* XXIV, 26; *Arc. Camb.* (1868), 271; *T.A.A.S.* (1956), 1–2
1832 F	Ty-Newydd, Llanfaelog	Cardiff 37.482.1–9	AOC?	W. 3; *Arc. Camb.* (1936), 93–9

Brecknock

Corpus no.	Site	Museum	Beaker group	References
1833	Dolygaer Cwm Car.	Lost?	S2(W)	W. 12, Fig. 1, 9, 10; (B9); *Arc. Camb.* (1902), 25–8
1834 F	Llanelieu, Ty-Du	Ridgebourne House, Kington	S2(W)?	Savory (1963), 39–40, Fig. 10, 7; W. 9, Fig. 6, 6 and 7; (A4); T. Jones, *Hist. of Brecknock* (1809), II, 369; *Arc. Camb.* (1871), 327–30
1835 F	Llanigon, Pen-y-Wyrlod	Cardiff 23.587.1 34.788.3	FN	W. 11; *Arc. Camb.* (1921), 296; Crawford; 'Long Barrows of the Cotswolds', 60–2; Grimes, 'Prehistory of Wales', 153, no. 172
1836 F	Penderyn, Cym Cadlan, Twyn Bryn Glas.	Cardiff 61.496.2	SH(?)	*B.B.C.S.* XIX, Pt. 1 (1960), 63, Fig. 4
1837 F	Penderyn, Nant Maden	Cardiff	Indet.	*P.P.S.* (1960), XXVI, 341
1838 F	Penderyn, Pant-y-Waen	Cardiff 34.473.1	N/MR	W. 8, Fig. 6, 5; (A3); *B.B.C.S.* V, 392; VI, 196; *Arch.* LXXXIX (1943), Pl. XXXIXb
1839	Pen Gloch-y-Pibwr, Cwm Du	Cardiff 24.353.A	SH4(B)	W. 10, Fig. 2, 1; (E1); *Arc. Camb.* (1924), 410; *Ibid.* (1925), 11
1840 F	Talgarth, Ty-Isaf	Cardiff 39.210.89	BW	*P.P.S.* V, 135; W. 7; (D1)
1840.1 F	Ystradfellte	Cardiff	FP	*Arc. Camb.* (1898), 248–64, Figs.

Caernarvonshire

Corpus no.	Site	Museum	Beaker group	References
1841	Bwlch-y-Gwrhyd, Below Drum	Bangor 3095	S2(W)	W. 14, Fig. 1, 6; (C4); Lowe, 'Heart of N. Wales', I (1912), 38–9; R.C.A.M. Caerns. I, LXIII, no. 26
	Clynnog, Penarth	Penarth Farm		W. 13; *Arc. Camb.* (1910),

Corpus no.	Site	Museum	Beaker group	References
1842		(1) *Ibid.*	N/NR	399; *Ibid.* Fig. 7, 4; (F8);
1843 F		(2) *Ibid.*	S2(W)?	*Ibid.* Fig. 4, 1; (F8);
				R.C.A.M. Caerns. II, no. 857
1844	Llithfaen, Pistyll	Bangor	N2	W. 15, Fig. 5, 2; (F3);
				Arc. Camb. (1939), 95–7
1845	Moel Hebog, Beddgelert	B.M.	N3	*P.P.S.* XXIII, 68,
		75 2–18 1		Fig. 5, 4; (F4)
1846	Tan-Yr-Allt, nr. Tremadoc	Bangor	S3(W)	W. 16, Fig. 3, 2; (E5);
				Arc. Camb. (1931), 363–4

Cardiganshire

Corpus no.	Site	Museum	Beaker group	References
1847	Banc Troed-Rhiw-Seiri, nr. Elerch	Private	N?	W. 17; (F11)
1847.1 F	Capel Cynon	Cardiff	BW	Unpub.
1847.2 F		58.460/7	Indet.	Unpub.

Carmarthenshire

Corpus no.	Site	Museum	Beaker group	References
1848 F	Cyffig, Little Pale	Cardiff	S2(W)	W. 18, Fig. 4, 6; (B8);
		25.46		*Arc. Camb.* (1925), 1–4
1849	Llannon, Cors-y-Dre	Cardiff	S2(E)	W. 19, Fig. 2, 2–5; (B7);
		30.196.1–4		*Arc. Camb.* (1930), 309–14

Denbighshire

Corpus no.	Site	Museum	Beaker group	References
1849.1	Bodtegir, Llanfihangel Glyn Myfyr	Cardiff	N3(L)	*Arc. Camb.* (1965),
				CXIV, 112–19
1850	Brymbo, Bryn-y-Ffynon	Cardiff	N2	*P.P.S.* XXV, (1959), 281;
				B.B.C.S. (1958–60), 192–3
1851 F	Capel Garmon	Cardiff	Indet.	*Arc. Camb.* (1927), 1;
		26.195.3–4		W. 22 (F1–2)
1852	Mynydd-y-Bryn, Llansilin	Lost	W/MR	W. 21, Fig. 6, 2; (A5);
				Arch. XLIII, 394;
				Arc. Camb. (1868), 268
1853	Plas Heaton, Henllan	Cardiff	FP	W. 20, Fig. 3, 3; (E3);
		50.24.1		*Arc. Camb.* (1851), 274;
				Ibid. (1868), 273; Davies,
				Prehistoric and Roman
				Remains Denbs. (1929), 140
1854	Ysgwennant, Llansilin	Offa	S2(W)	W. Day, 1965–6
1855		Ant. Soc.	S2(W)	
1855.1 F	Ysgwennant, Llansilin	Offa	Indet.	*B.B.C.S.* (1954–6), 229,
1855.2 F		Ant. Soc.	Indet.	(A8), Fig. 2, 7

Glamorgan

Corpus no.	Site	Museum	Beaker group	References
1856 F	Hendre'r Gelli, Rhondda	Cardiff	S2(W)	W. 25, Fig. 4, 5; (C5);
		25.224.24		*Arc. Camb.* (1906), 302–5;
				Ibid. (1926), 180–1
1857	Llancaiachisaf, Gelligaer	Cardiff	BW?	W. 27, Fig. 7, 1; (F7);
		22.149.1–3	Incised	*Ant. J.* III, 20–3
1858	Llanharry, Naaboth's Vineyard	Cardiff	S2(W)	W. 26, Fig. 5, 3; (C1);
		29.430		*Arc. Camb.* (1930), 402–5
1859 F	LLANMADOC, SPRITSAIL TOR, GOWER	Cardiff	S3(W)	*B.B.C.S.* (1932), 196;
		33.269.1–2		*P.P.S.* XXIII, Fig. 4, 2
				(as Prissens Tor)
	Merthyr Mawr Warren,	Cardiff		*Arc. Camb.* (1905), 211;
1860	Riley's Tumulus	(1) 19.65.1	S3(E)	W. 29, Fig. 2, 6; (B2);
1861		(2) 19.65–2	S3(E)	W. 30, Fig. 3, 4; (B3);
1862 F		(3) Swansea	S3(E)?	W. 31, Fig. 4, 3; (B4);
1863 F		(4) Lost	—	*Arc. Camb.* (1919), 336
1864 F	Merthyr Mawr Warren	Cardiff	Indet.	Grimes (1939), Guide
		01.353.1		to Nat. Mus. Cardiff Coll.
1865 F		53.459/1	S(?) }	179, no. 402;
1866 F		50.466.213	Indet. }	W. (A2) (C6) (D2)

Corpus no.	Site	Museum	Beaker group	References
1867	Sutton, Llandow	Cardiff 40.179.1	N/MR	W. 24, Fig. 6, 1, 8–14; *Arch.* LXXXIX, 101–4
1868 F	Tinkinswood, St Nicholas	Cardiff 19.210.20	Bowl	W. 32; (A1); *Arc. Camb.* (1916), 250–4
1869	Ty-Llwyd, Groeswen	Cardiff 50.295	BW	W. 28, Fig. 7, 2; (F6); *T.C.N.S.* LXXX, 39; *B.B.C.S.* XIV, 168–9
1870	Ty-Newydd, St Fagan's	Cardiff 01.112	S2(W)	W. 23, Fig. 1, 8; (B1); *Arc. Camb.* (1902), 28–32

Merionethshire

1871 F	Carneddau Hengwm, Llanaber Earth Circle	Cardiff 20.36.1	FP	W. 33; (E2); *Arc. Camb.* (1920), 107; Grimes, *Prehistory of Wales*, 54–6, Fig. 19
1872 F	*Ibid.* Stone Circle, South	Cardiff 20.36.2	FP	*Ibid.* W. 34; (E2)
1873 F	Dyffryn, Ardudwy	T. G. E.	Indet.	*Ant.* XXXVII, 24
1874 F		Powell	Indet.	
1875	Llanelltyd, Mynydd Foel-Uchaf	Cardiff 34.474.1 53.126.1	S2(W)	W. 35, Fig. 1, 5; (B11); *B.B.C.S.* VI, 195, 287

Montgomeryshire

1876 F	Darowen, Cefn-Coch-Gwyllt	Cardiff 47.164.174	S3(E)?	W. 36; (F10); *Arc. Camb.* (1926), 350–5 (misreconst. in above)
1877	Llanllwchaearn, Aber Bechan Hall	Welshpool Mus.	N3(L)	W. 37, Fig. 5, 5; (F5); *Mont. Coll.* III (1870), 426; R.C.A.M. Mont. no. 617

Pembrokeshire

1878 F	Caldey Is.	Cardiff 63.337.7		*Arc. Camb.* (1961), 40,
1879 F	Potters Cave	Wellcome Med. Mus. London	FP Cardium	Fig. 6; W (D3)
1880	Castlemartin, Linney Burrows	Cardiff 26.204	S4/FV Hybrid	W. 39; *Arc. Camb.* (1926), 186, 401
1881	Ludchurch, Croft Quarries	Cardiff 28.466	N/MR?	W. 38, Fig. 7, 3; (F9); *Arc. Camb.* (1928), 338–43
1882	Talbenny, South Hill	Cardiff 41.300.1	N/MR	W. 40, Fig. 6, 3–4; (A7); *Arch. J.* XCIX (1942), 1–32

IRELAND

Antrim

1883	Bushmills	—	FP	*Ant. J.* XIII, 262, Pl.
1884 F	Whitepark Bay	—	Indet.	*Man.* (1930), XXX, 134, Figs. 1 and 2

Clare

1885 F	Poulawack	Dublin	Indet.	*J.R.Soc.Ant.* I, 65, (1935), 191

Cork

1886 F	Moneen	—	N3	*P.R.I.A.* 54c (1952), 121

Down

Corpus no.	Site	Museum	Beaker group	References
1887 F	Ballynichol	—	Indet.	Unpub.; B.K. Davison (1959)
1888 F	Dundrum?	Dublin, Photo of Ward Coll.	Indet.	Unpub.

Dublin

Corpus no.	Site	Museum	Beaker group	References
1889 F	Ballyedmonduff	—	E.?	*P.R.I.A.* 55*c*
1890 F		—	S 2(W)?	(1952–3), 61
1891 F		— Cord	S 2(W)?	
1892 F	DALKEY ISLAND	—	AOC	Unpub.;
1893 F		—	E.	Davison (1959);
1894 F		—	S 2(W)?	De Paor (1958),
1895 F		—	FP	657, Fig. 3

Kerry

Corpus no.	Site	Museum	Beaker group	References
1896 F	Dingle	Cork Mus.	Indet.	*P.P.S.* 12 (1946), 142

Limerick

Corpus no.	Site	Museum	Beaker group	References
1897 F	BALLINGOOLA BARROWS I AND II	—	E.	*J.R.Soc.Ant.I*, 19 (1949), 139
1898 F		—	Undec.	
1899 F	Ballycullane	—	Indet.	*P.R.I.A.* 48*c* (1942–3), 272
1900 F	Caherguillamore	—	Indet.	*P.R.I.A.* 54*c* (1951–2), 71, note 45
1901 F	Grange	—	E.	*P.R.I.A.* 54*c* (1951–2), 72;
1902 F	Circle K.	—	Undec.	*P.R.I.A.* 30*c* (1913), 300
1903 F	Grange	Restored	S 3(W)	*P.R.I.A.* 54*c* (1951–2), 37
1904 F	Stone Circle	—	E.?	
	KNOCKADOON			*P.R.I.A.* 56*c*
1905 F	Site B	—	Indet.	(1953–4), 299;
1906 F	Site C	—	E.	*Ibid.*
1907 F	*Ibid.*	—	FN	*Ibid.*
1908 F	*Ibid.*	—	Undec.	*Ibid.*
1909 F	Site D	—	Bowl	*Ibid.* 398, Fig. 37;
1910 F	*Ibid.*	—	W/MR? N/MR?	*Ibid.* Fig. 35, 17; 36; 25;
1911 F	*Ibid.*	—	FP	*Ibid.*
1912 F	Site H	—	N/MR?	*Ibid.* Fig. 50, 28;
1913 F	Sites E., F., I.	—	Undec.	*Ibid.*
1914 F	*Ibid.*	—	Indet.	*Ibid.*
1914.1 F	Sites B–I	—	AOC?	*Ibid.*
1915 F	Lough Gur	—	E.	*J.R.Soc.Ant.I*, 85
1916 F	Megalith	—	FN	(1955), 34;
1917 F		—	Indet.	*Ibid.*
1918 F	RATHJORDAN BARROW III	—	E.	*J.C.H.A.S.* 53
1919 F		—	N/MR?	(1948), 22
	ROCKBARTON			*P.R.I.A.* 43*c*
1920 F	Bog. Site I	—	E.?	(1942–3), 255;
1921 F	Site II	—	E.	*Ibid.*
1922 F	*Ibid.*	—	Giant FN	*Ibid.* Fig. 6;
1923 F	Site III	—	Undec.	*Ibid.*

Londonderry

Corpus no.	Site	Museum	Beaker group	References
1924 F	Bann, River Mouth	—	AOC	Davison (1959)
1925 F		—	E.?	List B
1926 F	Gortcorbies	—	E.?	Davison (1959)
1927 F	Barrows I and II	—	N/MR?	List B
1928 F	Kilhoyle	—	Indet.	*P.B.N.P.S.* 1

Corpus no.	Site	Museum	Beaker group	References
1929 F		—	Undec.	(1938), 34;
1930 F		—	FP	*Ibid.*
1931 F	Well Glass	—	N/MR?	*Ulster J. Arch.* I,
1932 F	Spring,	—	N3	Pt. 2 (1938), 169, B1;
1933 F	Largantea	—	S3(W)	*Ibid.* B2

Mayo

1934 F	Ardcloon	—	E.?	*J.R.Soc.Ant.I.* 86 (1956), 204

Meath

1934.1 F	New Grange	—	W/MR Undec. Bowls	Unpub. Prof. O'Kelly (1967)
1934.2 F		—	E.	
1934.3 F		—	AOC	

Sligo

1935 F	Moytura	—	(1) E.	*P.R.I.A.* 38c (1928), 28;
1936 F		—	(2) E.	A. 39

Tyrone

1937 F	Cashelbane	—	FN	*J.R.Soc.Ant.I.* 70
1938 F		—	AOC	(1940), 143;
1939 F		—	E.	*Ibid.*
1940 F		—	Undec.	*Ibid.*
1941 F		—	E.	*Ibid.*
1942 F	Loughash, Giants Grave	—	N3?	*Ulster J. Arch.* 2 (1939), 254
1943 F		—	S2(W)	

Waterford

1944 F	Carriglong	—	Indet. Possibly FV	*J.C.H.A.S.* 46 (1941), 55; *P.P.S.* 12 (1946), 157

APPENDIX 7

DISTRIBUTION LISTS, BY BEAKER GROUP, OF THE BEAKERS IN THE CORPUS, SHOWN ON DISTRIBUTION MAPS 1–10

(1) All-Over-Cord beakers; (2) European Bell beakers; (3) Wessex/Middle Rhine beakers; (4) Northern/Middle Rhine beakers; (5) Northern/North Rhine beakers; (6) British and European list for Barbed-Wire beakers; (7) East Anglian beakers; (8) Primary Northern/Dutch beakers; (9) Developed Northern beakers; (10) Late Northern beakers; (11) Northern beakers with long necks, Developed and Late styles; (12) Final Northern beakers; (13) Primary Southern beakers; (14) Developed Southern beakers, eastern cylinder necked variant; (15) Developed Southern beakers, western funnel necked variant; (16) Late Southern beakers, eastern cylinder necked variant; (17) Late Southern beakers, western funnel necked variant; (18) Final Southern beakers; (19) Handled Southern beakers; (20) Undecorated beakers; (21) FN rusticated ware; (22) FP rusticated ware; (23) Bowls; (24) Distribution maps.

Prefatory notes to the distribution lists

(1) Where the classification of a particular beaker or sherd is uncertain and marked by a question mark, the inclusion of the site in the distribution list depends entirely on the merits of each case. In certain cases the query only reflects the absence of *absolute* certainty of classification whereas in other cases it may reflect an extremely tentative guess at the type. In this manner the limits of the material plotted can be kept narrowly defined but fully exploited;

(2) The position of the question mark in front of the site name, e.g. ?Ardcloon, reflects that the material is definitely from this site but of tentative classification in the particular beaker group list. When the question mark follows the site name, e.g. Nairn?, then the classification is not in doubt only the attribution to this particular site of this particular sherd or beaker;

(3) When a limited area or locus has yielded many sherds and vessels but apparently reflects only a single settlement or cemetery spot then the finds will be listed only once under the site name and the corpus number of the main find, e.g. in the AOC list Ashberry Windypit is included once only under 1228, although the site also includes the AOC beaker nos. 1229, 1230, 1231. To plot each vessel from individual domestic sites, even if it were possible, would clearly be incompatible with the aim of distribution mapping. However, if the site has yielded sherds of only one beaker then the indicator (F) is added, if sherds of many vessels then (FF);

(4) In a very few cases the corpus list is a little more up to date than the distribution lists that had to be finalised earlier for plotting. In such rare cases a vessel in the corpus may be absent from the distribution list, e.g. 486.1 Tallington.

7.1. All-Over-Cord beakers (AOC)

ENGLAND

Buckinghamshire
43   Win Hill, Hitcham

Cambridgeshire
80   Peacocks Farm, Shippea Hill (F)

Cumberland
112   Mecklin Park, Santon Bridge (F)

Derbyshire
154.1   Bee Low

Dorset
209   Maiden Castle (FF)
192   Melcombe Bingham (F)
199   Tarrant Launceston, barrow (1), 11 (F)

Hampshire
304   Boscombe Cemetery (F)
314   Furzy, Latch Farm (F)

Lancashire
415   Walney North End (FF)

Warton Crag, Carnforth
418 Dogs Hole Cave (FF)

Lincolnshire
444 Crosby Warren (FF)
454 Manton Warren
456 Manton Warren (FF)
468 Risby Warren (FF)
481 Skendleby (F)
460 Normanby Park (FF)

Northamptonshire
642 Fengate, Peterborough

Northumberland
651 Kirkhaugh, Alston (F)
699 Ross Links (FF)
697.1 Ponteland (Bowl)

Oxfordshire
730 Cassington (1947, 305)
732 Clifton Hampden (F)
771 Stanton Harcourt,
     Beard Mill (F)
774 Stanton Harcourt (1962.72)

Somerset
780 Brean Down (F)

Surrey
976 Mortlake
980 Mortlake

Westmorland
1023 Sizergh Fell

Wiltshire
1174 Wilsford G. (54) (F)
1191 Winterbourne Stoke 12 (F)
1064 Overton Hill, Sanctuary (F)
1107 Woodhenge (FF)
1068 West Kennet (FF)
1028 Knap Hill (F)
1056 Windmill Hill (F)
1096 Downton (F)
1085 Bulford Camp
1184 Winterbourne Gunner (F)
1089 Codford St Mary (F)

Yorkshire
1259 Kettlethorpe S. Cave
1376 Rudstone Cranswick
1317 Lea Green, Grassington
1235 Barnby Howes (F)
1215 Aldro 116
1220 Aldro 116 (FF)
1315 Goodmanham 113 (F)
1386 Sherburn 14 (F)
1345 Melton Quarry (FF)
1289 Garrowby Wold 39 (FF)
1357 Painsthorpe Wold 118 (F)
1222 Antofts Windypit (FF)
1228 Ashberry Windypit (FF)
1251 Bucklands Windypit (F)
1264 Green Howe, N. Deighton (F)
1278 Beacon Hill, Flamborough (FF)
1379 Rudston Woldgate (F)
1383 Sewell's Cave, Settle (F)
1408 Willerby Wold 235

SCOTLAND

Aberdeenshire
1414 'Aberdeenshire'
1445 Cuning Hill, Inverurie
1499 Sundays Wells, Torphins
1467 Loanhead of Daviot (F)
1426 Atherb Farm, Buchan (FF)
1465 Kintore
1448 East Finnercy, Dunecht (F)

Angus
1513 'Forfarshire'
1510 Castle Huntly

Argyllshire
1527 Ardnamurchan, Sana Bay
1528 Ibid. (FF)
1553 Salen, Mull
1548 Poltalloch (FF)
1535 Coll (FF)
1554 Tiree (FF)
1541 Cragabus Cists, Islay (F)
1543 Killelan Farm (F)

Ayrshire
1555 Loudon Hill (F)
1563 Muirkirk (FF)
1568 Shewalton Sands, Irvine (FF)
1570 Shewalton Moor (FF)

Banffshire
1573 'Banffshire'
1582 Forglen House
1574 Hill of Scatterty (?)

Berwickshire
1597 Gordon Moss (F)

Caithness
1607 Freswick Bay (FF)
1611 Lower Dounreay (FF)

Dumfriesshire
1615 Kirkburn, Lockerbie (FF)

East Lothian
1617 Archerfield Gullane (FF)
1628 Hedderwick Dunbar (FF)
1639 Tusculum N. Berwick (FF)

Fife
1663 Balnacarron
1664 Balnacarron (F)
1656 Brackmont Mill, Leuchars
1658 Brackmont Mill (FF)
1660 Tentsmuir, Garpit (FF)
1662 Tentsmuir, Morton Loch (FF)
1659 Tentsmuir, Leuchars

Inverness-shire
1669   North Uist, Geirsclett (F)

Kirkcudbrightshire
1695   Cairnholy II (FF)

Peeblesshire
1735   Drummelzier

Perthshire
1737.1   Aberfeldy
1738   Auchterarder, Bailielands

Ross and Cromarty
1750   Kilcoy, West Cairn (FF)

Shetland
1778   Stanydale, Sandsting (F)

Stirlingshire
1780   Blaeberry Muir, Falkirk (F)

Sutherland
1786.2   Embo Cairn (F)

West Lothian
1788   Linlithgow, Bathgate
1789   Linlithgow, Bathgate

Wigtownshire
1799   ⌠Glenluce Sands, Knockdoon (1) and (2)
1800   ⌡Glenluce Sands
1797   *Ibid.* N.M.A. (FF)
1820   *Ibid.* Hunterian (FF)
1816   *Ibid.* Kelvingrove (FF)
1819   ⌠Glenluce, High Torrs III (F)
1804   ⌡Torrs Warren, Dunragit (FF)
1813   Knockdoon Luce (FF)

WALES

Anglesey
1823   Newborough Warren (FF)
1832   Ty-Newydd, Llanfaelog (?) (F)

IRELAND

Dublin
1892   Dalkey Island (FF)

Limerick
1914.1   Knockadoon, Lough Gur (FF)

Londonderry
1924   Bann River Mouth (F)

Tyrone
1938   Cashelbane (F)

Meath
1934.3   New Grange (F)

7.2. European Bell beakers (E)

(A)—All-over horizontal comb impressions
(L)—Zoned lattice or fringe decoration
(R)—Zoned reserved triangle or lozenge decoration
(V)—Zoned oblique hatchings as in the Pan-European
beaker but including all variants

ENGLAND

Berkshire
22(L)   Cholsey
31(A)   Long Wittenham (F)
33(V)   Radley
34(A)   Sutton Courtenay

Buckinghamshire
44(A)   Win Hill, Hitcham

Cambridgeshire
85(A)   Burnt Fen, Plantation Fm.
77(A)   *Ibid.* Shippea Hill (F)

Cornwall
99(L)?   Gwithian (F)
99(V)?   *Ibid.* (F)

Derbyshire
146(A)   Rusden Low, Middleton (F)
136(A)   Calling Low, Middleton (F)

Devon
159(A)   Langcombe

Dorset
169(L)   Blackbush Down, Cranbourne
183(L)   Thickthorn Down, Gussage St Michael
184(L)   *Ibid.*
217(R)   Clandon, Winterbourne St Martin (F)

Essex
228(A)   Chitts Hill, Colchester (F)
261(A)   Shoebury II (F)
255(L)   St Osyth

Gloucestershire
289(A)?   Swell VI, Long Barrow

Hampshire
313(V)   Latch Fm., Furzy
318(A)   *Ibid.*
335(L)   Michelmarsh, Broom Hill
330(A)   Iford, Sheepwash
346(A)   Roebury, Southbourne (F)

Huntingdonshire
363.1(V)   Brampton

Isle of Wight
376(A)?   Arreton Down (F)

Kent
385(A)   Barham (F)
393(A)   Highstead, Chislet
394(R)   *Ibid.*
408(L)   Lower Fant, Maidstone

Lincolnshire
458(A)   Manton Warren (F)
491(A)   West Keal (F)
491(L)   *Ibid.* (F)

Norfolk
531(A)   Edingthorpe (F)
567(A)?   Whiteplot Drove, Methwold (F)
542(A)?   Grimston, barrow (A) (F)

Oxfordshire
767(R)   Stanton Harcourt, Beard Mill
768(V)   *Ibid.* (Oxon. 43)
770(L)   *Ibid.* (Oxon. 45)

Somerset
778(V)   Brean Down
796(A)   Chew Park (FF)
798 {(A)   Compton Martin
798 {(L)   Benbridge (FF)
818(L)   Wick Barrow, Stoke Courcy

Staffordshire
829(V)?   Ilam Moor (F)

Suffolk
844(A)   Barton Hall, Mildenhall
854 {(L)   Brantham Hall
856 {(A)   *Ibid.*
857(L)   Brantham Hall
893(L)   Glevering
909.2(A)   Ipswich, Grimwoods Pit (F)

Sussex
1009(L)?   Whitehawk Camp (F)
1009(V)?   *Ibid.* (F)

Warwickshire
1016(V)   Uncertain Loc.

Wiltshire
1027(A)   Alderbury, Whaddon
1045(A)   Nr. Amesbury
1070(V)   Avebury, W. Kennet Av.
1067(R)   *Ibid.*, Long Barrow
1067(A)   *Ibid.* (F)
1067(R)   *Ibid.* (F)
1173(V)   Wilsford (54)
1155(L)   Wilsford (G1)
1182(A)   Wilsford, 'Lake' (F)
1106(A)   Woodhenge Ditch (F)
1106(L)   *Ibid.* (F), Durrington
1057(A)   Windmill Hill (F)
1057(V)   Avebury (F)
1057(L)   *Ibid.* (FF)
1132(R)   Porton Down (F)
1201(L)   Easton Down (FF)
1201(A)   *Ibid.* (FF)

Yorkshire
1307(R)   Garton Slack, Craike Hill
1269(V)   Egton Bridge
1362(A)   Raindale
1387(L)   Skipsea Peat
1343(R)   W. Lodge Gate, Malton (F)
1380(A)   Rudston Woldgate (FF)
1276(L)   Flamborough Head (FF)

SCOTLAND

Aberdeenshire
1492(R)   Savock, Longside
1495(A)   Skillimarino (F)

Argyllshire
1550(V)   Poltalloch (F)
1537(R)   Coll, Torastain (F)
1529(V)   Ardnamurchan (F)

Ayrshire
1569(A)   Shewalton Moss (F)
1569(V)   *Ibid.* (F)
1569(L)   *Ibid.* (FF)
1565(A)   Muirkirk (F)
1565(V)   *Ibid.* (F)
1565(R)   *Ibid.* (F)

Bute
1603(A)   Glecknabae (F)

E. Lothian
1626(L)   Dunbar (?) (F)
1644 {(V)   N. Berwick (F)
1644 {(A)   Tusculum (FF)
1618(A)   Archerfield, Gullane
1629(A)   Hedderwick, Dunbar (FF)

Kirkcudbrightshire
1694(A)   Cairnholy I (F)
1696(A)   *Ibid.* II (F)

Perthshire
1741(R)   Fingask

Ross and Cromarty
1757(A)   Cairn Glas. Kilcoy (F)
1757(L)   *Ibid.* (F)
1753(A)   Kilcoy, W. Cairn (F)

Wigtownshire
1801(R)   Glenluce (F)
1807.1(A)   *Ibid.* (FF)
1809(V)   *Ibid.* (FF)
1817(L)   *Ibid.* (FF)

WALES

Anglesey
1825(A)   Newborough Warren (FF)

IRELAND

Dublin
1893(A)   Dalkey Island (F)
1893(V)   *Ibid.* (F)
1893(L)   *Ibid.* (F)

Limerick
1897(A)   Ballingoola II (FF)
1906(A)   Knockadoon, Lough Gur (FF)
1901(A)?   Grange Circle (F)
1915(A)   Lough Gur Megalith (F)
1915(V)   *Ibid.* (F)
1918(A)   Rathjordan III (FF)
1921(A)   Rockbarton (FF)

Londonderry
1925(A)   River Bann (F)
1926(A)   Gortcorbies (F)

Mayo
1934(A)?   Ardcloon (F)

Sligo
1935(V)   Moytura (F)
1936(L)   Moytura (F)

Tyrone
1939(A)   Cashelbane (F)
1941(V)   *Ibid.* (F)

7.3. Wessex/Middle Rhine beakers (W/MR)

ENGLAND

Bedfordshire
7   Kempston

Berkshire
25   Inkpen Hill and bowl
36   Sutton Courtenay
19   Slade End
32   Radley

Buckinghamshire
39   Bledlow, Cop (F) barrow and bowl
41   Chesham (?)

Dorset
162   Almer, Stag Lodge
201   Tarrant Launceston, Barrow 14 (5)
177   Dorchester, Masonic Hall

Essex
264   Thorpe Hall Pit

Hampshire
334   Martin
323   Fordingbridge
336   Silkstead/Otterbourne
337   (1) and (2); (F) (F)
352   Winchester, St James's Terrace
302   Boscombe Cemetery
339   Nutbane Longbarrow
348   Stockbridge Down
343   (?)   Micheldever, Roundwood barrow (F)

309 (?)   Bournemouth (F)
321   Wick Fm. Christchurch (F)
303   Boscombe Cemetery
337   Otterbourne, Poles Lane (F)

Northamptonshire
633   Brixworth
640   Fengate, (1) Peterborough (Giant)
641   (2) *Ibid.*

Oxfordshire
716   Cassington
735   Dorchester
749   Eynsham
750   And bowl
755   Little Rollright
773   Stanton Harcourt
761   Summertown, Oxford

Rutland
420   Glaston

Staffordshire
832   Normacott

Suffolk
882   Fakenham
883   Fakenham

Surrey
970   Ham, Dysart's Pit

Sussex

991   Devil's Dyke, Beggars Haven
1005 Selsey Bill

Wiltshire

1036 Amesbury (G51)
1081 ⎰Boyton 1
1082 ⎱Boyton 2
1084 Bulford
1108 Larkhill, Durrington
1115 Heytesbury, Imber
1125 Mere (6a)
1162 Normanton (2b), Wilsford
1076 Rotherly, Berwick St John
1135 Roundway (8)
1137 Roundway Down
1150 Upavon F.S.
1207 Upavon (?)
1151 Upton Lovell (2c)
1129 West Overton
1171 Wilsford (52)

1156 Wilsford (G1) No. 2
1157 *Ibid.* no. 3
1158 *Ibid.* no. 4
1159 *Ibid.* no. 5
1204 Winterslow Hut
1200 Winterslow Hut, Easton Down (FF)
1143 Sutton Veny (?)
1075 Rushmore, Berwick St John
1104 Woodhenge (Giant)
1181 Wilsford, 'Lake' (F)
1175 Wilsford (54) (F)
1117 Hilmarton, Goatacre (F)
1142 Savernake Forest (F)
1048 Stonehenge (F)
1109 Larkhill, Durrington (F)

Yorkshire

1247 Broxa Moor 4
1248 Broxa Moor 4
1378 Rudston 67 (F)

WALES

Denbighshire
1852 Mynydd-Y-Bryn, Llansilin

IRELAND

Limerick
1910 Knockadoon, Lough Gur (FF)

Meath
1934.1 New Grange (FF)

7.4. Northern/Middle Rhine beakers (N/MR)

ENGLAND

Cambridgeshire
53 Cambridge Fens (?) (F)

Herefordshire
354 Olchon 1
355 Olchon 2

Kent
389 Canterbury

Northumberland
682 Ilderton
694 Gryndan, Norham
698 Rock, Elsneuk

Oxfordshire
759 Polestead Rd, Oxford
772 Linch Hill, Stanton Harcourt

760 Summertown, Oxford
776 Yarnton
717 Cassington

Suffolk
908 Ipswich

Warwickshire
1014 Meriden

Wiltshire
1051 Avebury, Longstone Cove
1111 Monkton Farleigh
1200 Easton Down (F)
1169 Wilsford (51) (F)

Yorkshire
1321 Hanging Grimston 56 (F)

SCOTLAND

Aberdeenshire
1418 Aberdeenshire

Argyllshire
1551 Largie, Poltalloch

Ayrshire
1558 Dalry

E. Lothian
1632 East Barns

Kincardineshire
1689 Pityot, Fetteresso

Stirlingshire
1781 Buckieburn, Shankhead

APPENDIX 7

WALES

Brecknockshire
1838 Penderyn, Pant-Y-Waen

Glamorganshire
1867 Sutton, Llandow

Pembrokeshire
     (?) Ludchurch
1881 Croft Quarries
1882 Talbenny, South Hill

IRELAND

Limerick
1912 Knockadoon, (?) Lough Gur (FF)
1919 (?) Rathjordan III (F)

Londonderry
1927 (?) Gortcorbies II (F)
1931 (?) Well Glass Spring (F)

7.5. Northern/North Rhine beakers (N/NR)

ENGLAND

Cumberland
108 Broomrigg, Ainstable
114 Newton, Penrith

Derbyshire
147 (?) Rusden Low (F)

Gloucestershire
285 Prestbury

Huntingdonshire
373 Stanground

Lincolnshire
469 Risby Warren (F)
453.1 Kirkby-on-Bain

Northumberland
678 Dilston Park, Hexham 31.33
677 *Ibid.* 31.32
675 *Ibid.* 31.30
705 Borewell, Scremerston
671 Ford
693 Norham Castle
650 Alwinton, Harbottle
669 Horton Castle

647 Akeld, Wooler
647.1 Alnwick
647.2 Chatton

Oxfordshire
741 Eynsham

Westmorland
1020 Clifton, Penrith

Yorkshire
1213 Aldro 54
     Beverley
1238 Market Weighton
1246 Broxa 4
1279 Flixton
1281 Folkton 245
1299 Garton Slack 80
1300 Garton Slack 81
1310 Goodmanham 99
1361 Pickering
1369 Rudstone 62
1377 Rudstone 67
1391 Staxton
1365 Rossington (Giant)

SCOTLAND

Aberdeenshire
1491 Ruthven, Huntly
1496 Slap, Turrif
1507 Whitestone, Skene

Banffshire
1588 Lesmurdie

Berwickshire
1593 Hoprig, Cockburnspath

E. Lothian
1624 Drem
1634 Humbie, Windy Mains (F)

Inverness-shire
1668 Clettraval N. Uist (F)

Kincardineshire
1677 Balbridie, Durris
1685 Dunottar, Nether Criggie

Morayshire
1715 Gordonstown

Nairnshire
1723 Cawdor
1724 Cawdor (F)

Perthshire
1739 Pendreich

Ross and Cromarty
1746 Alness, Dalmore
1761 Blackstand, Rosemarkie
1764 Findon Urquhart

Roxburghshire

1775 Friars, Kelso
1769 Edenmouth

Shetland

1779 (?) Unst (F)

Sutherland

1783 Dornoch, Dunrobin
1784 Dunrobin Park
1787 Strathnaver

W. Lothian

1790 Cairnpapple

WALES

Caernarvonshire

1842 Clynnog, Penarth

7.6. Barbed-Wire beakers (BW)

ENGLAND

Berkshire

28 Lambourne Down (17)

Cambridgeshire

84 Plantation Farm, Shippea Hill (F)

Devon

156 Chagford Common

Essex

232 Fingringhoe
246 Lion Point, Clacton (FF)
249 Little Holland
260 Shoebury I
258 Shoebury I (FF)

Hampshire

353 Winchester

Kent

390 Canterbury, Littlebourne
400 Folkestone District
402 Gravesend District? (F)
403 Gravesend District? (F)
411 Sturry
413 Tovil

Norfolk

519 Cley
574 Overa Heath, Eccles (F)

Oxfordshire

752 City Farm, Eynsham (F)

Somerset

784 Burrington, Blackdown T. 5
817 Stoford Barwick

Suffolk

950 Stutton
889 Nr. Felixstowe 1927, 2674
887 Felixstowe, Golf Course (FF)
902 Ipswich (no. 14)
876 Foxhole Heath, Eriswell
841 Badwell Ash.
851 Palmersheath, Brandon (F)

Surrey

981 Mortlake (B.M. Bowl)
982 Putney (Lon. Mus. Bowl)

Sussex

952 Brighton, Ditchling Rd.
993 Church Hill, Findon

Wiltshire

1063 Sanctuary, Overton Hill

WALES

Glamorgan

1869 Groeswen, Ty-Llwyd
1857 Llancaiach-Isaf (incised beaker but of BW style)

Brecknockshire

1840 Ty Isaf (F)

Cardiganshire

1847.1 Capel Cynon (F)

Dutch Barbed-Wire beakers

(1) Gasteren, Anloo, Drenthe (F); Modderman (1955), 35
(2) De Vledders, Norg, Drenthe; *Nieuwe Drentse Volksalmanack*
(3) *Ibid.* (1959), 200, Fig. 69
(4) Vorstenbosch, Nistelrode, N. Brabant; *Ibid.* 280, Fig.

(5) Margijen Enk, Deventer, Overjissel (F); Modderman, 24, Fig. 3
(6) Eeze, Steenwijkerwold, Overjissel (F); Leiden Mus. (1918), VII, 29
(7) Hillegom-Lisse (F), N. Holland; Oppenheim, Oudheidkundig Mededeelingen, X (I), 8
(8) Ermelosche Heide V, Geld. (F): Modderman, 34

(9) Ermelosche Heide XVI, Geld (F); Modderman, 34
(10) Staverden Geld. (F); *Amersfoort Inst. Cat.*
(11) Elspeter Heide XI, Geld. (F): Modderman, 34
(12) Poolse Driesten, Geld. (F); *Amersfoort Inst. Cat.*
(13) Beek, Houtdorperveld, Geld. (F); *Amersfoort Inst. Cat.*
(14–15) *Ibid.*
(16) Huneschans (Hunnenschans?); *Ibid.*
(17) Barneveld, Geld. (F); *Ibid.*
(18) Garderen, Geld.; Modderman, 33, Fig. 1, 1
(19) Stegerse Veld, Ommen, Overjissel; Modderman, 33, Fig. 1, 2
(20) Wychense Ven, Wychen, Geld.: *Ibid.* Fig. 1, 3
(21) Ermelo II, Geld.; *Ibid.* Fig. 1, 4
(22) Vaasen, Geld.; *Ibid.* 37, Fig. 4, 1
(23) Gammelke, Weerselo, Overjissel; *Ibid.* Fig. 4, 2
(24) Weerselo, Overjissel; *Ibid.* Fig. 4, 3

(25) Hulzen, Hellendoorn, Overjissel; *Ibid.* Fig. 4, 4
(26) Weisel, Geld.; *Ibid.* Fig. 4, 5
(27) Garderen, Geld.; *Ibid.* Fig. 4, 6
(28) Gortel, Geld.; *Ibid.* Fig. 4, 7
(29) Ermelo (?), Geld.; *Ibid.* Fig. 4, 8
(30) Garderen-Voorthuizen, Geld. (F); *Ibid.* 39, Fig. 6
(31) Wageningse Eng., Geld. (F); *Ibid.* Pl. 1, 2
(32) Gasteren, Drenthe; *Ibid.* Pl. 11, 3
(33) Gelpenberg, Aalden, Zweeloo, Drenthe (F); *Ibid.* 35
(34) Nijmegen, Geld. (F); *Ibid.*
(35) Garderen barrow 3, Geld. (F); Bursch (1933), 70, Abb. 67
(36) De Schipborg, Anloo, Drenthe (F); *Drenthe Museum Bulletin* (1960–1), 237, Fig. 25
(37) Sleen, Drenthe (F); *Palaeohistoria* VIII (1960), 74

Belgian Barbed-Wire beakers

(1) Lanaken, Besemerberg, Limburg; Mariën (1951), 139, 144, Fig. 6

French Barbed-Wire beakers

(1) Abri de Perpétairi, Mollans, Drôme (F); *Gallia Préhistoire* IV (1961), 199, Fig. 12; 334, Fig. 33.

Note. The above list of sherds and vessels with 'barbed-wire' decoration can only be taken as an outline survey based on museum tours in the Netherlands and Germany, combined with existing published lists and illustrations. The most important badly mapped areas are E. Germany, Poland and France; reference to Danish and Swedish material will be found in the Barbed-Wire beaker group Chapter 11. The incorporated existing regional lists for this pottery are to be found in: Modderman (1955), 32–43—Netherlands; Müller (1952), 75, nos. 1–26 and Map no. 8—Rhineland, Westphalia; and Struve (1955), 51–2. 134—Northern Germany.

German Barbed-Wire beakers

Hesse

(1) Neustadt, kr. Marburg; Sangmeister (1951), 93, Taf. 13, 10
(2) Altendorf, kr. Wolfhagen (F); Müller-Karpe (1951), *Niederhessische—Urgeschichte*, Taf. 20, no. 9
(3) Fritzlar; *Fundberichte aus Hesse* (1961), 4–8

Lower Saxony

(4) Delmenhorst, kr. Oldenburg (F); Bremen Mus. 1297, Struve (1955), 134
(5) Hopels, kr. Wittmund; Struve (1955), 134
(6) Gegend Osnabruck (F); Hannover Mus. 10689
(7) Stocksdorf, kr. Diepholz; bowl, Struve (1955), 134
(8) Hemmingen, kr. Hannover; Hannover Mus. 8829
(9) Wittmar, kr. Wolfenbüttel (F); Braunschweig Mus.; Struve (1955), 134
(10) Quelkhorn, kr. Verden; Hannover Mus. 2575
(11) Holtorf, kr. Nienburg; Nienburg Mus.
(12) Addenstorf, kr. Uelzen (F); Lüneburg Mus.
(13) Bruchtorf, kr. Uelzen (F); Struve (1955), 134
(14) Achim, kr. Verden; Verden Mus.
(15) Langenbeck, kr. Harburg (F); Helms-Museum Harburg II 61708
(16) Emsen-Langenrehm, kr. Harburg (F); Struve (1955), 134
(17) Hambühren, kr. Celle (F); Struve (1955), 134
(18) Hamburg-Boberg site 12 (F); Schindler (1960), 84
(19) *Ibid.* 15 (F); *Ibid.*
(20) Hamburg-Boberg, Ohlendorf; Struve (1955), 51, Abb. 5

(21) Langenrehm (F); Wegewitz (1953), 178, Abb. 55, *Harburger Heimat*
(22) Ohrensen; Dehnke (1940), Taf. IX, 10, *Die Tiefstichtonware der Jungsteinzeit in Osthannover*
(23) Dösehof, kr. Kehdingen; Hannover Mus.
(24) Obereinzingen, kr. Fallingbostel; Struve (1955), 51
(25) Twistbostel, kr. Bremervörde; bowl, Stampfuss (1929), Taf. IV, 12
(26) Dümmer (F); Kilian (1950), Abb. 72, Taf. XIII, *Haffküstenkultur und Ursprung der Balten.*
(27) Beckdorf, kr. Stade; *Niedersachsisches Jahrbuch* (1933–4), Vols. 10–11, 38.
(28) Neerstedt, kr. Oldenburg; Struve (1955), 51
(29) Hammah, kr. Stade; Wegewitz (1949), 24–5, Abb. 26, *Die Graber der Stein und Bronzezeit im Gebiet der Niederelbe.*
(30) Dummersee, kr. Gross Diepholz (F); Hannover Mus.

Mecklenburg

(31) Gross Upahl, kr. Güstrow; *Bodendenkmalpfleger in Mecklenburg* 85, Abb. 51
(32) Sadenbek, kr. Ostprignitz; Struve (1955), 52

Middle Rhine (*Westphalia and Pfalz*)

(33) Roisdorf, Bucholz (F); Köln Mus. 6070–4
(34) Keppeln, Suckenheimer Hofe (F); Bonn Mus. 39.1338
(35) Kärlich; Koblenz Mus. 5367
(36) Kettig, Riffer; Koblenz Mus. 5426

(37) Mülheim Jagerhaus; Koblenz 2538, *Mannus* 17, 169, Abb. 5, 2

(38) *Ibid.* 2537, *Ibid.* Abb. 5, 1

(39) Mülheim, Löschalker; *Ibid.* 5556–60, *Bonn. Jahrbuch*, 143–4, Taf. 64

(40) Weissenturm, Koblenz; Bonn. 21767, Stampfuss (1929), Taf. 12, 4

(41) Köln-Fuhlingen; Köln Mus. 11363, *Ibid.* Taf. 11,4

(42) Krefeld, Gellep, Efe (F); Krefeld Mus. Gatermann, 82

(43) Moers, Alpen, Bonninghardt; Stampfuss, *Prähist. Zeitschrift.* (1931), 120

(44) Homberg, Hochheide (F); Bonn. Mus. 34.249

(45) Neuwied, Engers; Neuweid Mus. I.1179; Gatermann, 81

(46) Rockenfeld; Bonn Mus. 11714–5; Gatermann, 106

(47) Rees, Bislich (F); Hamborn Mus. 25.22; Gatermann, 79

(48) Damme (F); Hamborn Mus.

(49) Drevenack (F); Hamborn Mus.

(50) Haffen-mehr (F); Müller (1952), 75, no. (18)

(51) Halden (F); Bonn Mus. 41.215–27, 30

(52) Haldern, Wittenhorst, Efe (F); Hamborn Mus. 28.90

(53) Haldern, Hähe TP. 19; Hamborn Mus. 700

(54) Hamminkeln, Hülsenhorsterrott, Efe (F); Bonn Mus. 41.233–57

(55) Hamminkeln, Nähe Höhe 21 (F); Müller (1952), 75, no. (23)

(56) Opladen, Rosendahlsberg, Efe (F); Köln Mus. 10971

(57) Altenrath (F); Köln Mus. 10666, 13498

(58) Spich, Hollstein (F); Köln Mus. 10628

(59) Horcheim; Mainz Mus. Castillo (1928), *Lam.* CLXXXVIII, 2

(60) Nienborg-Heek; *Westfalen* (1934), h. 2, Taf. XIX, 2

(61) Rheinrillen kr. Neuwied; Eich (1933), 30, Abb. 20–1

(62) Worms, Adlerberg; Worms Mus. 17510/501.12

(63) Worms district; Worms Mus. 98.9

(64) Worms, Gueterhallenstrasse; Worms Mus. 95.2

(65) Hülsten, kr. Borken, barrow II (F); *Westfalen* (1934), h. 2, 138

(66) Bucholtwelmen, kr. Dinslaken (F); *Bonn. Jahrbuch* (1941), 141

(67) Gronau, kr. Ahaus (F); *Germania* 24 (1940), 183, Abb. 1

(68) Borkenberge, kr. Ludinghausen (F); *Ibid.* 184, Abb. 2

(69) Petershagen, kr. Minden (F); *Ibid.* 185, Abb. 3

(70) Selm, kr. Ludinghausen (F); *Westfalen* 19 (1934), 136, Abb. 19–23

(71) Waltrop, kr. Recklinghausen (F); *Ibid.* 16 (1931), 212, Abb. 22

(72) Herne kr. Herne (F); *Ibid.* 19 (1934), 128, Abb. 14

(73) Datteln kr. Recklinghausen (F); *Germania* 24 (1940), Taf. 18

Saxon-Anhalt

(74) Gross Garz, kr. Stendal; Struve (1955), 134, note 589

(75) Gross Ellingen, kr. Stendal; *Ibid.*

(76) Wahlitz, kr. Burg; *Ibid.* 52

Schleswig-Holstein

(77) Kummerfeld, kr. Pinneberg (F); Schleswig Mus.

(78) Satrup, Rüden Moor (F); Langenheim (1935), Taf. 9, *g*, *f*, *l* Tonware der Reisensteingräber im Schleswig Holstein

(79) Aasbüttel, kr. Rendsburg (F); Struve (1955), 52, Taf. 12, 9

7.7. East Anglian beakers (E. Ang.)

Cambridgeshire

54 Cambridgeshire (F)

Essex

225 Ardleigh
224 Arlesford
250 Little Holland
251 Furze Hill, Manningtree (F)
262 Shoebury II (F)
241 (FN) Piercys, Halstead
256 (FN) Shoebury I
257 (FN) Shoebury I

Huntingdonshire

368 Houghton

Kent

388 Bromley
395 Dover, Maison Dieu
398 Erith
399 Erith
407 Ightham Common
409 Preston, Ash
406 Ripple
414 Upper Deal
404 (?) Gravesend district (F)

386 (FN) Barham
396 (FP) Dover airfield

London and Middlesex

496 Old England, Brentford
499 (FN) Hammersmith

Norfolk

517 Chedgrave
588 Runcton Holme 37.8
586 Runcton Holme 31.3
584 Rollesby
613 Stowbridge, Wallington
603 Stalham
616 Syderstone
569 (FN) Methwold
589 (FN) Runcton Holme
590 (FN) *Ibid.* 37.9 and 9 *a*
596 Santon Warren East (F)
575 Overa Heath, Eccles (F)
576 Overa Heath, Eccles (F)
551 Hoe
505 Barton Bendish (F)
530 Edingthorpe (F)
533 Frettenham (F)

Oxfordshire

765 Stanton Harcourt
777 Yarnton

Suffolk

847	Bawdsey
848	Bawdsey Cliffs
850	Boyton
872	Creeting St Mary
892	Felixstowe Cliffs
886	*Ibid.* Chepstowe Rd
890	Felixstowe
891	Felixstowe
903	Ipswich District
905	Ipswich Dales Rd
920	Kettleburg/Brandeston
921	Kirton
961	Woolpit
852	(FN) Brandon Fields
853	(FN) Brandon Fields
919	(FN) Kersey
871	(FN) Creeting St Mary
906	(FN) Ipswich Dales Rd
922	(FP) Lakenheath
917	Ixworth, Newports Pit (F)

858	Brantham Hall (F)
873	Creeting St Mary (F)
945	Rushmere (F)
896	Great Bealings (F)
928	Joist Fen, Lakenheath (F)
880	Eriswell (F)
909	Ipswich

Surrey

972	Kew Gardens

Sussex

1007	Shoreham
989	Cissbury
996	(FN) Kingston Buci
1006	(FN) Shoreham, Slonk Hill

Yorkshire

1371	(?) Rudstone 62
1412	(?) Unknown county, bought in Yorks.

7.8. Primary Northern/Dutch beakers (N1/D)

ENGLAND

Lincolnshire

478	Salmonby

Norfolk

521	Cromer, Central Rd

Northumberland

665	Bellingham, Sneep

Yorkshire

1311	Goodmanham 99

SCOTLAND

Aberdeenshire

1487	Bankhead, Pitsligo
1494	Newhills, Skene
1440	Cairnie, Huntly

Angus

1521	Linlathen, Broughty Ferry
1525	Priestown, Edzell
1516	Kings Wells, Monikie
1523	Lunanhead, Pitscandly

Banffshire

1583	Forglen

E. Lothian

1630	Dunbar, Kirkhill Braes

Fife

1649	Collessie
1652	Denbeath

Kincardineshire

1688	Kineff

Lanarkshire

1704	Lanarkmoor

7.9. Developed Northern beakers (N2) including the long-necked variant (N2(L))

ENGLAND

Berkshire

21	(?) Curridge
29	Lambourne Down 17
11	Abingdon

Cambridgeshire

57	Chippenham Park
87	Snailwell
78	Burnt Fen (F)
69	(Ely, Springhead Lane, N2(L))
94	Wilburton Fen (N2(L))

Cumberland

109	Garlands, Carlisle

Derbyshire

135	Blake Low
134	Kenslow (F)
154	Bee Low, Youlgrave (F)
140	Minninglow (N2(L))

Durham

219	Brandon Hill, Brancepeth
223	Sacriston

Essex

227	Colchester (?) (N2(L))
242	Langham (N2(L))
265	Thorpe Hall (N2(L))

Gloucestershire

277	Barnwood

Hampshire

349	Stockbridge Down
331	Kinson (N2(L))

Huntingdonshire

364	Eynesbury (N2(L))
367	Houghton (N2(L))

Lincolnshire

429	Ashby Corner (F)
470	Risby Warren
476	Ryecliff, Roxby (F)

Norfolk

518	Cley Churchyard
560	Kelling Heath
591	Runcton Holme (F)
610	Stoke Ferry (F)
563	Little Massingham (N2(L))

Northumberland

658	Bamburgh 193
667	Blaydon
673	Fowberry
674	Fowberry
683	Jesmond
681	High Buston
686	Hawkhill, Lesbury
688	Lilburn Hill
691	Lilburn West
695	North Sunderland, Blue Bell Inn
659	Rosborough 197
710	West Wharmley
649	Whitehouse, Alnwick
684	Lesbury, Burney Knowes

Oxfordshire

764	Stanton Harcourt

Somerset

803	Culbone, Exmoor
822	Wincanton (N2(L))

Suffolk

899	Elveden, Bernersfield Fm.
933.1	Sahara, Lakenheath
942	Ousden
964	Woolverstone Park (F)
943	(?) Pakenham (F)
870	Coddenham (N2(L))

Surrey

973	Limpsfield (N2(L))

Sussex

988	Burpham (N2(L))

Warwickshire

1012	Bagington

Westmorland

1019	Clifton, Penrith

Wiltshire

1071	Avebury, W. Kennet Av. 25b
1073	Beckhampton, Grange
1140	Shrewton 5k
1187	Winterbourne Monkton (10)

Yorkshire

1212	Aldro 54
1260	Coates Moor, Nanny Howe
1322	Hanging Grimston 55
1334	Huggate and Warterwold (?) 254
1335	*Ibid.* 254
1366	Rudston 61
1367	Rudston 62
1368	Rudston 62
1375	Rudston 66
1381	Scampston Park
1384	Sherburn Wold 7
1402	Towthorpe 211$\frac{1}{2}$
1405	Weaverthorpe, Barrow Nook 297
1285	Ganton 22 (F)
1359	Painsthorpe Wold 118 (F)
1258	South Cave (F)
1396	Monklands, Thornton Le Dale (F)
1221	Amotherby (F)
1252	Burstwick (N2(L))
1282	Fraisthorpe (N2(L))
1265	Driffield (N2(L))
1303	Garton Slack 161 (N2(L))
1348	Middleton-on-the-Wolds (N2(L))

SCOTLAND

Aberdeenshire

1417	Aberdeenshire
1421	Aberdeen, King St
1423	Cruden, Ardiffery
1424	*Ibid.*
1506	Alford, Brux
1438	Broomhill, Tough
1435	Broomend, Inverurie
1436	*Ibid.*
1466	Chapel of Garioch, Leggats Den
1462	Nr. Kenmay (F)

1482	Leslie
1471	Mains of Leslie
1472	*Ibid.*
1473	*Ibid.*
1486	Old Machar, Persley
1480	Ord, Auchindoir
1484	Parkhill, Aberdeen
1489	Pittodrie, Oyne
1493	Skene, Blackhills
1497	Stoneywood
1498	Stoneywood

1501 Upper Boyndlie Tyrie
1475 Mid Clova, Kildrummy
1433 Broomend (N2(L))
1444 Cruden (N2(L))
1458 Johnston, Leslie (N2(L))
1481 (?) Glass (F)

Angus

1519 Kirkbuddo EG.79
1512 Fletcherfield
1518 Gallows Hill, Kirkbuddo (F)
1514 Greenlaw Farnell (F)
1526 Wellgrove, Lochee (N2(L))

Argyllshire

1552 Poltalloch

Ayrshire

1567 Muirkirk (F)

Banffshire

1584 Forglen
1575 Boharm, Achroisk
1578 Easter Gollachy, Buckie

Berwickshire

1594 Duns, Grueldykes (F)
1590 Edington Mill (F)
1592 Cockburnspath

Bute

1605 Great Cumbrae (F)

E. Lothian

1645 N. Berwick, West Links (F)
1623 Broxmouth, Waird (F)
1646 Nunraw Garvald (N2(L))
1635 Thornton Innerwick

Fife

1650 Collessie

1653 Dunshelt Fort
1651 Dairsie (N2(L))

Kincardineshire

1680 Balbridie, Durris
1682 Dunottar, Kernoon Fm.
1687 Canterland Hill (F)
1681 Banchory Ternan (N2(L))

Kirkcudbrightshire

1699 Woodfield

Midlothian

1709 Craigentinny (F)

Morayshire

1717 Acres, Knockando
1713 Nr. Elgin
1719 Urquhart, Law Fm.
1718 Lyne, Knockando (N2(L))

Nairnshire

1727 Auchindoun
1728 Auchindoun
1726 Cawdor Castle
1722 Cawdor (N2(L))

Perthshire

1743 Kincardine Castle

Ross and Cromarty

1756 Kilcoy, West Cairn

Roxburghshire

1772 Lanton Tower, Jedburgh (N2(L))
1771 Edgerston (F)

W. Lothian

1791 Cairnpapple (N2(L))
1792 Cairnpapple (N2(L))

WALES

Caernarvonshire

1844 Llithfaen

Denbighshire

1850 Brynbo

7.10. Late Northern beakers (N3) including the long-necked variant (N3(L))

ENGLAND

Cambridgeshire

93 Whittlesford

Cumberland

111 Cumberland
107 Ainstable nr.
113 Nether Moor, Hunsonby
110 Castle Carrock (N3(L))

Durham

220 Clara Vale, Ryton

Essex

263 Thorpe Hall (F)
272 Ulting (F)

Isle of Man

374 Lonan

Kent

392 Capel
401 Folkstone Links
397 St Margaret's Bay

Norfolk

508 Blakeney 1
509 Blakeney 2
545 Halvergate
577 Rackheath
595 Salthouse
617 Taverham

Northumberland

712 Northumberland
656 Ancroft
652 Amble No. 19
655 Amble 23, 2.1
657 Bamburgh, Rayheugh Fm.
664 Bellingham
661 Bedlington
666 Black Heddon
692 Norham
648 Shipley Alnwick
708 Trewhitt Hall
696 North Sunderland, Blue Bell Inn
676 Dilston Park 31, 31
679 Dilston Park 31, 34

Suffolk

842 Barnham Cross
874 Creeting St Mary
885 Felixstowe, Bath Rd
900 Icklingham, Mitchell's Hill
948 Sicklesmere

Surrey

979 Mortlake

Warwickshire

1013 Lillington (?)
1015 (?) Ryton Grange (F)

Westmorland

1017 Brougham
1021 Crosby Fells
1018 Clifton, Penrith

Wiltshire

1139 Shrewton 5 a

Worcestershire

1209.1 Pershore
1209.2 Pershore

Yorkshire

1291 Garrowby Wold 104
1292 Garrowby Wold 104
1327 Hempholme
1403 Weaverthorpe
1409 York, Bootham
1309 Goodmanham 99
1304 Garton Slack 163
1306 Garton Slack 163
1305 Garton *ibid.* (N3(L))
1370 Rudston 62 (N3(L))

SCOTLAND

Aberdeenshire

1415 Aberdeenshire (?)
1419 Aberdeenshire
1420 Aberdeenshire
1425 Ardoe
1454 Glasterberry
1432 Blairmore House
1434 Broomend, Inverurie
1457 Chapel of Garioch, Inveramsay
1441 Clashfarquhar 1
1442 Clashfarquhar 2
1443 Clinterty
1446 Ythan Wells
1449 Ellon
1450 Ellon
1452 Elrick Newhills
1453 Freefield
1500 Fyvie, Tifty
1439 Fyvie, Bruckleseat
1455 King Edward
1470 Mains of Leslie
1474 Memsie
1477 Newlands Oyne
1490 Oyne, Pittodrie
1485 Parkhill, Aberdeen
1488 Pitsligo, Boghead
1483 Strichen
1505 Turriff, Muiresk
1504 Upper Boyndlie
1508 Whitestone Skene
1463 Kinaldy, Dyce (F)
1464 Kinaldy, Dyce (F)
1451 Ellon, H:llhead (N3(L))

1502 Upper Boyndlie (N3(L))
1459 Keir, Belhelvie (N3(L))

Angus

1515 Kame Hillock
1511 Arbroath, Colliston
1509 Bandoch Inverkeiler
1524 Noranside, Fern
1517 Kirkbuddo

Argyllshire

1531 Callachally, Mull
1547 Poltalloch
1533 Balnabraid Kintyre
1549 Poltalloch (F)
1544 Kilmory Knap (N3(L))
1530 Kilmartin (N3(L))

Banffshire

1586 Lesmurdie EQ.30
1571 Aberchirdir, Whitefield
1576 Buckie
1577 Buckie, St Peters
1579 Deskford, Careston
1587 Lesmurdie (N3(L))

Berwickshire

1596 Gordon, Macks Hill
1591 Chirnside, Harelaw Hill, (N3(L))
1599 Manderston (N3(L))

Caithness

1606 Acharole, W. Watten

Dumfriesshire
1614 Auchencairn, Closeburn

E. Lothian
1625 Drem, W. Fenton
1648 Skateraw
1636 Thurston Mains, Innerwick
1633 Windy Mains, Haddington
1621 Archerfield, Gullane (FF)
1631 Dunbar, Little Pinkerton (N3(L))

Inverness-shire
1665 Corran Ferry
1666 Kirkhill, Kiltarlity
1674 Skye, Kraiknish
1667 Lochend
1676 Skye (F), Rudh an Dunain

Kincardineshire
1683 Dunottar (N3(L))
1684 *Ibid.* (N3(L))
1678 Balbridie, Durris (F)

Kinross-shire
1693 Tillyochie

Lanarkshire
1702 Crawfurd
1705 Lanarkmoor
1703 Whiteinch, Glasgow (N3(L))
1700 Carluke (N3(L))

Midlothian
1707 Cakemuir Hill
1710 Juniper Green (N3(L))

Nairnshire
1729 Auchindoun, Cawdor
1730 Inchnacaorach, *Ibid.*
1731 Easter Delnies, Cuthbertown
1732 Nairn (?)
1725 Cawdor (?) (F)

Orkney
1734 Rinyo, Rousay (F)

Peeblesshire
1737 Oliver, Tweedsmuir (N3(L))

Perthshire
1744 Methven, Tippermallo

Ross and Cromarty
1745 Achnasheen
1748 Eddertoun
1763 Tarradale

Roxburghshire
1767 Eckford
1774 Littleton Castle
1773 Jedburgh
1768 Wester Wooden, Eckford

Selkirkshire
1776 Ettrick

Stirlingshire
1782 Cambusbarron

W. Lothian
1794 Tartraven

WALES

Anglesey
1827 Pant-Y-Saer, Llanfair (F)

Caernarvonshire
1845 Moel Hebog, Beddgelert

Denbighshire
1849.1 Bodtegir, N3(L)

Montgomeryshire
1877 Llanllwchaearn, Aber Bechan (N3(L))

IRELAND

Cork
1886 Moneen (F)

Londonderry
1932 Well Glass, Spring, Largantea (F)

Tyrone
1942 (?) Loughash, Giants Grave (F)

7.11. Northern beakers with long necks, developed (N2(L)) and Late (N3(L)) styles

ENGLAND

Cambridgeshire
69 N2(L) Ely
94 N2(L) Wilburton Fen

Cumberland
110 N3(L) Castle Carrock

Derbyshire
140 N2(L) Minninglow

Essex
227 N2(L) Colchester (?)
242 N2(L) Langham
265 N2(L) Thorpe Hall

Hampshire
331   N2(L) Broadway, Kinson

Huntingdonshire
364   N2(L) Eynesbury
367   N2(L) Houghton

Norfolk
563   N2(L) Little Massingham

Somerset
822   N2(L) Wincanton

Suffolk
870   N2(L) Coddenham

Surrey
973   N2(L) Limpsfield

Sussex
988   N2(L) Burpham

Yorkshire
1252   N2(L) Burstwick
1265   N2(L) Driffield
1282   N2(L) Fraisthorpe
1305   N3(L) Garton Slack 163
1303   N2(L) Garton Slack 161
1348   N2(L) Middleton Wolds
1370   N3(L) Rudston 62

SCOTLAND

Aberdeenshire
1433   N2(L) Broomend, Inverurie
1444   N2(L) Cruden
1451   N3(L) Ellon, Hillhead
1459   N3(L) Keir, Belhelvie
1458   N2(L) Johnston, Leslie
1502   N3(L) Upper Boyndlie

Angus
1526   N2(L) Wellgrove, Lochee

Argyllshire
1530   N3(L) Kilmartin
1544   N3(L) Kilmory Knap

Banffshire
1587   N3(L) Lesmurdie

Berwickshire
1591   N3(L) Harelaw Hill
1599   N3(L) Manderston

E. Lothian
1631   N3(L) Little Pinkerton
1646   N2(L) Nunraw Garvald

Fife
1651   N2(L) Dairsie

Kincardineshire
1681   N2(L) Banchory, Ternan
1683   N3(L) Dunnottar, Criggie
1684   N3(L) Dunnottar, Criggie

Lanarkshire
1703   N3(L) Whiteinch, Glasgow
1700   N3(L) Carluke, Mossplate

Midlothian
1710   N3(L) Juniper Green

Morayshire
1718   N2(L) Lyne, Knockando

Nairnshire
1722   N2(L) Cawdor

Peeblesshire
1737   N3(L) Oliver, Tweedsmuir

Roxburghshire
1772   N2(L) Jedburgh, Lanton Tower

W. Lothian
1791   N2(L) Cairnpapple
1792   N2(L) Cairnpapple

WALES

Montgomeryshire
1877   N3(L) Llenllwchaearn, Aber Bechan

Denbighshire
1849.1   N3(L) Bodtegir

7.12. Final Northern beakers (N4)

Series I—broad, short everted necks

Aberdeenshire
1460   Keir, Belhelvie
1461   Keir, Belhelvie
1478   Newlands, Oyne

Kincardineshire
1692   Upper Mains Of Catterline

Morayshire
1716   (?) Hopeman Duffus (F)

Ross and Cromarty
1747   Alness
1749   Fyrish, Evanton

Series II—slack biconical, sinuous profile

Aberdeenshire
1429   Auchrynie

1456 Insch (?)
1476 Rathen, Fraserburgh
1503 Upper Boyndlie

Banffshire
1580 Cullen
1589 Auchmore, Portsoy
1572 Afforsk, Trouk

Caithness
1609 Heathfield, Glengolly

Inverness-shire
1675 Skye, Rudh an Dunain

Midlothian
1708 Borthwick, Caickmuir Hill

Ross and Cromarty
1745.1 Bruachaig

7.13. Primary Southern beakers (S1)

Bedfordshire
2 Clifton
4 Harrowden (1) (F)
5 Eastcotts (2) (F)
6 *Ibid.* (3) (F)
8 Kempston
10 Turvey Abbey

Cambridgeshire
66 Doddington
92 Soham

Derbyshire
115 Green Low, Alsop Moor
117 Haddon Field, Bakewell
130 Long Low, Grindlow

Essex
266 Thorpe Hall 1
267 Thorpe Hall 2
269 Thorpe Hall 3

Huntingdonshire
365 Eynesbury
370 Ramsey St Mary

Kent
387 Brendly
391 Capel, Folkestone

Leicestershire and Rutland
421 Glaston
425 Melton Mowbray (?)

Lincolnshire
445 Denton
463 Revesby Abbey

Middlesex
(?) London
501 Leadenhall St, Leadenhall

Norfolk
504 Barton Bendish
520 Coltishall (F)
523 East Tuddenham
525 East Winch
559 Hockwold Cum Wilton, Camboritum

Staffordshire
826 Rams Croft field, Stanshope 1
827 *Ibid.* 2
833 Rocester

Suffolk
860 Brantham
953 Lakenheath
925 Lakenheath, Joist Fen (F)
941 Needham Market
967 Worlington

Surrey
975 Mortlake A. 13471

Wiltshire
1126 Netheravon
1127 Netheravon
1113 Figheldean
1190 Winterbourne Stoke 10
1194 Winterbourne Stoke

Yorkshire
1210 Acklam Wold 124 (F)
1216 Aldro 116
1244 Boltby Scar (F)
1328 Cordner Heslerton Wold 5
1275 Ferrybridge
1298 Garton Slack 75
1296 Garton Slack 37
1332 Huggate Wold 216
1389 Staxton
1390 Staxton
1395 Thornton Dale
1350 Newton Mulgrave
1352 Painsthorpe Wold 4

7.14. Developed Southern beakers (S2), eastern cylinder necked variant (S2(E))

ENGLAND

Bedfordshire
9 Shefford

Berkshire
14 Abingdon

Derbyshire
123 Gospel Hillock, Buxton
149 Stoney Middleton

Essex
229 Colchester, Flagstaff Rd
254 Rainham

Hampshire
311 Brown Candover
301 Lower Farringdon
328 Sheepwash Iford

Hertfordshire
358 Hitchin (?)
363 Ware

Leicestershire
426 North Kilworth
428 Noseley

Lincolnshire
484.2 South Willingham

Norfolk
516 Castle Acre
621 Trowse
631 Wortwell

Northamptonshire
644 Fengate Pit 1, 4–5 Vessels (FF)
645 Fengate Z.12
634 Brixworth

Northumberland
707 Seahouses, North Sunderland
711 Woodhorn

Somerset
792 Charmy Down 1

Staffordshire
835 Castern
825 Mouse Low, Deepdale

Suffolk
904 Ipswich (?)

Sussex
1008 Telscombe Tye

Wiltshire
1037 Amesbury (G51)
1146 Swindon Okus
1102 Woodhenge Circle 1

Yorkshire
1142 Boltby, Hesketh Moor 1
1143 Hesketh Moor 2
1320 Hanging Grimston 56
1323 Hanging Grimston 55
1329 Heslerton 6(F)
1374 Rudston 66
1397 Thwing 60
1331 Warterwold

WALES

Carmarthenshire
1849 Llannon, Cors-Y-Dre

7.15. Developed Southern beakers (S2), western funnel-necked variant (S2(W))

ENGLAND

Berkshire
27 Lambourne

Cambridgeshire
64 Chippenham 5 (FF)
68 Ely, Newbarns Lane
83 Plantation Fm., Shippea Hill (F)

Cornwall
101 Praa Sands, Gernoe (F)
105 Trevedra

Derbyshire
153 Bee Low, Youlgrave
143 Hay Top Hill, Monsal

118 Hazelbadge Hills (1)
119 Bradwell (2)
145 Rusden Low, Middleton
120 Sliper Low, Brassington
139 Smerril Moor, Middleton
148 Rusden Low, Youlgrave (F)
125 (?) Crackendale (F)
137 (?) Calling Low (F)

Devon
155 Broad Down, Honiton (F)
158 Fernworthy

Dorset
178 Dorset (F)

179 Dorset (F)
197 Tarrant Hinton 20*b*, Racedown
181 Frampton 2 (F)

Essex
226 Berden (F)

Gloucestershire
300 Woodchester Park

Hampshire
326 Holdenhurst (FF)
333 Lymore
351 Weeke

Hertfordshire
359 (?) Royston (FF)

Isle of Wight
379 (?) Gore Down, Chale (F)
378 (?) Bonchurch (F)

Lincolnshire
436 Billinghay
450 Grantham, Harlaxton Rd
482 Skendleby (FF)
447 Denton (F)
486 (?) Sudbrook (F)
453 Grantham, Wyndham Park (F)
461 (?) Osgodby (F)
433 (?) Bagmoor Mine (FF)
438 Burton on Stather (F)

Northamptonshire
636 Newark, America Fm. (FF)

Norfolk
609 Stoke Ferry, Wissey (FF)
506 Barwick (F)
597 Santon Warren East (F)

Northumberland
660 Beanley Moor
703 Old Rothbury
690 Lilburn Steads, Wooler

Somerset
787 Bos Swallet, Sidcot (FF)
800 Corston
802 Corston
808 Gorsey Bigbury (FF)
820 Wick, Stoke Courcy

Suffolk
937 (?) Mildenhall Fen (F)

929 Rabbit Hill, Lakenheath (FF)
931 *Ibid.* Sahara (FF)
923 *Ibid.* Right Up Drove (F)
894 West Row

Surrey
971 Kew, Thames

Sussex
986 Church Hill, Brighton (I)
999 (?) Sompting (F)

Wiltshire
1046 Amesbury, Fargo Plant
1034 Amesbury, Stonehenge 36
1078 Bishops Cannings 4
1087 Calne Without 2*c*
1101 Durrington 36
1130 Overton, West Lockeridge
1131 Overton West 6*b*
1145 Swindon, Okus
1185 Winterbourne Monkton I
1186 *Ibid.* II
1195 Winterbourne Stoke (54)
1039 Amesbury (54), Stonehenge 39
1047 Stonehenge Ditch (F)
1044 (?) Amesbury 78/81 (F)
1180 Lake 72.9 (F)
1179 Lake 72.7 (F)
1122 Little Bedwyn (F)
1120 Kilmington, Whitesheet 4 (F)
1066 West Kennet, Longbarrow (FF)
1086 (?) Bulford 65 (F)
1059 Windmill Hill Ditch (FF)
1199 Easton Down (F)

Yorkshire
1217 Aldro 116
1218 Aldro 116
1283 Ganton 21
1293 Garrowby Wold 104
1324 Hanging Grimston 55
1351 Painsthorpe Wold 4
1399 Tinshill, Leeds
1400 Towthorpe 21
1312 Goodmanham 111 (F)
1313 Goodmanham 113 (F)
1404 Weaverthorpe 52 (F)
1372 Rudston 62 (F)
1253 Calais Wold 100 (F)
1290 Garrowby Wold 42 (F)
1401 Towthorpe 21 (F)
1354 (?) Painsthorpe 4 (F)
1287 Garrowby Wold 32 (F)
1319 Halton East (F)
1382 (?) Castle Hill, Scarborough (F)

SCOTLAND

E. Lothian
1620 (?) Archerfield, Gullane (F)

Perthshire
1742 (?) Whitecairn, Glencochil (F)

Roxburghshire
1770 Edgerston

WALES

Anglesey
1829   Porth Dafarch, Holyhead (F)
1831   Rhosbeirio

Brecknockshire
1833   Dolygaer, Cwm Car
1834   (?) Llanelieu (F)

Caernarvonshire
1841   Bwlch-Y-Gwrhyd
1843   (?) Clynnog, Penarth (F)

Carmarthenshire
1848   Cyffig, Little Pale (F)

Denbighshire
1854 ⎫
1855 ⎬ Ysgwennant, Llansilin

Glamorganshire
1856   Hendre'r Gelli (F)
1858   Llanharry, Naaboth's Vineyard
1870   Ty-Newydd, St Fagan's

Merionethshire
1875   Mynydd Foel-Uchaf, Llanelltyd

IRELAND

Dublin
1894   (?) Dalkey Island (F)
1890   (?) Ballyedmonduff (F)
1891   (?) *Ibid.* (F)

Tyrone
1943   Loughash, Giants Grave (F)

7.16. Late Southern beakers (S3), eastern cylinder-necked variant (S3(E))

ENGLAND

Cambridgeshire
47   Barnwell

Derbyshire
128   Dowel Sterndale

Dorset
172   Bradford Peverell, Frome (30)

Essex
233   Great Chesterford
234   *Ibid.* (?)

Gloucestershire
278   Bourton-On-The-Water

Isle of Wight
380   Freshwater
382   Nodgham, Carisbrooke

Lincolnshire
437   Broughton
493   Woolsthorpe
472   Risby Warren Pits (FF)
487   (?) Thealby Mine (F)

Norfolk
514   Castle Acre
515   Castle Acre (F)
532   Feltwell (F)
585   Runcton Holme 32.6
587   *Ibid.* 32.563
612   (?) Stowbridge, Luddingtons Pit (F)

Northamptonshire
646   Peterborough 1907

Oxfordshire
738   Dorchester 1962.245
744   Eynsham 1937.886
758   Polestead Rd, Oxford
756   North Stoke 1957.110

Staffordshire
828   Ramscroft, Stanshope
834   Top Low, Swinscoe
839   Three Lowes, Wetton (F)

Suffolk
877   Eriswell
868   Butley (F)

Sussex
998   Park Brow

Wiltshire
1147   Okus, Swindon (F)

Yorkshire
1214   Aldro 54 (F)
1284   Ganton 21
1272   Brough, Mill Hill
1274   (?) Eston Nab, Mt Pleasant (F)
1256.3 ⎫
1256.4 ⎬ Castleshaw (F)
1256.5 ⎭

SCOTLAND

Argyllshire
1532   Callachally, Glenforsa Mull

E. Lothian
1638   Boglehillwood, Longniddry

Inverness-shire
1672   Kilmarie, Skye
1673   Kraiknish, Skye

Lanarkshire
1706   Shieldhill, Libberton

WALES

Glamorganshire
1860   Merthyr Mawr, Riley's Tumulus (1)
1861   *Ibid.* (2)
1862   *Ibid.* (F) (3)

IRELAND

Antrim
1883   Bushmills (FF)

7.17. Late Southern beakers (S 3), western funnel-necked variant (S 3(W))

ENGLAND

Berkshire
20   (?) Caversham (F)

Cambridgeshire
72   Little Downham

Cornwall
104   St Buryan, Tregiffian Fm.

Dorset
202   Tarrant Launceston (16)

Hereford
356   Mathon, Southend Fm. (F)

Leicestershire
424   Knipton

Somerset
786   Bos Swallet, Sidcot (F)
809   Gorsey Bigbury (F)
813   Nettlebridge (F)
821   Stoke Courcy, Wick Barrow

Suffolk
914   Fifty Fm.

Wiltshire
1119   East Kennet
1088   Cherhill, Calne
1164   Wilsford 170, Longbarrow
1188   Winterbourne Monkton 10

Yorkshire
1245   Brantingham
1326   Eddlethorpe, Hedon Howe
1355   Painsthorpe 83

WALES

Anglesey
1822   Bedd Bronwen (F)

Caernarvonshire
1846   Tan-Y-Allt

Glamorgan
1859   Llanmadoc, Spritsail Tor. (F)

IRELAND

Limerick
1903   Grange Circle (F)

Londonderry
1933   Well Glass Spring (F)

7.18. Final Southern beakers (S 4)

ENGLAND

Berkshire
37   Theale

Cambridgeshire
70   Ely
82   Plantation Fm., Shippea Hill

Derbyshire
142   (?) Monsal Dale, Hay Top Hill (F)

Devon
159.1   Sidmouth

Dorset
176   Colliton Park
204   Weymouth

Essex
270   Southminster (F)

Hampshire
306   Glenferness Av. Talbot Woods (1)
308   Ibid. (2)
332   Kinson, Bournemouth

Lincolnshire
488   Thornton, Horncastle
473   Risby Warren (FF)
479   (?) Salmonby (F)
483   (?) South Kelsey (F)
431   Stainsby (FF)

Norfolk
534   Gayton Thorpe
550   Hilgay Fen
561   (?) Kings Lynn, S. Wooton Lane (F)
608   Stoke Ferry (F)
529   Edingthorpe (F)
565   (?) Massingham (F)
558   Hockwold Cum Wilton (F)
581   Reffley, Gaywood (FF)

Northamptonshire
635   Loddington

Northumberland
672   Ford 174 (F)
687   Lilburn Hill Fm.
647.3   Alnwick, Chatton

Nottinghamshire
713   Clumber Park, Worksop (1)
714   Ibid. (2)

Oxfordshire
731   Cassington, 1947.306
722   Ibid. 1933.1622
719   Ibid. 1933.1620
729   Ibid. 1943.10
751   Eynsham, 1941.12
743   Ibid. 1937.1619
745   Ibid. 1938.405
747   Ibid. 1938.406
753   Hardwick

Staffordshire
837   Gratton Hill, Leek (F)
838   Three Lowes, Wetton (F)

Suffolk
849   Bawdsey Cliff
913   Fifty Farm, Isleham (FF)
865   Bury St Edmunds, Gainsborough Rd (F)
962   Woolverstone Park (FF)
936   Martlesham Plant (FF)
910   Ipswich, Chantry Estate (F)
867   Butley (FF)
956   Wattisfield (FF)

Wiltshire
1072   Beckhampton, Avebury
1083   Brigmerston
1138   Salisbury, Ashley Hill
1141   Shrewton (5 k)
1177   Wilsford (62)
1197   Winterbourne Stoke Rd

Yorkshire
1211   Acklam Wold 204
1280   Folkton, Sharp Howe
1316   Goodmanham 116
1349   Newton Mulgrave
1373   Rudstone 63
1392   Staxton
1394   Thirsk, Sutton Bank
1407   Whitwell Hill
1261   Old Sledmere, Cottam (FF)
1358   (?) Painsthorpe 118 (F)

SCOTLAND

1913.2   Scotland EG.10

Angus
1522   Lochlee, Milton Hill
1520   Linlathen, Cairngregg

Argyllshire
1545   Slaterach, Kerrera

E. Lothian
1637   Lennoxlove, Abbey Mains
1647   Skateraw, Innerwick

Fife
1654   Kinghorn, Grangehill
1655   Kirkcaldy
1662.1   Methilhill

Kincardineshire
1691   Stonehaven

Morayshire
1720   Urquhart, Sleepies Hill

Ross and Cromarty
1762   Brahan Castle (?)

Wigtownshire
1803   (?) Stoneykirk Glenluce

7.19. Handled Southern beakers (SH) with experimental finer subdivision

	Simple zones	Filled neck, filled belly	All-over dec.
SH1 Handled Primary Southern beaker	SH1(A)	SH1(B)	SH1(C)
SH2—Handled beaker unspecialised shape	SH2(A)	SH2(B)	SH2(C)
SH3—Handled beaker barrel/cylinder shape	SH3(A)	SH3(B)	SH3(C)
SH4—Handled beaker collared/biconical shape	SH4(A)	SH4(B)	SH4(C)

H(FV)—Vessel intermediate between a true Handled beaker and the derived Handled Food Vessels
H(DO)—Handled Bowls of Dorset type but with beaker decoration

On domestic sites the *minimum* number of handled vessels present is given in the brackets after the site name, thus SH4(C) ?Wattisfield (FF) (5) represents at least five fragmentary beakers, probably SH4(C) type.

ENGLAND

Berkshire
13 SH2(B)   Abingdon

Cambridgeshire
48 SH3(A)   Bottisham
71 SH3(B)   Fordham
75 SH2(B)   March
63 SH2(?)   Chippenham (1)(F)

Cornwall
106 SH4(C)   Try, Gulval

Dorset
165 SH4(C)   Ridgeway, Bincombe
208 SH3(C)   Winterbourne St Martin (34b)
171 H(DO)   Bradford Peverell
213 H(DO)   Winterbourne St Martin

Essex
245 SH4(B)   Lion Point (F)
262.1 SH2(A)   Sible Hedingham
262.2 SH2(B)   Sible Hedingham

Hampshire
315 SH3(C)   Latch Fm., Furzy

Huntingdonshire
372 H(FV)   Somersham

Lincolnshire
446 SH3(C)   Denton
451 SH4(B)   Grantham, Harrowby
475 SH4(B)   Risby Warren
  ? SH4(B)   *Ibid.* (FF) ⎫ (15)
474 SH4(C)   *Ibid.* (FF) ⎭
435 SH?   Barrowby (F)
432 SH4(C)   Stainsby (FF) (3)
484.1 SH3(C)   South Willingham

Norfolk
510 SH3(A)   Bodney
511 SH4(B)   Brancaster
541 SH4(B)   Gresham
571 SH4(B)   North Creake
606 SH3(C)   Stoke Ferry
607 SH4(C)   (FF) (2)
528 SH4(C)   Edingthorpe (F) (1)
582 SH4(C)   Reffley (FF) (4)

Northamptonshire
632 SH3(B)   Brixworth
638 SH3(B)   Newton-In-The-Willows

Oxfordshire
721 SH4(B)   Cassington 10
740 SH2(B)   Eynsham 30.761
742 SH4(B)   Eynsham 37.1618
734 SH3(B)   Dorchester (F)

Somerset
807 SH?   Gorsey Bigbury (F) (1)
785 SH?   Bos Swallet (F) (2)

Suffolk
952 SH2(A)   Tuddenham
932 SH4(C)   Lakenheath, Sahara? (F) (2)
912 SH4(C)   ? Fifty Fm., Isleham (FF) (3)
957 SH4(C)   ?Wattisfield (FF) (5)

Wiltshire
1205 SH?   Wylye 2 (F)
1060 SH4(C)   ?Windmill Hill Ditch (F)

Worcestershire
1208 SH2(B)   Draycott, Kempsey

Yorkshire

1219 SH3(C)	Aldro 116	
1302 H(FV)	Garton Slack 141	
1314 SH4(B)	Goodmanham 113	
1318 SH3(C)	Guisborough	

1337 H(FV)	Huggate and Warterwold 264	
1388 H(FV)	Snip Gill (FP)	
1360 SH4(C)	Pickering	
1406 SH4(B)	Whitby Area	
1241 H(FV)	Littlewood 1 (F)	

SCOTLAND

No true handled beakers, i.e. no Northern handled tradition. Balmuick, Comrie (Perth.) is a FV clearly based on Rillaton metal type. Cairnhill, Monquhitter, (Aberdeen.) is a corded FV.

WALES

Brecknockshire
1836 SH?   Penderyn (F), Cwm Cadlan
1839 SH4(B)   Cwm Du, Pen Gloch-Y Pibwr

IRELAND

No handled beakers yet found.

7.20. Undecorated beakers

Undecorated beakers, excluding the special undecorated Dorset Ware of Wessex II (Undec. Dorset). The remaining undecorated beakers mainly represent the common domestic fabric of the AOC, E, W/MR, N/MR, N/NR, beaker groups.

ENGLAND

Essex
260.2   Shoebury II (1904)
268   Thorpe Hall, Southchurch, E. Ang.

Hampshire
350   Warsash, Newbury Pit (W/MR)

Lancashire
417   Walney, North End

Leicestershire and Rutland
422   Glaston Sand Pit (E)

Northumberland
701   Ross Links

Sussex
990   Cissbury Barrow
995   Hassocks Sand Pit (W/MR)
1003   Rodmell, Heathy Brow (W/MR)?
1011   Whitehawk Camp

Wiltshire
1102   Durrington Walls Barrow (W/MR)?
1160   Wilsford Barrow (G 1) (W/MR)
1161   Wilsford Barrow (G 1) (W/MR)

Yorkshire
1225   Antofts Windypit, Helmsley
1227   *Ibid.*
1346   Melton Quarry, Hull. 'Hut Circles.' (FN)

SCOTLAND

Aberdeenshire
1416   Aberdeenshire
1427   Atherb Fm., Buchan

Argyllshire
1539   Coll, Torastain, Cornaig

Caithness
1612   Lower Dounreay (Indet.)

E. Lothian
1640   North Berwick, Tusculum, I
1643   *Ibid.*

Inverness-shire
1671   North Uist, Unival

Kincardineshire
1686   Dunnottar, Resting Hill (N/MR?)

Wigtownshire
1805   Torrs Warren, Dunragit, Glenluce Sands
1810   Glenluce Sands
1815   *Ibid.*

WALES

Anglesey
1826   Newborough Warren, Bryn Llwyd

IRELAND

Limerick
1898 Ballingoola barrows I and II
1902 Grange Circle K
1908 Knockadoon Site C
1913 *Ibid*. Sites E, F, I
1923 Rockbarton, Bog Site III

Londonderry
1929 Kilhoyle

Tyrone
1940 Cashelbane

7.21. FN rusticated ware

FN rusticated beaker pottery, mainly with non-plastic paired and single fingernail impressions but including similar bone and stick impressed vessels.

ENGLAND

Berkshire
23 Farncombe Down Barrow
35 Sutton Courtney

Buckinghamshire
42 Hitchin, Win Hill
46 Saunderton Lodge Hill Barrow

Cornwall
96 Cataclews Bay, Harlyn (?)

Derbyshire
124 Cow Dale, Gospel Hillock

Dorset
170 Bloxworth Down, Barrow (1)
185 Gussage St Michael (163a)
191 Handley Down, Nr. Wor Barrow
198 Tarrant Launceston (1)
210 Winterbourne St Martin

Durham
221 Hasting Hill, Nr. Offerton (N/MR-FN)

Essex
230 Dovercourt, Mill Bay
235 Gt Clacton, Bull Hill
240 Hallsford Sand Pit
248 Lion Point, Jaywick
252 Great Oakley
253 Pledgdon Sand Pit
256 Shoebury I (1909) (E. Ang.)
257 *Ibid*.
274 Walton-on-the-Naze, Stone Point
276 West Mersea

Hampshire
312 Brown Candover
329 Iford, Cattle Lane Sheepwash
344 Southbourne, Whitepits
345 *Ibid*. Heatherlea
347 *Ibid*. Roebury

Lancashire
416 Walney, North End

Lincolnshire
443 Crosby Warren
448 Flixborough

455 Manton Warren
456 *Ibid*. (AOC)
457 *Ibid*. (AOC)
492 West Keal, Hall Hill

London and Middlesex
497 Bow, Victoria Park

Norfolk
527 Edingthorpe
536 Gt Bircham, Boiler Common
538 *Ibid*. Hurm Covert
548 Heacham
552 Hoe, East Dereham
556 Hockwold-Cum-Wilton
568 Methwold, Whiteplot Drove
573 Overa Heath, Eccles
594 Runcton Holme
605 Stoke Ferry, River Wissey
620 Tottenhill Church

Northumberland
700 Ross Links

Oxfordshire
718 Cassington, Grave I
748 Eynsham
762 Oxford Summertown
766 Stanton Harcourt

Somerset
779 Brean Down
781 *Ibid*.
797 Chew Park
799 Compton Martin, Benbridge
819 Stogursey Wick, Barrow

Staffordshire
830 Ilam Moor

Suffolk
855 Brantham Hall, Woman's Grave
862 Bury St Edmunds District
871 Creeting St Mary (E. Ang.)
875 *Ibid*.
881 Eriswell, Blacksmith Pit
884 Fakenham
888 Felixstowe Golf Course
927 Lakenheath, Joist Fen

951	Sudbury		1080	Boscombe Down East
960	Wherstead Thorington Hall		1097	Downton, Pit 56
866	Butley		1202	Winterslow, Easton Down
			1203	*Ibid.*

Sussex

1010 Whitehawk Camp

Yorkshire

1236 Barnby Howes, Barrow II, E. Cleveland
1277 Flamborough Head, Beacon Hill
1346 Melton Quarry 'Hut Circles' (Undec.)

Wiltshire

1054 Avebury Ditch
1069 *Ibid.* (22)

SCOTLAND

Argyllshire

1538 Coll, Torastain Cornaig

Fife

1661 Leuchars, Tentsmuir (AOC)

Ayr

1560 Merkland Knowe
1562 Muikirk Circle 2 (FV)
1564 Muirkirk Circle 2

Kirkcudbright

1696.2 Cairnholy II

Ross and Cromarty

1755 Kilcoy, W. Cairn (Giant)
1758 Kilcoy, Cairn Glas

Bute

1604 Glecknabae, Bute

Dumfriesshire

1616 Kirkburn, Lockerbie (Undec.)

Wigtownshire

1798 Clachsiant, Stoneykirk
1807 Torrs Warren
1809 Glenluce Sands (E)
1812 *Ibid.*
1814 *Ibid.*
1817 *Ibid.* (E)

E. Lothian

1619 Archerfield, Gullane
1627 Dunbar, Hedderwick
1642 N. Berwick, Tusculum, II

WALES

Anglesey

1824 Newborough Warren

Brecknockshire

1835 Llanigon, Pen-Y-Wyrlod

IRELAND

1907 Knockadoon
1916 Lough Gur, Megalith
1922 Rockbarton, Site II (Giant)

Tyrone

1937 Cashelbane

7.22. FP rusticated ware

FP rusticated beaker pottery, mainly ribbed, plastic finger-pinched surface.

ENGLAND

Bedfordshire

1 Bedford District

Berkshire

15 Blewbury

Cambridgeshire

49 Bottisham, Lode
55 Cherry Hinton
59 Chippenham I
62 Chippenham III
65 Chippenham V

74 Little Downham
76 Milton
81 Shippea Hill
86 Snailwell

Derbyshire

116 Ashford Shacklow
122 Buxton
141 Ryestone Grange
144 Ravenscliffe Cave
151 Swarkeston Barrow

Dorset

188 Angle Ditch
203 Crichel 17
211 Maiden Castle
216 Winterbourne St Martin
218 Forth Matravers

Essex

239 Hallsford Sand Pit
244 Lion Point, Jaywick
271 Southminster Cutting
273 Unprov.

Hampshire

307 Bournemouth, Talbot Woods
310 Bournemouth, Nursery Road (Bowl)
316 Christchurch, Latch Farm
317 *Ibid.*
320 *Ibid.*
322 Danebury West
324 Hengistbury Head
325 Holdenhurst, Long Barrow
327 *Ibid.* (Bowl)

Hertfordshire

360 Tewin Chalkpit

Huntingdonshire

371 Somersham

Kent

405 Gravesend District

Leicestershire and Rutland

423 Harston

Lincolnshire

430 Ashby Puerorum
434 Barrowby
439 Caythorpe
440 Conesby Mine
441 Crosby Warren
452 Grantham
464 Risby Warren
471 *Ibid.*
484 S. Kelsey
490 Bunkers Gorse

London and Middlesex

495 Brentford
498 Hammersmith
500 Hammersmith, Thames

Norfolk

502 Arminghall Henge
507 Bergh Apton
524 East Tuddenham
526 Edingthorpe
544 Grimston Heath
546 Harpley Common
549 Hilborough
553 Hockwold-cum-Wilton
557 *Ibid.*
562 Kings Lynn
564 Massingham
578 Reffley

580 *Ibid.*
599 Santon Warren (W)
600 Santon Firebreak
604 Stoke Ferry
611 Stowbridge
614 Sutton
622 Wallington
625 Grimes Graves
626 Fengate Fm., Weeting

Northamptonshire

637 Newark, America Fm.
643 Peterborough

Northumberland

668 Dalton, Huntlaw

Oxfordshire

724 Cassington
746 Eynsham
757 N. Stoke Barrow
763 Standlake

Somerset

782 Brean Down
788 Bos Swallet
791 Cannington
794 Cheddar
795 Cheddar, Sun Hole
804 Ebbor Gorge
806 Gorsey Bigbury
814 Nettlebridge

Suffolk

843 Barnham Heath
863 Bury St Edmunds
864 *Ibid.*
869 Butley
895 Great Barton
898 Honnington Tumulus
907 Ipswich, Dales Road
911 Isleham
915 Isleham, Haylands House
924 Lakenheath
926 *Ibid.* Joist Fen
930 *Ibid.* Rabbit Hill
933 *Ibid.* Sahara
934 Martlesham Heath
935 Martlesham Plantation
938 Mildenhall
939 Needham Market
954 Undley Barrow, Lakenheath
955 Wattisfield
958 West Stow Barrow
965 Woolverstone Park

Sussex

994 Findon Church

Wiltshire

1058 Avebury, Windmill Hill Ditch
1065 *Ibid.* (22)
1095 Collingbourne (3)
1114 Figheldean (25)
1124 Martindown Camp
1152 Wanborough Barrow (1)

1168 'Lake 22'
1172 'Lake 24'
1198 Winterslow

Yorkshire

1256.1 Castleshaw
1256.2 Castleshaw
1255 Calais Wold
1257 Cave, Sandpit
1262 Old Sled Mere

1268 Driffield Area
1273 Elloughton
1288 Garrowby Wold (32)
1295 *Ibid.* (143)
1333 Huggate Wold (216)
1341 Kilham
1353 Painsthorpe
1364 Riggs Barrow
1410 Yorkshire Wolds
1411 ? Yorkshire

SCOTLAND

1413.1 Scotland ?

WALES

Anglesey

1828 Pentraeth, Merddyn-Gwyn

Denbighshire

1853 Plas Heaton, Henllan

Merionethshire

1871 Carneddau Hengwm, Llanaber
1872 *Ibid.* Stone Circle

Pembrokeshire

1878 Caldey Is. Potters Cave

IRELAND

Antrim

1883 Bushmills (S 3(E))

Dublin

1895 Dalkey Is.

Limerick

1911 Knockadoon

Londonderry

1930 Kilhoyle

7.23. Bowls

Probable or certain beaker bowls from Britain.

ENGLAND

Berkshire

26 Inkpen Hill

Buckinghamshire

40 Bledlow, Cop Barrow, Wain Hill

Dorset

164 Bincombe Down, Ridgeway Hill, Barrow (II)

Essex

243 Linford, Hall's Pit

Hampshire

327 Holdenhurst, Long Barrow (FP)
310 Bournemouth, Nursery Rd (FP)

Isle of Wight

375 Afton, nr. Freshwater

Norfolk

531.1 Edingthorpe

Northumberland

697.1 Ponteland (AOC)

Oxfordshire

750 Eynsham

Suffolk

930.1 Lakenheath

Surrey

983 Walton-on-Thames

Worcestershire

1209.3 Hill and Moor, Pershore

Yorkshire

1233 Ashberry Windypit, Helmsley

SCOTLAND

Fife

1657 Leuchars, Brackmont Mill (AOC)

Morayshire

1721 Urquhart, Sleepie's Hill

WALES

Glamorgan
1868   Tinkinswood (F)

IRELAND

Limerick
1909   Knockadoon

7.24. Distribution maps

The maps that follow are based on the distribution lists above—map captions give relevant list references. For maps showing the Continental background, see Figs. VIII (AOC), IX (W/MR), X (BW), and XI (N I/D).

Map 1. All-Over-Cord beakers (Appendix 7.1)

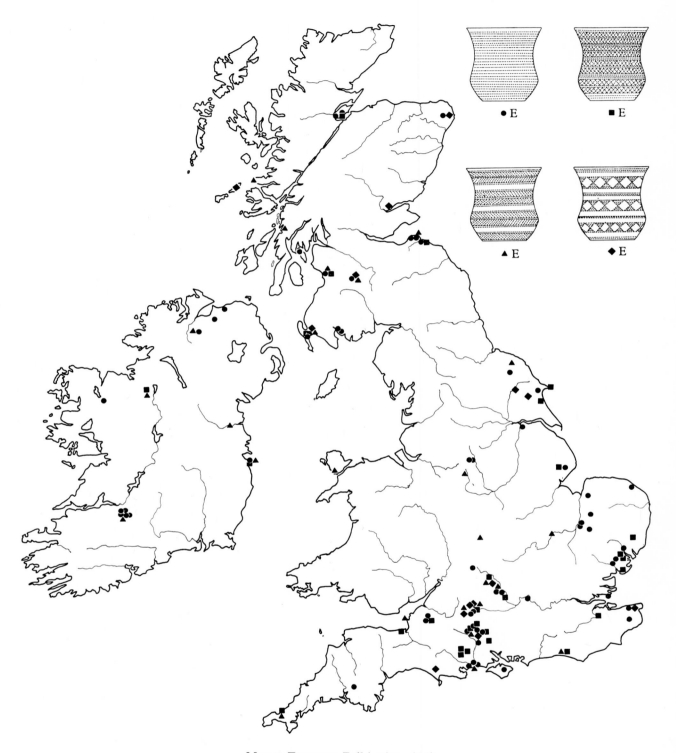

Map 2. European Bell beakers (7.2)

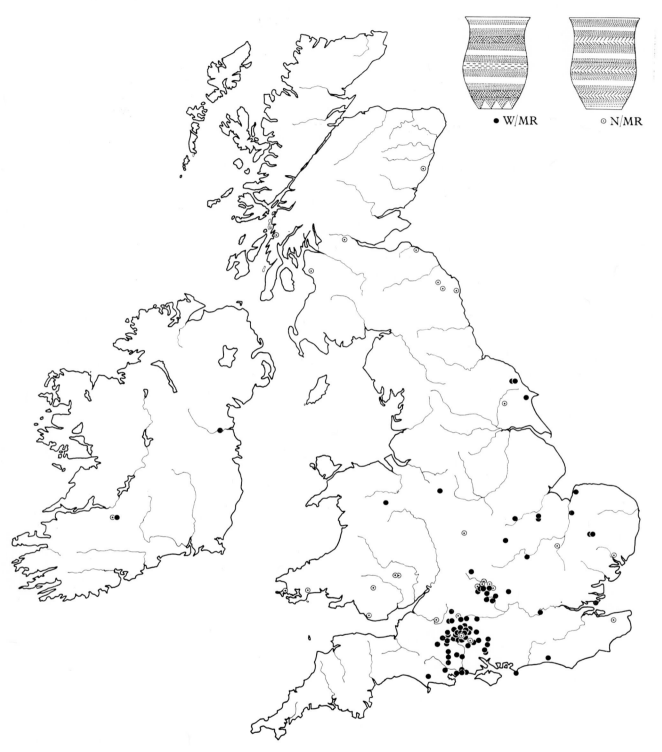

Map 3. Wessex/Middle Rhine beakers (7.3) and Northern/Middle Rhine beakers (7.4)

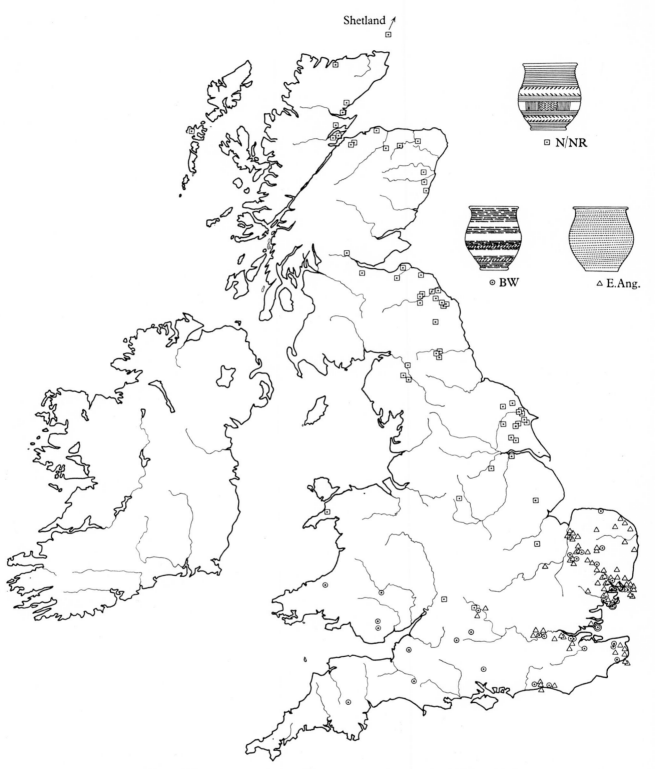

Map 4. Northern/North Rhine beakers (7.5), Barbed-Wire beakers (7.6), and East Anglian beakers (7.7)

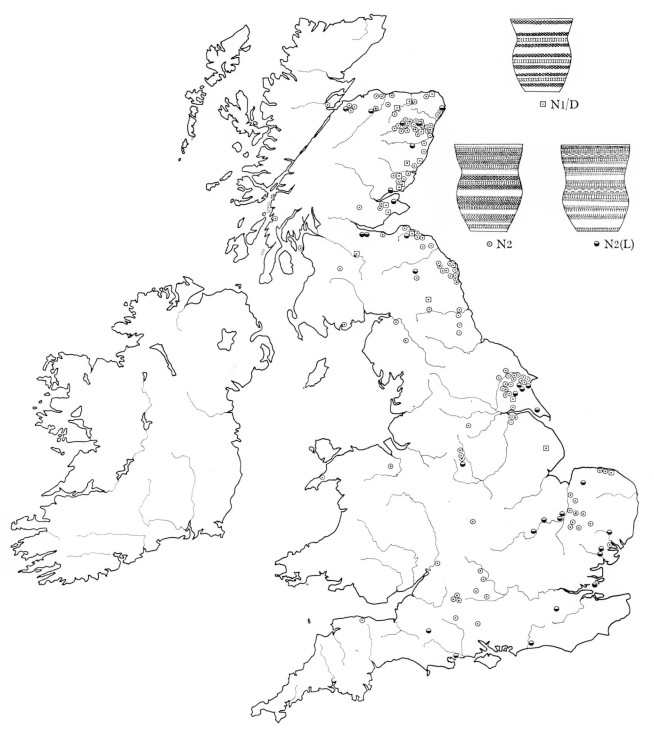

Map 5. Primary Northern/Dutch beakers (7.8), Developed Northern beakers (7.9), and the long-necked variant (7.11)

Orkney

N3

N3(L)

Map 6. Late Northern beakers (7.10) and the long-necked variant (7.11)

Map 7. Primary Southern beakers (7.13)

IO-2

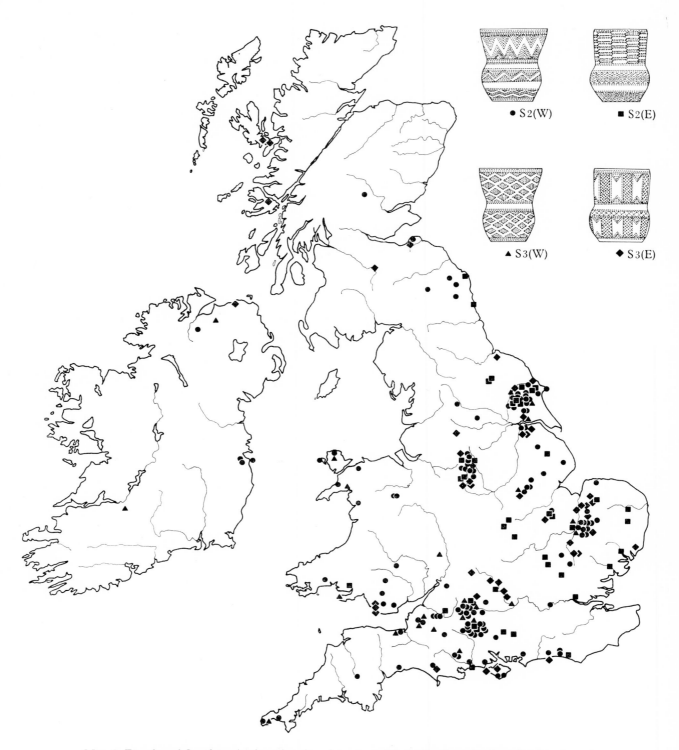

Map 8. Developed Southern beakers (7.14) and 7.15), and Late Southern beakers (7.16 and 7.17)

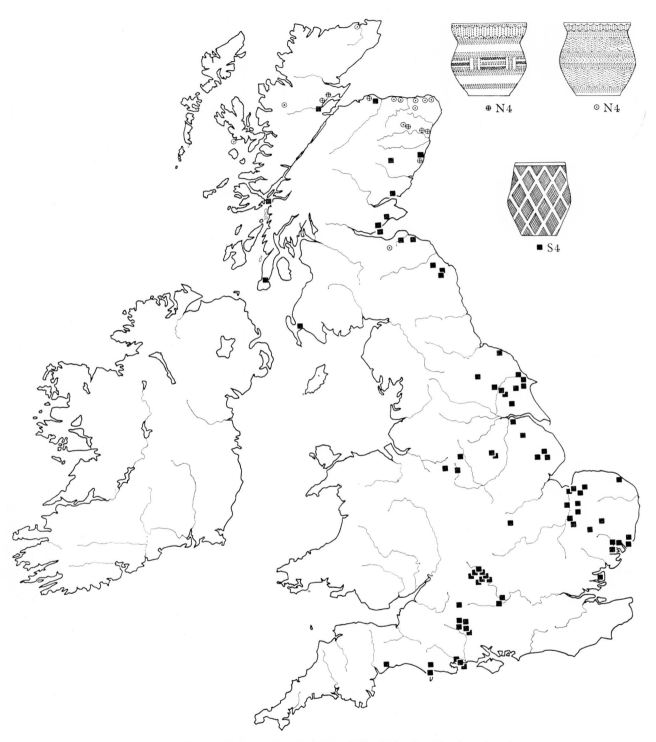

Map 9. Final Southern beakers (7.18), and Final Northern beakers (7.12)

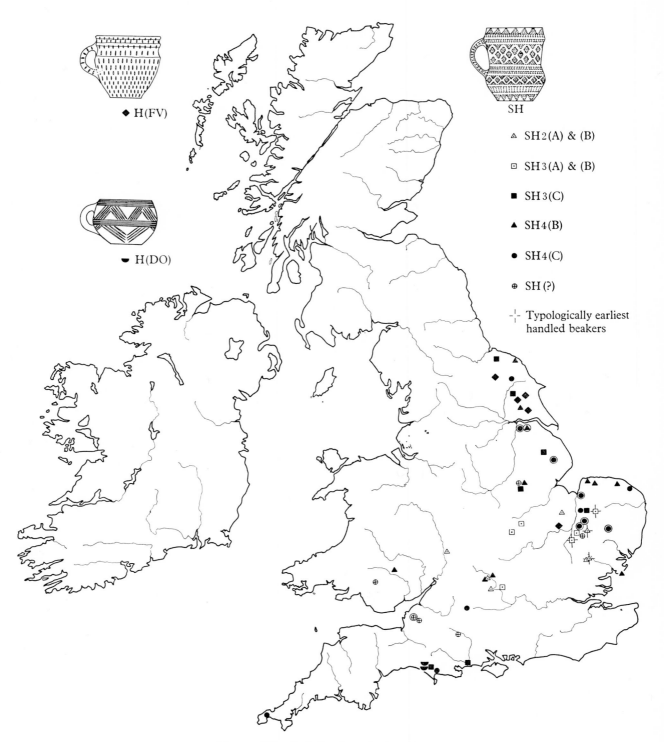

◆ H(FV)

◖ H(DO)

SH

△ SH 2(A) & (B)

⊡ SH 3(A) & (B)

■ SH 3(C)

▲ SH 4(B)

● SH 4(C)

⊕ SH (?)

-¦- Typologically earliest handled beakers

Map 10. Handled Southern beakers (7.19)

1. The list of Welsh beaker sites in this corpus (corpus nos. 1822–82) is based upon a synthesis of the two recent corpuses of Welsh beakers, by Savory (1955) and by Griffiths (1957). These latter works have been checked with the Welsh museum material and corrected where necessary. The Irish beakers have been covered from the published material, especially the lists made by Davison (1959) and by De Paor (1958). I am particularly indebted to Mr B. K. Davison for the loan of his unpublished work on Irish beakers (Davison, 1959).

2. The peculiarities of recent British beaker terminology have caused some confusion in Continental circles, since in several cases an accepted Continental notation has been given a quite different British meaning. In this way the term 'Bell' beaker has always been accepted as referring to the whole of the European beaker epoque—hence the Bell beaker culture. In Britain alone, the term 'Bell' beaker has been restricted to the actually 'bell-shaped' beakers of the earliest beaker phase (Piggott, 1963). This confusion has been avoided in the present work by accepting the Continental designation for the whole 'Bell Beaker Culture' and defining the All-Over-Cord and the European Bell beaker groups for those British beakers formerly lumped under 'Bell beakers'. Another example of the same kind of confusion has been the British use of the term 'cord zoned' beaker for the types called all-over cord beakers on the Continent (Piggott, 1963), especially when the same term 'cord zoned' is already used for a quite different European beaker category in which the beaker has zoned decoration, with the horizontal zone borders in cord and the motif filling in comb (Gersbach, 1957).

3. The Gwithian bone comb is illustrated in Fig. I. A careful search through the scanty beaker bone work has not yielded any more British examples. However, an early reference mentions another possible example (*Arc. Camb.* (1918), 45, n. 1):

> Mr A. C. Wright informs me that there is in the Joslin Collection, Colchester Museum, a toothed instrument made from the shoulder blade of some animal. Its thin edge about three inches long is serrated like a saw, and the serrations are about the size of those of a rather coarse joiner's saw. He suggests that it was a potter's tool for producing dotted lines like those on prehistoric beakers.

This tool can no longer be found in the museum collection.

4. I have been able to collect seven cases in which the white encrustation, filling British beaker dentated designs, has been chemically analysed. Three of these analyses are old published examples and four more I have had tested at Cambridge; a note on these analyses follows:

(1) Dairsie, Fife, no. 1651: calcium phosphate and carbonate, probably made from burnt bones (Abercromby (1912), 51);

(2) Mill Farm, Rathen, Aberdeen., no. 1476: mainly calcium phosphate and some carbonate; possibly from burnt bones (*P.S.A.S.* LXIX, 384);

(3) Johnstone, Leslie, Aberdeen., no. 1458: mainly calcium phosphate also some carbonate and chloride; possibly from burnt bones (*P.S.A.S.* LXIV, 220).

The four remaining analyses were made on my behalf by Dr R. Binns at the Department of Geology, Cambridge.

(4) Stoke Ferry, Norfolk, no. 607: calcium carbonate with fine grained calcite, chlorite and quartz impurities, foraminifera fossils found in chalk; certainly impure crushed chalk;

(5) Stoke Ferry, Norfolk, no. 608: exactly as above (4), with traces of iron stain on the grain surfaces, suggesting some form of cement with organic traces; certainly impure crushed chalk, with the usual foraminifera fossils;

(6) Ely, Cambs., no. 68: calcium carbonate with foraminifera fossils, plentiful fine quartz impurities with iron staining on the grain surfaces together with organic traces perhaps suggesting a binding gum or cement; impure crushed chalk;

(7) Bottisham, Cambs., no. 48: calcium carbonate with foraminifera fossils, small grains of quartz and chlorite; impure crushed chalk.

The minute fossil foraminifera shells in the analyses above, prove that the chalk deposit was not a precipitation from waterlogged surroundings. The particular foraminifera identified indicate chalk deposits varying from Carboniferous, Upper Jurassic to Eocene, and possibly Devonian strata. Other British beakers with unanalysed white encrustation include: nos. 212, 1135, 1480, 1481, 1868.

5. Fragments of chalk rock in beaker settlements are mentioned at Plantation Farm, Cambs., no. 82 (*Ant. J.* XIII, 268); Sahara, Lakenheath, Suffolk, no. 931 (*C.A.S.* XLII, 96); Chippenham barrow 5, Cambs., no. 63 (*C.A.S.* XXXIX, 63).

6. The two Welsh beakers with the atypical, reversed style *d* decoration—zoned neck/filled belly—are the vessels from Porth Dafarch, Anglesey, Wales, no. 1829 and Llannon, Carmarthenshire, Wales, no. 1849 (see *P.P.S.* XXIII, 61–3, Figs. 1, no. 7; 2, no. 2).

7. The available Carbon dates for Continental All-Over-Cord and Maritime Bell beakers are as follows:

All-Over-Cord beakers

2145 ± 110 B.C.	Heidelberg laboratory (*Ant.* XXXIV, 17)
2190 ± 70 B.C.	GrN-851, Anlo 49, Holland (*Radiocarbon* 5 (1963), 180)
1980 ± 65 B.C.	GrN-851, Anlo (uncorrected? *Ant.* XXXIV, 17)
2015 ± 50 B.C.	GrN-1976, Anlo, a *terminus ante quem* date (*Radiocarbon* 5 (1963), 180).

Maritime beakers

1930 ± 25 B.C.	GrN-2158, 2419, 2497, 3097; Vlaardingen, Holland, an extremely precise determination from a large series of tests (*Helinium* 2 (1962), 233).
c. 1900 B.C.	GrN-609, 610; Oostwoud, Holland, *indirect* date from comparable strata at Hawert, which gave a bracket 2130–1790 ± 120 B.C.
c. 1900 B.C.	Heidelberg; Oldesloe-Wolkenwehe, Germany, *indirect* date from containing strata (*Helinium* 2 (1962), 233).

8. It should be noted that the total number of beakers possessing particular decorative styles is different in the unsorted 45 by 45 matrix (Appendix 1.5) from the similar totals for the 39 by 39 matrix (Appendix 5.2–4). The reason for this difference is that the sample for the 45 by 45 motif matrix includes the intact or restorable Welsh beakers, also including the wider definition of the 'fully contracted' zone style *c*; rusticated beakers not being included. Whereas the 39 by 39 matrix includes only the English and Scottish sample and does include the rusticated vessels.

9. A single British exception to the all-over style *o* of the All-Over-Cord beaker decoration is the sherd from the Island of Coll, Argyll., no. 1536 (fig. 51*c*). This sherd has alternate zones blank and the remainder with grouped cord horizontals in style *a*; although unique in Britain this form of decoration is well known as a European All-Over-Cord variant (L'Helgouach (1963), Fig. 3, II, 2*a*).

10. The beaker chequer motif no. 10 (Appendix 1.4) has a striking similarity to the same motif, used in the same manner, on Chassey A pottery from the same distribution area. The following are beaker examples:

South France: several sites, e.g. Embusco (Taffanel (1957), 53–71, Figs.)

Pyrenees and Catalonia: many examples—Castillo (1928), *Lam.* LXV, 3; LXVI, 1; LXVIII, 12; LXXII, 8; LXXV, 2; XC; LXXVII, 2; LXXX; LXXXII; XCI.

Meseta: several sites—Castillo (1928), *Lam.* XIV, 2; XXII, 3; XXIII; LXXXVI.

Portugal: many sites—Castillo (1928), *Lam.* XXXVIII, 1; XXXIX, 2; XL, 1; XLIII, 1–3; XLIV, 2, 9; XLV, 4; XLIX, 2; LXXXVIII; LXXXIX.

Middle Rhineland: more than fourteen sites; see list under n. 36.

11 The truncated and outlined triangle motif no. 10 is typical of the Corded Ware culture group of Northern Europe: see Struve (1955), 136, Abb. 14*d*; Sangmeister (1951), Taf. XVII, 17; Stampfuss (1929), 58, Abb. 7 nos. 1, 2, 4; Childe (1929), Figs. 80*d*, 88, 94 (1 and 2), 135.

12. The three Dutch beakers which display a fringe motif approaching the hexagon form in Fig. IV are: Groevenbeeksche Heide, Gelderland (van der Waals and Glasbergen (1955), pl. XV, 44); Uddelermeer (Leiden Mus. *e*1929/3/38); Noord Veluwe (Leiden Mus. *e*1920/8/2).

13. An excellent example of the appearance of the exotic Saxo-Thuringian assemblage in the Middle Rhineland is the grave from Darmstadt Waterworks, Darmstadt (fig. 198). The crouched inhumation was accompanied by a shanked bone belt ring, a curved section four-hole bracer, and a polypod bowl with metope decoration; thus this one burial includes almost all the exotic elements in a closed association (Jorns (1961), 58, Figs. 6–7).

14. The matrix in Appendix 1.5 studies the cross-correlation of the individual motifs and styles of decoration; this can be compared with the broader study of matrix Appendix 5.4 in which the Motif Groups so defined are correlated with both shape and style variations.

15. The technique and application of matrix analysis remains a controversial topic in many fields besides archaeology, the arguments usually centring around the choice of traits and the interpretation of sorted diagrams. The background to these issues and to this matrix chapter can only be fully understood by reading the literature surrounding the technique; a short bibliography has been appended in Appendix 5.9. Fortunately an expert assessment of these methods and techniques is now available in R. Sokal and P. H. A. Sneath (1963), *Principles of Numerical Taxonomy*, matrix section, pp. 207–9, 284.

16. All the beaker diameter and height measurements were taken from the beaker profile as drawn for the corpus. These measurements were therefore arbitrarily taken for the vessel's 'best' profile.

17. The range of thirty-nine traits chosen for the coding of the beaker matrix sample makes no claim to be exhaustive. At the time when these were prepared (1961–2), a 39 by 39 matrix sort was the limit of the computer capacity; since that date, EDSAC II has been improved and now replaced by a larger capacity machine TITAN.

18. An initial series of experiments with matrix analysis and beaker data were conducted in 1959–60 by the author and Mr W. Easterbrook; the results of these experiments were submitted as part of Mr Easterbrook's Diploma Dissertation at the Cambridge Mathematical Laboratory. Subsequently, at the same laboratory, Dr J. Grant prepared and advised on the program for the matrices based on the corpus data collected in 1960–1. Further help and advice was very kindly given by Dr R. Needham and Dr P. H. A. Sneath. I am very deeply indebted to this team of mathematicians who have made possible this series of experiments in matrix analysis and archaeological data.

19. A short account of the computer program used for sorting the 39 by 39 matrix (Appendix 5.4) has been prepared by Dr J. Grant and included as Appendix 5.8.

20. The list that follows contains an abstract of 'significant zeros' from the matrix Appendix 5.3 and 5.4, being those traits which can occur together but do not, in the sample treated (760 beakers). The traits are numbered according to the key, Appendix 5.2, and listed so that 12/30 represents a zero correlation between traits 12 and 30:

12/30, 13/3, 13/20, 13/32, 16/25, 17/24, 17/25, 17/33, 20/29, 20/30, 21/27, 21/29, 21/30, 22/31, 25/27, 25/29, 25/30, 25/31, 26/29, 26/30, 27/30, 27/31, 27/32, 27/33, 28/30, 29/30, 29/31, 29/39, 30/32, 30/36.

If these zero cross-occurrences of traits are checked by the sherd material, not catered for in the matrix sample, then one finds twenty-five out of the thirty negatives still apply. However, traits 20/30, 26/29, 27/30, 28/30, 30/36, do occur together on the sherd material, but only rarely so. The remaining nucleus of zero correlations between traits then provides a significant set of observations for breaking down the material into groupings.

21. The Motif Groups into which the individual beaker motifs have been sorted must be treated with some reservations. It must be carefully emphasised that the range of motifs used by the beaker folk was cumulative. In this way the simple motifs of the Basic Motif Group 1 continued to be used throughout the history of beaker decoration, similarly the other Motif Groups survive after their conception (Appendix 1.5 and 1.6). Likewise, Motif Group 5, the panels and metopes series, is not a motif assemblage in the same sense as the other Motif Groups but rather a special motif class. Further difficulties arise from particular motifs that lie between groups; the filled triangle motif appearing rarely on early Bell beakers as part of Motif Group 1 and yet forming the basis for the reserved motifs of Motif Group 4.

22. Continental collared and cordoned beakers are illustrated here in figs. 47, 90, 157, 463, 466. Cordons are everywhere more common than collars on beakers and, as one might expect with a utilitarian feature, both forms are much more plentiful in sherds from domestic sites than on complete vessels selected for the graves. A good example of this latter observation and of the general European beaker domestic pattern, is given by the assemblage from Embusco in the South of France (Taffanel (1957), 53–71, Figs. 4, 15, 16).

23. An analysis of the types of vessel present in the All-Over-Cord beaker assemblage can be found for a selection of sites in Table 4. A more extensive list of All-Over-Cord beaker domestic sites, or probable domestic sites, can be abstracted from the distribution list Appendix 7.1, where the sites yielding many sherds are marked (FF) and are set in capitals in the corpus Appendix 6.

24. A short list of British beaker and neolithic pottery with cardium shell decoration can be found in Appendix 2.2.

25. A list of British beakers on which the lower part of the body has been left undecorated can be found in Appendix 2.10.

26. The All-Over-Cord beaker domestic sites with a few Maritime beaker sherds in them, once again suggests that in Britain at least, the All-Over-Cord beaker folk were earlier than, or contemporary with, the people making Maritime beakers. The references to the details of the sites listed can be obtained from the corpus. One new piece of evidence, however, refers to the famous paired-zone Maritime beaker from Latch Farm, Christchurch, Hants., no. 313. This beaker came into the Druitt collection from a workman who excavated the vessel from a pit four feet deep in the gravel, along with pieces of charcoal. Amongst the pieces of charcoal now in the beaker there is a small sherd of All-Over-Cord beaker, no. 314, never previously published or mentioned. It is no longer possible to be certain that the All-Over-Cord beaker sherd came from the original find but the evidence suggests that the Maritime beaker may have been contemporary with, or later than, an All-Over-Cord beaker interment, whose beaker is smashed. This explanation would agree with the evidence already cited and parallel the case from Stanton Harcourt, Oxford. nos. 770–1, where a European Bell beaker grave probably smashed an All-Over-Cord beaker from an earlier burial (Appendix 4).

27. For details about the Irish All-Over-Cord beaker sherds and for Irish beakers in general, I am deeply indebted to Mr B. K. Davison (Davison, 1959).

28. Most of the sherds from the Lough Gur excavations are small and abraded; amongst these sherds there seem to be some which are most probably from All-Over-Cord beakers (Co. Limerick, Ireland, no. 1914.1). However, some of these sherds also have small zones of chequer or chevron cording, elsewhere unknown on All-Over-Cord beakers. Then again, there is the unique survival in Ireland of cord decoration for a Developed Southern beaker from Ballyedmonduff, Co. Dublin, no. 1891, and beaker-influenced cord impressed motifs on Irish Middle Neolithic Sandhill pottery. The evidence is enigmatic but perhaps the Irish Sandhill pottery represents the same Middle Neolithic reaction to the All-Over-Cord and European Bell beaker landings as the Mortlake Ware does in England. This would explain the parallels between Peterborough and Sandhill Wares and suggest an Irish tradition from which the cord decoration might be borrowed by the intrusive Southern British beaker group.

29. Cremation burial is an exception to the rule amongst the British beaker folk, there being only eleven probable cases and another nineteen possible cases (Appendix 3.6). Crouched inhumation was the normal method of burial, most of the probable cremations being associated with the atypical Northern/North Rhine and Barbed-Wire beaker groups and most of the possible cremations almost certainly being mistaken interpretations; these figures must be compared with c. 1,235 cases of probable and certain beaker inhumation graves in Britain. Most of the possible beaker cremations depend on old reports of charcoal, scorching, burnt bone, ash or simply the absence of a skeleton. These reports and some modern interpretations elevating them to 'cremation' burials ignore the point that scorching and charcoal are normal and frequent in beaker inhumation graves, possibly part of the pre-burial ritual; burnt food bones have also been found in ordinary beaker inhumation graves; many old accounts of grey 'ash' reflect decayed timber coffins or cists, not burnt material. Thomas Bateman regularly describes white patinated flint as 'calcined' (Bateman, 1861); therefore the probable cremations here include only those accounts apparently describing cremated human bones (Appendix 3.6).

30. Amongst British beaker groups there is a steady trend from undecorated domestic ware and non-plastic fingernailing or stick jabbing, towards the complete abandonment of undecorated ware and the dominance of increasingly more plastic, ribbed and moulded, finger-pinch rustication. These trends are related to similar changes in European beaker assemblages, especially in the Netherlands; the problem as a whole is further discussed in Chapter 22. For these purposes I propose to define three main classes of beaker domestic ware:

Undec.—undecorated ware, usually small undecorated beakers and small bowls (lamps?) (figs. 33–4, 36, 97–100, 226).

FN—non-plastic rusticated ware, the surface of the vessel is usually impressed with paired fingernail impressions giving a 'crowsfoot' effect; the same class includes cuneiform bone and stick impressions. The overall surface of the vessel is still virtually smooth and only slightly roughened (figs. 49, 50, 113–26).

FP—plastic rusticated ware, in which the surface of the vessel has been raised by finger-pinching into ribs and cordons, usually in alternating horizontal and vertical bands, sometimes smoothed-over to remove the finger marks (figs. 461–9, 790–806).

31. Undecorated beakers seem to have formed part of the early European Bell beaker domestic assemblage and are consequently found from the entire area of the Bell beaker distribution, from Spain to North Germany, from Britain to Hungary. The non-plastic rusticated ware (FN) is certainly found in the same contexts, from the whole of Northwestern Europe including Britain, Germany, the Netherlands, Belgium and Northern France; in this same Northwestern area the later plastic rusticated ware evolves from this common basis (FP). Outside this Northwestern area, in Southern France, Spain, Italy and Eastern Europe, the evidence for rusticated beaker ware is exiguous; it is precisely in these areas that the beaker plain ware is most plentiful, since it continues throughout the local beaker sequences. Nevertheless, for many years rusticated ware has been arbitrarily separated from the parent beaker assemblages and there are indications that simple beaker fingernailed rusticated ware may exist in Southern Europe, particularly amongst the domestic material of all ages lumped together in the Spanish 'Cave Culture'. It is also in these areas adjacent to the Mediterranean that one suspects a rather arbitrary division has been established between Impressed Ware with rustication and comb impressions and beakers with the same decoration.

Possible examples of Spanish and Moroccan rusticated beaker ware may be found in the following references: Castillo (1928), *Lam.* III, 1, 2, 3, 12, 16, 17; XXV; LXVI, 1; *Ampurias*, 19–20 (1957–8), 166; *Bulletin D'Archéologie Marocaine*, tome III (1958–9), 306.

32. The two large sherds of the beaker bowl (?) from Oatlands Park, Walton-on-Thames, Surrey, no. 983 (fig. 111), were found by a workman digging house foundations. After keeping the sherds for a few years as a curiosity, the workman handed them in to Weybridge Museum in 1911; apparently the vessel was found in sherds but was originally more complete.

33. I am indebted to Mr A. M. ApSimon for details about the beaker sherds from the Calais dunes.

34. Good examples of early 'European' Bell beakers, with the broad, low silhouette, are rather rare in the Low Countries, probably for reasons made clear by the many feet of clay overlying the Vlaardingen site (*Helinium* II, 23–7). On the interpretation favoured here (Chapter 2, Table 1), the equal-zoned and paired-zoned beakers of van der Waals' 2.1*a*–2.1*b* belong in the same stylistic assemblage and suggest by their slim proportions that they mainly belong to the latter half of the 'European' Bell beaker floruit (van der Waals and Glasbergen (1955), 18, Fig. 9, Pl. IX, 26). For the same reasons and for others made clear in Chapter 8, the Odoorn beaker whilst continuing the archaic Maritime hatched motif must yet be separated from the 2.1*b* group on the basis of the contracted zone styling, the shape with the angular neck, the sealing-wax red fabric and above all by the associations. Indeed, the closest British parallels to the Odoorn beaker are Southern British beakers with archaic motifs (S1, S2; see figs. 742, 745, 748, 754, 902); the common basis here being the Wessex/Middle Rhine beaker origin of both the Odoorn beaker and the Southern British beakers.

35. The only Breton beaker displaying chequer motif no. 9 is the sherd from the megalith at Mané-er-loh, Locoal-Mendon (L'Helgouach (1963), 75, Fig. 9, no. 6), using the slanting version of the motif (Appendix 1.4, no. 9). The same version of the chequer motif appears on the West Kennet beaker no. 1067 (fig. 76) and on another from Woodhenge ditch, no. 1106; both of the latter beakers show influence from the Wessex/Middle Rhine influx (see Chapter 7, Section 8). These unique Breton and English beakers, together with the Breton parallels to the West Kennet vessel (Castillo (1928), *Lam.* CVII, 1) can be explained in terms of contact between Wessex and Brittany at the time of the arrival of the Wessex/Middle Rhine settlers in both areas.

36. The chequer motif no. 9 (Appendix 1.4) is to be found on the following Rhenish beakers, the ancestors of the Wessex/Middle Rhine group:

Giessen Strasse, Rödgen (Sangmeister (1951), II, 3)
Butzbach (*Ibid.* 8)
Ilvesheim (*Ibid.* IV, 7)
Seckenheim (*Ibid.* V, 7)
Worms-Rheingewann (*Ibid.* 13)
Fühlingen, Köln (Stampfuss (1929), VI, 6)
Heidesheim (*Ibid.* 18)
Nierstein (*Ibid.* VIII, 25)
Urmitz (i) (*Ibid.* XI, 2)
Gabsheim (Castillo (1928), *Lam.* CXC, 4)
Weissenturm, Koblenz (Bonn Mus. 21768)
Urmitz (ii) (Bonn Mus. 41123)
Andernach (Bonn Mus. 391044)
Forschheim (Childe (1929), Fig. 105, centre)

37. There are two or three Dutch beakers which may tentatively be attributed to the same flux that brought Middle Rhenish influence into Wessex and Brittany. These vessels are rather uncomfortable in van der Waals' 2.1*b* classification and together with the exotic Moravian influence to be noted in the Netherlands and in Britain (W/MR fig. 179) clearly contribute a great deal to the rise of the indigenous Dutch Veluwe tradition. A superficial knowledge of the Dutch material points to the beakers from:

Odoorn, Drente (van der Waals and Glasbergen (1955), Pl. VIII, 24)
Ede, Gelderland (Fig. 234; Leiden Mus. cast)
Solseberg, Apeldoorn, Gelderland (Leiden 1952/5)

These beakers may belong to the Wessex/Middle Rhine group and have tentatively been included in the map Fig. IX.

38. I am much indebted to Mrs E. Proudfoot for advance information about the excavation and beakers from Wilsford (G1), Wilts., nos. 1154–61.

39. I have followed R. J. C. Atkinson's bracer typology in order to test the manner in which the new beaker and bracer classification agree. Since Atkinson's bracer typology is unpublished I am indebted to him for the outline quoted below. The total number of holes is given for the bracer.

Type A1: the long sides are generally convex, the ends generally rounded, and the transverse section flat or slightly bi-convex. Two holes only.

Type A2: as type A1, but with plano-convex transverse section.

Type B1: generally rectangular in plan, with flat or slightly bi-convex cross-section. Two holes only.

Type B2: as type B1, but with four holes.

Type B3: as types B1 and B2 but with six or more holes.

Type C1: waisted in plan, with straight ends. Concavo-convex transverse section, convexo-concave longitudinal section in most cases. Four holes.

Type C2: characteristics allied to type C1, but with V-perforations through the ends. Two holes only.

A rough guide to the distribution of these is as follows:

Type A1: from Aberdeen., Skye, Mull, Fife, Lanark., Lincs., Cambs., Co. Antrim.

Type A2: from Moray., Lancs., Cos. Antrim, Derry, Down, Westmeath, Kildare, strays from Northern Ireland generally.

Type B1: from Wigtown., Yorks., Beds., Oxford., Kent, Wilts., Co. Armagh.

Type B2: from Lincs., Suffolk, Salop, Worcs., Wilts., Devon, Cos. Antrim, Sligo.

Type B3: from Aberdeen., Lincs., Berks., Wilts.

Type C1: from Ross., Aberdeen., Skye, Lanark., Yorks., Worcs., Herts., Oxford., Wilts., Cos. Tyrone, Donegal, Antrim.

Type C2: from Cos. Antrim, Meath.

The rough distribution list by counties, given above, has been compiled from my own list of bracers in British museums, amplified by a more extensive list prepared by Atkinson, to be published shortly.

40. In 1891, workmen excavating foundations at St James' Terrace, Winchester, uncovered a grave containing a crouched skeleton or skeletons accompanied by a large broken beaker and a smaller intact vessel with a hole near the base made by the workmen's pick. Subsequently, the sherds of the larger beaker (Hants. no. 352, W/MR, fig. 222) were presented to Winchester museum, where they remain today. Meanwhile, the smaller intact vessel passed into private hands and was sent to America for display at the 1893 Chicago Exhibition; all further trace of this latter vessel was then lost until 1963.

Through the good offices of Professor Cunliffe I was told that a beaker had recently (1963) been loaned to Portsmouth City Museum from the collection of Councillor G. Barter of Winchester (Mus. no. H: 63: 47). A photograph and measurements quickly revealed that this was in fact the missing beaker of the St James' Terrace pair, correct in every detail including the pick hole and the remains of a Chicago Exhibition label. The importance of this re-identification resides in the fact that the missing beaker belongs to the Barbed-Wire group and was probably associated or at least roughly contemporary with, the Wessex/Middle Rhine beaker no. 352. The Barbed-Wire beaker is Hants. no. 353, illustrated in fig. 223.

41. The small group of Dutch beakers which seem to be ancestral to the indigenous Veluwe tradition, 2.1c–f, lie between van der Waals' classes 2.1b–2.1c (van der Waals and Glasbergen (1955), 18, Fig. 9). These intermediate beakers already display a sharpened neck profile and a slim, slightly accentuated short-neck shape (fig. 234) but the motifs are still simple and archaic and the zonal styling still paired-zone or incipient contracted-zone. These vessels do not yet display the full Veluwe range of fringe motifs (Appendix 1.4, Motif Group 2), full zone contraction, or the angular, pronounced neck and waist. The vessels that fall into this category are precisely those few beakers from the Netherlands noted as having Wessex/Middle Rhine connections (see list, n. 37).

42. The following note represents a very brief outline sketch of the overall distribution of prehistoric belt rings of the simple and shanked variety (Class I, fig. 143; further discussed in Chapter 23). The rings in question are usually about 2–4 cms external diameter with a large central perforation, made in bone, amber, stone, occasionally in copper and probably originally in wood. Deliberate roughening, a shank, or perforations are often present for prehension and a contrasting, smoothly worn or polished rim area may show the running edge for the belt. The examples listed below are a sample taken from a swift survey of the literature.

GREAT BRITAIN

British examples of bone and jet belt rings are discussed at length in the text, Chapters 9 and 23 (figs. 136, 139, 143, 144 etc.). In addition to these beaker associated examples there are many strays which may belong to the same group of early simple bone belt rings:

(1) Silverhill Barrow, Boltby to Hawnby Road, Yorks.: dug in 1864, crouched male skeleton with bone belt ring (lost?) with 'two lateral extensions' (*P.Y.G.P.S.* IV (1865–6), 500);

(2) Ravenscliffe Cave, Derby.: a simple bone ring in loose association with rusticated beaker ware (Derby., no. 144; *J.D.A.S.* XXXII, 141–6, Pl. III, 8);

(3) Carew, Pembroke., Wales: bone pulley belt ring with a barbed and tanged arrowhead, an inhumation and an 'earthenware vessel' (lost) (*B.B.C.S.* XVI, 238, no. 6).

NORTHERN EUROPE

Sweden: Corded Ware/Battle-Axe culture; common type fossil, more than twenty-five associated examples in bone and one in amber (Malmer (1962), 271, 287–95, Abb. 69, 71, 74). A very important example from Olinge,

Knislinge, Scania, combines belt ring and 'V' button in a single unit (Forssander (1936), Taf. XXXI, 3; also Taf. XXIV, right).

Denmark: Corded Ware/Battle-Axe culture; common type, in amber and bone, shanked and unshanked. More than thirty associated amber belt rings are known from Jutland alone, bone examples less common because of the acid soil (Malmer (1962), 271; Glob (1952), *II Yngre Stenalder*, Figs. 325–8, 616–19).

North Germany: Corded Ware/Battle-Axe culture, Schönfeld culture, Bell beaker culture, Straubing and Adlerberg cultures:

Schleswig—Corded Ware/Battle-Axe culture, common in amber and bone (Struve (1955), Taf. 2e; 15b; Kat. no. 572, Abb. 8);

Prussia and Pomerania—amber simple and shanked examples in amber hoard from Schwarzort, kr. Memel (Ebert (1927–8), *Reallexikon* XI, 374, Taf. 119). With Schönfeld bowl and facetted battle-axe, Schönfeld, kr. Stendal and in a similar context at Gross-Ammensleben, kr. Wolmirstedt (C. Engel (1935), *Vorgeschichte der Altpreuszichen Stämme*, Taf. 33, Abb. 31, 102). At least twelve bone belt rings are known from Schönfeld sites in the Elbe valley (*Jahresschrift für die Vorgeschichte de Sächsisch-Thüringischen Länder* (Halle, 1937), Band 25, 65–123, Taf. 23, 27, 28), Vahldorf, Saxony, mistakenly reconstructed as a pin (Struve (1955), Taf. 25, no. 3), with Oder-type Corded Ware. From Arnstadt with a bone hammer-head pin and early Aunjetitz vessel (E. Caemmerer (1945), *Vor und Frühgeschichte Arnstadts*, Arnstadt Museum 1940–5, 32, Abb. 38). Central Prussian belt rings in amber (R. Klebs, *Der Bernsteinschmuck der Steinzeit*, Taf. VIII, nos. 8, 9, 10, 12). Schönfeld example, combining belt ring and bow-shaped toggle in bone (W. Bohm (1937), *Die Vorgeschichte des Kreises Westprignitz*, Taf. 14, no. 3). Bucholz, Pomern, Corded Ware belt ring (Forssander (1936), Taf. VIII);

Middle-Rhineland—from Bell beaker contexts, as at Darmstadt Waterworks (fig. 198; Jorns (1961), 58, Figs. 6–7). From Straubing and Adlerberg contexts (H. J. Hundt (1958), *Katalog Straubing I*, Taf. 7, no. 5; Taf. 11, no. 51; Stampfuss (1929), 137, Abb. 41, no. 4).

The Netherlands: a large amber ring related to this series and particularly to the Scandinavian and British Class IV (fig. 143) comes from Wychen, field K, Kruisberg, together with fragmentary bronze bracelets, possibly of British Knipton type (Leiden Mus. e1933/2, 3, 4, 5).

CENTRAL AND EASTERN EUROPE

Bohemia: in Bell beaker contexts, in bone from Jičin, Bohemia (Stocký (1924), *La Bohême à l'âge de la pierre*, Pl. XLVI, no. 11). Similarly, a shanked example in bone from Prague-Šárka (J. Schranil (1928), *Die Vorgeschichte Böhmens und Mährens*, Taf. XVII, no. 8).

Poland: in Corded Ware/Battle-Axe and TRB Middle Neolithic contexts, as at Jordansmühl and Nalenczów (Forssander (1936), 12, Abb. 2; Childe (1929), 123).

Middle Danube: in Vinča and proto-Aunjetitz sites, including an antler form with a row of joined rings: at several Vinča tell sites, e.g. Vinča, Tordos, Csóka (Childe (1929), 30–1; Childe (1957), *The Dawn of European Civilization*, 91, Fig. 47). At proto-Aunjetitz sites such as Ó Beba (Childe (1929), 218).

Russia: common on Corded Ware sites as an alternative to the flat, bone belt-plaque form (Gimbutas (1956), 77, Fig. 41, B4; Pl. 39, nos. 31, 32; Pl. 50, nos. 10, 11).

The Balkans, Greece and Turkey

Gumelnitza culture: in forms close to the Vinča examples, as at Vidra II (Childe (1957), *The Dawn of European Civilization*, 98). Greek Early Neolithic contexts: antler and stone rings found at Tsangli (Wace and Thompson (1912), *Prehistoric Thessaly*, 125, 129, Fig. 78 *h*). It is possible that some of the large, barbless bone 'fishhooks' from pre-pottery neolithic sites in Thessaly, e.g. Tsufli (unpublished) really equate with the similar large bone belt hooks from similar Turkish sites, definitely used in conjunction with the bone belt rings as belt fasteners (see below).

Troy: various bone and stone rings of belt ring form (Childe (1957), *The Dawn of European Civilization*, 44).

Chatal Hüyük, Turkey: in this *tell* there have been found several elaborate bone belt rings, used in conjunction with large bone belt hooks; these objects come from the pre-pottery neolithic assemblage, now dated between 6000–4000 B.C. (*Anatolian Studies*—the Journal of the British Institute at Ankara—(1963), Vol. XIII, Pl. XXVII(*c*) and (*d*)).

Summary

Simple belt rings, of various related kinds, appear to have been part of the male dress of various prehistoric cultures, widespread in space and time. All that can be pointed out here is their first appearance with the earliest farmers of Turkey and the Balkans, followed by their appearance with many other 'Anatolian' features in the Vinča tell culture, in the Middle Danube. Subsequently the same device appears in the Corded Ware/Battle-Axe culture group and in some neighbouring Danubian II and Bell beaker groups. With the Bell beaker groups the device spreads from the Middle Rhineland to Britain, where an indigenous series commences (fig. 143).

43. Details about individual Barbed-Wire beaker sites can be found under the following references: Altendorf, kr. Wolfhagen (H. Müller-Karpe, *Niederhessische Urgeschichte* (1951), Taf. 20, 9); Boberg, Fpl. 12 (Schindler (1960), 84); Roisdorf, Bucholz (Gatermann (1943), 107; Köln Mus. 6070–4); Gellep, Efe, Krefeld (Gatermann (1943), 82; Krefeld Mus.); Hamminkeln, Efe (*Bonn. Jahrbuch.* (1948), 338, 371, Abb. 22, Taf. 62; Bonn Mus. 41, 233–57); Haldern, Efe (*Germania*, Vol. 22, 71, Taf. 12, nos. 1, 7, 13; Hamborn Mus. 28.90); Gronau, Westphalia (*Germania*, Vol. 24, 182).

44. For the last fifty years quantities of prehistoric material of all periods have arrived at Colchester Museum from the vast brickearth pits at Shoebury, which cover many acres. Formerly, these objects have been classified by their period but all the sherds and vessels in each period have only one covering number for each 'lot' arriving; each 'lot' is in fact a rough assemblage from a different area being worked in the pits at different dates. Therefore, amongst the beaker material it has seemed worthwhile to distinguish *Shoebury I*—the area being excavated in 1909, mainly a Barbed-Wire beaker site (1824.09); *Shoebury* II—being the area excavated in 1904, mainly a neolithic assemblage with a beaker scatter, lying much closer to Southchurch (mainly under 480.A.12.04).

45. The overwhelming contemporary evidence is in favour of regarding Barbed-Wire beaker pottery as an indigenous Northern European phenomenon. However, there are one or two small but disturbing features which may be accidental or may suggest that this view could be modified in the future. Principal amongst these awkward facts is the occurrence of Barbed-Wire decorated sherds, apparently in an Impressed or Cardial Ware context from Morocco and Spain (*Bulletin D'Archaéologie Marocaine* III (1958–9), 305, Pl. XI, 1, 3, 4, 6; *Ampurias* 19–20 (1957–8), 166). It would conceivably be possible to link these finds with what appears to be Barbed-Wire beaker sherds from the South of France, at the Abri de Perpétairi, Mollans, Drôme (*Gallia Préhistoire* IV (1961), 192–205, Fig. 12, no. 9, Fig. 33). Then again, we now have evidence of Barbed-Wire beaker sherds as far south in the Rhine valley as Worms (Appendix 7.6, Middle Rhine BW list, nos. 62–4). It could therefore be claimed that there is some evidence for the use of the 'barbed-wire' technique spreading from the Mediterranean to Northern Europe via the Rhône-Rhine route, or more plausibly from Black Sea Impressed Ware to the early 'pit-comb' wares of the Dniepr and thence to Late Corded Ware Europe. However, the evidence is as yet sketchy, the technique may not be quite the same in both areas and in any case the technique may have developed independently as a method of imitating comb impressions. Therefore, the alternative theory of an independent Northern European origin is followed here for reasons elaborated in Chapter 11, Section 6.

46. Huggate and Warterwold barrow 254 covered a central pit in which were crouched two skeletons, each with a beaker. One of these two beakers is certainly no. 1334, a Developed Northern beaker; the other beaker certainly went into the Mortimer collection but up to this time could not be traced. Since both the beakers appear to have been contemporary burials, the missing beaker, described by Mortimer as 'similar in form' to the survivor, should also be a Developed Northern beaker. In the present Mortimer collection is a box labelled 'Barrow 25X Body 2', where X is unreadable. This box contains most of a Developed Northern beaker no. 1335, charcoal, burnt bone and a charred amber fragment (see fig. 508). I suggest that this is the missing beaker since between Mortimer's barrows nos. 250–9 only no. 254 has a body 1 and body 2 numeration; barrow 254 is almost the only Mortimer barrow whose beaker has not been traced; burnt bones and charcoal were found beneath the beaker burials in barrow 254. Whether the amber fragment goes with the beaker or with some different interment must remain debatable.

47. The metal of the British single-rivet daggers is not certainly known, although the Shrewton dagger has been said to be copper, not bronze (fig. 549). It is, however, at least possible that some of the later single-rivet daggers may be of true bronze (fig. 676).

48. I am indebted to Miss R. Crawford of Edinburgh University for preliminary information about Scottish jet artefacts.

49. It is difficult to come to any conclusion about the authenticity of the Leadenhall Street beaker no. 501 (fig. 747). The beaker was bought by a collector from the workmen laying foundations for the Midland Bank, at the end of the last century. Workmen on London building sites of this period were notorious for their fraudulent antiquities sold to a regular circle of antiquarians. This beaker is unique in Britain in shape and decoration, the fabric is unusually thick and poor but not impossibly so; the gritting surprisingly seems to be crushed quartz or Millstone Grit. On the other hand, if a fake, the careful zonal decoration, the row of reed impressions and above all, the use of a barely visible dentated comb, all combine to suggest a remarkable knowledge of beaker ceramic possibilities. I am inclined to think this beaker to be genuine but possible not originally from the claimed site, quite possibly even an antiquarian import from North Germany. The faintly similar Newton Mulgrave beaker, no. 1350 (fig. 744), was destroyed at Liverpool in the last war. In the latter case the authenticity is not in doubt, only the accuracy of the surviving drawing.

50. There are a number of incised or grooved bowls, or fragments of bowls, that have always been treated as part of the Grooved Ware or Food Vessel tradition. At Risby Warren such a bowl was found in the same pit as a Late Southern beaker assemblage, including handled beaker sherds, nos. 472–5 (*P.P.S.* XXIII, Pl. X, 3). At West Runton, Norfolk, a similar bowl came from a pit with an indeterminate beaker sherd no. 629, probably a Late or Final Southern beaker sherd (*Ant. J.* XXIX, 81). Similarly, a related bowl appears in the Mildenhall Urn assemblage with that group's clear Final Southern beaker elements (*Ant. J.* XVI, 42, Fig. 8, no. 4). Another of the same class was buried against a stone of the Avebury Avenue (*Ant.* X, 423, Fig. 3). These miscellaneous bowls have in common their relationship to Grooved Ware vessels on one hand and their definite association with Late and Final Southern beaker influences on the other. It is precisely these relationships which can be shown in more detail for the rest of the Developed-Final Southern beaker assemblage and Southern Grooved Ware (figs. 879–82). A tentative solution to these relationships is outlined in Chapter 24, Section 3, where it is suggested that the Grooved Ware of Southern England integrates features from the Fengate tradition and the incised/grooved Developed-Final Southern beaker tradition.

51. I am indebted to the excavator, Mr Gavin Simpson, for advance information about the Tallington, Lincs. no. 486.1, Southern beaker burial with two undecorated, stout bronze basket-earrings (S2(E)?).

52. There is confusion in the literature about the origin and associations of the beaker possibly from Borough Field, Great Chesterford, no. 234. This vessel is one of a pair of closely similar beakers, figs. 924, 953, excavated by Lord Braybrooke and originally in his collection at Audley End. One beaker, no. 233 (fig. 953), is firmly identified as the vessel excavated by Lord Braybrooke in 1860 from Borough Field, no mention is made in the original field notes of a second beaker. However, before the collection at Audley End was dismantled, in 1919, the then curator of Saffron Walden Museum supplied Mr R. Smith with a very inaccurate sketch showing the two beakers in question, nos. 233–4, and a notched flint dagger, all apparently then displayed under the label 'from Balsham, Cambs.' (*P.S.A.L.* XXXII, 15, Fig. 9). Now one of these beakers, no. 233, certainly never came from Balsham and was never associated with a flint dagger. The remaining beaker may have come from Balsham with the flint dagger, or perhaps only the flint dagger came from Balsham as a stray find. There remains the strong resemblance between the two beakers, suggesting a pair from a single grave or from a single cemetery. Therefore, the whole association is in question but perhaps the two beakers come from Great Chesterford and the flint dagger from Balsham.

53. There are a number of Cinerary Urns showing strong Final Southern beaker influence, especially in their small biconical shapes or reserved motifs. A few of these hybrid vessels are noted below:

Fen Ditton, Cambs. (Fox (1923), 38, Pl. III, 1);

King's Weston, Bristol (*B.U.S.S.* no. 3, Vol. 2, 241, Fig. 3);

Wytham, Berks. (herein fig. 1007, Ashmolean Museum);

Totternhoe, Beds. (herein fig 992; C. L. Matthews (1963), *Ancient Dunstable*, 17, Fig. 4, 1);

Kirk Ireton, Derby. (Ashbee (1960), 124, Fig. 42, 3);

Garrowby Wold, Yorks. (Mortimer (1905), 138–9, Pl. XLIV, 367–8).

54. Copper or bronze daggers associated with Dutch Beakers:

2.1*b*—Odoorn, Drente (van der Waals and Glasbergen (1955), 32 (Note 24);

2.1*b*—Ginkel, Ede, Gelderland (*Ibid.* 32, Note 26);

(2.1*b*?)— Lettenseberg, Ede, Gelderland (Leiden Mus. *e*/1936.1). (All the daggers noted above are tanged, probably copper daggers, only that from Lettenseberg has a single rivet in the tang);

2.1*d*—Stroeërzond, Barneveld (Sangmeister (1963, 41, Fig. 11);

2.1*d*—Doesburg Heide, Ede, Gelderland (verbal information Mr van der Waals, 1962).

(The last two daggers are of the riveted or rivet-notched rhomboidal form).

The Lettenseberg dagger did not accompany a beaker but the accompanying amber buttons compare with the Odoorn amber.

55. The burial rite of the Barbed-Wire beaker group in Britain exactly matches the Continental evidence. In Holland and Germany there are quite certain cases of ordinary crouched inhumation burials with Barbed-Wire beakers, e.g. Rheinrillen, Neuwied (Appendix 7.6, Middle Rhine, no. 61). Equally, there are many certain cases of Barbed-Wire beaker cremations, e.g. from Lower Saxony (Appendix 7.6, no. 7) and from the Middle Rhineland (Appendix 7.6, nos. 33, 41, 43). The very frequent occasions in the Netherlands, Germany and England, when Barbed-Wire sherds are found scattered beneath otherwise empty sand barrows, together with carbon and scorched earth, also hint at completely calcined cremations with deliberately smashed accessories. The giant Barbed-Wire or related rusticated vessels found as strays with their bases ploughed-off, from the same countries, also suggest inversion over calcined cremations; a rite certainly known with other Barbed-Wire beakers, e.g. Findon, Sussex, no. 993 (for Dutch examples, see Modderman (1955*a*), 32–43, Figs. 1, nos. 2, 4; 7). It seems probable that this mixture of burial rites may reflect the same mixture of Bell Beaker and late Corded Ware elements visible in the pottery and its associations.

56. Careful study of a small series of selected and polished igneous stone hammers and anvils, sometimes from beaker contexts, has independently led J. J. Butler, van der Waals and myself to identify these objects as metalsmithing tools (2nd Atlantic Symposium, Groningen, 1964). These objects fall into three or four classes: highly polished hammerstones, ovate or rectangular in shape, made of hard and dense rock with faceted corners around flat hammer surfaces (figs. 890, 897–8); larger flat-faced cushion shaped anvils; small bevel-edged triangular 'chasers'; possibly small discs of soft sandstone (figs. 897–8). These implements seem to be the hammers, anvils, chasing-tools and grinders or rasps, necessary for the production of hammered *blechstil* trinkets in copper or gold and also for finishing and hardening cast copper implements like the tanged daggers and thick-butt axes.

In Britain these tools are known from at least three graves, in every identifiable case with Developed Southern beakers, with unusually rich associations and elaborate graves, e.g. Amesbury, Wilts., no. 1039 (fig. 890), Winterbourne Monkton, Wilts., nos. 1185–6 (figs. 897–8), Winterbourne Stoke, Wilts., no. 1194 (but with the earlier inhumation, not with the beaker). The manner in which this kind of tool was used, especially the ingenious use of the angled facets for shaping sheet metal, can be read in the contemporary Spanish accounts of Inca smiths using precisely similar stone tools for precisely the same purposes on the same metals—copper and gold, in sheets and in simple castings (*American Antiquity* XVI (1950–1), 160–3).

57. Unpublished, new W/MR male grave from Sewell, Totternhoe, Beds., with bone belt toggle, bronze pin and B2 bracer (Plate 3). Not entered in this corpus, in which it would be no. 8.1 (Beds.). The pin is 8.2% tin bronze and with the W/MR tin bronze knife from Dorchester (fig. 128) provides the earliest evidence for bronze in Britain. The double spiral pin has close parallels in Saxo-Thuringia and the Alpine area; the bronze spectrum suggests the same areas, favouring the Alpine source (see Odoorn). Roundway racquet pin (fig. 132) thus confirmed; paralleled same areas—perhaps this also bronze? Beaker fringe motif also relates to N/MR and Proto-Veluwe developments.

REFERENCES

ABERCROMBY, *Hon.* John (1904). 'A proposed chronological arrangement of the Drinking-cup or Beaker class of Fictilia in Britain.' *P.S.A.S.* 11, 45, 323.

— (1912). *A study of the Bronze Age pottery in Great Britain and Ireland and its associated grave-goods* Vol. I.

ANDERSON, Joseph (1886). *Scotland in Pagan times; the Bronze and Stone ages*. Rhind Lectures in Archaeology, 1882.

APSIMON, A. M. (1954). 'Dagger graves in the Wessex Bronze Age.' *University of London, Institute of Archaeology, Annual Report*, 1954, pp. 37–61.

— (1958). 'Food Vessels.' *Bulletin of the Institute of Archaeology, University of London*, 1958, No. I, pp. 24–36.

APSIMON, A. M., DONOVAN, D. T. and TAYLOR, H. (1961). 'The stratigraphy and archaeology of the Late-Glacial and Post-Glacial deposits at Brean Down, Somerset.' *Proc. of the Spelaeological Soc., University of Bristol*, IX, pt. 2, 1960–1, pp. 67–136.

ARMSTRONG, E. C. R. (1920). *Catalogue of the Irish gold ornaments in the collection of the Royal Irish Academy*. Dublin Museum of Science and Art, Guide.

ARTEMENKO, I. I. (1967). 'Plemena Verkhnego i Srednego Podneprovya v Epokhu Bronzy.' *M.I.A.*, S.S.R., no. 148.

ASHBEE, Paul (1960). *The Bronze Age round barrow in Britain*.

ATKINSON, Richard John Copland (1960). *Stonehenge*.

BAILLOUD, G. and DE BOOFZHEIM, P. M. (1955). *Les civilisations néolithiques de la France dans leur Contexte Européen*.

BATEMAN, Thomas (1848). *Vestiges of the antiquities of Derbyshire, and the sepulchral usages of its inhabitants...*

— (1861). *Ten years' diggings in Celtic and Saxon grave hills in the counties of Derby, Stafford and York from 1848–1858*.

BEHRENS, H. (1958). *Archaeologische Kostbarkeiten im Landesmuseum für Vorgeschichte*. Halle/Saale.

BEVERIDGE, Erskine (1911). *North Uist: its archaeology and topography*.

BORLASE, William Copeland (1872). *Naenia Cornubiae*, a descriptive essay.

— (1897). *Dolmens of Ireland*.

BOSCH-GIMPERA, P. (1967). *L'Anthropologie*.

BRAINERD, G. W. (1951). 'The place of chronological ordering in archaeological analysis.' *American Antiquity* 16, 301–13.

BRITTON, Dennis (1963). 'Traditions of metal-working in the later Neolithic and Early Bronze Age of Britain: Pt. I.' *P.P.S.* XXIX, 258–97.

BROHOLM, H. C. and HALD, M. H. (1934). *Danske Bronzealders Dragter*.

BURSCH, F. C. (1933). *Oudheidkundige Mededeelingen van het Rijksmuseum van Oudheden te Leiden*, NS. XIV, 39–123.

BUTLER, J. J. (1956). 'The late Neolithic gold ornament from Bennekom.' *Palaeohistoria* V, 53–71.

— (1961). 'A Bronze Age concentration at Bargeroosterveld.' *Palaeohistoria* VIII, 101–26.

CASTILLO, A del Yurrita (1928). *La Cultura del Vaso Campaniforme*.

— (1954). 'El Vaso Campaniforme cordado en la Peninsula Ibérica.' *Crónica del IV Congreso Internacional de Ciencias Prehistóricas y Protohistóricas*, pp. 445–58.

CHADWICK, Hector Munro (1950). 'The early cultures of north-west Europe.' *H. M. Chadwick Memorial Studies*, ed. Sir C. Fox and B. Dickins.

CHILDE, Vere Gordon (1929). *The Danube in prehistory*.

— (1935). *The prehistory of Scotland*.

— (1940). *Prehistoric communities of the British Isles*.

— (1946). 'The significance of cord ornamented Bell Beakers.' *Actas Y Memorias* 21, 196–201. Madrid.

CLARK, J. G. D. (1931). 'The dual character of the Beaker invasion.' *Antiquity* V, 415–26.

— (1950). *Prehistoric Europe—the economic basis*.

CLARKE, David L. (1962). 'Matrix analysis and archaeology with particular reference to British Beaker pottery.' *P.P.S.* XXVIII, 371–83.

— (1968). *Analytical Archaeology*.

CLARKE, David L. and CONNAH, G. (1962). 'Remanent magnetism and Beaker chronology.' *Antiquity* XXXVI, 206–9.

COGHLAN, H. H. and CASE, H. (1957). 'Early metallurgy of copper in Ireland and Britain. *P.P.S.* XXIII, 91–123.

CORDINER, Charles (1788–95). *Remarkable ruins, and romantic prospects, of North Britain*. 2 vols.

CRICHTON MITCHELL, Margaret E. (1934). 'A new analysis of the early Bronze Age Beaker pottery of Scotland.' *P.S.A.S.* LXVIII, 132–89.

CROFTON CROKER, T. (1854). 'Notes on gold plates chiefly in the south of Ireland.' *Collectanea Antiqua III*.

CUNNINGTON, Maud Edith (1926). 'List of Bronze Age "Drinking Cups" found in Wiltshire.' *W.A.M.* 43, 267–84.

(1927). *The pottery from the Long Barrow at West Kennet, Wilts.*

(1929). *Woodhenge, 1926–28.*

CURWEN, Eliot Cecil (1937). *The archaeology of Sussex.* (Methuen's County Archaeologies.)

DAVIS, J. B. and Thurnam, John (1865). *Crania Britannica.* 2 vols.

DAVISON, B. K. (1959). 'Irish Beaker sites.' (Unpub. thesis, Belfast.)

DEHN, W. (1941). *Kreuznach Katalog, Kreuznach Museum.*

DEHNKE, R. (1940). *Die Tiefstichtonware der Jungsteinzeit in Osthannover.*

DE PAOR, M. (1958). 'Notes on Irish Beakers.' *Bericht über den V Internationalen Kongress für Vor- und Frühgeschichte,* pp. 653–60. Hamburg.

DEVIZES MUSEUM (1911). *Catalogue of antiquities in the Museum of the Wiltshire Archaeological and Natural History Society at Devizes.* Compiled by Mrs M. E. Cunnington and E. H. Goddard. Part 2.

DOBSON, Dina Portway (1931). *The archaeology of Somerset.* (Methuen's County Archaeologies.)

DUDLEY, Harold Edgar (1949). *Early days in north-west Lincolnshire; a regional archaeology.*

EICH, F. (1933). *Der Siedlungsstand im Kreise Neuwied zur Stein und Bronzezeit.*

ELGEE, Frank (1930). *Early man in north-east Yorkshire.*

ERITH, F. H. and LONGWORTH, Ian H. (1960). 'A Bronze Age Urn Field on Vince's Farm, Ardleigh, Essex.' *P.P.S.* XXVI, 178–92.

FORSSANDER, J. E. (1933). *Die Schwedische Bootaxkultur und Ihre kontinentaleuropäischen Voraussetzungen.*

(1936). *Der Ostskandinavische Norden Während der Ältesten Metallzeit Europas.*

FOX, Sir Cyril Fred. (1923). *The archaeology of the Cambridge region.*

(1943). 'A Bronze Age barrow in Llandow Parish, Glamorganshire.' *Arch.* 89, 89–126.

GATERMANN, H. (1943). *Die Becherkulturen in der Rheinprovinz.*

GERSBACH, Egon (1957). 'Schnur- und Häkelmaschenverzierung auf west-europäischen Glockenbechern.' *Jahrbüch der Schweizerischen Gesellschaft für Urgeschichte,* Bd. 46, 1–12.

GIMBUTAS, Marija (1956). 'The prehistory of Eastern Europe, Part I.' *Bulletin of the American School of Prehistoric Research,* 20.

GLASBERGEN, W. *see* VAN DER WAALS, D.

GLOB, P. V. (1944). 'Studier over men Jyske Enkeltgravskultur.' *Aarbøger* (1944), 1–283.

GREENWELL, William (1877). *British barrows; a record of the examination of sepulchral mounds in various parts of England; with description of skulls etc. by G. Rolleston.*

GRIFFITHS, W. E. (1957). 'The typology and origins of beakers in Wales.' *P.P.S.* XXIII, 57–90.

GRINSELL, Leslie Valentine (1959). *Dorset barrows.* (Dorset Natural History and Archaeological Soc.)

HACHMANN, R. (1957). *Die frühe Bronzezeit im Westlichen Ostseegebiet und ihre Mittel- und Südosteuropäischen Beziehungen.*

HEAD, John Frederick (1955). *Early man in South Buckinghamshire; an introduction to the archaeology of the region.*

HOARE, Sir Richard Colt (1810–21). *Ancient Wiltshire.* Part I. *The ancient history of South Wiltshire.* Part II. *The ancient history of North Wiltshire,* 2 vols.

HOLSTE, F. (1953). 'Die Bronzezeit in Süd und West Deutschland.' *Handbuch der Urgeschichte Deutschlands;* herausg. von Ernst Sprockhoff, Bd. I.

HORNE, J. (1905). *Evolution of an English town.*

HUNDT, Hans-Jürgen (1958). *Katalog Straubing, I.* Heft II, 'Materialheft zur Bayerischen Vorgeschichte'.

HUTCHINS, John (1861). *The history and antiquities of the County of Dorset.* 3rd ed. Vol. I.

INVENTARIA ARCHAEOLOGICA (1855–1960). An illustrated card-inventory of important associated finds in Archaeology...Great Britain.

JACKSON, J. Wilfrid (1913). Third report on the Explorations at Dog Holes, Warton Crag, Lancashire.' *Transactions of the Lancs. and Cheshire Antiquarian Soc.* 30, 99–130.

JACOB-FRIESEN, K. H. (1939). *Einführung in Niedersachsens Urgeschichte.*

JESSUP, Ronald Frederick (1930). *The archaeology of Kent.* (Methuen's County Archaeologies.)

JEWITT, Llewellyn (1870). *Grave-mounds and their contents: a manual of archaeology.*

JORNS, W. (1961). *Aus der Welt der ältesten Darmstädter von der Steinzeit bis zum frühen Mittelalter.* Darmstadt Museum.

JUNGHANS, S., SANGMEISTER, E. and SCHROEDER, M. (1960). *Metallanalysen Kupferzeitlicher und Frühbronzezeitlicher Bodenfunde aus Europa.* Römisch-Germanisches Zentralmuseum.

KENDRICK, Sir Thomas Downing (1928). *The archaeology of the Channel Islands.* Vol. I: *The Bailwick of Guernsey.*

KENDRICK, Sir Thomas Downing and HAWKES, Christopher F. C. (1932). *Archaeology in England and Wales, 1914–1931.*

L'HELGOUACH, J. (1963). 'La céramique campaniforme en Armorique. Répartition—Formes—Décors.' *Les Civilisations Atlantiques du Néolithique à l'Âge du Fer.* Actes du Premier Colloque Atlantique. Brest, 1961.

LONGWORTH, Ian H. (1961). 'The origins and developments of the Primary series in the Collared Urn tradition in England and Wales.' *P.P.S.* XXVII, 263–306.

LONGWORTH, Ian H. *et al.* (1960). 'Hurst Fen, Mildenhall, Suffolk; Pottery Report.' *P.P.S.* XXVI, 228–43.

McINNES, I. J. (1961). 'The prehistoric pottery from the Sands of Glenluce.' (Unpub. thesis, Edinburgh.)

MAGNUSSON, M. (1948–49). 'Wulstkeramik in Skandinavischen Funden aus dem Spätneolithikum.' *Årsberättelse; Bulletin de la Société Royale des Lettres de Lund,* 1948–9.

MALMER, M. P. (1962). 'Jungneolithische Studien.' *Acta Archaeologica Lundensia,* Series in 8°, no. 2.

MARIËN, M. E. (1951). *Oud-België.*

MELLAART, J. (1967). *Chatal Hüyük; a Neolithic Town in Anatolia.*

MODDERMAN, P. J. R. (1955). 'Margijnen Enk, Deventer.' *Berichten van de Rijksdienst voor het Oudheidkundig Bodenomderzoek* VI, 22–31.

(1955a). 'Late Beaker-ware decorated with impressions made by a thread-wound stamp.' *Berichten van de Rijksdienst voor het Oudheidkundig Bodenomderzoek,* VI, 32–43.

MORTIMER, J. R. (1905). *Forty years' researches in British and Saxon burial mounds of East Yorkshire.*

MÜLLER, G. (1952). 'Die Keramischen Stilarten das Späten Neolithikums in der Rheinprovinz.' (Bonn dissertation.)

MURDOCH, J. (1889). *Ethnological Results of the Point Barrow Expedition.*

NEEDHAM, R. M. (1962). *A method for using computers in information classification.* The International Congress on Information Processing, Munich.

NEUMANN, E. (1929). 'Die Gliederung der Glockenbecher in Mittel Deutschlands.' *Prähistorische Zeitschrift*, 20.

PIGGOTT, Stuart (1938). 'The early Bronze Age in Wessex.' *P.P.S.* IV, 52–106.

— (1940). 'A trepanned skull of the Beaker period from Dorset and the practice of trepanning in prehistoric Europe.' *P.P.S.* VI, 112–32.

— (1954). *The Neolithic cultures of the British Isles.*

— (1962). *The prehistoric peoples of Scotland.*

— (1962 a). 'The West Kennet Long Barrow; Excavations, 1955–56.' *M.O.W. Archaeological Reports*, 4.

— (1963). 'Abercromby and after: the Beaker cultures of Britain re-examined.' *Culture and Environment; Essays in honour of Sir Cyril Fox*, ed. Foster and Alcock, pp. 53–91.

PITT-RIVERS, A. H. L. F. (1887–1905). *Excavations in Cranborne Chase.* (Excavation Series, vols. 1–5.)

POLLITT, W. (1935). *The archaeology of the Rochford Hundred.*

REID, Robert William (1924). *Illustrated catalogue of specimens from pre-historic interments found in the North East of Scotland.* Anthropological Museum, Marishal College, Aberdeen.

ROBINSON, W. S. (1951). 'A method for chronologically ordering archaeological deposits.' *American Antiquity* 16, 293–301.

SANGMEISTER, E. (1951). 'Die Glockenbecherkultur und die Becherkulturen.' *Schriften zur Urgeschichte*, Hesse, Bd III, 1.

— (1963). 'La Civilisation du Vase Campaniforme.' *Actes du premier Colloque Atlantique*, Brest, 1961.

— (1964). 'Die Datierung des Rückstroms der Glockenbecher und ihre Answirkung auf die Chronologie der Kupferzeit im Portugal.' *Palaeohistoria* XII, 395.

SAVORY, H. M. (1955). 'A corpus of Welsh Bronze Age pottery.' *Bulletin of the Board of Celtic Studies*, pp. 215–41.

— (1963). 'The personality of the Southern Marches of Wales in the Neolithic and early Bronze Age.' *Culture and Environment; Essays in honour of Sir Cyril Fox*, ed. Foster and Alcock, pp. 25–52.

SCHINDLER, R. (1960). *Die Bodenaltertümer der Freien und Hansestadt Hamburg.*

SCHLETTE, Friedrich (1948). 'Die neuen Funde der Glockenbecher-kultur im Lande Sachsen-Anhalt.' *Strena Praehistorica: Festgabe zum 60 Geburtstag von Martn Jahn*, pp. 29–77.

SCHROEDER, R. (1951). *Die Nordgruppe der Oderschnurkeramik.* Vorgeschichtliche Forschungen von Ernst Sprockhoff, Heft 14.

SCHWABEDISSEN, H. (1958). 'Untersuchung mesolithisch-neolithischer Moorsiedlungen in Schleswig-Holstein.' *Neue Ausgrabungen in Deutschland*, 1958, 26–42.

SMITH, Alfred Charles (1884). *Guide to the British and Roman antiquities of the North Wiltshire Downs in a hundred square miles round Abury.*

SMITH, Isobel F. (1955). 'Late Beaker pottery from the Lyonesse Surface and the date of the transgression.' *University of London, Institute of Archaeology, Annual Report*, 1955, p. 29.

— (1956). 'The decorative art of Neolithic ceramics in S.E. England and its relations.' (London University thesis.)

— (1961). 'An essay towards the reformation of the British Bronze Age.' *Helinium* I, no. 2, 97–118.

SOKAL, R. R. and SNEATH, P. H. A. (1963). *Principles of Numerical Taxonomy.* San Francisco.

SPROCKHOFF, E. (1938). 'Die nordische Megalithkultur.' *Handbuch der Urgeschichte Deutschlands*, 3.

STAMPFUSS, R. (1929). *Die Jungneolithischen Kulturen in Westdeutschland*, Bd. II. Rheinische Siedlungsgeschichte, Bonn.

STOCKÝ, A. (1929). *La Bohême à l'Âge du Bronze.*

STONE, J. F. S. (1958). *Wessex before the Celts.*

STRUVE, K. W. (1955). *Die Einzelgrabkultur in Schleswig-Holstein und ihre kontinentalen Beziehungen.*

TAFFANEL, O. and J. (1957). 'La Station préhistorique d'Embusco.' *Cahiers Ligures de Préhistoire et d'Archéologie*, 6, pp. 53–71.

TANIMOTO, T. T. (1958). 'An elementary mathematical theory of classification prediction.' (IBM Paper.)

THURNAM, J. (1871). 'On ancient British barrows, especially those of Wiltshire and the adjoining counties.' *Arch.* XLIII, 285–552.

TUGBY, D. J. (1958). 'A typological analysis of axes and choppers from Southeast Australia.' *American Antiquity* 24, 24–33.

TURNER, William (1899). 'Ancient remains, near Buxton.' (Reprints of papers by the Rev. J. C. Cox, J. Ward and W. H. Salt regarding the archaeological explorations of Micah Salt.)

VAN DER WAALS, D. and GLASBERGEN, W. (1955). 'Beaker types and their distribution in the Netherlands.' *Palaeohistoria* IV, 5–46.

VAN DER WAALS, D. and Glasbergen, W. (1958). 'Een laat-neolithische Tweeperiodentumulus te Harskamp.' *Gelre—Bijdragen en Mededeelingen der Vereeniging Gelre*, LVII, 1–14.

VAN DER WAALS, D. and GLASBERGEN, W. (1959). 'De Twee Bekerculturen Honderd Eeuwen Nederland.' *Antiquity and Survival* (1959), 100–24.

VULLIAMY, Colwyn Edward (1930). *The archaeology of Middlesex and London.* Methuen County Archaeologies.

WARNE, Charles (1866). *The Celtic Tumuli of Dorset.*

WHEELER, Sir Robert Eric Mortimer (1943). 'Maiden Castle, Dorset.' *Society of Antiquaries of London, Reports of the Research Committee*, 12.

WILSON, Sir Daniel (1863). *Prehistoric annals of Scotland.* 2 vols. 2nd ed.